I0815452

Thoroughbred
NATION

Thoroughbred NATION

MAKING AMERICA AT THE RACETRACK 1791–1900

NATALIE A. ZACEK

LOUISIANA STATE UNIVERSITY PRESS
BATON ROUGE

PUBLISHED WITH THE ASSISTANCE OF THE V. RAY CARDOZIER FUND

Published by Louisiana State University Press
lsupress.org

Manufactured in the United States of America
First printing

DESIGNER: Barbara Neely Bourgoyne
TYPEFACE: Whitman
PRINTER AND BINDER: Sheridan Books, Inc.

JACKET ILLUSTRATION: *Horse Race with Spectators*, 1883, by Edward P. Sanguinetti. Library of Congress, Prints and Photographs Division.

Library of Congress Cataloging-in-Publication Data

Names: Zacek, Natalie, author.
Title: Thoroughbred nation : making America at the racetrack, 1791–1900 / Natalie A. Zacek.
Description: Baton Rouge : Louisiana State University Press, [2024] | Includes bibliographical references and index.
Identifiers: LCCN 2024010877 (print) | LCCN 2024010878 (ebook) | ISBN 978-0-8071-8282-6 (cloth) | ISBN 978-0-8071-8322-9 (epub) | ISBN 978-0-8071-8323-6 (pdf)
Subjects: LCSH: Horse racing—United States—History—19th century. | Horse racing—Social aspects—United States—History—19th century. | Thoroughbred horse—United States—History—19th century. | Horse racing—Southern States—History—19th century. | Horse racing—Social aspects—Southern States—History—19th century. | Horse racing—New York (State)—History—19th century. | Horse racing—Social aspects—New York (State)—History—19th century. | Thoroughbred horse—Southern States—History—19th century. | Thoroughbred horse—New York (State)—History—19th century.
Classification: LCC SF335.U5 .Z33 2024 (print) | LCC SF335.U5 (ebook) | DDC 798.40097309/034—dc23/eng/20240509
LC record available at https://lccn.loc.gov/2024010877
LC ebook record available at https://lccn.loc.gov/2024010878

In loving memory of

William Fleming MacLehose

(1967–2020)

and

Judith Cohen Zacek

(1937–2021)

CONTENTS

ILLUSTRATIONS

ACKNOWLEDGMENTS

This book has been a work in progress for a very long time. When I began it, Tony Blair had just stepped down as British prime minister, Barack Obama's name was familiar only to political junkies, and Facebook seemed unlikely to achieve greater longevity than Friendster or MySpace. I thought that I was going to write a book about the symbolic meaning of horses in colonial Virginian culture, a project whose limitations soon became all too obvious. Fortunately, a chance conversation with Michael P. Johnson, in which he suggested that I examine racetracks as social and physical spaces in nineteenth-century America, helped me reconceptualize what I was at that point calling "the horse project," and from that point onward, in what I promise is the only horse-related pun in this book, I was on the right track and off to the races.

Researching a book that examines more than a century of American history in locales throughout the eastern half of the United States necessitated visits to many libraries and archives. I am grateful for the assistance of the reference and research staff at the Henry E. Huntington Library, the Harry Elkins Widener Memorial Library of Harvard University, the main branch of the Boston Public Library, the American Antiquarian Society, the Beinecke Rare Book and Manuscript Library of Yale University, the John A. Morris Library of the National Racing Museum and Hall of Fame, the Milton S. Eisenhower Library of Johns Hopkins University, the Virginia State Library, the Virginia Historical Society, the Valentine Richmond History Center, the John D. Rockefeller Library of Colonial Williamsburg, the Albert and Shirley Small Special Collections Library of the University of Virginia, the Charleston Library Society, the South Carolina Historical Society, the main branch of the Charleston County Public Library, the Marlene and Nathan Addlestone Library of the College of Charleston, the Filson Historical Society, the Hill Memorial Library of Louisiana State University, the

Earl K. Long Library of the University of New Orleans, and the main branch of the New Orleans Public Library. I am also indebted to librarians of my home institution, the John Rylands University Library of the University of Manchester (UoM), none of whom ever said, "We can't get that for you."

I have benefited greatly from presenting work in progress at conferences, including the annual conferences of the British Association for American Studies, British American Nineteenth-Century Historians, and the North American Conference on British Studies. I thank Philip Morgan for inviting me to share the early fruits of my research at Oxford's Rothermere American Institute and Jordana Dym for allowing me to talk about the history of horse racing at Skidmore College, less than two miles away from my original inspiration, the Saratoga Race Course. My fellows' talks at Colonial Williamsburg and the Virginia Historical Society offered much-needed early encouragement, and the latter introduced me to Mitchell Merling, who gave me a private tour of the amazing collection of sporting art at the Virginia Museum of Fine Arts. The University of Manchester provided funding for many of these visits, along with fellowships from the British Academy, Colonial Williamsburg, and the Virginia Historical Society. Gabrielle Spiegel kindly allowed me to be a visiting scholar at Johns Hopkins University in autumn 2007, and I am grateful to Andre O'Neil, Matthew Mulcahy and Jenny Turnham, Larry Peskin, Franz Schneiderman, Max and Jen Edelson, Sally and Mike Flynn, and Alisa Plant and Jim Boyden for providing homes away from home during research trips. I'm also deeply thankful for the counsel of Sven Beckert, Andrew Fearnley, Elaine Frantz, Michal Rozbicki, Randy Sparks, Audra Wolfe, and Kirsten Wood, each of whom offered invaluable feedback on the project.

My Manchester American studies colleagues have been an ongoing source of support, not least through our works-in-progress seminar. I'm especially grateful to Peter Knight for helping me understand the rise of finance capitalism in the Gilded Age and Andrew Fearnley and Molly Geidel for co-organizing our 2017 workshop "Spectacle and Spectatorship in American Culture" and the resulting special issue of the *European Journal of American Studies.* Friends throughout UoM have heard about this project over many years and have provided both intellectual inspiration and nonacademic enjoyment; my thanks to Naomi Baker, Francesca Billiani, Caroline Bithell, Ana Carden-Coyne, Douglas Field, Emma Griffiths, Steven Pierce, Elizabeth Toon, Anastasia Valassopoulos, and Zheng Yangwen. The same is true of Manchester-area friends Fazila Bhimji, Julie Gottlieb, Laura Sandy, Morag Rose and the Loiterers Resistance Movement, Jonathan Spangler, and the Hot Tub Book Club. Farther afield but just as important are Lina de Montigny, Bret Empie, Maura Gallagher, Sheryllynne Haggerty, Christine Johnson, Lara Kriegel, Linda Morrison, Joe Morgan, Bidisha Ray, Glyn Redworth, and Philip Vogt, along with academic "parents" Trevor Burnard, Catherine Clinton, and, of course, Jack Greene.

My greatest regret about this book's long gestation is that some people who were especially important to me did not live to see its publication. Michal Rozbicki was on my side from our first meeting in 1999, always offering gentle encouragement and sly humor. Sidney Mintz was and remains my model of who I hope to be as a scholar and a human being. I can't imagine a day when I wouldn't wish for more time with my beloved friend Bill MacLehose or my mother, Judy Zacek, but if there's an afterlife I hope they're up there together, expressing their pleasure, and probably their amazement, that I finally got this thing done.

Thoroughbred
NATION

Introduction

On May 18, 2019, more than 130,000 people passed through the turnstiles of Baltimore's Pimlico Race Course to attend the 144th Preakness Stakes. Chronologically, the Preakness is the second of the Triple Crown races, the most celebrated annual events in American Thoroughbred racing. Although the number of spectators that year represented a small decline compared to the record-breaking crowds of 2016 and 2017, the "handle" (the total amount wagered) was the largest in the race's history. As both a sporting and a social event, and in terms of the profits it generated, the 2019 Preakness was a grand day for Pimlico, the second-oldest currently operating racetrack in the United States.[1]

But it was also a highly atypical one. While both locals and visitors throng the course each year for the Preakness, few return on any other day of Pimlico's annual racing season. As a result, whereas in 2016 the track offered twenty-eight days of sport, the following December the Maryland Racing Commission announced that that number would be cut to twelve for the 2017 season. The course's proprietor, the Maryland Jockey Club, informed the public that it would no longer sell food at the course, other than from vending machines, despite many attendees' affection for traditional trackside fare such as the Hilltop crab cake and the Triple Crown club sandwich.[2] And worse news was to come: just before Christmas 2018, the Maryland Stadium Authority (MSA) issued a report that stated that the complex's historic facilities, including the grandstand and the clubhouse, had deteriorated beyond repair; the best option, according to the MSA, was to tear down all of the structures and replace them, at a cost of nearly a half billion dollars and with a construction period estimated at three years. During this time the Preakness would have to be staged elsewhere, most likely at the Laurel Park course in Prince George's County, more than twenty miles away, although this change would alienate many racegoers and almost certainly cause a significant drop in attendance and profits.[3] But Pimlico's physical decline had raised complaints from both turf fans and sports journalists for several decades, and while purists claimed to love the complex's aura of history, seeing its dilapidation as a form of authenticity, to many others it was a "miserable eyesore." Some track aficionados had hoped for the introduction of either a casino or slot machines that might boost visitorship and generate revenues to fund the most pressing repairs, but these plans were blocked by the state legislature, and the racecourse continued its steady decline.[4]

Long-term Pimlico fans such as George Eastwood waxed nostalgic about earlier times, when even an ordinary race day might attract ten thousand people,

Looking from grandstand at Pimlico, 1943.
Library of Congress, Prints and Photographs Division.

among whom, he claimed, "there was a camaraderie . . . this is where you met. 'I'll see you at the track.'" Cricket Goodall, the executive director of the Maryland Horse Breeders Association, argued that the availability of slot machines at downtown Baltimore's Horseshoe Casino, which opened in 2014, now satisfied the gambling urges of many people who in previous years would have come to Pimlico to place their bets, and that even those who enjoyed the sport for its own sake now preferred to watch the races on television or online, avoiding the course's shabby facilities and what some perceived as the unsafe neighborhood that abutted it. Eastwood recalled a time when Baltimorean parents brought their children to Pimlico, introducing them to the pleasures of racing spectatorship and raising them to become the next generation of turf enthusiasts, but this practice had waned in recent decades, and by the beginning of the twenty-first century, track audiences, other than at the Preakness, were increasingly elderly and rarely replenished by younger fans.[5] These factors produced a vicious cycle: as Pimlico became more run-down, its attendance dropped, and the resulting decrease in revenue forestalled the financing of improvements that might attract more visitors. Although Pimlico has muddled along through many years of decay, it cannot continue along this path for much longer; it may now be necessary to destroy the track in order to save it.

Pimlico is far from unique among American racetracks in its story of decline. Horse racing was the most popular sport in the United States throughout the nineteenth century, and although it was eclipsed at the end of that century by the rise of professional team sports such as baseball, basketball, and football, it retained considerable popularity up to the 1950s. Even during the Depression, men and women flocked to tracks across the nation, hoping to improve their financial situation with a lucky wager or just to distract themselves with the spectacle of blooded horses, silk-clad jockeys, and the various "characters," from glamorous women to professional gamblers, who filled the stands. But by the 1960s racecourse attendance began its long fall. Postwar American children who were introduced to sports through participation in Little League or Pop Warner programs often became passionate baseball or football fans as adults, but, in the words of Philip H. Iselin, the president of New Jersey's Monmouth Park track from 1968 to 1976, "how many young people today ever see a horse, much less ride one? . . . Physical participation on the most amateur level in the sport of horse racing is virtually non-existent."[6] As options for home-based entertainment proliferated, racing became less alluring to some fans, and others often preferred to engage with the sport via television or, later, the internet. For many years Nevada was the only US state that permitted off-track betting, but New York's approval of this practice in 1970 paved the way for its proliferation via the Interstate Horseracing Act of 1978; with gamblers across the country now able to place their bets in these alternative venues, track attendance fell still further.[7] Throughout the nation, racetracks came to be seen less as sites of wholesome family leisure or raffish glamour than as seedy places patronized primarily by lonely retirees and sleazy hustlers. At the same time, concerns about the welfare of horses and jockeys alike have alienated many potential spectators and encouraged them to experience equine competition through dressage, which boasts an "upmarket and clean-cut image" and lacks the elements that undermine the health of mounts and riders alike at the track.[8] Since 2000, forty-three courses in seventeen states have closed, including Washington's Walla Walla Fair, which had hosted competitions for nearly a century and a half, and Los Angeles's Hollywood Park, whose founding stockholders included such celebrities as Bing Crosby, Irene Dunne, and Al Jolson, and which in its midcentury heyday had attracted so many famous faces, from Jack Benny to Betty Grable, that "you could see a celebrity just about every time you looked up into one of the boxes."[9]

The fact is that today the vast majority of Americans know little and care less about racing. Even the Triple Crown victories of American Pharaoh in 2015 and Justify in 2018 failed to capture the public imagination in the way that Secretariat's record-shattering exploits did in 1973, or Affirmed's rivalry with Alydar in 1978. But even those instances of high drama paled in comparison with the passionate engagement with racing that was shared across races, regions, classes, and genders in the United States throughout the nineteenth century. In the early national era, Congress frequently adjourned for the duration of the local races, and the Washington, DC, track's visitors included the "black, and white, and yellow; of all conditions from the President of the United States to the beggar in his rags, of all ages, and of both sexes," while the first traffic jam in the history of New York City supposedly occurred in 1823, as sixty thousand spectators headed to Long Island's Union Course for a "match race" between the northern champion Eclipse and the southern star Sir Henry.[10] The physical locations of the nation's leading racecourses may have shifted northward after the Civil War, but the public's devotion to the sport endured; at New York's Belmont Park, the audience "was not restricted to any one locality nor to any one class. They came, men and women, old and young, from . . . Boston and Cambridge . . . Philadelphia . . . Chicago and the coast cities," and "the Bowery and the [Fifth] Avenue mingled in the surging democracy of the betting ring."[11]

Moreover, memorable days at the track lingered in national memory; trainers, jockeys, and, most of all, horses were incorporated into American folklore. An estimated twenty thousand men and women watched the Kentuckian Lexington defeat Louisiana's Lecomte at New Orleans's Metairie Association Course on 14 April 1855, a competition in which the former set a record for a four-mile race that stood for decades and that was "the last of that series of events which have lent to New Orleans a turf history perhaps more brilliant than that possessed by any racing city in the United States." But, according to the turf historian Charles E. Trevathan, it was not only the attendees who thrilled to the action, or even those who were keenly interested in racing; "far up into the North, even into parts where the race-horse was not known, travelled the word 'Lexington,'" and for years afterward "any little child of America could have told you the story of Lexington." Writing a half century after this celebrated competition, Trevathan claimed that "there are still aged gentlemen living in the South who refer to the time 'when we came back from New Orleans with a boatload of money'" from wagers on the winner.[12] Other noteworthy track competitions transcended their time and place by becoming immortalized in popular music, as with the oft-recorded folk song "Molly and Tenbrooks" (also known as "The Racehorse Song"), which was inspired by an 1878 race at Louisville's Churchill Downs. Supposedly composed by an African American banjo player who witnessed the event, and most famously recorded by bluegrass pioneers the Stanley Brothers and Bill Monroe in the 1940s, it was revived by folk musicians in the 1960s and has become a standard among younger contemporary roots and country performers, many of whom are unaware of its historical context.[13] It is difficult to overestimate how much cultural space horse racing occupied in the United States throughout the nineteenth century, particularly in comparison with the very narrow bandwidth it maintains today.

The plight of Pimlico shows that neither a long and glorious history nor the hosting of a Triple Crown race can prevent a racecourse's decline. For a track to remain successful, those who manage and promote it need to ensure that it provides not just sport but story; that they craft and maintain a narrative that asserts that those who patronize this track are not merely sports spectators but actors in a social drama that positions them as members of a cohesive and distinctive community, one that boasts a long tradition to which outsiders crave at least temporary membership. The very nature of racing makes this aim challenging: the individual horses change each year, and while jockeys, trainers, and owners may remain onstage over the longer term, only the most devoted turf enthusiasts engage with them on more than a superficial level. By contrast, fans of baseball, basketball, or football, although they may have a special regard for an individual player or coach, tend to identify throughout their lives with their team as a unit, even as its members cycle in and out; spectators, like participants, constitute what the literary scholar Joseph Roach has described as an "everlasting club."[14] A team's physical and social milieu is often of great significance to the fans; many Boston Red Sox supporters accept the inconveniences associated with the antiquated Fenway Park because the site creates and maintains their feelings of "fan identity and place bonding." Similarly, many teams' followers feel a deep attachment to particular aspects of the game-day experience, such as chants, songs, or mascots.[15] But today, when social, economic, and technological factors threaten racing's future, the tracks that remain successful are those that offer their visitors something beyond the sport itself, and that something is a sense of membership in a prestigious community. Throughout the nineteenth century, upon which this study focuses, when racing held a far more dominant position in the world of American leisure than it does today, the racecourses that were the most successful, in both cultural and financial terms, were those that were redolent not just of sporting history but of a broader social narrative. Some tracks never achieved this goal; others initially succeeded but then lost this attribute. To maintain its prestige and profitability over the long term, a track had to retain its hold on its story, and to ensure that it continued to be one in which its visitors would want to play a part.

Like Pimlico, Louisville's Churchill Downs hosts a Triple Crown race, the Kentucky Derby, and, as at the Baltimore track, that day marks the high point of attendance of each year's racing season. But in contrast to Pimlico, Churchill Downs' profits and visitor numbers have soared over the past decade. Some of that success is probably due to dramatic improvements to the course's facilities: in addition to resources that are open to all, such as expanded parking areas and enormous video screens, the complex's management has invested in those reserved for the very rich, including the fine-dining Turf Club, whose annual membership costs several thousand dollars; the Mansion, which can be accessed only through a concierge and which boasts a Chanel cosmetics counter in its ladies' lounge; and the Starting Gate Suites, whose unparalleled view of the action on the track is available to those who are willing to pay six figures for a few hours' enjoyment.[16] These luxurious amenities have helped to attract celebrities, from Jeff Bezos to Kim Kardashian, to Churchill Downs, but for visitors with more modest budgets much of the track's appeal lies with its aggressive promotion of the concept of "southern hospitality," a set of practices associated with wealthy planters of the antebellum era that over the past century has become "an essential, foundational narrative" of the region's alleged distinctiveness and has been deployed to promote everything from Delta Air Lines flights to foot care products.[17] At the racecourse, particularly on Derby Day, "the kind of Southern heritage fashion displayed . . . is flamboyant," especially for the rich and famous attendees who occupy the best seats and can avoid the mud, heat, and crowding of the infield.[18] But although celebrity-watching is far from unique to the Downs, it adds to the site's broader appeal even to fans of tradition. Even a Bezos or a Kardashian is expected to drink a mint julep from a commemorative glass, to sing along when the University of Louisville band plays Stephen Foster's "My Old Kentucky Home," and, for women, to wear a huge, extravagant hat, likely purchased exclusively for this event.[19]

But at a sporting event that is "known for its atmosphere as much as its thoroughbred racing," it is the men and women of the local elites, rather than those who represent global celebrity, whose presence is essential to the venue's atmosphere, and thus to the day's popularity.[20] Spectators may gawk at famous faces, but it is the affluent yet anonymous "southern belles" and "good ol' boys" in their floral dresses and seersucker suits who give the race its flavor of regional identity and historicity; their presence provides a sense of connection over generations, from the inaugural Derby in 1875 to today, and it is they, not the actors, athletes, or politicians in attendance, whose appearance and behavior spectators emulate. The desire to see oneself, even for a day, as a southern lady or gentleman from a long-established family is so strong that even those who watch the race at a Derby Day party in California or Maine often opt to do so while sporting a wildly patterned Vineyard Vines blazer or a feathered fascinator. The availability on Churchill Downs' website of more than a hundred items for off-site Derby parties, from invitation cards to garden flags, testifies to the venue's ongoing success in creating and maintaining a story of which people across the nation, and beyond, wish to be a part. And that desire has been extremely lucrative for both the course and its city; in 2019 Churchill Downs' shareholder return was 69 percent, a figure well above that of the S&P 500, and the Derby alone generated more than $200 million for Louisville and its environs.[21] The course attracts visitors not only to each day of its several-months-long season but throughout the year; in 2019 the on-site Kentucky Derby Museum attracted almost a quarter million visitors and hosted more than three hundred non-racing-related events, including weddings and corporate galas.[22] In stark contrast, the Pimlico complex is deserted and shuttered outside of its scant racing season.

We will return to Churchill Downs in this book's final chapter, but its role here is to introduce the topic of this study, which is how American racetracks functioned throughout the nineteenth century as social spaces as well as sites of sport, and, more specifically, how and why those who managed each of the major tracks of this period fashioned these sporting venues into a sort of theater, with the attendees taking the place of actors in a social drama. Some visitors, particularly those outside the ranks of the local social elite, were no doubt oblivious to or unconcerned with this drama, attending the races because of their love of the sport, desire for entertainment, or hope for profit, but nonetheless their social and economic superiors, especially the members of the local jockey clubs that administered the courses, served as its stage managers. To them, their tracks were a crucial element of the story that they told to themselves and of whose accuracy and significance they hoped to convince others: that their town, city, or region had been and continued to be a place of social, political, cultural, and/or economic importance within a rapidly expanding and changing nation and that the men and women of that locale's elite still held a hegemonic position in a wider community.

In the decades that separated the American Revolution from the Civil War, horse racing was the preeminent sport of the United States. Its only real competition was boxing, but championship bouts were staged only in the larger cities, and as this activity, associated as it was with drunkenness and violence, was not considered respectable, it could not attract the patronage of women, or of men who wished to be viewed as genteel or godly.[23] By contrast, most antebellum Americans held a favorable view of racing, other than evangelical Christians who frowned upon activities involving gambling, and even they might relax their hostility in venues in which wagers were prohibited. The affluent, socially prominent, and nearly all Anglo-Saxon Protestant men who made up the membership of local jockey clubs throughout the South from the mid-eighteenth century until the outbreak of the Civil War were intent upon maintaining their courses' reputations as sites of polite, law-abiding, and elegant leisure, at which women, children, and even clergymen could feel at ease. The loss of such a reputation, whether via word of mouth or through unfavorable commentary in local and national newspapers and sporting periodicals, would be both prompted and reflected by the presence of "blacklegs," men of no fixed address whose interest in the turf was entirely pecuniary. It was perfectly acceptable for male racegoers to bet with their friends and kin, based upon their knowledge of the qualities of a particular horse or jockey, or their allegiance to the state or region associated with a mount, rider, or owner—and women and children could also gamble, though for confectionery or trinkets rather than cash—but those who attended the races solely to make money were anathema to turf enthusiasts, and to people of quality in general. At Charleston, South Carolina's Washington Course, which from its opening in 1791 to the beginning of the Civil War was the nation's most socially prestigious racetrack, the men of the aristocratic South Carolina Jockey Club were convinced that "gambling rooms" and "tables spread to catch the unwary stranger" were facilities that "abus[ed] the object and real intent of our meetings, and defeat[ed] the legitimate ends, for which our Club was initiated." At the Washington Course, "it will be expected, that every one who visits our Race Grounds, will do so, to enjoy the sport, 'itself alone.'" Indeed, a few leading turfmen were so aggrieved when the club's members opted to "depart . . . from the good old customs of their fathers" by replacing pieces of plate with cash prizes that they withdrew from racing entirely.[24]

But a racecourse whose management did its utmost to discourage the presence both of blacklegs themselves and of the types of gambling that attracted them faced another challenge: then, as today, few tracks could survive financially if their appeal was limited to the ranks of the local racing fancy, those who were knowledgeable and passionate about the sport. The hallmark of a successful course was its ability to attract a sufficient number of visitors of elevated or at least respectable social status, and although it is easy to imagine that race and class were the preeminent, even the sole, components of that status, whiteness and a facade of affluence did not always result in social approbation. The enslaved, free people of color, and working-class whites, as long as they knew their place and did not challenge the social order, were often more welcome at the track than were flashily attired gamblers or vulgar *nouveaux riches* of the "black-satin-vest gentry." Elite white southerners of the antebellum era believed that men and women of the lower orders could improve their behavior through contact with their betters, as "inferiority naturally submits itself to the guidance of education and talents . . . [because] the language and manners of the polite are closely imitated" by such people, whereas blacklegs neither sought nor were capable of such improvement, and thus their presence tarnished any racecourse at which they appeared.[25]

These issues are indicative of the challenges faced by jockey clubs and track owners and managers in the nineteenth-century United States. Their responsibilities were not limited to the organization and promotion of their courses' activities but included managing both the behavior and the nature of those who attended these events. Such endeavors were particularly difficult in the southern states, in which the majority of American racetracks were located in the century prior to the Civil War.[26] For decades, scholars have hotly debated the nature of the relationship between elite and "common whites" in the antebellum South, but for the most part they have concurred that it behooved the former to treat the latter with a degree of respect and amity, in order to maintain at least a façade of racial unity and forestall alliances between low-income and -status white men and people of color, whether free or enslaved.[27] Jockey club members could not afford, in economic or social terms, to alienate local poor whites, but accommodating them could undermine the prestige not only of their tracks but of the communities of which they saw themselves the leading citizens. They hoped that the courses with which they associated themselves would attract the most celebrated horses of their locality, state, or region; that the spectators would be both numerous and well-behaved; that the less elite among them would emulate the privileged or at least avoid offending them; and that their activities would generate sufficient profits that they would not be called upon to dip into their own pockets to finance the club's next season. But above all they aimed to portray themselves and their communities in the most positive light and to the widest public. For those who took the sport the most seriously, it was not simply a pastime but an institution that allowed a community to present its most favorable self-image for public consumption—in other words, to tell its story, and to impress that story's truthfulness and significance upon others. The ways in which this process of communal self-fashioning served as both cause and effect of various communities' engagement with Thoroughbred horse racing throughout the nineteenth century—from the sport's revival after its virtual disappearance during the American Revolution through the onset of its eclipse by team sports toward that century's end—is the issue upon which this study centers. In so doing, it works to bring into dialogue with one another the fields of cultural, urban, and sports history, with the goal of illuminating the processes through which racing both influenced and reflected the values of the societies in which it flourished.

One might ask, if racing was throughout the nineteenth century truly integral to the self-definition of many American communities, or at least to the elites thereof, why a study such as this one has not been previously undertaken. Such a project faces the challenges, as well as the opportunities, inherent in engaging with several distinct historiographies, each of which has its own methodologies, parameters, and idiosyncrasies. The history of sports attracted little interest from scholars until the early 1970s, at which time the rise of the "new social history," emphasizing the quotidian experiences of ordinary people, encouraged a reevaluation of the significance of popular forms of leisure.[28] The year 1972 saw the foundation of the North American Society for Sport History, which two years later established the *Journal of Sport History*. But it would be fifteen years before works in this subfield, such as Melvin L. Adelman's *A Sporting Time: New York City and the Rise of Modern Athletics, 1820–1870* (1986), Steven A. Riess's *City Games: The Evolution of American Urban Society and the Rise of Sports* (1989), and Bruce Kuklick's *To Every Thing a Season: Shibe Park and Urban Philadelphia, 1909–1976* (1991), attracted a readership within the wider historical profession. However, the focus of these studies, and of many others that followed, was on sports in which participants and spectators alike were drawn from the urban working classes, especially those of the North and the Midwest, which made racing, particularly in the antebellum era, a topic of limited interest.[29]

This is not to assert that previous decades saw no significant studies of horse racing in colonial or antebellum America; historians, sociologists, and scholars of literature and visual culture produced some impressive work on this topic. But it has been examined, at least within a scholarly context, either within narrow geographic boundaries or as part of a wider project.[30] Historians such as Patricia J. Click, Katherine Brash Jeter, Lara Otis, Randy J. Sparks, Nancy L. Struna, and Maryjean Wall have produced important studies of one or more individual racetracks and the communities in which they existed, while Katherine C. Mooney's recent monograph *Race Horse Men: How Slavery and Freedom Were Made at the American Racetrack* ranges across the principal courses of the nineteenth-century United States, in both the pre–Civil War South and the postwar North, but focuses on the contributions and experiences of African American jockeys, trainers, and grooms. Another recent study, Kenneth Cohen's *They Will Have Their Game: Sporting Culture and the Making of the Early American Republic*, deals in some depth with colonial and early national American racing practices but situates them less in particular locales than within a national culture of popular leisure activities that also included theatrical performances, card games, and various types of informal sporting contests. The works that have offered the broadest perspective on nineteenth-century American racing are those of amateur enthusiasts, such as the railroad company executive Fairfax Harrison, the sports journalist John Hervey, the writers Walter D. Osborne and William H. P. Robertson, and the genealogist Lyman Horace Weeks. They are replete with information, but their treatment of this material tends to be narrative rather than analytical and frequently reflects the authors' opinions rather than aspiring to scholarly objectivity. On the whole, the historiography of American horse racing engages with the sport's history at either a micro or a macro level, whereas this study aims to occupy a place in between, examining a number of racing sites both individually and in dialogue with each other. At the same time, it locates these sites within a wider sociocultural context, exploring the ways in which the sport simultaneously shaped and was shaped by the communities in which it flourished.[31]

In investigating the social context of the nineteenth-century American racetrack, it is essential to engage with seminal works in the fields of sport, urban, and cultural history. Within the first genre, T. H. Breen's 1977 article "Horses and Gentlemen: The Cultural Significance of Gambling among the

Gentry of Virginia" is foundational in its exploration of the ways in which popular recreations simultaneously reflect and influence the dominant values of the societies in which they take root. Although it focuses on the informal quarter-racing tradition of prerevolutionary Tidewater Virginia rather than on the Thoroughbred competitions of the early national era with which this study begins, Breen's deployment of the anthropologist Clifford Geertz's influential ethnographic practice of "thick description" encourages him to conclude that "the wild sprint down a dirt track" was not only a major source of entertainment within this largely rural society but also an activity that "served the interests of Virginia's gentlemen better than they imagined," as it simultaneously encouraged a sense of social cohesion among these privileged men and upheld a class-based hierarchy among its white inhabitants.[32] Within the field of urban history, Sven Beckert's 2001 monograph *The Monied Metropolis* depicts the emergence in mid- to late nineteenth-century Manhattan of a new elite whose wealth came from business and finance, and illuminates the combination of economic confidence and social insecurity that motivated these *nouveaux riches* to devote so much of their time and money to horse racing, and to re-create the sport in the North as it declined in the postbellum South. Beckert's work is also integral to this project in a broader sense, as it provides a model for inquiries into the emergence of local elites and the practices through which they develop networks, create institutions, and articulate their worldviews, not only among themselves but within their real and imagined communities.[33] Finally, with respect to cultural history, Rhys Isaac's Pulitzer Prize–winning 1982 monograph *The Transformation of Virginia* covers some of the same ground, in both historical and methodological terms, as Breen's essay, but although Isaac deals only briefly with racing, or with sporting activities in general, his conception of a local culture as a "social theater" and his use of nontextual sources, including the built environment and the ways that its inhabitants experienced it as "statements," is central to this book's exploration of the cultural meaning of the racetrack in general and of particular racetracks in the nineteenth-century United States.[34]

Beyond these several historiographies, my hope is that this study will appeal more broadly to scholars of the nineteenth-century United States, particularly those whose work focuses on the decades immediately before and after the Civil War. A detailed analysis of the shifting practices and meanings of horse racing can offer insights not only to those who are concerned with antebellum and postbellum cultural differences between the North and the South but also to those interested in how social classes formed and reformed over the century in a society in which even the concept of class was often seen as either alarming or irrelevant. It can contribute to our understanding of the development of mass culture in a nation whose popular culture would become a dominant force within and beyond the Anglosphere, adding further nuance to Lawrence W. Levine's influential formulation of the "high" and "low" cultures of the United States on either side of the Civil War.[35] And it can illuminate the paradoxical nature of tradition in a country that prided itself upon its recent birth and independence from long-established hierarchies and practices, yet simultaneously felt unmoored in their absence.

The structure of this book is simultaneously chronological and geographical; each chapter examines the racetrack(s) of a single location but does so in relation to the time period in which racing flourished there, thus reflecting the ebb and flow of social, cultural, and economic dynamism between various localized elites of the nineteenth-century United States. The first part of the book focuses on the southern states from the years immediately following the end of the American Revolution to the outbreak of the Civil War and illustrates the transit throughout this period of economic and social energy from the long-settled coastal regions to the Lower Mississippi Valley. Chapter 1 briefly describes the emergence of horse racing in the Tidewater region of colonial Virginia before examining the rise of the state's new capital city, Richmond, which became the epicenter of American racing in the early decades of the nineteenth century but soon forfeited this role as Virginians moved westward in search of better opportunities in Kentucky and Tennessee, draining the state of its financial, human, and equine capital. By contrast, as chapter 2 argues, the racing enthusiasts of Charleston, South Carolina, particularly the members of the compulsively self-mythologizing South Carolina Jockey Club, succeeded in maintaining the prestige and popularity of their Washington Course from its opening in 1791 until the first shots were fired at Fort Sumter, despite the fact that the city not only suffered a prolonged economic decline over these decades but lost its status as the state's capital to the Upcountry hamlet of Columbia. Chapters 3 and 4 follow racing into the Lower Mississippi Valley, the region that revivified the institution of slavery in the second quarter of the nineteenth century and became the wheelhouse of American capitalism in that period. In 1860 this area was the home of the highest concentration of millionaires in the nation. It was these families who established Natchez, Mississippi's Adams County Jockey Club, and it was their vast wealth that allowed them to make their course, Pharsalia, an ongoing celebration of their economic and social preeminence, to such an extent that, while they were happy to permit both neighbors and strangers to witness their pomp, they did not require the financial support of a wider public to fund their activities.[36] The city of New Orleans was a relative latecomer to the antebellum racing scene, due primarily to a general lack of enthusiasm for the sport among the Francophone Creoles who dominated its culture until the 1830s. The emergence of racing rendered the "City That Care Forgot" more American, and its courses' combination of top-class competition and myriad other forms of luxury and spectacle reflected its self-image as a place in which money could purchase pleasures unavailable in longer-settled and more decorous parts of the nation.

The second half of the book centers on three racetracks that were established during or soon after the close of the Civil War. The first of these, discussed in chapter 5, is upstate New York's Saratoga Race Course. In the late antebellum era Saratoga Springs had become a fashionable summer destination for rich southerners, and in their absence during wartime the resort's entrepreneurs introduced racing in the hope of attracting a new clientele. Chapters 6 and 7 focus on the Bronx's Jerome Park, founded in 1866, and Louisville's Churchill Downs, which opened in 1875; these two tracks represent the competing impulses that characterized the sport in the final third of the nineteenth century. The former became a favored venue for the city's society women, renowned as "the seat of elegance [and] the home of fashion," but it was also a site of entertainment for the city's working classes.[37] Jerome Park combined the plebeian with the patrician in a manner similar to that of English racing of this era. In sharp contrast, although Churchill Downs' practices were highly mimetic of those of the English turf, its founders developed and deployed an atmosphere of old-fashioned "southern charm," characterized by an adherence to tradition (much of which had been recently invented), a more leisured pace of activity, and an emphasis on alleged southern authenticity in opposition to the aggressive modernity of the North and the Midwest.

Through a detailed exploration of the histories of these racetracks, their promoters, and their patrons, this study hopes to illuminate the cultural work that these places and people performed, and the ways in which they simultaneously reflected and shaped both the communities in which they were enmeshed and these communities' images in a broader regional and national context throughout the nineteenth-century United States. That such relationships existed might seem axiomatic. Even the most casual observer of professional sports is aware that many people around the world make deep emotional investments in athletes and teams that go far beyond enjoyment of their performances. The bitter and sometimes violent rivalry between the supporters of Glasgow's two soccer teams—the Catholic-backed Celtic and the Protestant-supported Rangers—has far less to do with sporting competition than with issues of religion, class, gender, and nationhood.[38] A milder example might be the 1980 victory of the American Olympic ice hockey team over that of the Soviet Union; this shocking upset's mass celebration as the "Miracle on Ice," and, nearly twenty years later, its designation by *Sports Illustrated* as the greatest sporting moment of the entire twentieth century, indicates the extent to which this match represented not just an intensely dramatic athletic contest but a crucial moment in the Cold War.[39] And it is not difficult to call to mind instances in which a venue normally used for sporting activities has been transformed, temporarily or permanently, into a very different type of *lieu de memoire:* Savannah, Georgia's Ten Broeck racecourse, which is notorious in African American history as the site in 1857 of the "Weeping Time," the largest individual sale of enslaved people in the history of the United States; Santiago, Chile's Estadio Nacional, a venue for the 1962 World Cup that for several months in 1973 became a facility for the imprisonment and execution of opponents of General Augusto Pinochet; New Orleans's Superdome, which in the wake of Hurricane Katrina became a symbol of the suffering of the city's residents and the failures of its leadership. Finally, examples abound of sports promoters' attempts to control the narrative of a particular venue: the largely occluded history of the destruction of the Mexican American community of Chavez Ravine to build Los Angeles's Dodger Stadium, or the linkage between the local and the imperial embedded in the designation of the terraced seating at Liverpool's Anfield soccer ground as Spion Kop, after a Boer War skirmish in which hundreds of British soldiers were killed. But despite these and other examples, the racetracks of the nineteenth-century United States, specifically the ways in which they were created, experienced, and depicted by their promoters and their publics, offer a distinctive and important story of the mutually constitutive relationship between the era's most popular sport and the ways in which the men and women of a number of locales—southern and northern, large and small, rural and urban, rising and declining—used horse racing as a way to tell what they considered to be their most important stories, to themselves and to a wider world.[40] To understand the protean nature of local, regional, and national identities over a century of constant and rapid change, horse racing is, to paraphrase Claude Levi-Strauss's oft-cited observation regarding animals, "good to think with." What follows represents the results of such thinking.[41]

1

Virginia

GENTILITY AND DECLINE

At a large dinner party composed of the judges, owners of the horses and others, invited guests, the following, among other toasts, were drank [*sic*]: By a gentleman: "Old Virginia never tire."

—"The Races," *Niles' Weekly Register*, 1823

Yet *Old Virginia* had both wind and speed . . . *Huzza, for "Old Virginia never tire."*

—JAMES B. RANSOM, "The Charleston Races," 1838

The evening of 28 October 1824 was an occasion of great satisfaction for the members of Richmond's Tree Hill Jockey Club. The semi-annual three-day meeting at their track, which was located on the eponymous plantation on the city's western outskirts, had seen particularly fine sport, especially in its last and most hotly contested race, in which all three of the competitors for the thousand-dollar club purse were the offspring of Sir Archy, "the best *American bred* stock-getter that ever covered in this country, getting racing stock out of all sorts of mares, being on both sides, of the best English blood." The presence trackside throughout the meeting of Colonel William Ransom Johnson, who was renowned among racing enthusiasts throughout the nation as the "Napoleon of the Turf," and the participation of several of his most prized horses, was a further sign of the gathering's social and sporting prestige.[1] On the final day the crowd was exceptionally large and enthusiastic, on account not only of the quality of the races' entrants but of the visible presence in the club members' stand of Gilbert du Motier, the Marquis de Lafayette. Few, if any, international visitors were better known or more revered among Americans of the early national era than the man who nearly a half century before had emerged not only as a military hero of the struggle for independence but as a surrogate son to George Washington. When the sexagenarian marquis began his tour of the United States in August 1824, he attracted crowds of admirers everywhere he went, and local elites throughout the country vied to lure him to their social gatherings, but, according to his secretary, Andre-Nicolas Levasseur, he was in particular demand in Richmond, as "this city in proportion to its population contained a greater number of witnesses of his efforts in favour of American independence." "All business was suspended" during Lafayette's visit, a "multiplicity of entertainments were laid on for him and his entourage, and the members of the Tree Hill Jockey Club not only rescheduled their fall meeting to accommodate his schedule but limited to one the number of "strangers, distinguished citizens, and revolutionary officers and soldiers" each member could invite to the track on the day of his visit, "to avoid the unpleasant confusion of a promiscuous crowd." Lafayette's willingness to devote his first full day in Richmond to the activities of the club both reflected and contributed to the prestige not only of Tree Hill and its supporters but of Virginian horse racing more generally.[2]

When the races ended in the early afternoon, Lafayette and his party joined the club members in their dining room, in which "they partook of a splendid and sumptuous repast" prepared by James Selden, owner of the Tree Hill estate and proprietor of the track.[3] "The cloth being removed" at the feast's end, the attendees proposed a series of toasts. The first, predictably, saluted the memory of George Washington and the presence at the table of his illustrious associate, after which Lafayette paid tribute to "the surviving patriots of the revolution" and "the spirit of our country." Several of those that followed linked the sport of racing to the winning of American independence. William H. Roane, Selden's brother-in-law and a grandson of the Virginia patriot Patrick Henry, described the Revolution as "the glorious race of '76," in which "America [was] the field—Virginia the starting post—Liberty the stake," and the King and Queen County planter Temple Gwathmey praised Lafayette as a man who "from youth to age has been running the race of true glory," and who, like the best Thoroughbreds, was "quick at the starting place, good in all heats, and foremost at the coming in." John Marshall, the chief justice of the Supreme Court of the United States and a Richmond resident since 1790, praised "the sports of the turf" as having

Tree Hill, Richmond, Virginia. Virginia Department of Historic Resources.

functioned as a training ground for the Virginia cavalry, which had played an important military role in the Revolution, and John C. Calhoun of South Carolina, then serving as secretary of war and visiting Tree Hill as the guest of his friend Roane, proclaimed that "the generous sport of the turf when pursued with honor, [is] calculated to improve the race of men as well as horses." As they departed Tree Hill to attend the club ball at Richmond's Eagle Hotel, ordinarily the "great centre of business for strangers" visiting the city but which on that night "floral and evergreen decorations, banners and twinkling lights had turned into a fairyland," the men of the jockey club and their guests had every reason to believe that horse sport, both at their track and throughout their region, represented an ideal combination of private pleasure and public spirit and that it would continue to reflect and display the most cherished values of the Virginian elite, who were simultaneously homegrown aristocrats and the heirs of the Revolution.[4]

Lafayette's visit to Tree Hill attests to the prestige with which horse racing in early nineteenth-century Virginia was imbued, due to the quality of the horses, the gentility of the spectators, and the involvement of such national luminaries as Marshall and Calhoun. The members of the Tree Hill Jockey Club were well aware of the sport's long history in the Tidewater region of the state, and the participation therein over several generations of men of the highest eminence, including many members of the "First Families of Virginia," not least George Washington and Thomas Jefferson. But by the time of Lafayette's visit, horse racing in Virginia was on the verge of an inexorable decline, as the state, and particularly the Tidewater, confronted a series of intertwined challenges. As cotton replaced tobacco as the United States' most valuable export crop, many Virginians relocated across the Appalachian Mountains to Kentucky or Tennessee in search of better opportunities, and as a result the state's population dropped and its influence in national politics waned. Among those who remained, the abolition of primogeniture and entail resulted in the breaking up of some of the great estates of the prerevolutionary era.[5] Many of the families that had supported horse racing for decades found themselves unable to carry on this tradition. In their absence, the turf, particularly that which had developed around the racing center of Richmond, soon became the haunt of professional gamblers, creating a cycle through which a perceived loss of trackside decorum attracted still more blacklegs and other undesirables, thus further discouraging genteel men and women from attending. Virginia, and the Tidewater in particular, had played a dominant role in the emergence of Thoroughbred racing and breeding in Britain's North American colonies and had taken an equally important part in their reemergence in the wake of the Revolution, but the second quarter of the nineteenth century would see the locus of the sport move ever farther to the south and the west of the Old Dominion, paralleling the movement of human and financial capital and symbolizing the decline of the first, and perhaps the most compulsively self-mythologizing, American elite.

It was a source of some irritation to Virginian racing enthusiasts that their state could not boast of having staged what turfmen and historians alike believe to have been the first organized race between blooded horses in British North America. It was Richard Nicholls, the first royal governor of New York, who in 1665, as one element in his program of "Anglicization" of the formerly Dutch colony, laid out a racetrack at Hempstead, on Long Island, which he named Newmarket, after the Suffolk course at which Charles II had established and often enjoyed "the sport of kings." There, "once a year the best horses in the Island are brought hither to try their swiftness, and the swiftest rewarded with a silver cup, two being annually provided for the purpose."[6] But the Virginian colonists were soon engaged in the sport, the first reference to which dates from September 1674, when the York County court fined a tailor named James Bullock a hundred pounds of tobacco for having arranged a race for his mare against a horse belonging to his neighbor Matthew Slader. Bullock was censured because local society deemed horse racing "a Sport only for Gentlemen" and viewed him, a nonlanded artisan, as a mere "labourer." The next five decades saw the establishment of a number of "race-paths" in Henrico County, at Bermuda Hundred, Conecock, Malvern Hill, Varina, and The Ware, as well as at Coan in Westmoreland, Devil's Field in Surry, Old Field in Richmond, Smith's Field in Northampton, and Fair Fields, Scotland, and Yeocomico in Northumberland. But although these events were usually governed by rules regarding the weights of the riders and regulated by judges and starters, they occurred only at irregular intervals, usually as a result of one horse owner's challenge to another, and thus were organized on an ad hoc basis.

It would not be until the 1730s, when the colony's prosperity increased dramatically as a result of the House of Burgesses' decision to regulate the quality of tobacco sold on the English market, that the wealthier Virginians would be both willing and able to consume imported luxuries and could purchase blooded horses from England, allowing their engagement with racing to reach a new and much more elevated level.[7] These horses, often acquired from London-based factors whom planters charged to purchase "the best racing stallion[s] [they] could find," had been bred and trained for competitions that consisted of multiple heats, each of two to four miles, which were customary at Newmarket and England's other leading racecourses, in contrast to the quarter-mile competitions that had typified Virginian sport thus far. While quarter races remained popular among ordinary people, particularly those who inhabited the Southside, as the more recently settled piedmont and Appalachian regions of the colony were known, the British colonel Thomas Anburey (or Anbury, or Asbury) claimed that such "ridiculous amusements" were "much laughed at and ridiculed" by the inhabitants of the Tidewater. Whether or not his comment was accurate, many of the "topping people" of the area created one-mile tracks, usually circular or oval in shape on the English model, in contrast to the straight "race paths" used in quarter racing, and set up breeding operations with the aim of producing champions for this new, costly, and self-consciously elite and metropolitan form of racing. More than two dozen Virginian planters established stud farms prior to the outbreak of the Revolution, and, as Jane

Carson observed, their names, which included those of Byrd, Carter, Harrison, and Randolph, constituted "a roll call of the tidewater aristocracy."[8]

In the four decades between the arrival in Virginia of the first Thoroughbred horse (Bulle Rock [also known as Bull Rock and Bully Rock], a star of the English track who was believed to be the get of the Darley Arabian, out of a Byerley Turk mare, and whom the Hanover County tobacco merchant Samuel Gist purchased in 1730) and the outbreak of the Revolution, subscription-based races took place on a regular basis in a number of the larger Tidewater communities, principally Yorktown, Leedstown, Fredericksburg, Gloucester, and the colonial capital, Williamsburg.[9] In these competitions, the fees, or subscriptions, paid by the owners of the competing horses and the event's attendees generated substantial purses, and thus the events were more carefully regulated than the majority of quarter races. Philip Vickers Fithian, a recent graduate of the College of New Jersey (subsequently Princeton University) who spent the years 1773 and 1774 as tutor to the children of the leading planter Robert Carter III at Carter's Nomini Hall plantation in Westmoreland County, attended a subscription race for a purse of five hundred pounds in Richmond County. Having studied for ordination as a Presbyterian minister, Fithian was initially skeptical of the morality of the sport—another Virginia Presbyterian clergyman of this era, Samuel Davies, excoriated racing, along with cockfighting and gaming, as "lawless pleasures" that were nothing more than "fashionable methods of killing time"—but he admitted in his journal that his anxieties had been misplaced, as he found that the timing of the competition was "precise" in order to forestall any possibility of cheating, the rules were meticulously observed, and the sizable audience was "exceeding polite in general."[10]

Because many Tidewater residents inhabited dispersed plantations and farms or small towns, they eagerly anticipated gatherings such as county court days and fairs, which offered them the opportunity to conduct business, purchase both necessities and luxuries, and, most importantly, socialize beyond the circle of their households and near neighbors.[11] As a result, at these events horse races were usually combined with other sports and pastimes to attract the largest number of attendees and convince them to spend an entire day, or even several, in town. This tendency is evident in the eclectic program of entertainments at a Saint Andrew's Day (30 November) gathering in 1737 in Hanover County, which was home to many Scots migrants. Although a three-mile subscription race was the first of the activities listed in the announcement of the event, and it was described in greater detail than the others, "several other Diversions, for the Entertainment of the Gentlemen and Ladies" were on offer, including a series of competitions for prizes (twelve-year-old boys sprinting to win a hat; "a number of brisk young men" wrestling for a set of silver shoe buckles; a pair of silk stockings to be awarded to "the handsomest young Country Maid that appears in the field"), along with "many other Whimsical and Comical Diversions." The organizers emphasized that these festivities had been organized and funded by the "Gentlemen, Merchants, and creditable Planters" of the county, with the aim of "cultivating Friendship, and innocent Mirth . . . [among] the best Sort, of both Sexes." To that end, they provided booths that offered subscribers a space in which they could enjoy a "handsome entertainment," dining with their wives or other female kin in a manner appropriate to the ladies' modesty and refinement, and they informed potential attendees that they were expected "to behave themselves with Decency and Sobriety"; any failure to do so would be "discountenanced . . . with the utmost Rigour."[12] Although fairs and court days were open to Virginians of all classes and races, they were dominated by the values of the gentry, who cast themselves as the principal actors in these social dramas, and who dictated that plebeian white men and women would, like slaves and free people of color, function as enthusiastic but respectful observers, with the occasional exception by which nonelite young white people—"brisk young men" and "handsome Country Maids"—might compete for normally unattainable but highly desirable luxury items such as silver shoe buckles or silk hosiery.[13]

The rapid increase in the number and quality of Thoroughbred horses in the colony encouraged the leading turfmen of the Tidewater to begin to organize themselves into jockey clubs, in imitation of that which had been established at England's Newmarket course in 1750. The presence of these clubs changed prerevolutionary Virginian horse racing from a male-dominated and sometimes rowdy activity that generated at least some degree of cross-class and, occasionally, cross-racial participation into one whose rituals and overall tone increasingly separated the plebeian from the patrician, as well as the white from the Black and the free from the enslaved. The presence of women and girls of the upper ranks was not merely allowed but actively encouraged by club members; the culmination of a race meeting was no longer an all-male banquet marked by the free flow of liquor but a formal, invitation-only ball that in many instances became the most prestigious social event within its locality. In order to draw women to the races, a club might designate one competition at each meeting as a "ladies' purse," upon which only female attendees were permitted to bet. Jockey club–sponsored race meetings soon became occasions at which members of the Tidewater gentry could forge or strengthen their relationships with those whom they viewed as their peers or superiors, while simultaneously providing them with a venue in which they could impress those they deemed their inferiors. In order to allow members of this latter group to attend, clubs refrained from charging admission fees to their events; they valued racing more as an exercise in the display of deference and hierarchy than as a source of profit.[14]

The most prestigious races in prerevolutionary Virginia, in both sporting and social terms, took place in Fredericksburg and Williamsburg. The former, the seat of Spotsylvania County, on the southern bank of the Rappahannock River, was, despite its small size, renowned for the high style in which its residents lived. The Philadelphia businessman Ebenezer Hazard, who passed through the town several times in 1777 in his capacity as surveyor of the colonial postal service, remarked in his journal on what he considered to be the "Luxury & Extravagance of its Inhabitants," epitomized by their having built via subscription a facility "entirely devoted to Dissipation," in the form of dancing and card-playing.[15] The Fredericksburg fair, established in 1738 and held twice each year, became the most popular of such events in prerevolutionary Virginia, due at least in part to the organizers' provision of activities such as "masquerades, river-festivals, and all manner of gaieties" aimed at more affluent visitors, as well as the presence of many young women, who transformed the town into "a bazaar of beauty" in which "many marriages of the Rappahannock region were arranged." The less privileged attendees, who were not included in the nightly balls, were entertained with "Puppet shows, roape dancings, &c."[16] But the races on offer, which by the 1770s were organized by a jockey club with nearly four dozen members, were at least as enticing to plebeian and patrician alike, due to the high quality of the horses that competed for "genteel purses" of up to one hundred guineas, and included such "first running nags" as Alexander Spotswood II's Fearnought and Eclipse, William Fitzhugh's Kitty Fisher and Regulus, and Mann Page's Damon. It was at Fredericksburg that the young George Washington, a friend of avid local turfmen such as Fitzhugh, Spotswood, and John Baylor, watched a number of races, as part of the "genteel company" that the Scots indentured servant John Harrower described as the principal audience for such events. Whether or not these activities were indeed replete with what one particularly romantic chronicler of colonial Virginia described as "three-cornered hats, silver knee-buckles, and powdered wigs . . . [and] consorts and daughters . . . with panniers, hoop skirts, and hair craped high, and poke bonnets over charming faces, and chivalry and beauty, and gallantry," the Fredericksburg Jockey Club succeeded in setting a tone at its races and at the balls that accompanied them that was both highly fashionable and eminently respectable and that served as the model for other Tidewater jockey clubs.[17]

If a reputation for elegant sociability helped to attract audiences to the Fredericksburg races, those staged at Williamsburg, which in 1699 replaced Jamestown as the colony's capital, offered still greater possibilities for such pleasures. Writing of both the town's year-round inhabitants and those who resided there when the legislature was in session, the Anglican clergyman Hugh Jones observed that "they live in the same neat manner, dress after the same modes, and behave themselves exactly as the Gentry in London . . . Thus they dwell comfortably, genteelly, pleasantly, and plentifully" in their "delightful, healthful city," which offered its residents and visitors "rich Stores, of all Sorts of Goods" and "convenient Ordinaries or Inns for Accommodation of Strangers."[18] Jones, who relocated to Maryland in the mid-1720s, did not experience the formation of Williamsburg's Jockey Club and the advent of horse racing in the town in 1737, which drew ever more visitors to its fairs and "Publick Times," the biannual two-week court sessions during which the town's population might increase from two thousand to three times that number. By 1739 the town boasted a track known as the "Mile Course" and hosted races that, like those at Fredericksburg, attracted the best-blooded horses of the colony's elite, such as Brazure Cocke of Henrico County's evocatively named Sing'd Cat, who competed for luxury items including as a "a Silver Soop Ladle, of 45 Shillings Value." Within a few decades, sizable purses would replace these objects; by the 1760s, the "Williamsburg Purse," the prize for the first day's race, was a hundred pounds, and a few years later those on offer on each of the six subsequent days of competition were set at fifty pounds. In addition, sweepstakes and matches were frequently convened "for considerable sums."[19]

The British army officer Captain J. F. D. Smyth, who visited Williamsburg in the early 1770s, attested to the outstanding quality of the horses in competition there, describing them as "very capital" and "such as would make no despicable figure at [England's] Newmarket." The Tidewater gentry, whom he depicted as "quite devoted to the diversion of horse-racing," invested considerable money, time, and effort to the acquisition of the best available bloodstock from Britain, which, Smyth asserted, they improved further through "proper and judicious crossing" with domestically bred horses. Smyth, who had studied in the sophisticated urban milieu of Edinburgh, was far less impressed than Hugh Jones had been a half century earlier by the amenities on offer in Williamsburg—he scoffed at the town's many wooden houses, complained about its unpaved, sandy thoroughfares, and opined that, were it not the legislative center of the colony, it would be entirely devoid of consequence, as "her share of commerce is very inconsiderable, and she does not possess a single manufacture"—but he was effusive in his praise of the local racing culture, which in the 1760s and 1770s was dominated by the horses owned, bred, and/or trained by Colonel John Tayloe II. The colonel, who was one of the richest men in the American colonies, and who maintained a stud farm and a private track at his Mount Airy plantation in Richmond County, was such an overwhelming presence at the Williamsburg races that in April 1767 his horse Bel Air "galloped over the course . . . no horse appearing to dispute the prize [of the hundred-pound Williamsburg Purse] with him."[20]

On the eve of the Revolution, horse racing in Tidewater Virginia was in robust health, attracting the region's elite as both participants and observers, and maintaining a tone of glamour and exclusivity without alienating ordinary men and women, including people of color, from enthusiastic spectatorship. The region was responsible for the breeding and training of the colonies' best racing, driving, and saddle horses, and, in the words of an early twentieth-century turf historian, "long before Virginia became the Mother of Presidents she was the dam of the thoroughbreds that presidents could not withstand."[21] But the outbreak of warfare between the colonies and the metropole caused racing in Virginia, and in the other locales, notably South Carolina, in which the sport had flourished, to come to an almost complete halt. During the conflict it would in many instances have been difficult, if not impossible, to keep racing going; "the racing gentlemen became cavalrymen, and the blooded horses were the spoils of battle," and the semi-annual fairs at which the majority of prewar races had been held were canceled for the duration of the hostilities. And even if these logistical challenges had not forced the temporary abandonment of the track, racing attracted increasingly hostile scrutiny from most advocates of American independence. Even before the first shots were fired, the delegates to the Continental Congress, in the hope of "encourage[ing] frugality, oeconomy, and industry" among their fellow colonists, urged them to abandon "every species of extravagance and dissipation, *especially all horse-racing*," as well as cockfights, plays, and "other expensive diversions and entertainments."[22] Four years later the congressmen reiterated this message, enumerating racing, along with theater-going and gambling, as an activity "productive of idleness, dissipation and a general depravity of principles and manners," especially at a moment at which the minds of patriotic Americans should be fixed on more important issues.[23] But racing, unlike plays and games of chance, was not simply a form of frivolity that was considered inappropriate in a time of war; to many patriots, particularly those from the northern colonies, the sport was all too redolent of their conception of Britain as a society based upon aristocracy and hierarchy. Any sport that was deemed to be "of British extract, and brought in[to] practice by British gentlemen" would be anathema in what they hoped would be a new nation founded on principles of democracy and equality.[24]

Although its jockey clubs did not stage competitions during the war, racing did not completely disappear from Virginia during the Revolution. Philip Fithian, who left his post as tutor at Nomini Hall to become a chaplain in the Continental Army, attended a Virginian militia muster in 1775, at which he was irritated to find the assembled men staging impromptu races rather than improving their military skills. These activities, however, were not uncommon among Virginian soldiers, particularly in areas such as the Northern Neck and the Southside, in which racing had long been popular in peacetime.[25] The *Virginia Gazette* published a number of announcements of upcoming competitions, such as purse races in Manchester, in Chesterfield County, in September 1779, and a month later at Joseph Seawell's ordinary near Gloucester, which had been a site of such contests for nearly half a century. In the late 1770s, numerous issues of the *Gazette* included advertisements for the stud services of horses who had gained renown in prewar races, such as William Fitzhugh's Regulus, whom his owner described as having won sixty pounds at Leedstown as well as taking the Fredericksburg Jockey Club prize, in which competition he had defeated Spotswood's Eclipse, Page's Damon, William Brent's Figure, and other equine champions.[26] The frequency of these announcements suggests that the leading turfmen of Virginia were confident that, once the conflict was over, racing would revive throughout the region and that it would match prewar standards, thus necessitating the continued availability of horses of the best breeding and training.

Such confidence was not misplaced. When Johann David Schopf (also spelled Schoepf), surgeon to one of the Hessian regiments that fought for Britain in the Revolution, visited the Virginia House of Assembly in 1783, he found many of the legislators dressed in riding clothes and loitering in an anteroom discussing horse racing. Schopf was not surprised by this conversation, as he noted that blooded horses were a "prime object" among the residents of the Old Dominion and that "the coming together of so many gentlemen from all parts of the province brought hither a great number of very fine horses," to such an extent that a visitor to Richmond, which in 1780 had replaced Williamsburg as Virginia's capital, "could almost fancy it was an Arabian village." He sensed the elevated place of the horse in Virginian culture, observing that "they give their attention chiefly to racers and hunters, of which indubitably they have the finest in America," while deploring the fact that "the province has no good draught and work-horses" and that, while racehorses were tended with care by their owners, working horses were treated with "great negligence."[27] Traveling through the Chesapeake in 1785, the New Englander Noah Webster stated that horse races were held regularly in Virginia each spring and autumn, and that they were "holidays; like the Election & Thanksgiving in Connecticut." At this time, Virginian mercantile firms Malcomb Hart and Alexander McDonald of Louisa and Benjamin Hyde of Fredericksburg were dispatching buyers across the Atlantic to purchase new bloodstock for the state's resurgent racetracks, returning with such outstanding mounts as Medley, "an excellent Racer and foal getter," and Shark, renowned in England as "the most capital horse of his time" for both his speed and his stamina.[28]

The combination of wartime damage and the loss to Richmond of its status as Virginia's capital, which caused Webster to state that the town "decays since Government was removed," forestalled a significant postwar revival of racing in Williamsburg, but "racing was still the ruling diversion" among local elites, and thus the sport was not entirely absent from the Tidewater region after the Revolution. The patronage of the enormously wealthy Tayloe family underwrote the emergence in 1795 of a new jockey club at Tappahannock, the seat of Essex County, whose races were advertised in the Richmond and Fredericksburg newspapers.[29] But horse sport, along with population and prosperity, was shifting westward within the state, which perhaps accounts for the claim made in 1788 by the French radical and abolitionist Jacques-Pierre Brissot de Warville, when passing through Alexandria, that "the practice of races, borrowed from the English by the Virginians, is fallen into disuse. The places renowned for this business are all abandoned."[30] Nonetheless Petersburg, in Dinwiddie County, saw the establishment of a jockey club in 1785, largely at the instigation of the town's tavern landlords; its course was at Pride's Field, adjacent to Pride's Tavern, at which informal racing had been conducted since 1766. The English-born architect Benjamin Henry Latrobe, who attended the races there in the spring of 1796, estimated the audience at 1,500 and complained that "everyone here is so engaged in talking of Lamplighter, the Shark mare, the Carolina horse, etc. that I am as much at a loss for conversation as if I were among the Hottentots." So many visitors had flocked to this event that Latrobe was forced to share the attic at Mrs. Armistead's boardinghouse with seven other racegoers. The Irish topographical writer Isaac Weld Jr. was similarly impressed by the number of people whom he encountered at the Petersburg track; visiting that same year, he observed that "great crowds were assembled . . . attracted by the horse races."[31]

In the early nineteenth century the Petersburg races retained their popularity; the visiting English agriculturist Morris Birkbeck reported in 1817 that they offered him "the opportunity of seeing a large assemblage of planters, and of being introduced to a number of well-informed persons of that class." At the same time, they became considerably more socially elevated in tone, due in large part to decisions taken by the members of the Newmarket Jockey Club. As the sports historian John Eisenberg has noted, the Newmarket course existed "for the classes, not the masses," and thus it had no difficulty attracting the participation of respectable women, who watched the goings-on from inside coaches parked at the summit of Hare's Hill, named in honor of club president Otway P. Hare; the four-mile events they attended were "the closest thing in southern Virginia to a secular holiday."[32] Unlike several other racetracks in the area, Newmarket continued to attract sizable crowds up to the outbreak of the Civil War; the fall races of 1854, as reported in the New York–based but nationally circulated sporting periodical *Spirit of the Times*, saw such an influx of carriages and pedestrians that the course "presented the appearance of a living ocean of human beings." The Newmarket races were so popular that in 1826 the local newspaper, the *Petersburg Intelligencer*, inaugurated a regular column called "Annals of the Turf," which not only reported doings at the course but commented on broader questions of pedigree and breeding. Compiled by George Washington Jeffreys, these articles became the foundation of Richard Mason's *The Gentleman's New Pocket Farrier*, the first attempt to create an American stud book modeled on that established in England in 1791.[33]

Much of the credit for Newmarket's success was due to the deep and longstanding commitment of the aforementioned William Ransom Johnson, the leading breeder, trainer, and racer of Thoroughbreds in the Upper South in the first half of the nineteenth century, who from 1815 to 1845 headquartered his racing stable at this course, located fewer than twenty miles from his vast breeding and training establishment, Oakland, in Chesterfield County. Johnson's racing success and personal charisma had gained him the favor of the First Families of Virginia, despite the fact that he had been born and raised in North Carolina and did not boast a particularly long or distinguished lineage; the man whose good looks earned him the nickname "the Irish Beauty" was considered the leading authority on every aspect of the turf, and his reputation blossomed further as he gained many victories with Sir Archy, whom he purchased in 1808 from Ralph Wormeley, a great-nephew of Colonel John Tayloe II.[34] But as successful as Johnson was throughout his sporting career, perhaps his greatest contribution to Newmarket was his understanding that, while the members of its jockey club, like those of others throughout Virginia and elsewhere in the southern states, needed to be men of unimpeachable gentility in order to make the course attractive to the right audience, the clubmen's elevated social status rendered the majority of them incapable and/or unwilling to run the track in the most profitable way, or even to be seen as attempting to do so. Johnson was aware that many high-status turfmen were deeply suspicious of track managers, considering them hardly better than the much-loathed blacklegs, so his selection for this post of Otway P. Hare, who had previously been engaged in the towing business along the Appomattox River, was particularly fortuitous. Hare had a reputation for great integrity and public spirit, particularly after

Col. William Ransom Johnson, "The Napoleon of the Turf," ca. 1852. Library of Congress, Prints and Photographs Division.

1831, when he participated in suppressing the rebellion of the enslaved led by Nat Turner, yet he was also a shrewd and extremely capable administrator with "the keenest black eye you ever did see." He was familiar with current business practices and was determined to prevent Newmarket from falling victim to the problems that afflicted other tracks in the region, reorganizing the jockey club and its events as he deemed best from his appointment in 1834 until the course's destruction during the Siege of Petersburg in the summer of 1864.

Despite Petersburg's success, from the mid-1780s, when Virginia was the wealthiest, the most populous, and most politically influential state in the new nation, the center of the Old Dominion's racing lay twenty-five miles to the north, in Richmond and its environs. The new capital city was the locus of the state's political life, and although many Virginians of the late eighteenth and early nineteenth centuries felt that dominance over the governance of the new nation was their birthright, few appear to have taken seriously the words of Nicholas Collin (*né* Nils Colin), the Swedish-born pastor of the Gloria Dei Lutheran congregation in Philadelphia, regarding what he considered the frivolous and unpatriotic nature of the sport and its incompatibility with statesmanship. Collin was dismayed that "so many gentlemen follow horse-racing and know the genealogy of an English horse better than the history of their own country"; in his view, "an American with a great estate, whose ambition should be to figure in Congress" should not play the "silly boy . . . spending his time among jockeys and grooms." Collin expressed admiration for the "beauty, strength, and valour" of cavalry horses, but he had no such respect for those whose distinction came from the winning of races, nor for their owners. Many inhabitants of the northern states, as well as numerous southern evangelical Christians, agreed with Collin about the incompatibility of such "fashionable amusements" with the spirit of public service upon which the republic's success depended, but their excoriation of racing had little effect in Virginia, in which even such political icons as Washington and Jefferson were open in their love of the sport, as when a colt belonging to the latter defeated the former's beloved Arabian horse Magnolio at the Alexandria Jockey Club races in 1790.[35]

Richmond's emergence as the center of Virginian racing culture came at a time at which the sport's infrastructure was undergoing major changes. The jockey clubs that prior to the Revolution had waived admission fees for rich and poor alike were now instituting charges for attendees other than club members and their guests. This alteration was due in part to financial pressures; the prewar Tidewater tracks were in most cases located on lands that had been donated on a temporary or permanent basis by local planters, whereas those established in this later period were the property of profit-seeking landlords, with the clubs as their tenants. The membership of the clubs themselves was also changing; they were increasingly dominated by urban professionals and businessmen rather than by plantation owners, as many of the latter were experiencing financial difficulties that prevented them from supporting the sport as they and their fathers and grandfathers had done in the prerevolutionary era. Even some of the First Families of Virginia who remained prosperous were reluctant to involve themselves in racing, as they felt that it was becoming increasingly professionalized and commercially oriented. If prewar Tidewater races had functioned not merely as sporting events but as showcases for performances of deference and hierarchy, those of the postwar era saw these events' "social value . . . tied to profit motives."[36]

This shift altered the composition of the audiences at Virginian racetracks. Before the war, poor whites, free people of color, and, at least on some occasions, the enslaved were welcome at the races; the presence of these alleged inferiors bolstered the prestige of the elite, as long as the former behaved in a polite and deferential manner. Allowing individuals whom they considered socially and economically subaltern to share their space and, as at the Fredericksburg fairs, excluding them from the balls but providing them with alternative entertainments was part of the culture of "treating," by which elite men provided the common folk with alcohol or other material rewards in return for their political support. But by the early nineteenth century such practices had fallen out of fashion. Status-conscious urbanites did not want or need the approbation of the white lower classes; they preferred to keep them at a distance, and admission fees served a social as well as a financial purpose by helping to exclude such "vagabond intruders."[37] By contrast, people of color remained an important element of racing. Enslaved men and women might accompany their owners to the track, in the capacity of coachmen, grooms, and ladies' maids, helping the men and women they served appear at their best on these occasions. Moreover, men and boys of color, enslaved or free, were central to the action on the course, as it was they who served not only as grooms but as jockeys, it having become disreputable for the owners of racehorses to participate directly in competitions of this nature. It would not be until some years after the end of the Civil War that white men and boys would replace African Americans as jockeys at the nation's leading racetracks.

Richmond's reputation over the first three decades of the nineteenth century as not just "the capital of the upper south" but "the greatest race center of the United States" stemmed from the fact that it boasted three major tracks in its environs, Fairfield, Broad Rock, and the aforementioned Tree Hill, each of which at various moments succeeded in attracting the participation of the nation's most renowned horses, as well as their owners, breeders, jockeys, and trainers. Several factors combined to support this primacy. The most basic was geographic; with the disappearance of racing from Williamsburg, many of that city's inhabitants were unable or unwilling to travel to the tracks located in and around the newly established District of Columbia, which was twice as far from them as Richmond. At least as importantly, the area around the city was home to some of the southern states' most enthusiastic turfmen, who did much to promote the sport.[38] Among these was Thomas Goode of Chesterfield County, whose purchase of the imported horse Diomed in 1800 electrified Virginian, and indeed American, racing. At more than twenty years of age, Diomed was far too old to compete, but his stellar reputation in England, where he had won the inaugural Epsom Derby in 1780, made him an extremely desirable stud, and despite his venerable age, in the eight years that he lived at Goode's estate he "virtually founded our native Thoroughbred line" by siring fifty-five colts. These included Captain Jessie Haynie's Maria and her great rival, Andrew Jackson's Truxton, whose achievements made Jackson "the leader of the turf for some years" in Tennessee, as well as the previously mentioned Sir Archy. So appealing was Diomed to many Americans, including those who otherwise had little interest in turf matters, that "there was almost as much mourning in the old colony land [Virginia] over his demise as there was at the death of George Washington," and the Virginians' sorrow was "assuaged only by the thought that he had left behind him numerous sires who should carry on the glories of the family."[39] The Richmond area's residents also included Major John Pryor, a Revolutionary War veteran and prosperous businessman who owned a number of blooded horses and was locally renowned as "a judge of horse flesh and an all around sport," and the planter-politician John Minor Botts, whose Half Sink plantation was home to such outstanding horses as Tobacconist and Revenue, and who "gave much study to the horse, bred on a large scale, and forgot questions of State to participate in the excitements of the race-course." It was also the home of Congressman, Senator, and Minister to Russia John Randolph of Roanoke, whose encyclopedic knowledge of turf history and pedigrees and status as a member of one of Virginia's oldest and most eminent families—he claimed descent from both William the Conqueror and Pocahontas—made him "one of the great figures of racing in an age when our greatest men were frequently to be seen at the races." Finally, the city's reputation for refined sociability attracted many visitors from abroad, particularly from England.[40]

The earliest of the Richmond tracks, Fairfield, which was laid out either just before or during the Revolution, soon gained a reputation for poor maintenance and a "slow" surface for racing, but its convenient location, just outside the city limits on the Mechanicsville Turnpike, made it a popular *rus in urbe* venue for local residents. It was also a scene of the utmost respectability, patronized by many local professionals. In the words of one aficionado, on race days, "grave judges adjourned their courts, presidents of banks deserted their seats, and distinguished lawyers dropped their briefs" and made their way to Fairfield to watch "the very flowers of the thoroughbred stock of the South"; when John Randolph of Roanoke challenged Colonel Miles Cary Selden, the first owner of the Tree Hill estate, to race his Diomed colt against the former's chestnut filly, for a purse of a thousand dollars, Fairfield was the ground of their choice. But its heyday was short-lived; by 1810 it was supplanted for many by Petersburg's Newmarket, which, under the proprietorship of Banks Moody, offered not only a "faster" track that was smoother and firmer under the horses' hooves but a large and elegant grandstand in which attendees could indulge in "sumptuous dinners," "feasting on the fat of the land and quaffing the choicest liquors."[41] In the face of this more appealing, though less convenient, option, many of the area's more elite racing enthusiasts abandoned Fairfield, and those who remained loyal to it were troubled by the increasing numbers of working-class white men and women who began to attend its races, to such an extent that in 1813 the former demanded that the booths from which the latter purchased food and drink be relocated away from the course to a distant corner of the grounds. Moreover, unlike its nearby rival tracks, Fairfield could not boast a well-funded and energetic jockey club, a sharp-witted manager, or the participation in its affairs of the region's leading turfmen, although from the 1830s to the 1850s Colonel John Belcher, who made Fairfield his headquarters, became renowned both for his training of equine stars such as Colonel William Johnson's Boston, a son of Sir Archy, and for being, according to the jockey and horse trainer John Davis, "a man of the highest standard of morals" and "a model example to the race track." It was Belcher who in 1853 staged a series of widely anticipated competitions between his horse Red Eye, a son of the great champion Boston, and Red Eye's half sister Nina, the property of T. J. Bacon of South Carolina; Red Eye was the victor in the first race and Nina in the second, though it is noteworthy that the rivalry was settled in Red Eye's favor by a third contest held not at Fairfield but at the Broad Rock track.

The former course continued to operate until the outbreak of the Civil War, shortly before which time its supporters attempted to organize a new jockey club in the hope of raising the track's tone, but the quality of the sport on offer was decried in both the local and the national press. In 1851 a commentator for *Spirit of the Times* contrasted an era when "the recurrence of the fall and spring races [at Fairfield] was regarded with the liveliest interest" with the present time, at which, he claimed, "they fail to excite the smallest degree of interest . . . save in the very small circle yet devoted to sports of the Turf." Similarly, in 1856 a local journalist complained that, while Charleston's Washington Course offered elegant accommodations for its female attendees, thus attracting large numbers of elite women to the track, where they "by their attendance give an amount of dignity to [racing] which it could never possess" in their absence, the "young racers" of Fairfield had allowed their facilities to decay and failed to prevent disreputable individuals from attending the competitions, with the result that the course was "no place to take a lady." The Fairfield Jockey Club's updated racing regulations for 1853 stated that "any person desirous of becoming a member for the purpose of starting a horse may do so, he being approved of by the Club, and paying a double entrance [fee]," which implies that both clubmen and horses were in short supply at this time.[42]

Broad Rock, named for a large rock located by the side of the road that led to the track, lay to the south of the city, and although its origins are obscure, it, like Fairfield, appears to have been founded in the 1780s. Although it too remained in operation until the outbreak of the Civil War, its heyday appears to have been limited to the first decade of the nineteenth century, when it attracted the participation of the now District of Columbia–based Colonel John Tayloe II. Tayloe's chestnut Hamlintonian won several proprietor's purses at Broad Rock against "race nags of the first order" in 1804 and 1805, but the colonel's greatest moment on this stage was the 1805 match race between his Peacemaker and William Ball's Florizel, for three thousand dollars a side, in four-mile heats. The combination of Tayloe's fearsome reputation as a turfman and the opportunity to watch two sons of the famed Diomed (one, Florizel, notorious for his vicious temper) race against one another for such high stakes led at least one turf historian, albeit the colonel's grandson, to state that "no match-race has ever produced the like sensation in Virginia." Perhaps stung by his horse's defeat in such a widely publicized competition, Tayloe largely withdrew from racing at Broad Rock in favor of the tracks of his adopted home city, and from then onward the course struggled to attract "the full strength of Virginia . . . the best horses in the State." Although it was the site of the inaugural appearance in 1836 of Colonel Johnson's Boston, Florizel's grandson, within two years the horse was no longer a "welcome visitor" there, as the contrast between his obvious excellence and the indifferent quality of the competition meant that the purses for the four-mile heats would be "surrendered at discretion." Broad Rock also appears to have struggled, even in its early days, to attract respectable patrons and to forestall the presence of blacklegs; for example, it permitted the notorious gambler Robert Bailey to enter his horse Buciphulus in one of its early nineteenth-century competitions. There Bailey rubbed shoulders with "gentlemen of the first respectability," despite the fact that he had been "shunned and persecuted" elsewhere in the state for more than a decade on account of his reputation for chicanery.[43]

Of the Richmond tracks, it was the Tree Hill course that epitomized the qualities that elite Virginians cherished in racing and that they wanted to believe typified their society. The structure of this course's governing body, which was officially known as the Richmond Jockey Club, was initially based on that of Petersburg's Newmarket, due at least in part to the involvement in both organizations of William Ransom Johnson but also because, by the mid-1820s, it was Newmarket that attracted both the finest horses and the most genteel audiences, in contrast to the declining appeal of both Broad Rock and Fairfield. The determination of the club's members to locate Tree Hill on a higher plane than its neighboring tracks was apparent from their first organizational meeting in the spring of 1824, at which they agreed that "every member starting a horse shall select some colour for his rider's cap & jacket . . . and thereafter always [dress] their riders in the same livery," as had since 1762 been the standard practice on the English track, in contrast to the randomly selected and even ragged clothing worn by many enslaved African American jockeys. The clubmen were also keen to learn from the mistakes of other racing venues, setting out elaborate regulations to ensure that every member pulled his weight with respect to the financing and administration of each year's spring and fall racing seasons; any man who failed to pay his subscription for two consecutive meetings would be excluded from the club, and one who had been delinquent in paying his forfeits for two meetings would be barred from starting a horse in any of its races. They were also aware that a racetrack that aimed to attract and retain a clientele that was both affluent and respectable had to make its premises appealing to women; although Virginian society frowned upon the participation of the "ladies" in trackside gambling, their presence was seen as lending elegance to the events as well as encouraging male visitors to behave properly, thus upholding a venue's reputation in the face of the threat of infiltration by blacklegs and other unsavory types. By providing "a suitable Building for the accommodation of Ladies," separate from that for the general public, almost from its opening, Tree Hill did not have to struggle in later years to repair a damaged reputation.[44]

Attracting a visit from a figure of such renown as Lafayette, especially just two years after Tree Hill's opening, attested to the club's success in achieving its goals, but this was not its only triumph. In 1829 John Stuart Skinner, the founding editor of the New York–based *American Turf Register and Sporting Magazine*, at that time the nation's preeminent sporting periodical, attended Tree Hill's October races, and although the Manhattan resident was initially skeptical, he soon changed his tune. He had expected to be favorably impressed by the quality of the sport and the facilities, including not only the ladies' stand but the clubhouse, which was located on a rise overlooking the James River, the sleeping quarters for fifty members and their guests, the dining room that could seat several hundred, and the stables that accommodated fifty horses, but he was surprised to find himself awed by the social aspect of the event, pronouncing the club's members "gentlemen of the highest respectability and moral worth." Under their direction, guests "unite around the social board with excellent cheer and the kindest feelings. The champagne foams, the wit sparkles, and the song goes round." Moreover, Skinner "did not see a beastly drunkard or an uncivil man" anywhere on the grounds during his time at Tree Hill.[45] The track impressed him as the epitome of the "well attended and well managed race course" at which genteel men could engage in the "friendly rivalries and contentions that characterize field sports" without becoming aggressive toward one another or seeking to enrich themselves through high-stakes gambling. Skinner's experiences at Tree Hill were echoed by the sentiments expressed soon thereafter by a Richmond theatrical impresario, Mr. Dickson, who performed a comic song that asserted that "Full blooded nags, the Southerns boast . . . / The mare . . . is old Virginia breed, sirs / And Old Virginia's up to tricks / No matter what the case is / Her horses, men, and politics / Have run some famous races."[46]

Not all Virginians, even among the elite, shared this enthusiasm for racing. As they had done since well before the Revolution, Presbyterians, now in the throes of the Second Great Awakening, fulminated against the sport. A contributor to the *Virginia Religious Magazine* who signed himself "Philander" presented a laundry list of his objections to racing. In addition to the usual complaints regarding the gambling, drinking, and brawling that he claimed typified trackside behavior, he deplored the sport on the grounds that, even if it could be purged of these forms of misconduct, it represented a tremendous waste of time and mental energy. Racing enthusiasts, according to Philander, abandoned worthwhile topics of inquiry, such as "the state of crops, the prices of wheat and tobacco, the news from abroad, and even the political discussions," in order to devote their fullest attention to what he described as nothing more than "*the pleasure of seeing one horse run faster than another horse.*" When Philander asked a neighbor who loved the sport why he was so fond of it, the latter responded that "there is a very great pleasure in the business, I assure you; but it is a pleasure which I don't suppose myself able to make you understand," an answer that his interlocutor deemed entirely unsatisfactory.[47] And while the colonial era had seen "sporting parsons" of the Church of England flock to the races, including the Reverend James Blair, the president of the College of William and Mary, who is believed to have been involved in founding the Williamsburg Jockey Club in the 1730s, by the early republican era the Episcopal Church of Virginia had adopted a far stricter stance toward such behavior. At its convention in May 1818 the delegates decreed that racing, along with the frequently associated activities of theater-going and attendance at public balls, "should be relinquished by all communicants of this church, as having the bad effects of staining the christian character; of giving offense to their pious brethren; and of endangering their own salvation." But Philander and his fellow clergymen were all too aware that, while evangelical Christianity was expanding its hold throughout Virginia and the South in general, few of their fellow Virginians shared their distaste for racing. Ministers occasionally succeeded in convincing turfmen to change their ways, as when Major Hezekiah Anderson and Captain Richard Jones, respectively the president and the owner of the Bellefonte track near Blackstone, in Nottoway County, gave up the sport in the face of a coordinated campaign by local clergymen, but such victories were rare. "Doc," a frequent attendee of Richmond-area races and a contributor to *Spirit of the Times*, ridiculed what he considered the "crocodile tears and pharisaical prayers" of evangelical Christians, claiming that "racing neither leads to drinking nor rowdyism, and cannot be held accountable for any vices over which it has no control." It would, he argued, be equally illogical to decree that all cities should be abandoned because "men make blackguards of themselves and violate the laws" within them.[48]

According to the Bostonian Henry Adams, "in 1800 the Virginia race-course still remained at the head of American popular amusements." If Adams was right, why might a local turfman mourn in 1833 that "from a review of the racing this past spring, I am reluctantly brought to the conclusion that the sceptre has in a measure departed from the Ancient Dominion"?[49] Blacklegs were a convenient element for many to blame for this turn of events; their very presence, or even the rumor thereof, supposedly discouraged the respectable men who owned the state's finest horses from participating in the sport. John Randolph of Roanoke lamented that, once the "gambling spirit" took hold at Virginian tracks, "the best horses are now found, where the racing spirit has not been suffered entirely to die," in rural communities on both sides of the Virginia/North Carolina border, but elsewhere in the state, including at its leading tracks, turfmen had "turned up the whites of their eyes, [and] our horses as well as our men have degenerated." His plaint was echoed by the Richmond-based merchant Samuel Mordecai, who asserted that "in olden times Virginia racing was the sport of gentlemen," but in recent decades it had devolved into "a scene of mere gambling"; an anonymous contributor to the *American Turf Register* complained that few men remained who "blended with the character of the *Virginia sportsmen* that of *Virginia gentlemen.*" This unwelcome change discouraged not only the participation of "many of the kind of men who had maintained its tone in the olden times" but also the attendance of their wives and daughters, to such an extent that "few ladies of the present generation ever saw a race," and their absence in its turn contributed to the further degradation of the sport.[50]

Gamblers and the vices they were seen as bringing in their train were a tempting target for disgruntled Virginian turfmen, as the latter could portray the advent of the former as an unfortunate circumstance against which they struggled in vain. But if blacklegs supposedly diminished the refined milieu of Virginian racing, they could not be blamed for the decline of the quality of the state's blooded horses, which stemmed largely from the decisions made by their breeders, even those of such repute as Randolph and Johnson. Of particular concern was an overreliance on the bloodline of Sir Archy and his get; the horse and his immediate offspring, including Timoleon, Sir Charles, Gohanna, and Flirtilla, were indubitably fine racers, but Virginian breeders soon came to rely far too much on this particular strain, effectively inbreeding to excess, which "brought about the decay of the [Archy] family and the passing of Virginia as the Race Horse Region." One Virginia breeder lamented in 1833 that "we have been satisfied to breed almost exclusively from our Sir Archy stock," and doing so from locally bred mares rather than those descended from "the old English stock," such as Diomed, whose maternal line produced the best Archy colts. "*The best horses* that have run in America for the last twenty years, *almost without an exception,* were from mares *got by imported horses.*" The Charleston artist John Beaufain Irving, who was also the chronicler of the South Carolina Jockey Club, cut to the heart of the problem: Virginia had sold too many of its finest mares of English lineage out of the state and thus had "distribute[d] among her sister States . . . weapons that were destined from time to defeat herself with."[51] These decisions affected the realm of warfare as well as that of sport; a contributor to the *Richmond Examiner* in the midst of the Civil War claimed that the weakness of the Virginia cavalry was the result of "allow[ing] our race of horses to become a mongrel abortion" by breeding impeccably pedigreed Virginian horses to inferior mares or stallions "whose history cannot be traced more than a dozen or two years back."[52]

Finally, some of those who bemoaned the perceived decline of the Virginia turf laid the blame on the proliferation of jockey clubs within the state, particularly in comparison with South Carolina, in which Charleston's South Carolina Jockey Club, like that of England, was essentially without rivals as the arbiter of horse sport. In a situation in which both money and top-quality horses were in limited supply, many clubs struggled to survive, let alone to offer the quality of competition that reflected Virginia's glorious racing heritage. In 1857 a contributor to the *Richmond Whig,* having read Irving's recently published history of the South Carolina Jockey Club, suggested that the turfmen of the Old Dominion should imitate their neighbors not only by chronicling their racing heritage but by forming "a very grand Southern institution, to be known at all times as 'The Virginia Jockey Club.'" This organization would enroll five hundred members who would subscribe at the rate of fifty dollars for the inaugural year and twenty thereafter, generating sufficient capital to allow them to purchase a course near Richmond, erect the necessary stands and other structures for the comfort of their human and equine guests, and fund generous purses, all "under the exclusive direction of the Club and its own officers and agents."[53] The author's plea appears not to have gained significant support from his fellow Virginians, due probably at least in part to the reluctance of the members of the existing clubs to abandon their courses, meetings, and histories and agglomerate themselves into a far larger and less cohesive statewide organization, even if doing so might benefit the sport as a whole.

In theory, all of the factors that contemporary observers believed undermined the social and financial security of the Virginia turf could have been dealt with through concerted efforts on the part of the state's racing enthusiasts, particularly those who inhabited the area around Richmond. But these challenges were symptomatic of far more serious problems that had afflicted the Old Dominion since the end of the Revolution and that had grown more severe throughout the first half of the nineteenth century. Put simply, Virginia's prosperity, population, and political influence all diminished dramatically between the end of the War of Independence and the outbreak of the Civil War, as "the epoch when merely owning land and slaves could secure a family's prosperity was over."[54] Even before the Revolution a number of the leading planters of the Tidewater were experiencing considerable financial difficulties, as they had for decades focused their energies on acquiring and wielding political and social power in their localities rather than on improving the profitability of their estates. Many were living well beyond their means, incurring vast debts, and after the Revolution some had no option but to withdraw from political life as they attempted to repair their fortunes, a task made more challenging by the extensive destruction of property during the war and the exhaustion of the soil after two centuries of cultivation; a Boston newspaper claimed that, by the 1840s, "Eastern Virginia, like a fast driven horse, is panting for breath; it has been taxed to its utmost capacity." Writing in 1824, John Randolph of Roanoke expressed his nostalgia for the lifestyle of the Virginian elites that he remembered from his childhood in the 1770s, when the First Families were "living in their palaces, and driving their coaches and sixes," but he feared that such days would never again be seen in the Old Dominion. His anxieties were echoed by the editor John Stuart Skinner, who, despite his highly favorable impression of Tree Hill, pronounced himself moved to "melancholy admiration" by the sight of "splendid old mansions . . . formerly the seats of opulence, refinement, talent, chivalry, and beauty" that represented "olden and better times" in comparison with Virginia's present and future. Still less attainable was the ideal of agrarian autarky described in the 1720s by the planter and surveyor William Byrd II: "I have a large Family of my own and my Doors are open to Every Body, yet I have no Bills to pay, and a half-a-Crown will rest undisturbed in my Pocket for many Moons together. Like one of the Patriarchs, I have my Flocks and my Herds, my Bond-men and Bond-women, and every Soart of trade among my own Servants, so that I live in a kind of Independence on every one but Providence." If, as the English literary critic Cyril Connolly famously claimed, "there is no more sombre enemy of good art than the pram in the hall," "Bills to pay" constituted a comparable threat to the continued success of Virginian horse racing throughout the antebellum era.[55]

Some members of the state's most elite families followed the ranks of less affluent Virginians in seeking new opportunities across the Appalachian Mountains or still farther afield. In 1834 Henry Augustine Tayloe, a grandson of Colonel John Tayloe II, purchased more than 1,500 acres of cotton land in Alabama and declared that he "came here to make money"; he brought with him his family's love of racing and became a leading figure in the establishment of the sport in Tuscaloosa. Charles T. Botts, brother of the Tree Hill turfman John Minor Botts, made his way to the San Francisco Bay area in the wake of the Gold Rush, where he became first a lawyer and then a newspaper publisher. Even William Ransom Johnson, who for decades had been the state's leading turfman, sought opportunities elsewhere in his later years; in 1845, deeply in debt, he sold a small number of his horses and a much larger one of his slaves, closed down his stable at Newmarket, and relocated his breeding operations from his Oakland estate to Tennessee and Kentucky and his racing endeavors to the newly established racetracks at New Orleans and Mobile, managing before his death in 1849 to make back the money he had lost in Virginia. But while Tayloe, Botts, and Johnson, like many of the approximately one million men, women, and children who left Virginia in the period between the Revolution and the Civil War, may have improved their individual situations, the departure of so many inhabitants weakened their home state in both political and economic terms. As Virginia's share of the nation's population dropped, it lost a number of its seats in the US House of Representatives, and the "Mother of Presidents," which had been home to four of the first five chief executives, became ever less influential in national affairs; meanwhile Virginia-born men, such as Henry Clay, were elected to Congress from other states. Many of the remaining inhabitants could have echoed the plaint of Benjamin Watkins Leigh, a Richmond delegate to the state's constitutional convention of 1829–30: "Whither has the genius of Virginia fled? Of all the old States, none has contributed more to the peopling of the New States than Virginia . . . Virginia has declined and is declining—she was once the first state in the Union—now she has sunk to be the third, and will soon sink lower in the scale." These challenges became still more pronounced in the wake of the Panic of 1837, whose effects hit Virginia particularly hard.[56]

As Virginia's wealth, population, and political importance declined, it is not surprising that the same processes would characterize its turf world and that "so many of the best Virginia horses [were] taken to the west." In the words of the frequent *American Turf Register* contributor Allen Jones Davie, a North Carolinian plantation owner, the "equine ark of the covenant" would continue to move westward, whether to the famed bluegrass country of Kentucky or to the booming sugar and cotton plantations of the Lower Mississippi Valley.[57] For the state's many racing enthusiasts, these losses were tragic, striking as they did not only at their favored leisure activity but at their sense of themselves as Virginians, and of their state's importance to the nation. But they developed two distinct yet intertwined strategies with which to cope with the relocation of that "equine ark," both of which looked to the past to inspire the present. The first was the development of what historians have termed the "Cavalier mythology," a version of the history of Virginia that claimed that the majority of the colony's white settlers in the middle third of the seventeenth century were Englishmen of noble blood and royalist allegiance, who developed in their new home "a society based on the values of the English country gentry," in contrast to those who made their way to the northern colonies, who were transplanted Cromwellians and whose culture thus became simultaneously puritanical and commercial.[58] The very term "cavalier," in both the seventeenth and the nineteenth centuries, exalted the mounted man and imputed to him not just skill in horsemanship but the values associated with chivalry and aristocracy, which elite Virginians considered central to their society and attempted to epitomize through their racing practices.

But if that sport was in decay by the second quarter of the nineteenth century, and if in its current state it was no longer capable of representing and transmitting those virtues, Old Dominion turf enthusiasts could at least defend their cherished ideals by claiming that, although times had recently changed to their detriment, they were the heirs of a glorious past. This nostalgia was abetted by a number of antebellum Virginian novelists, beginning with George Tucker and including John Pendleton Kennedy, William Alexander Caruthers, William Wirt, and most notably, with regard to the role of horse racing, John Esten Cooke. In Cooke's *Henry St. John,* published on the eve of the outbreak of the Civil War, the titular hero's idyllic plantation, Flower of Hundreds, includes a stable that is home to "as fine a collection of thorough-breds, 't was said, as any in the colony," but it is in Cooke's earlier work *The Virginia Comedians* (1854) that the author portrays racing as the ideal representation of the values intrinsic to Virginia's Cavalier heritage, in a scene set at the Williamsburg track prior to the Revolution. He longs to know "where are they now, those stalwart cavaliers and lovely dames that filled that former time with so much light, and merriment, and joyous laughter? Where are those good coursers, Selim, Fair Anna, and Sir Archy; where are black and white, old and young, all the sporting men and women of the swaying crowd? What do we care for them today? . . . What do we care for all those happy maiden faces—gallant inclinations—graceful courtesies—everything connected with the cavaliers and dames of that old, brilliant, pompous, honest, worthy race?"[59]

Those Virginians who preferred to try to live out the Cavalier myth rather than to read about it were the earliest adopters in the United States of the pseudomedieval tournament, a pastime inspired by the enormously popular novels of Sir Walter Scott, particularly *Ivanhoe.* Scott's heavily romanticized depictions of aristocratic life in medieval England and Scotland inspired numerous attempts to bring from page to life what Mark Twain scathingly dismissed as the "sham grandeurs, sham gauds, and sham chivalries of a brainless and worthless long-vanished society" by staging ring tournaments, meticulously choreographed and elaborately costumed rituals of equestrian combat, which from the early 1840s to the beginning of the Civil War were extremely popular at the springs resorts in western Virginia. These events centered on the attempts of individual riders to spear metal rings of two to three inches in diameter, which were suspended around eight feet above the ground from a series of arches placed along the course. The man who gained the largest number of rings was the victor and could crown the female spectator of his choice as the

"Queen of Love and Beauty," either at the competition's end or at a subsequent "Coronation Ball."[60]

But while the prospect of a public sporting triumph observed by eligible young women may have been the most attractive element of the tournament for many of the participants, to its observers much of the competition's appeal lay in its equestrian focus. A skillful performance therein allowed a young man to display his physical grace, manual dexterity, and ease in the saddle, and accredited him as a participant in a long-established tradition in which "the elegant accomplishment of horsemanship" represented an ideal combination of martial skill and masculine character, one that affluent southerners valued above even the "midnight revels of the ballroom" as a training ground for genteel manliness. For these audiences, the tournament ground could complement or even replace the racecourse as a site for the display of both horses and horsemanship in a region in which many inhabitants were fascinated by horse breeding and proud of their (or their ancestors') ownership of blooded stock, and in which racing had long been a prized element of the culture, even for those outside the ranks of the elite. Moreover, this sport, in comparison with racing, required little in terms of funding or infrastructure to flourish. The horses involved were usually those that their owners rode in the course of their everyday activities rather than expensive Thoroughbreds that were reserved for the track; the riders were the owners themselves, or their friends or kin; and the rewards on offer were social and emotional rather than financial. Under these circumstances there was no need to hire a track manager, rent a course, or provide lavish hospitality, and the exclusive nature of the summer colonies blocked the involvement of blacklegs and other disreputable individuals. Finally, and at least as importantly, the medieval trappings of the tournament—the homemade armor of the competitors, the banners that decorated the field, the titles under which the contestants entered the lists, such as Brian de Bois-Guilbert or the Knight of the Valley—though redolent of an epoch centuries prior to that of the Cavaliers, appealed to similar conceptions of honor, chivalry, and aristocracy.[61]

For Virginian turfmen, the colonial and early national eras had been times of glory, in which racing was both a cause and an effect of the Old Dominion's exalted position within the social, political, economic, and cultural life of its region, and even that of the nation. Yet for the half century prior to the Civil War, the decline of this polity led to a corresponding waning of the prestige and profitability of the sport. But this declension model was not universal throughout the antebellum South, even in states that, like Virginia, were dominated by a long-established planter class that was struggling to cope with rapid shifts in the region's and the nation's economy as the nineteenth century progressed. As we shall see in the following chapter, the racing enthusiasts of the South Carolina Lowcountry succeeded where those of Tidewater Virginia failed in maintaining both the popularity and the prestige of the sport and ensuring that it reflected their sense of themselves and what they saw as their well-deserved dominance within their society. The lyrics of the old song could well have been adjusted to declare that it was South Carolina that "had both wind and speed," and thus would "never tire."

2

Charleston

THE CARNIVAL OF THE SOUTH

Charles-Town is in the north what Lima is in the south; both are capitals of the richest provinces of their respective hemispheres; you may therefore conjecture, that both cities must exhibit the appearances necessarily resulting from riches.

—J. HECTOR ST. JOHN DE CREVECOEUR, *Letters from an American Farmer,* 1782

So luxury in [South] Carolina has made the greatest advance, and their manner of life, dress, equipages, furniture, everything denotes a higher degree of taste and love of show, and less frugality than the northern provinces . . . Pleasures of every kind are known, loved, and enjoyed here.

—JOHANN DAVID SCHOPF, *Travels in the Confederation, 1783–1784,* 1911

In January 1931 the writer DuBose Heyward was hard at work on his latest novel, *Peter Ashley,* which was set in Charleston in the period between South Carolina's secession from the Union in December 1860 and the outbreak of the Civil War four months later. In a letter to his friend Henry Ravenel Dwight, an amateur historian of South Carolina and, like Heyward, a descendant of one of the state's longest-established planter families, he wrote that he was "trying to give an honest impression of the mental attitudes, and the habits of life of the period," and thus had decided to set a lengthy section of the book at "the great Albine–Planet race that took place on the Washington Race Course in the midst of those trying days. What a marvelous sporting event that was!" Heyward's family had lived in Charleston for generations, and many of his ancestors, and Dwight's, had attended competitions at this track, possibly including the match race on 6 February 1861 in which Major Jack Cantey's South Carolina–bred mare Albine, trained by an enslaved man named Hercules, won a dramatic and unexpected victory over the previously undefeated Planet, owned by Colonel Thomas Doswell, the proprietor of the celebrated Bullfield stud farm in Hanover County, Virginia.[1] Held during what would turn out to be the city's final Race Week, the contest was described by eyewitnesses as one of the most exciting in the seventy years since the Washington Course's opening. John Beaufain Irving, the historian of the South Carolina Jockey Club (hereafter SCJC), attended the event and reported that "the excitement was immense" when the competitors approached the starting post and that the spectators "view[ed] the animated scene with unmitigated delight" as the horses "passed like a whirlwind." Although Albine was victorious, both animals, according to Irving, "display[ed] such undeniable manifestations of their racing qualities as to ennoble the sport and enroll their names upon the annals of our club as having made the best time in a four mile race ever run on our course."[2] While those who had wagered on Planet's victory were disappointed by the outcome, partisans of both competitors agreed that it had been a great privilege to watch such a dramatic match between two of the nation's most celebrated horses, held at what was at that time the most distinguished course in America in terms of both its social status and its sporting excellence.

Four years later, the scene at the Washington Course had altered nearly beyond recognition. The Ohio-born journalist Whitelaw Reid, who visited Charleston shortly after the war's end in the course of an official inspection tour of the former Confederacy, led by Salmon P. Chase, the chief justice of the Supreme Court, made his way through the "shabby suburbs" to "the track where, of yore, all the beauty and fashion of Charleston was wont to congregate—the Race Course." But the site was greatly changed from the day that Albine had defeated Planet. Transformed at the beginning of the hostilities into a venue for Confederate military training, in 1863 the track been repurposed as a "prison-pen," or prisoner-of-war camp, which the following year was used to house the overflow of captives from the notoriously overcrowded Camp Sumter, in Andersonville, Georgia; "here, without shelter, without clothing, and with insufficient food, were confined the Yankee prisoners; and in a little inclosure, back of the judges' stand, may be seen their uncounted graves."[3] Public opinion in the North was inflamed by the revelation of the sufferings of the soldiers in this makeshift prison, which were extreme even in comparison with those at

A clubhouse at the Washington Course in Charleston, South Carolina, where federal officers were confined, April 1865. Library of Congress, Prints and Photographs Division.

Andersonville and other Confederate POW camps. Captain Henry O. Marcy, a Massachusetts surgeon of abolitionist sympathies who served as the medical director of the Union forces occupying Charleston, described "the inhuman treatment of our defenceless prisoners" as an "unforgettable and unforgivable crime" on the part of the Confederate military authorities. But at least the miserable deaths of these prisoners had not been forgotten; as Marcy noted, members of the city's sizable population of free people of color commemorated them with a lengthy procession of children, "laden with floral offerings . . . singing patriotic songs as they decorated these long rows of graves with their beautiful flowers . . . This was the origin of the day since dedicated, both North and South, to the memory of our soldier dead." Through these actions, Black Charlestonians took control of the racetrack, a space that before the war had epitomized the social, economic, and above all racial distinctions upon which antebellum plantation society had rested, and created the Memorial Day tradition by which Americans of all races would honor military veterans, both living and dead. As David Blight has noted, "the symbolic power of the planter aristocracy's Race Course (where they had displayed their wealth, leisure, and influence) was not lost on the freedpeople."[4]

One might view the transformation of the Washington Course from a racetrack to a prison camp, and then to a site of martyrdom and memory, as encapsulating a story of the decline of South Carolinian horse racing that paralleled that which, as we have seen, played out in Virginia in the decades prior to the Civil War. This claim, however, would be a misreading of the situation. In comparison with the racing fancy of the Old Dominion, that of the Palmetto State was far more successful in maintaining racing's prestige in both social and sporting terms throughout the nineteenth century, up to the very outbreak of the war. Even apart from the headline-making match race between Albine and Planet, the Race Week of February 1861 attracted numerous spectators from throughout the South, who pronounced the event as splendid as ever, despite the prospect of war having thinned the numbers of younger men in attendance.[5] And in the conflict's aftermath, the ruination of the Washington Course notwithstanding, the state's turf enthusiasts had a least a small measure of success in reviving the sport. By the century's end, it was clear to even the most dedicated SCJC members that the economic situation of club and city alike could no longer support racing, at least not in the style to which the members remained committed, but the winding up of the club and its course was carried out in a way that greatly impressed influential members of the new Manhattan-based racing elite, and encouraged them to incorporate the memory of the palmy days of Charlestonian horse sport into their vision of the history of American racing.

As noted in chapter 1, in 1857 an unsigned article in the *Richmond Whig* offered glowing praise not only for Irving's recently published history of the SCJC but for the club itself and the South Carolinian turf in general, in comparison with which that of Virginia, the writer claimed, was in a dismal condition. Irving himself had commented reprovingly on the willingness of some Virginia turfmen to sell their best mares to South Carolinian breeders, a process that he described as "distribut[ing] among her sister States . . . weapons that were destined from time to defeat herself with." And a contributor to Richmond's *Daily Dispatch* in 1856 had excoriated the management of the city's Fairfield track for allowing its facilities to deteriorate and the course to become the haunt of gamblers and other disreputable individuals, thus discouraging respectable people, especially women, and the owners of many of the South's best horses, from attending its events. Only by following Charleston's example, "erect[ing] a comfortable long house [stand] at a distance from the public booths" and "giv[ing] the ladies an assurance of comfort and pleasure," could the Old Dominion hope to regain "the enviable reputation she once enjoyed, of being the land of race horses of the highest order."[6] But in order to understand the very different position that the sport occupied in these two states on the brink of the Civil War, it is necessary to go back to the beginnings of racing in South Carolina, from which vantage point we can observe the development of a quite different sort of planter elite than that that evolved in Virginia, one that deployed horse racing in ways and for reasons distinct from those that characterized its neighbor to the north.

Perhaps the most important difference between the racing fancy of these two locales is that separating jockey clubs from *the* Jockey Club. As we have seen, Virginians established these organizations in every community in Tidewater and Southside Virginia with the requisite number of inhabitants who were interested in turf matters and sufficiently wealthy not only to own blooded horses but to make a financial contribution toward renting or purchasing a course and organizing the associated social events that rendered the sport genteel. The area around Stafford County, in the Tidewater region, alone boasted seven clubs before the Revolution. South Carolina, by contrast, largely followed the English model of a single jockey club, whose members were drawn from the ranks of a wider elite.[7] This club was, and would remain, more accurately known as the Charleston Jockey Club, as it was headquartered first at the city's York Course, then at its Newmarket track, and finally at the Washington Course, and although its members included men who were not usually resident in the city, its most active participants were those who lived there year-round.

This is not to say that South Carolina had no other jockey clubs prior to the Civil War; although they were not nearly as numerous as in Virginia, they developed in a number of communities throughout the Lowcountry. The earliest, in Georgetown, on the coast sixty miles north of Charleston, constituted itself in 1744, a decade before the formation of the SCJC. Although this club's suspension of its competitions during the War of Independence ended up lasting for a half century, in the 1820s it was revived and began to stage its own Race Week, during which "the entire society of the district joined together to enjoy the present and to share memories of a common past," in a manner more redolent of homespun Independence Day festivities than of the glamourous sociability associated with the Charleston races. The St. George's Jockey Club formed in 1786 in Dorchester County, about fifty miles inland from Charleston, an area in which racing had existed on an informal basis for decades; it developed from a prewar hunting club and included eminent local horse breeders, including Ralph Izard, a United States senator who "excelled in horsemanship and manly exercises," and Wade Hampton I, who would become one of the richest planters in the entire South. Five years later in St. Stephen's Parish, in Berkeley County, local planters such as the Scots migrant Captain James Sinkler and his brother Peter combined with Charlestonians William Alston, Stephen Mazyck, Henry Ravenel, and others to form the Santee Jockey Club, named for the nearby river. And that same year, also in Berkeley County, the planters of the nascent community of Pineville laid out the St. Stephen's course and established a jockey club that in its first year enrolled nearly a hundred members and that would remain in operation until the Civil War.[8]

These groups existed largely as supplements to rather than competitors of the Charleston club, in contrast to the situation in Virginia. Many of those who joined one of the former also belonged to the latter but also sought the opportunity to race their horses closer to their plantations, or enjoyed being the proverbial big fish in small ponds. They might not boast the level of wealth or social status that would allow them to play a leading role in the SCJC, but they could do so in a smaller club, most of whose members were their kin and their neighbors. For others, the smaller size and lesser formality of these groups' events offered a more relaxed atmosphere than that of Race Week in Charleston; the rural sociologist W. H. Mills described the Santee club's meetings as offering "pleasure divested of every attraction for the mere business men of the Turf, and many worthy old gentlemen, surrounded by their descendants of the second generation, came out to have a day's enjoyment." Even the ritual formulae of these clubs—the precisely minuted meetings, the proliferation of offices, and the elaborate rules for the admittance or blackballing of new members and the exclusion of established ones—may have held a special appeal for participants. Some of the clubs advertised their races in the metropolitan newspapers, as the Pineville Jockey Club did in the *Charleston Mercury* throughout the early 1850s, but this publicity was probably aimed at informing their members' urban friends and relations of their activities rather than convincing Charlestonian readers to travel to attend them.[9] For the members of these smaller jockey clubs, as for so many people throughout the state and beyond, Race Week in Charleston was the only event that really mattered, both for those who loved the sport and those who attended in pursuit of other agendas. The SCJC was fully aware of and untroubled by the fact that some of its members were also involved in other clubs; the 1828 revision of the club's rules stated that "gentlemen residents of this State, shall not be considered as entitled to any of the hospitalities of this Club," because such individuals, regardless of where in South Carolina they resided or whether or not they belonged to other clubs, would presumably be eligible to join the SCJC, and if they opted not to do so, or were not sufficiently affluent or respectable to receive such an honor, they could not expect the trackside reception and amenities afforded to those who had chosen to join.[10]

The colony of South Carolina was established in 1670, more than six decades after the beginning of English settlement in Virginia, and although it seems that some type of horse racing existed on an informal basis during its first fifty years, it appears not to have evolved any type of vernacular horse sport comparable to the Old Dominion's quarter-racing tradition. But the dramatic growth in the European market for rice meant that, by the 1730s, South Carolinian planters were as willing and as able as wealthy Virginian tobacco cultivators to adopt at least some elements of the lifestyle of the English gentry, and to purchase expensive imported items, including blooded horses. According to the Charleston-born Quaker missionary Sophia Hume, the inhabitants of her native city were all too keen to "mimick *Great Britain* in every Foppery, Luxury and Recreation." By the time that Hume made this comment, more than fifteen years had passed since the 1734 opening of Charleston's, and the colony's, first racecourse, the York Course, located at the Quarter House inn approximately five miles beyond the city limits. For most of its first decade, this course hosted only sporadic meetings, but after 1743, when John Hanbury became both the landlord and the track manager, it scheduled races nearly every month, usually not for purses but for luxury items such as a gold watch or a piece of silver plate. This practice may have resulted from a shortage of specie in the region, but it also increased the course's appeal to members of the nascent Charleston elite, some of whom felt that money prizes were "beneath the dignity of a gentleman to give or receive." Hanbury capitalized on this social cachet by constructing a "Gallery for the Ladies" and another for male racegoers, making the York Course the first racetrack in Britain's American colonies to offer its attendees the opportunity to segregate themselves from the hoi polloi.[11]

The York Course's inconvenient distance from the city caused it in 1754 to be succeeded by one named, rather predictably, Newmarket, which was located on the Common at Charleston Neck, and was managed from 1760 to 1770 by a Yorkshire-born saddler named Thomas Nightingale, and then by James Strickland, until the outbreak of the War of Independence curtailed its activities. It was at Newmarket that the SCJC was formed in 1758, and within a few years the club became the sponsor of three races, the Charleston Plate, the Colt's Plate, and the Sweepstakes, at meetings held in February and March. Like its predecessor, Newmarket usually offered the winners of its events not money prizes but what a nostalgic commentator at the beginning of the twentieth century hymned as the "pieces of plate that still grace the sideboards of old Charlestonians, which were won by their ancestors, who owned race horses in the days in which the sport still had something noble about it."[12]

On the brink of the Revolution, the Newmarket course had developed an elaborate program of competitions to which the local newspaper, the *South Carolina Gazette,* and other publications devoted considerable attention, offering detailed accounts of the horses scheduled to compete and the odds on each of them, as well as on the weather conditions that were likely to affect the outcomes. Many Charlestonian shopkeepers and merchants, aware of the large number of city residents and visitors who attended these events, made their way to the track, where they held auctions (locally known as vendues) or rented booths in which to display their goods. The races became a central element in the development of a winter social season in Charleston, which also included concerts, theatrical performances, lectures, and, above all, balls, activities that enticed many planters and their families to the city. But unlike these other pastimes, the races were attended not only by men and women of the upper classes but by poor whites, free people of color, and sometimes even enslaved men and women. Elite Charlestonians engaged in "performances of consumption" at balls and concerts in order to impress one another, but at the racetrack their audience was both larger and more varied, and their expenditures on fashionable clothes and accessories, lavish carriages, and large wagers, and, for the members of the SCJC, on blooded horses and jockey silks, helped justify their political and social dominance not only to their peers but to those whom most considered their inferiors, reinforcing the seemingly immutable nature of the community's social hierarchy, the paternalistic relationships between elite and plebeian whites, and the universal subalternity of people of African descent. By the 1760s, the colony's legislature recessed for the first week of February to allow delegates to attend the races, whether to watch their horses in competition, place wagers, or simply enjoy the spectacle that John Randolph of Roanoke, visiting from Virginia, described as an "unusually brilliant" gathering of "beautiful women, gallant fellows, and elegant equipages." The Boston lawyer Josiah Quincy Jr., on a trip to Charleston in 1773, wrote flippantly in his journal of his intention to attend "the famous races" and was both amused and disgusted by the fact that the owner of a winning horse "assumed the airs of a hero or German potentate" and that local society seemed to consider "the ingenuity of a Locke or the discoveries of a Newton . . . infinitely inferior to the accomplishments of him who knew when . . . to start a fleet horse," but few Charlestonians shared his skepticism about their values.[13]

In South Carolina, as in Virginia, horse racing essentially ground to a halt during the American Revolution, but the war's end saw the state's turfmen eager to revive the sport, as in the Old Dominion. As noted above, the late 1780s and early 1790s saw the formation of a number of jockey clubs in the plantation districts of the Lowcountry, but it was, inevitably, in Charleston that racing, in the opinion of both participants in and historians of the sport, entered a new and glorious era. Although the Newmarket course reopened in 1785, according to Irving, "the number of horses trained [for the track] was few, and not many races were run in public," and a Scots visitor described the state of the track as "very indifferent," in spite of the reorganization of the SCJC in 1783, and again in 1788, in the hope of placing Charleston racing on a more secure financial footing. But in 1792 the club, after a fourth and, as it turned out, final

Washington Course, Charleston, S.C., by H. Bosse, after a daguerreotype by B. Y. Glen, 1857. Library of Congress, Prints and Photographs Division.

restructuring, abandoned Newmarket in favor of the newly established Washington Course, formerly part of John Gibbes's Orange Grove plantation, which lay just north of the contemporary city limits, in what is now Hampton Park. Irving described this moment as the beginning of "a period destined to be the commencement of a new era in the annals of racing in this State," as well as throughout the South.[14]

That this "golden age" of Charlestonian racing began in the early 1790s is a noteworthy development, because at this time the city had not merely declined from its prerevolutionary economic apex but was no longer the capital of South Carolina, a status it had held since the colony's establishment. In 1786 the state legislature, under pressure from delegates from the increasingly populous "Upcountry," or western, part of the state, voted to designate a site that they proposed to name Columbia, located just over a hundred miles northwest of Charleston, in Richland County, as a new, "more centrical" seat of government from 1790 onward. Many Charlestonians were appalled that their city was being supplanted in this way, and that its replacement was not even a rival conurbation but a "wilderness of pines" that had only its geographic situation to recommend it. An architectural historian described the public buildings that were erected in Charleston after its loss of capital status as reflecting a "decline in civic aspiration," but the city was far from devoid of ambition in other areas, in which racing figured significantly. If it could no longer be a political center, it would become a "planters' city," a "resort for the region's wealthiest," in which "wealthy men, of ancient name" who had infused Charleston and its environs with their "aristocratic ideas" would continue to exert their influence through what today would be described as "soft power." Columbia might have become the locus of South Carolinian politics, but Charleston would maintain its dominance in the social, economic, and cultural spheres, and would continue to attract those who sought every type of asset or advancement, from fashionable clothing to marital alliances to business partnerships, even in the absence of its role as the seat of government. And what could be more appealing than the presence of top-quality racing, in a milieu of unquestionable respectability that could nonetheless accommodate participants of diverse backgrounds, to attract visitors from throughout the state, as well as from elsewhere within and beyond the United States? Such social and sporting capital was unattainable by the small and provincial town of Columbia, which sank into a torpor when the Assembly was not in session.[15]

What was it about the fourth iteration of the SCJC that facilitated the reestablishment of racing in Charleston on a far grander scale than it had attained before the Revolution, especially in a city that had just lost its position as the capital and a state that was still recovering from the destruction it had endured during wartime? The short answer is that the men who led the club at this time were determined that its activities would promote not just outstanding sport and an atmosphere of gentility, its goals since its formation, but also the continued social and cultural primacy of Charleston within South Carolina and the wider South. This broadening of the club's remit did not gain the approval of every Lowcountry turfman, some of whom would have preferred that Charlestonian racing remain the preserve of an inherently limited number of long-established local families of irreproachable dignity, and who were particularly incensed by the replacement of pieces of silver plate with sizable purses as prizes. A few of these men, including the former York Course manager Nightingale and the Berkeley County planter and turfman Daniel Ravenel of Wantoot, so despised this "departure from the good old customs of their fathers" that they withdrew both themselves and their stables from competitions at the Washington Course, but the other club members were undeterred by their absence, and by 1797 the SCJC's races offered purses as large as $1,200 for a sweepstakes victory.[16]

The Charlestonian who made the most significant contribution to the success of the newly reorganized and relocated jockey club was the lawyer and planter Charles Cotesworth Pinckney, a Revolutionary War veteran and a delegate to the Constitutional Convention. Pinckney neither owned, bred, nor trained blooded horses, and according to his friend Christopher Gadsden, the rector of Charleston's St. Philip's Church, he "neither made bets nor played cards," yet he, along with the former state governor William Moultrie, the architect Gabriel Manigault II, the military hero and state senator William Alston, Edward Fenwick Jr., who owned the renowned John's Island stud farm, and the aforementioned Wade Hampton I, was one of the twenty founding proprietors of the Washington Course. Such an involvement might seem a peculiar choice for a man who did not own horses or wager on races, but for Pinckney the continued existence of the jockey club as an institution was far more important than the activities it promoted. As Marvin R. Zahniser observed, in Pinckney's eyes, the club was "more than an organization which promoted horse racing; it was a social club of such pre-eminence that to be admitted was a recognition of pedigree and an indication of acceptance into the social establishment." Although he was involved in many of the other clubs and organizations that proliferated in the city, playing a leading role in the Charleston Library Society, the Society for Relief of Widows and Orphans, the Charleston Bible Society, and the Society of the Cincinnati, as well as contributing to the foundation of South Carolina College in Columbia (now the University of South Carolina), he expended tremendous energy on the jockey club, not only serving as its president for a number of years but devoting much of his time to its administration. Margaret Izard Manigault, the wife of Pinckney's fellow club member and track proprietor Gabriel Manigault II, who was Charleston society's leading hostess at the beginning of the nineteenth century, wrote in 1805 to her mother, Alice DeLancey Izard, that Pinckney was "always very much occupied with the Jockey Club . . . that employs him all day long." During Race Week, he not only attended all of the club's sporting and social events but turned his large house on Broad Street into a center for entertaining the most elite visitors to the Washington Course.[17]

Although Race Week's existence predated the American Revolution, and thus Pinckney's involvement with the SCJC, it was in the era of his leadership that it took on a significantly expanded role in Charlestonian social life. This change is epitomized by the fact that, by the late 1790s, the principal events organized by the city's St. Cecilia Society were scheduled in order to accommodate the club's schedule. The membership of the society, which had formed in 1737 to promote the performance and enjoyment of concert music, at any time included a number of members of the SCJC, but the former was notably more socially exclusive than the latter. A Carolinian turfman who was generally considered to be well-mannered and of good character was likely to be admitted to the jockey club, even if his antecedents were humble, whereas participation in the St. Cecilia Society passed from father to son within Charleston's oldest families, and its door "was shut to the plebeian and the man of business." But while the society outranked the club in terms of social prestige, the men of the former, whether or not they were members of the latter, were all too aware that they would struggle to attract audiences to their concerts if attending meant missing the club's dinner or ball, and thus they opted to reschedule or even cancel their activities during Race Week. For the SCJC it was unthinkable to move Race Week to another date, just as it would have been to hold it more than once a year, despite the fact that nearly all other antebellum tracks had meetings in both the spring and the fall. According to Irving, whenever the question of an additional annual event was raised, club members "invariably set their faces against it, with great wisdom, feeling the force of the reasoning of [the ancient Roman poet] Juvenal: 'Voluptates commendat rarior usus.' Our pleasures have a higher relish when they are rarely used. The keenest sense of delight is sure to be blunted by a too frequent repetition."[18]

Perhaps it was Pinckney's very lack of personal commitment to racing that allowed him to understand what so many antebellum Virginian turfmen appear to have missed: that in order for a jockey club to become and remain successful it could not rely exclusively on the local racing fancy, and thus its members needed to focus their energies as much on the social aspects of its activities as they did on the sporting elements thereof. It was essential that the former evoke not just respectability but glamour, making the track a place at which elite women were not merely willing but eager to appear, regardless of the degree of their interest in racing. And in physically large states with widely dispersed populations, such as Virginia and South Carolina, the most effective way to convince those who lived at some distance from a racecourse to expend the time, money, and effort to make a multiday visit was to locate the race meeting within a broader spectrum of social and cultural events, which might be enjoyable for their own sake but which were also venues in which familial, financial, and political business could be transacted.[19] Under such circumstances, a visit to Charleston for February's Race Week would appear to many as not just a pleasure but an imperative, and those who had little commitment to racing would nonetheless feel obligated to make an appearance trackside in order to display their clothing, horses, and carriages (showing both their taste and their presumed wealth), meet their friends and kin, and make themselves known in the city that continued to portray itself as the social and cultural center not merely of the state but of the entire South. The pleasures of this "season of incessant gaiety" were set out in an 1846 issue of the *Charleston Mercury:* "The Race Course in the morning—dinner parties in the afternoon, and Balls in the evening, occupy pleasantly the thoughts and attention of that very large portion of our community, who look forward to participate once a year in the sports of our Turf, and the good things of our *little World.*" It was not surprising that, according to a northern visitor of the previous decade, "at the races, all Carolina comes up to Charleston, as the tribes of Greece met at Olympia."[20]

The prevalent impression of Charleston during Race Week that emerges from the testimony of those who attended it at any point between the beginning of the nineteenth century and the outbreak of the Civil War is of a "great assemblage of people," both at the course and throughout the city. For those who could not rely on relatives or friends for accommodation, lodging was difficult to come by, as "the town was crowded with strangers, [and] the hotels overflowing." The English lawyer James Stuart, who came to Charleston in 1830 in the course of a multiyear tour of the United States, was turned away first from Jones' Hotel on Broad Street, which was "unquestionably the best in the city," and then from Angus Stewart's Carolina Coffee House on Tradd Street before he found a room at the "respectable" Planters' Hotel at the corner of Church and Queen Streets.[21] At the previous year's Race Week, the German-born merchant

John Christopher Schulz, whose wife was Susan Flud Cantey, the daughter of the owner of the celebrated Albine, had found when he arrived in Charleston from his home far upcountry in Pendleton that "there never was so great a crowd of strangers in this City before, every boarding house is filled, even the steam boats and other vessels lying at the wharves have their cabins filled with lodgers." It was almost as difficult to find accommodation for horses, other than those scheduled to compete; Schulz had to make his way to the "lines," the old fortifications at the city's northern edge, to stable his mount in a wagon yard. The situation was no better in the mid-1840s, when the Virginian agricultural scientist Edmund Ruffin found the Carolina Hotel on Broad Street so full that his only option was "a cot mattress in a large room where some half a dozen were placed." Even those who were able to find rooms at the city's leading hotels were not always pleased with their accommodation; the Pineville planter Robert Cahusac, who attended Race Week in 1822 and stayed, like Stuart, at the Planters' Hotel, complained to his friend William Porcher that the establishment was "so much crowded, & such a continual riot kept up, that no satisfaction was to be enjoy'd either day or Night," and that this "scene of dissipation was not very congenial" to "sober fellows" like himself. Even the aforementioned Alice Izard, whose husband was a turfman and who for decades was one of Charleston's leading hostesses, admitted that any newcomer to the city in the weeks surrounding Race Week "would think it the most dissipated place in the world."[22]

The next challenge for racetrack-goers was to get from their homes or lodgings to the course itself. According to the Charleston physician David Ramsay, for several hours prior to the opening of each day's races "the road leading to the course is so crowded that access to the city is very difficult"; the streets were thronged both by track attendees and by those—generally people of lower socioeconomic status, including "countrymen of the 'cracker' type," free people of color, and the enslaved—who could not afford admission, and "thronged to the race . . . on foot or in primitive carts and wagons" to watch this cavalcade as it passed by. As post time approached, "a solemn stillness reign[ed] throughout the streets," which were "for the most part deserted," as Charleston itself was "transferred to the race ground." And while the local and visiting gentry left the course as soon as the races concluded, returning to town to attend dinner parties, followed by concerts or balls, those of middling and lower status remained trackside, "divert[ing] themselves with some hack races, after which they repaired to the booths [food vendors], and finished the day in humble imitation of their superiors."[23] James Shoolbred, the British consul in the city, painted a similar picture, writing to his father that "the Town is absolutely depopulated" during the races, and "the race grounds become the promenade of Fashion and the Exchange for men of Business." Although Shoolbred's local residence and his lack of interest in the sport prevented him from having to struggle to find a place to stay or to fight his way through the crowds to the track, he nonetheless felt the effects of Race Week, expressing his relief when it ended and his hope that "people will now recover their senses which like an Incumberance they are usually in the habit of laying aside" while the races were on.[24]

Shoolbred was far from the only Charleston resident who disliked and disapproved of the races. As in Virginia, a number of Charlestonians deplored the sport on religious grounds. By the time the Washington Course opened, they had succeeded in ensuring that "no sports or pastimes, as . . . horse-racing . . . shall be allowed on the Lord's day"—Race Week commenced on a Wednesday and concluded the following Saturday—but their claims that racing was at best a waste of time and at worst the promoter of numerous sins had little effect.[25] The young William Plumer Jacobs, who would later found South Carolina's Presbyterian College and serve for almost a half century as a pastor in the Upcountry town of Clinton, admitted as much in an imaginary dialogue that he composed in his diary as Race Week loomed in February 1859:

> The races, the races! I am going up to the race-course, are you? "Yes." Such is the conversation I hear all around me; everyone is full of the races, the horses, betting and gambling, and I care for none of them. The races, what good is there in making two or more poor horses run themselves to death? Why on earth don't they get two steamcars and set them running? "No sport." O, no sport, eh! Put you on behind. "Dangerous." O, it is not dangerous to the horses and their riders to run at such a rate. "None of my look-out." Go heartless wretch and learn Philanthropy. "Well, but I can win money." Yes, and lose it too and that is your lookout. "What's money to me?" It would be a great deal to the starving and dying poor. "I can do as I please with my money." It is wrong to use it for gambling. "I made my own money." God gave it to you and God can take it from you again. "Mind your own business." Tis no use arguing with such breath-wasters.[26]

Evangelical Christian denominations made significant inroads among the inhabitants of the Upcountry but had little impact in Charleston and the surrounding plantation districts, and thus their critiques of the morality of racing are unlikely to have discouraged many of the inhabitants from participating in Race Week. Nor did the state's Episcopal hierarchy concur with that of Virginia that racing was sinful; the Charlestonian artist Charles Fraser, writing in 1854, claimed that the city's "clergymen thought it no impropriety to see a well contested race," and the Presbyterian minister Moses Waddel's disgust for what he perceived as the problematic worldliness of Charleston society was epitomized by the fact that men of the cloth could often be found at the newly opened Washington Course, cheering for the horses on whose success they had wagered.[27]

Had Waddel overcome his scruples and visited the track, he would almost certainly have agreed with the Methodist minister Francis Asbury, who passed through Charleston that same year, that the city was "the seat of Satan, dissipation and folly," and he would have been still more alarmed if he had been aware that some of his fellow attendees had traveled great distances in order to be part of Race Week because of, not despite, their belief that it was "a season of much dissipation." He would undoubtedly have observed a good deal of gambling, not only among the turfmen but also by women and people of color. The industrialist Joseph Wharton, visiting from New Jersey in search of investors, wrote to his fiancée, Anna Lovering, that at the track "the darkies were there in shoals and are as great bettors as their betters among whom I saw many bank notes change hands while the darkies passed round their half and quarter dollars with much noise." Women were expected to abstain from gambling with money, but it was acceptable for them to wager with small personal items, such as pairs of gloves, boxes of sugarplums, or books; their male escorts were expected to allow them to bet on the favorite in each competition. Female guests might pass this favor on to young children, "initiat[ing] [them] in the art of gambling in sugarplums" and wagering on the horse with the shortest odds in the hope of gaining "a shower of bonbons" for the youths. But even such an innocuous form of speculation was anathema to "Theodore," who wrote in the *Charleston Courier* in 1842 that "horse-racing and the race course are monstrous evils" because they were beset by "betting, gambling, and profanation," which he believed constituted a far more powerful lure to the track than the mere "pleasures of the turf." His sentiments were echoed by Mr. Miles, who taught English at a local boys' school, but sixteen-year-old Alexander Cheves Haskell, later a Confederate colonel and a South Carolina Democratic politician, reasoned that, because he "never bet and did not mean to," despite his "love for Miles" he could go to the course in 1855, where he encountered his mathematics teacher. "It became bliss when I found that he had picked the same horse that I had," but Haskell does not report whether or not Mr. Searle also forbore placing a wager on Charley Ball.[28]

While the possibility of gambling attracted many people to the Charleston races, opportunities for the public display of fashion and other forms of consumerism held at least as much appeal. The Scotsman J. B. Dunlop, who attended 1811's Race Week, considered this materialism the event's most noteworthy characteristic, noting the "grand display of new carriages" and the fact that "all are envious which should carry off the public opinion with regard to taste." In accordance with the stereotype of Scots as penny-pinchers, Dunlop objected not to any perceived frivolity or irreligion in this display but rather to its financial implications; he claimed that "the custom is carried so far that a Planter will embarrass himself for one half of the year for the gratification of shewing on this occasion something superior." But when one considers that the races attracted most people of economic and political as well as social influence from throughout the Lowcountry, in addition to many affluent visitors from outside the region, any financial "embarrassment" engendered by the purchase of a lavish and heavily taxed new vehicle (such as the coach-and-four, with outriders, that carried the women of the Alston family to the course in the 1820s, and from which, like other elite female attendees, they watched the competitions) or stylish new clothing was insignificant in comparison with the humiliation of being seen trackside in a dilapidated conveyance or wearing worn or outdated clothing. Such a shabby appearance could be interpreted as evidence of one's poverty, miserliness, or failure to understand the nature of the event, all of which might result in failure to raise a loan, make a match for a son or daughter, or influence a piece of legislation. It is not surprising that the "gentlefolks" would make every attempt to "outdo" one another, whether through "splendid Equipages" or via "dress bonnets and gay costume." Colonel Henry Wilton, the lightly fictionalized father of the Charlestonian memoirist Caroline Howard Gilman, disapproved of flamboyant fashions and outfitted his adolescent daughter in a simple dark-colored riding dress for her first appearance at the Washington Course, but as he was "something of a jockey, and had a direct interest in the races . . . it was with no small care that he fitted out his equipage" in which he and his family drove to and from the track.[29] Wilton considered Caroline's inconspicuous attire a sign of his family's refinement, but to travel to the Washington Course in a modest carriage drawn by unspectacular horses would have offended his sense of himself as a leading local turfman.

While men needed only to be neatly attired and well-groomed, it was incumbent upon women, especially those who were young and unmarried, to appear at the track in new clothes of the latest fashion, perfectly coiffed and elegantly accessorized. The "Rice Prince" J. Motte Alston, scion of one of the oldest and wealthiest Lowcountry families and grandson of the prominent turfman Colonel William Alston, first attended the races circa 1826, at which time he was still "a little fellow with long ringlets," but even in his old age he remembered his pleasure in seeing "the ladies of Charleston . . . turned out in full feather," not least his famously glamorous aunt, Maria Alston Nisbett, who as a leading belle of the city had married the British aristocrat Sir John Nisbett of Dean in 1797. Sally Baxter Hampton, the Manhattan-bred wife of Frank Hampton, younger brother of the immensely rich planter and future Confederate commander Wade Hampton III, writing to her unmarried sister Lucy, urged her to "brisk up" for the "topping time" she would have when she attended Race Week when she visited the Hamptons, and reminded her to "bring your prettiest ball dresses—you won't need much else."[30]

Observers' opinions varied significantly with regard to the fashions on parade at the Washington Course and the SCJC's Race Ball. The architect Robert Mills, visiting from Baltimore in 1817, wrote to his wife that "the ladies displayed a great deal of good taste, nothing gaudy," and he was particularly pleased to see that many wore simple white dresses, set off to advantage by colorful accessories that were "judiciously disposed" and of "delicate character." Another mid-Atlantic visitor, Henry Wharton of Philadelphia, whose sister Emily had married the Lowcountry planter and racing enthusiast Charles Sinkler, was similarly impressed by the "handsome dressing" he saw at the 1848 ball.[31] But the New England–born writer John Milton Mackie, who had heard so much about the "*grande toilette*" of Charlestonian women in Race Week, was disappointed to find that, though they were "sufficiently pretty and high-bred," many of them were "over-dressed for the occasion," attending the races "in full feather; in ermine and point lace; in light brocades and cashmeres of India," while some older women wore costly jewels that Mackie considered "more appropriate for a ballroom." He was more favorably impressed by the appearance of the male attendees in their "easy morning attire" and was pleased to report that he did not see "a single specimen of the black-satin-vest gentry." Caroline Howard Gilman, the author of the fictionalized memoir *Recollections of a Southern Matron*, sneered at the eye-catching outfits of the "city belles" she encountered at the Washington Course, whom she criticized further for their apparent lack of interest in the horses; in her opinion, the ladies had missed the point of the February races by seeing them as sites of fashion rather than sport.[32]

Gilman's fictive stand-in, Cornelia Wilton, described herself as having been "brought up in a kind of companionship" with her father's blooded horses, so for her to watch these "noble creatures" compete at the Washington Course offered sufficient romance, beauty, and excitement. But the principal attraction of Race Week for many women was the "gay and brilliant" Race Ball, which was held on Friday evening, after the end of the third and penultimate day of racing, at the St. Andrew's Society Hall on Broad Street, the site of many of the city's "self-affirming rituals," including SCJC meetings. Even John Beaufain Irving, who was both passionate and deeply knowledgeable about the horses, jockeys, trainers, and races that he had observed over many years' attendance at the Charleston track, or about which he had read in historical accounts thereof, rhapsodized about the event as "the ball, par excellence, of all balls." An attendee of 1848's event was equally impressed, noting "the tables ornamented with appropriate devices, and covered with nick-nacks of all sorts," "the pyramids of confectionery and classically formed temples, glittering with precious *bon bons*," and the "extensive display of ice cakes, tasteful specimens of *l'art de confiseur*." Such lavish display did not come cheaply; in 1831 the club authorized an allocation of seven hundred dollars for the evening, which equates to around twenty thousand dollars in modern money.

For many SCJC members and their male guests, it was the club dinner that was the true highlight of the week, "the culinary apex of the social year," at which attendees feasted upon "real turtle soup, wild turkies, venison, grouse, partridges, pheasants, shad, and all the smaller fry of delicacies, not forgetting pate de foie gras in great abundance, and wines of great value, such as [the German Riesling] Johannisberg of 1822." Held on Wednesday evening following the first day of the races, this entertainment centered upon animated discussions of equine lore and racing history, capped by the club's president leading the attendees in the SCJC's anthem, "The High-Mettled Racer." By contrast, the ball, although it too was organized by the club, followed a similar formula to that of its sole rival in prestige, that of the St. Cecilia Society, which was also held in February; both took place at the St. Andrew's Hall and featured "the same silver and cut glass, and probably the very same servants waited on the guests of both."[33] At these dances it was the female guests who took center stage; not only was their appearance considerably more colorful, fashionable, and varied than that of the men, but the unmarried girls and women among them were very much on display to potential husbands. Parents who might have little interest in the sport on offer at the Washington Course would nonetheless come to the city for Race Week in the hope that their daughters, who would be on view both in the trackside ladies' grandstand and on the floor of the St. Andrew's Hall, might attract the attention of single men of appropriate social status, and thus invitations to the ball were both greatly coveted and strictly limited to individuals of the most impressive lineage and the greatest respectability. For men and women who spent much of the year on isolated plantations the ball offered their best opportunity to meet a suitable spouse, and they would have known of many who had found, as in the title of a poem published in the *Charleston Courier* in 1822, "Love at the Jockey Club Ball." Sally Hampton's instruction to her sister Lucy to bring her most becoming ball gowns with her for her Race Week visit may have been made in the hope that this New Yorker would follow her sister's path and, by joining the "band of Sylphs, in their mystic round / [who] will lightly dance to the music's sound," would captivate, and wed, a rich and genteel Carolina turfman.[34]

All of this is not to imply that Race Week was bereft of top-class horse sport or that much-anticipated competitions such as the famous match race between Albine and Planet were few and far between. The SCJC succeeded up to the outbreak of the Civil War in ensuring that the horses, jockeys, trainers, and owners it attracted to the Washington Course remained among the finest that the South, and thus the nation, could offer. Although, as we will see in a subsequent chapter, the quarter century prior to the beginning of the conflict saw racecourses in the Lower Mississippi Valley, particularly those in and around

New Orleans and Natchez, rise to prominence, the latter throughout the Lower South and the former on a national basis, the Palmetto State continued to boast outstanding stables, particularly those of Wade Hampton II and his namesake son at the family's Millwood plantation near Columbia and William Sinkler at Eutaw in Berkeley County, whose owners considered Charleston the most important venue in which to display the mettle of their bloodstock and their jockeys, the majority of whom were also their slaves. For a South Carolinian turfman, no amount of money or acclaim gained at an out-of-state venue, or achievement in commerce or politics, could trump the satisfaction of appearing before one's peers in the "inner circle of triumphant owners" at a February Race Week at the Washington Course.[35]

On the brink of the Civil War, Carolinian racing aficionados expressed their confidence that, were the United States to follow the English precedent and establish a national jockey club, Charleston was the obvious choice for its location. Not only, they claimed, was it ideal in geographical terms, as it was reachable by sea from Virginia and Maryland, and by rail from Louisiana, Alabama, Georgia, Tennessee, and Kentucky, but, at least as importantly, it had developed and for many decades maintained a turf that was of "high character . . . free from any taint or stain," as it had been entirely "in the hands of gentlemen" of "moral force." The creation of a national racing organization headquartered in Charleston, they claimed, "would make racing in this country what it is in England—the acknowledged favorite sport of the best classes in society."[36] As we have seen, such a claim might have been made about racing in Virginia in the years just before the American Revolution, and perhaps also in the early decades of the nineteenth century, but, Lafayette's visit to Tree Hill notwithstanding, it was no longer plausible beyond that point. And, as will be discussed later in this work, the newer tracks of the Lower Mississippi Valley, although they boasted richer patrons and horses at least as fine as those of the Washington Course, did not attract large numbers of the "best classes" to the same extent as did the latter. But the outbreak of war just over a year later, and the cessation of racing throughout the Confederate states during this conflict, forestalled further exploration of this possibility.

Considering how much more successful South Carolinians seem to have been than Virginians in maintaining both the prestige and the popularity of horse racing within their state, it may be a surprise to learn that the long-established planter families of the former group were experiencing financial struggles that were almost as challenging as those faced by the latter. Although the Lowcountry did not undergo processes of soil exhaustion as severe as those that afflicted the Tidewater, the cultivation of rice was no longer as profitable as it had been in the final two-thirds of the eighteenth century, when the Lowcountry planters had made their fortunes and become known as "rice princes." As a northern visitor noted in the 1840s, by that time Charleston "depends alone on her commerce—her exports, her imports, her receipts and sales of produce from the interior, and the supply afforded in return, for an increase in prosperity."[37] The relocation of the capital to Columbia symbolized the realignment of the state's economy, away from the rice and indigo that had for more than a century been cultivated along the coast and toward the cotton that was the staple of the ever-more-populous Upcountry and that, after 1760, was the colony's, and later the state's, most lucrative product. The British naval officer Basil Hall, who attended Race Week in 1828, found the Washington Course far less crowded than he had expected and reported that he "was informed by at least twenty different persons, that this was a most unfavourable specimen of the races, which of late has been falling off, chiefly, it has been suggested, in consequence of the division of property, by which so many of the large estates had been melted down. These great landed proprietors . . . who used in former days to give such éclat to the Charleston races, are no longer to be found on the turf."[38] Unlike some of Britain's North American colonies, South Carolina had never established primogeniture or entail within its laws regarding inheritance; at the Constitutional Convention the SCJC stalwart Charles Pinckney had urged its abolition across the new nation, fearing that the republic's integrity would be compromised if a few men acquired "large amounts" of money and land in this way. But, as in Virginia, the practice of partible inheritance meant that over a few generations even a vast estate could be divided into tracts that could not generate sufficient profits to fund a lavish way of life.[39]

By the early years of the nineteenth century Charleston's economy was also suffering from the end of the transatlantic slave trade in 1807. As Gregory E. O'Malley has shown, the sale and purchase of Africans was "not just big business in colonial Charleston, it was *the* business—the commerce around which all other economic activities pivoted." The city was the landing point for almost half of the captives imported to North America, and for some Carolinians the opportunity to buy slaves was the only truly compelling reason to travel there. As it was not possible for planters to conclude their business within a day, socialites and entrepreneurs alike organized the winter social season to coincide with the peak arrival time of ships from Africa in order to take advantage of the influx of visitors. Of course, Charleston was not alone in forfeiting much of its economic vitality when importation of enslaved Africans was outlawed, but no other southern city was as dependent on this type of commerce, and thus as affected by its conclusion.[40]

Some Charlestonians were moved to draw dispiriting comparisons between their city and Venice. They were aware of the physical resemblance between the two locales' low-lying, marshy landscapes that gave the impression both of "ris[ing] out of the water" and "growing out of the waves" and flattered themselves that their conurbation had developed a similarly distinctive architectural and cultural style. Some of the city's old Huguenot families, "tracing their descent even back to a prior emigration from Italy into France, claim[ed] as their ancestor one of the Doges," the leaders of Venice from its beginnings to Napoleon's conquest. But they feared that their fate might be similar to that of the Venetians, that their city too would lose its political and commercial dominance and become a beautiful ghost of what it had been in its glory days. If the transfer of the state capital to Columbia symbolized the displacement of the Lowcountry "rice princes" in favor of the inland "cotton snobs," the emergence of New York to the north and New Orleans to the south dethroned Charleston from its position as the United States' great Atlantic port. At the time of the Constitutional Convention, the city was the fourth-largest in the new nation, but its population, white and Black alike, declined dramatically over the second quarter of the nineteenth century, and in 1860 it was not even among the twenty-largest American metropolises. The lawyer and writer Henry Cruger's claim that Charleston's "deserted and sepulchral streets" and its "time-worn, rusty, and mouldering edifices" were reminiscent of the "blank, icy, and desolate aspect of that other city afar" would have seemed hyperbolic to the majority of his neighbors, but from 1830 onward many of them found reasons to worry about their city's prospects in a nation with whose practices and values it appeared increasingly out of step. Fanny Kemble, the English actress who married one of Georgia's leading planters, confirmed these fears during her visit to the city in 1838; she praised it as "highly picturesque" and noted its "look of state, as of quondam wealth and importance," but described it as "a little gone down in the world," although clearly aware of its "former dignity"—much like Venice.[41]

Some members of the city's elite responded to this sense of decline in much the same way as the Virginians, retreating from the unwelcome changes and challenges of the moment into nostalgia either for an idealized version of the times of their youth—like John Randolph of Roanoke—or for a still more romanticized and distant past centered on medievalist fantasy or an obsession with aristocratic lineage. But others, after reflecting upon their city's situation, emerged with a reinvigorated sense of communal self-confidence. The Nullification Crisis of 1832–33, in the course of which South Carolinians refused to abide by the "Tariff of Abominations" that Congress had passed in 1828, and threatened to secede from the Union if they received no redress of their grievances, resulted in their eventual defeat by the obdurate Andrew Jackson, but at the same time it allowed the state to gain regional power as the cradle of southern nationalism. Although Nullification was an issue in the Upcountry as much it was on the coast, it was Lowcountry planter-politicians such as James Hamilton Jr., Robert Barnwell Rhett, and Robert Y. Hayne who emerged as the leaders of this struggle. And although it would be nearly thirty years before South Carolina or any other state actually seceded from the Union, the growing conflict between northern and southern economic interests, in tandem with the steady rise in antislavery sentiment in the North, encouraged the slave states toward closer cooperation with one another, based upon a sense that the federal government was increasingly unsympathetic to their economic needs and cultural values alike. With South Carolina emerging as the leader of the proslavery and states' rights causes, it did not seem impossible that Charleston, rather than following the Venetian model of slow decline into decorative irrelevance, might revive its fortunes and become the "'spiritual capital' of the South, a place dedicated at all costs to maintaining the institution of slavery and all that went along with it."[42]

Charleston's increasing political prominence within the South encouraged ever more people from outside of the state to visit the city, while at the same time it continued to be a magnet for the more affluent residents of the Upcountry and the Lowcountry alike. For both groups, Race Week was as much of a draw as ever. Racing enthusiasts wanted to see top-class sport and to bask in the refined aura of the SCJC, which offered a dramatic contrast to the perceived decline of racing's social capital in cities such as Baltimore, Norfolk, and, of course, Richmond, and those who visited the city purely for social reasons felt that they could not pass up the opportunity to appear at such a prestigious public event. Those like the scientist Edmund Ruffin, who cared neither for the sport nor for its social milieu, and who came to Charleston in the hope of furthering a financial, legal, or political concern, knew that the people with whom they sought audiences would almost certainly be found trackside and that they would likely be relaxed and in good humor in such a setting. These factors, along with the SCJC's meticulous integration of Race Week within the city's winter season of amusements, meant that it was far easier for Charlestonians to maintain the appeal and reputation of their course than it was for Richmonders. At tracks such as Broad Rock and Newmarket it was the sport itself that was the sole attraction, and once these venues gained a reputation for moving down market and being overrun by blacklegs and other unsavory types, they lost their allure to many men and nearly all women of the local gentry, leaving too few reputable attendees to keep the courses either financially or socially sustainable. Charleston, by contrast, had little difficulty up to the outbreak of the Civil War in attracting the South's rich and respectable, including the women and girls whose presence at the Washington Course both attested to and buttressed the track's spotless reputation, and which far more than recompensed the considerable expenses the SCJC had incurred in 1835, at which time the members commissioned the eminent Carolinian architect Edward C. Jones to design an elegant and comfortable new stand for female attendees, "a handsome building with porte-cocheres and balconies." The presence of these ladies was proof of the Washington Course's gentility, even at times when its other guests included "a number of sailors . . . with their girls" and "the negroes, with their dingy misses," who after the departure of the elite sector of the audience proceeded to drink heavily and, by the evening, would "come reeling into town, well charged with wine, rum-punch, gin sling, and sangaree."[43]

Eliza Middleton Fisher was the daughter of Henry Middleton, an exceptionally wealthy South Carolina rice planter who had served as the state's governor, in Congress, and as US minister to Russia. Her letters to her mother, Mary Hering Middleton, after Fisher married into one of Philadelphia's oldest families and relocated to the North, epitomize the pull of Race Week to the American gentry, particularly the women. In October 1839 Fisher, vacationing in Newport, Rhode Island, wrote to Middleton that she was about to visit Mrs. Pierce Butler, also known as Fanny Kemble. Mrs. Butler, according to Fisher, was soon to head back to the South, bringing with her May Appleton, the daughter of the very successful Bostonian businessman Nathan Appleton, one of the founders of the Lowell textile mills. Mrs. Butler and Miss Appleton would then travel to Charleston to ensure their presence "at the time of the races." The following January, Fisher wrote to Middleton regarding Fisher's brother Arthur and his Italian wife, Countess Paolina Bentivoglio, the daughter of an old Roman family, advising her mother that she doubted that the couple would leave their Washington, DC, home to visit their southern relatives "before the *Race Time*, in Charleston." Come mid-February, Middleton reported to her daughter, she and her husband, Henry, would depart Middleton Place, the family's plantation in Dorchester County, and cross the Ashley River to travel the fifteen miles to Charleston "to enjoy the gaieties of the race week—if gaieties they can be called." Mary Middleton returned home some days in advance of her husband, who appears to have found Race Week significantly more enjoyable than his wife did, and who was delighted to recount to her the number and eminence of the events to which Paolina, as an exotic and aristocratic newcomer to the city, had been invited, which included both the St Cecilia and the Jockey Club balls.[44]

Examples such as these bear out Irving's claims regarding the "*peculiar attractiveness of our own Race Course in Charleston*," that it was "a place of sport somewhat different from the generality of Race Grounds" because the SCJC, particularly after it purchased the course from its proprietors in 1836, had consciously developed it not just as a sporting venue but as a site that would "link town and country together, and our State with her sister States, binding them to each other by mutual interests, and the promotion of a common object—to bring together from all parts of our own State, and from racing regions beyond . . . that they may, at least once in twelve months, 'smoke the calumet' of kind feeling and cheerful intercourse, to the continuance of old and the formation of *new* friendships." Given that Irving was not only an enthusiastic participant in the SCJC but its chronicler, one might suspect him of hyperbole, but these claims were borne out by others, including those not native to Charleston. A contributor to the *Southern Literary Messenger*, writing twenty years earlier, described the social pull of Race Week in strikingly similar terms, asserting that the February races "bring strangers together from all parts of the country;

they tend to strengthen the bonds of brotherhood, to create mutual interests, and to bind town and country, and even neighbouring states in more enduring relations of kind feeling and friendly intercourse." The Irish actor Tyrone Power Sr., who visited Charleston in November 1834, lamented that at that time of the year the place was extremely dull, as the planters and their families were in the country, and the city was "abandoned to the cotton-shippers," but he was aware that the situation would be entirely different come February, "when the race-meeting draws the whole State together; and, for a period of four or five weeks, few places, as I learn, can be more lively or more sociable."[45]

But no matter how deftly the SCJC entwined horse racing with the "pleasures of every kind" with which Charleston was intimately associated for a hundred years prior to the Civil War, the outbreak of that conflict dealt a mortal blow to the sport, just as it did in Virginia.[46] As depicted by Whitelaw Reid at the beginning of this chapter, at the war's end the Washington Course was not only in a state of ruin but it was no longer under the SCJC's control, having been confiscated by the Freedmen's Bureau. Yet over the following three decades, while the club's remaining members were unable to resurrect the sport as it had existed in the antebellum era, they did the next best thing: they made the death throes of Charleston racing appear so noble and attractive that they ensured that the memory of Race Week would become integral to the history of horse racing in America, despite the fact that the current pages of that story were being written not by Carolinians but by a new breed of turfmen: northern financiers and industrialists, most of whom were based in or around Manhattan.

Eighteen months after Appomattox, the SCJC managed to regain control over the racetrack and its grounds from the Union authorities, in exchange for waiving all claims for damages, and by 1875 it began to stage races again, although they were shorn of the affiliated amusements, particularly the ball, that had characterized Race Week. The club continued as much as it could to function as it had done before the war, although its numbers were greatly reduced; some members had died or were elderly and ailing, and others could no longer afford to participate even in a reduced manner. The organization made a decision that maintained its prestige while also undermining its chances of survival; it stopped accepting new members, and it abolished the annual membership dues. In so doing, it refused to compromise its standards of social exclusivity by allowing the "carpetbaggers" and blacklegs, whom one commentator described as "infest[ing] the State" in the postwar years, entrance into this hallowed institution, but it also ensured that the club's end would be inevitable, as it ran low on both funds and participants.[47]

Although, according to the *New York Times*, the three-day race meeting at the Washington Course in January 1875 was "the largest turf gathering seen in Charleston for fifteen years," the event was in no way comparable, in style or attendance, to those of the prewar era. The SCJC had managed to "make the repairs necessary to put and keep the track in perfect order"—it had raised the needed funds by hosting events, such as art exhibitions, at the course, and allowing local residents to exercise their horses on it in exchange for their financial support—but it was unable to attract a sufficient number of equine champions to make the competition exciting. South Carolina, like most of the Confederate states, had been drained of its blooded horses during the Civil War; many had been co-opted into the cavalry and had died in service, while others had been confiscated during Sherman's invasion of the South—his forces are estimated to have seized thousands of Carolinian horses, including the famous Albine.[48] Even had the standard of the competitors been higher, it would probably not have resulted in a significantly larger audience. Some people stayed away because, they claimed, despite the best efforts of the SCJC, the races were no longer "patronised by the best class of people" and were now overrun with gamblers and with others who represented a more "professional" approach to turf matters. Although the club hosted race meetings on an occasional basis until 1883, the fact remained that the planter society that it had epitomized no longer existed, and each year fewer people were willing to take the time and spend the money to attend what must have struck them as a pale imitation of this formerly beloved sporting and social event. Club members took advantage of every opportunity to raise money, which they hoped would allow them to restore the course and its events to something like their former glory—selling more than seven hundred bottles of the club's famous madeira and renting out the reviewing stands for the storage of agricultural equipment and the course to a local riding and driving club—but by 1900 the remaining members were forced to admit that "the prospect of restoring the amusement of horse-racing on a respectable and safe footing has proved to be hopeless" and that the club "finds itself the owner of property which can no longer be utilized for the purpose for which [it] was formed."[49]

But if the SCJC were to dissolve after operating for a century and a half, its members, under the leadership of their final president, Major Theodore G. Barker, formerly adjutant to Lieutenant General Wade Hampton III, were determined that "it should die as nobly as it had lived," and set about ensuring that its assets, rather than falling into what it deemed "unworthy hands," were disposed of in a responsible way, and that the proceeds, which after the sale of the course to the city amounted to approximately $100,000, be donated to the Charleston Library Society, a private membership library founded in 1748. The society was selected over other local institutions because club members viewed it as in many ways comparable to their own association, and many of them, including Charles Cotesworth Pinckney, had been involved in its affairs; in Barker's words, it was "an old and honourable Society which . . . had lived from the middle of the eighteenth century an honourable and useful life, and had, like our club, come down to our generation as an inheritance from colonial days." The club also donated its papers, covering the years from 1842 onward, to the Charleston Library Society, ensuring that future generations of Charlestonians who had no personal memory of the SCJC's heyday might learn about it through its records.[50]

This transfer of assets from one long-established pillar of Charlestonian society to another facilitated the persistence of the SCJC's local renown after its dissolution, but, as it turned out, the club's fame would also be revived in an unexpected and more distant venue. In 1902 August Belmont Jr., one of turn-of-the-century America's most prominent turfmen, the president of the American Jockey Club and the son of the cofounder of New York City's Jerome Park racetrack, wintered his stable in Garnett, South Carolina, in Hampton County, near the Georgia border. Belmont was in the process of building the largest racing complex in the United States, and when he learned that the four massive gateposts that had stood at the Washington Course's entrance since its opening in 1792 had been abandoned at the now disused track, he made a bid to purchase them, with the aim to install them at the entrance to his new Belmont Park course in Hempstead, Long Island. After some debate, Charleston's municipal leaders decided that they were not willing to place a financial value on these evocative objects, and the posts were "presented to Mr. Belmont with the compliments of the city." Although the enormously wealthy Belmont would likely have been willing to pay a substantial sum for them, funds that the struggling city could certainly have used, the gift burnished elite Charlestonians' sense of themselves as gracious donors rather than ruined aristocrats selling off their last assets to the northern *nouveaux riches*. Once installed on Long Island, the gates would bear "a tablet describing briefly the history of the turf in South Carolina."[51]

Why would Belmont, who had been raised in Manhattan, and whose father was a German Jewish immigrant to the United States, be, in his own words, "anxious to perpetuate the record" of Charleston's racing heritage at his New York track? He had been a young child at the outbreak of the Civil War and thus had never had the opportunity to experience Charleston racing at its zenith. As the first president of the American Jockey Club, he played a dominant role in the transformation of the racing culture of the United States in the final years of the nineteenth century, in ways that rendered it nearly unrecognizable to those who had attended the Washington Course's races in the antebellum era. As will be discussed in a later chapter, he encouraged the metamorphosis of what had been a distinctively American sport, centered in the South and organized on a highly localized basis, into one that was self-consciously emulative of British racing traditions, based largely in the state of New York, and dominated by a single, national jockey club. To Belmont, racing as practiced before the war at the Washington Course bore little resemblance to that that he intended to showcase at Belmont Park. But at the same time he envisioned himself as the heir to and custodian of the United States' antebellum racing traditions, not merely their supplanter, and he wanted to portray himself in this light not only to his fellow elite turfmen but to the crowds of racing fans whom he hoped to attract to his new track.[52]

Charlestonians were not universally convinced of Belmont's benevolence, and some complained loudly in the local newspapers that his track, like other northern courses, was home to activities that would have been anathema to Carolinian turfmen in general, and to SCJC members in particular, as it made most of its profits from organized gambling. It might be patronized by members of Manhattan's financial and industrial aristocracy, but old Charlestonians dismissed such individuals as parvenus. Others, however, were convinced that, even if Belmont's track were home to practices that would have been unacceptable in the glory days of the Washington Course, his motivation for installing the gateposts there was to honor the memory of the SCJC, which "left a record which will be the glory of horsemen for ages to come." Reassuring themselves of the New Yorker's knowledge of and reverence for this history, they claimed that "he has reason to remember the days when gentlemen raced thoroughbreds for silver cups and tankards, and, like many other true sportsmen, he would be glad to see horsemen emulate the sport as it was carried on in Charleston before the war." Perhaps these men, many of whom had been educated in the classical tradition, thought of Horace's frequently cited claim that "Captive Greece took captive her fierce conqueror and introduced her arts into rude Latium."[53] Whether their hopes were fulfilled will be the subject of chapter 6.

3

Natchez

NABOBS AT PLAY

The passion for the turf is, I find, yet stronger here [in Natchez], if that be possible, than in the North.

—Tyrone Power, *Impressions of America; during the Years 1833, 1834, and 1835*

The great attraction for the day in the vicinity of the City [of Natchez] was the Pharsalia Race Track, where Capt. Ben Pryor had made the most ample arrangements for comfort, convenience and luxury.

—"The Fourth of July in Natchez," 1850

In the course of his travels in the southern states between 1852 and 1857, the New England–born journalist and landscape architect Frederick Law Olmsted was repeatedly struck by the dedication of the region's inhabitants to horses and horse sport. With regard to Virginia, he quoted from an article published in the Richmond-based agricultural journal the *Southern Planter,* which asserted that "horse-racing was a favorite amusement of all classes; some of the farmers owned and ran race-horses, and nearly all reared horses of the high blood, and at the high cost required for the turf." Upon his arrival at a plantation on the "Rice Coast" of South Carolina, he was enthralled to see "the clean and neatly-dressed negroes grooming thorough-bred horses. They pawed the ground, and tossed their heads, and drew deep inspirations, and danced as they were led out, in exuberance of animal spirits, and I felt as they did."[1] But in his opinion it was the white male residents of Natchez, Mississippi, who were the most passionate aficionados of horses and racing to be found anywhere south of the Mason-Dixon Line, and thus throughout the United States. As soon as he arrived in the town, Olmsted was struck by the distinctive nature of both its horses and its men, writing that he "never saw such a large number of fine horses as there is here, in any other town of the size. In the stable and the hotel there is a remarkable number of young men, extraordinarily dressed, like New York clerks on their Sunday excursions, all lounging or sauntering, and often calling at the bar; all smoking, all twisting lithe walking-sticks, all 'talking horse.'"[2]

The writer Joseph Holt Ingraham, who spent several years in Mississippi as a teacher of languages, concurred with Olmsted that the men of Natchez were, even by southern standards, particularly devoted to all things equine and equestrian. He described the town's streets as filled with private carriages but noted that most of these vehicles belonged not to inhabitants of the city of Natchez itself but to the families who owned the vast cotton plantations that surrounded it, and who ventured into town to do business, shop, or socialize. As a newcomer to the region, the Maine-born former sailor and self-described "Yankee" was fascinated by plantation society and its inhabitants, and, after visiting a local racetrack, he wrote that "home is, perhaps, the proper scene for studying the planter's character; but it will never be perfectly understood until he is seen, booted and spurred, with his pocket-book in one hand, and bank bills fluttering in the other, moving about upon the turf."[3]

The men to whom Olmsted and Ingraham referred represented two distinct racing traditions in Natchez and its vicinity. The dandyishly attired youths whom the former encountered in town were most likely to have frequented the racetrack located in Natchez-under-the-Hill, the area surrounding the landing at which the Mississippi River steamboats docked. This "town under the hill" was the oldest section of Natchez, and it was notorious throughout the Lower Mississippi Valley for the alleged criminality of its residents and the availability there of all types of vice. The Philadelphia Quaker Thomas B. Taylor, who landed at the port in 1847, called it "a wretched looking place," and, as he believed that it was not "any too safe for a stranger to pass through except in open daylight," he and a New Orleanian man he had befriended aboard the steamboat "delayed our scramble up the hill . . . until the business population were astir." A Mrs. Gaines, the daughter of the steamboat captain John W. Russell, described the neighborhood in the antebellum era as "the very festering focus of vice in all its odious, its disgusting and horrible forms." Visitors to Natchez-under-the Hill, she claimed, could not avoid contact with "the most lewd and abandoned of women" and with "men who were refugees from every nation under the sun," who "committed crimes with impunity" and joined the women for "continued orgies." James R. Creecy, who spent several weeks on business in Natchez shortly before the Civil War, described the "lower town" as "the terror of all decent and moral people," a place in which "gambling, drunkenness, and beastialities of the most infernal description were known to be perpetrated." Even at the beginning of the nineteenth century the then nascent settlement appalled its visitors, appearing to the Methodist missionary Jacob Young as surpassing in wickedness "anything I had ever seen or thought of," due to the presence of the numerous Kentuckian flatboatmen who traveled up and down the river, "acting like demons" when they landed in the town.[4]

Natchez-under-the-Hill was especially notorious for providing opportunities for all types of gambling, facilitated by the frequent arrivals and departures of the steamboats that carried not just "demonic" boatmen but professional gamblers up and down the Mississippi. As blacklegs became increasingly unwelcome in the longer-settled and more law-abiding communities throughout the South, they transferred themselves and their activities onto the riverboats and into the often lawless port towns at which they called. It is not surprising, then, that a town in which so many inhabitants and visitors alike were devoted to games of chance and to the general pursuit of pleasure would support a racetrack. But the sport on offer "under the hill" bore little resemblance to that which existed in the first half of the nineteenth century in cities such as Richmond or Charleston; it consisted mostly of quarter racing, and its competitions were not the genteel community-based pastimes that, as we have seen, the elites of Virginia and South Carolina supported, but free-for-alls centered on wagering. The track at Natchez-under-the-Hill was not supported by a jockey club, nor were the results of its races reported in the pages of the *Spirit of the Times* or the *American Turf Register*, as were those at Tree Hill and the Washington Course. It functioned in conjunction with the community's taverns, brothels, and gambling dens rather than in partnership with elite civic organizations or other elements of polite society.[5]

According to Eugene Genovese, the racecourse under the Hill "appealed to both unsavoury locals and the most respectable gentlemen from the bluff," the 800-foot "Hill" upon which the middle- and upper-class neighborhoods of Natchez were located. This claim is supported by the novelist and amateur historian Harnett T. Kane, who, in typically florid prose, asserted that "the plantation men with lace cuffs and ruffled shirts" were known to spend time in this "hell-raising, rampaging sin spot . . . [which was] the turbulent meeting-place of a willful crew of hard-faced humanity."[6] It is quite possible that the sons of the area's leading planters occasionally visited the landing to enjoy the activities on offer there, safe in the knowledge that they were unlikely to encounter the more respectable men, let alone the women, of their class in such venues, but the turf at which the carriage-owning families of the area's plantation gentry, as described by Ingraham, were ordinarily to be seen, "booted and spurred," sat atop the hill, several miles outside the city limits and a world away from the "village of ragged buildings" that lay below. And while churchmen such as Young deplored what they considered the immorality of the "Lower Town," they chose not to alienate the affluent residents of upper Natchez by including racetrack gambling in their list of the "social crimes" that occurred below the bluff.[7]

At these tracks—first Fleetfield, then St. Catherine's, and finally Pharsalia—the cotton planters of Adams County, of which Natchez was the seat, established jockey clubs and a racing tradition that, as in Richmond and Charleston, aimed at combining top-quality sport with an ambience that exuded gentility and reinforced local hierarchies of rank and race.[8] But while those East Coast racecourses and their supporters, as we have seen, struggled throughout the first half of the nineteenth century to cope with the declining economic and political power of their communities, and to maintain the sporting and social standards of their racing venues, the Natchez track's existence was both considerably shorter and far more successful. Although Natchez acquired its first racetrack during the 1790s, the sport's heyday therein came in the three decades prior to the outbreak of the Civil War, while in 1861 both Virginia and South Carolina could boast of more than a century of organized Thoroughbred racing. But the people who gained national renown as the "Natchez Nabobs," a group of approximately forty intermarried families who had made their fortunes in commerce and agriculture, were some of the richest individuals not only in the South but in the entire United States throughout the first six decades of the nineteenth century, as Mississippi produced an ever-increasing share of the nation's cotton, and the state's plantation owners reaped immense rewards on their investments. In 1860 Adams had the highest per capita wealth of any county in the United States and had produced nearly a dozen millionaires, each of whom owned at least fifty slaves, and some five times as many.[9] The First Families of Virginia and the "Rice Princes" of the South Carolina Lowcountry might look askance at Natchez, considering it a crude and uncultured town whose elite were *nouveaux riches* in comparison with those whose social, economic, and political ascendancy had begun in the seventeenth century, but to residents of the Lower Mississippi Valley it was the home of the state's most influential families and functioned as the region's social and cultural center as well as its "principal emporium of commerce," and eventually as one of the world's greatest cotton ports. In Sven Beckert's words, the Natchez District and the Yazoo–Mississippi Delta to its north constituted "a kind of Saudi Arabia of the early nineteenth century," the leading site for production of "the industrial world's most important commodity" in this era. Stefan Link and Noam Maggor make this point still more baldly, commenting that in 1850 the United States' place in the global economic order was that of "a supplier of slave-produced cotton to industrializing Europe," and the conjunction of cotton and slavery was more intense in western Mississippi than anywhere else in the antebellum South.[10]

Under these circumstances, the Nabobs felt little need to impress either the subaltern members of their community or the wider public with the gentility of their racing practices or, by extension, that of their society. They were pleased to preside over a course at which the attendees "maintained the greatest decorum and order" and that, as a result, attracted "quite a number of the fairest and most respectable ladies of the town," but their chief goal was to impress the spectators, whether they were present trackside or heard of these events at secondhand, with their immense wealth; beyond that, they simply wished to enjoy their favored leisure activity, one that allowed them to view themselves and be seen by others as southern aristocrats, despite the newness of their fortunes and of the Natchez community itself.[11] The members of the Mississippi Association and, later, the Adams County Jockey Club (hereafter ACJC) had little interest in evoking past glories in the hope of resuscitating them; they were entirely confident about their present and, up to the outbreak of the war, their future.[12] They saw little reason to indulge in nostalgia, as they had every reason to believe that their best days lay before them, and racing offered them an opportunity to "publicly display their self-assertion, their competitiveness, and their liberality," attributes more assertive than those valorized by the Virginians and Carolinians of this era.[13]

While Virginians and South Carolinians might debate the moment at which racing first developed in their midst, always attempting to push that date farther back into the colonial era, antebellum Mississippians were able to pinpoint the sport's origin within their state, which occurred at a time at which the Natchez District had yet to establish schools or to display "other signs of culture, aesthetics, or education." In 1795 thirty-nine investors pooled their resources to build the Fleetfield course in Natchez, which at that time was part of the Natchez District of the Spanish Province of Louisiana.[14] Little is known of the track's manager, tavern-keeper Richard King, but Fleetfield's early subscribers included the district's governor, Manuel Gayoso de Lemos Amorin y Magallanes, the Catholic priest Francisco Lennan, and a number of local planters who bred blooded horses. These men included the Scots-born William Dunbar, a member of the American Philosophical Society and frequent correspondent of Thomas Jefferson, who contributed his architectural expertise to the new course's layout, and Stephen Minor, an "opulent planter" and Gayoso's secretary of state, who in 1799 would succeed the latter as governor, due to his popularity among the American settlers who were flocking to this "El Dorado" of opportunity on the southern frontier. Minor's descendants would over the following decades rise to the highest eminence in the economic and sporting spheres of Mississippi and the neighboring state of Louisiana, becoming both the grandest of the Nabobs and the leaders of the turf world of the Lower Mississippi Valley in the era of its greatest prosperity.[15]

That the Fleetfield track existed, that it hosted stakes races, and that it was at least briefly popular among some of the most influential inhabitants of the Natchez District is clear, but beyond that it is difficult to discover anything regarding the nature or longevity of its sporting endeavors, other than that it was still in operation in 1800. Natchez had no local newspaper before 1805 or from 1809 to 1817, when the state entered the Union, and in October 1807, when the *Misissippi* [*sic*] *Herald and Natchez Gazette* printed a notice concerning the formation of a Mississippi Jockey Club in the town of Washington, on Natchez's outskirts, it stated that this organization's competitions would take place at a location to which it referred as "the Turf," with no specific reference to Fleetfield. By early 1819 the legislature had passed an act "to prevent Horse racing in any town or village in the State of Mississippi," and it would be more than a decade before political opinion altered to the extent that the ever-wealthier grandees of the Natchez District felt confident enough to establish the Mississippi Association, whose aim was to promote racing among blooded horses bred and raised within the state.[16]

It was at this time that racing in Natchez assumed the form that it would take until the coming of the Civil War. By 1829 the Mississippi Association had opened a track at St. Catherine's Creek, which was located three miles east of the town along the Old Washington Road, the northbound post road, and which was described in the *American Turf Register* as "a gently inclined plane, in the form of an eccentric *ellipse*, on a light clay soil, and in length forty feet over one mile." A few years later, Ingraham praised this course not only for its location in "a delightful intervale" but because it consisted of a "perfectly level plain . . . whose centre is slightly convex, so that the spectators can obtain a full view of the horses while running." The course was generally referred to as St. Catherine's (though occasionally also as Toll Bridge Turf, due to its proximity to the Washington Road toll bridge), but in 1835, at which time the Mississippi Association reconstituted itself as the Mississippi Association for the Improvement of the Breed of Horses, the members renamed it Pharsalia, in reference to Lucan's epic poem of the same name, which described the civil war of 49–45 BC between Julius Caesar and the forces of the Senate of Rome. It is not clear whether the members of the association chose this name for a reason beyond a desire to display their sophistication, via their knowledge of the classics, but they were not the only antebellum Americans to select it; it was also the name of a short-lived settlement in the state's Tallahatchie County, of a large Virginia plantation established in 1814 near Charlottesville, and of a town in Chenango County, New York, first settled in 1808.[17]

At first glance, the history of the Pharsalia course does not look much different from that of other southern tracks in the three decades preceding the Civil War. Sporting periodicals and local newspapers alike described the size and composition of the crowds it attracted—in 1838 a local commentator stated that "the town [was] full of strangers to see the Races"—the improvements that the proprietors made to the course, and the effects of local weather on the outcomes of its competitions. Perusal of the *American Turf Register* and the *Spirit of the Times*, and of the relevant sections of the Mississippi newspapers, implies that Pharsalia's clubmen and track managers encountered little difficulty in maintaining an atmosphere of "the greatest decorum and order," despite the course's

PHARSALIA TRACK.

RACES! RACES! RACES!
FOURTH OF JULY.

FIRST RACE—Dash of a mile—catch weights—
John Jaquemine enters b. m. Goose.
J. Curtain enters b m. Eliza Bemen.

This is an exciting match. Both mares are among the fastest in the United States. Betting is equal.

Second Race—Dash of a mile—three entries—an exciting contest may be expected.

Many citizens have requested the Proprietor of the Pharsalia Race Track to make extensive arrangements for the celebration of the *Nation's Birth Day*. He has done so on a scale that will entertain all who may join in the celebration. The citizens of Natchez, Concordia Parish, Adams and Jefferson Counties, will assemble in numbers to testify their devotion to our National Union. july 3

Pharsalia track notice and the Pharsalia track on a map, ca. 1864.
"Horse Racing in Natchez," Historic Natchez Foundation.

location just a few miles from Natchez-under-the-Hill. On many occasions, "the ladies' stand was graced by some of the fairest daughters of the country," a situation encouraged by the fact that the female kin of ACJC members were admitted free of charge, and because the club barred entry to any man "who has been expelled from a [Jockey] Club, or ruled off any Course in the Union," and forbade the use of "improper language" trackside.[18] Moreover, by 1852 the course's manager, the celebrated horse trainer John Benjamin Pryor, had provided female guests with a separate stand that had its own entrance and had decorated it with "carpets, sofas, arm-chairs, mirrors, pictures, &c.," endowing it with the atmosphere of an elegant private residence.[19] At the majority of the meetings, spectators attended in "sufficient numbers to testify to the high interest felt for the growing benefits of the Association, and in the fond anticipation of seeing fine sport," although local weather conditions, particularly dry air that stirred up vast clouds of dust, sometimes kept numbers down. Not only were these dust storms unappealing for the attendees, as they both limited their view of the action and besmirched their clothes, but they rendered the track "heavy," which limited the speed at which the horses could run.[20]

Although the majority of turfmen and spectators alike came from Natchez and its environs, Pharsalia at times attracted the participation of horses from the surrounding states, and of their owners, such as the renowned Louisiana Whig politician T. J. Wells, the "owner of many of the celebrated racing horses of ante-bellum days." Manager Pryor "does everything possible to welcome people and horses from a distance," and the ACJC openly encouraged "our friends [from] abroad, who have fine stock to run or sell, [to] come here and contend for our liberal purses given by our Jockey Club, which is as well managed as any in the United States."[21] Given this record of achievement, it is unsurprising that, in a narrative of the racing career of Adam L. Bingaman, who along with William J. Minor, son of the aforementioned Stephen, was for several decades the leading light of the ACJC, a *Spirit of the Times* contributor who signed himself merely as "A Turfman" described "time-honored 'Pharsalia'" (which was at the time actually just a few decades old) as being "renowned for its fair fields, and its distinguished patronage."[22]

Pharsalia was also widely known for gambling, a fact that complicated its reputation. A report in the *Spirit of the Times* from 1837 described the level of betting at the course as "pretty severe," and wagers might mount into the thousands when two or more Nabobs matched their finest horses against one another. Attendees who were less wealthy or more cautious also placed bets, but usually on the secondary races in which less illustrious horses competed for lower stakes.[23] For some inhabitants of Natchez and its environs, the prevalence of this type of gambling undermined Pharsalia's image as a site of genteel, well-managed leisure and caused it to develop an unwelcome resemblance to the debauchery associated with the lower part of the town. Nonetheless, the course was selected to host a variety of events of unimpeachable civic respectability, including an 1848 rally in support of Lewis Cass, the Democratic candidate for the presidency, and a "Grand Military Encampment" in 1858, which attracted the participation of units from Alabama and Louisiana as well as Mississippi. The devoutly Catholic planter John Nevitt, the president of Natchez's Roman Catholic Society, was a regular at Pharsalia, and even the scientist and historian Benjamin L. C. Wailes, who considered horse racing "scarcely respectable," and who excluded "Sportsmen" from those he termed "the *better class* of our community," gave in to his son's pleading and accompanied him to the course in 1855 in order to watch a much-hyped competition between the Mississippi horse Lecomte and Louisiana's Arrow.[24]

The fact was that gambling was a highly class-dependent phenomenon. Many people considered it a deplorable activity when it was practiced by individuals of low economic and social status. Not only were such people wasting what little money they possessed rather than using it to better their situations, but the gaming sites in Natchez-under-the-Hill and other Mississippi River port towns were known as places of interracial sociability, and thus of a potentially dangerous blurring, if only a temporary one, of the racial boundaries upon which every aspect of antebellum southern society rested. Like blacklegs, even those whose endeavors made them rich, these poor white men were viewed by those of elite status as devoid of honor, and thus among them wagering could never be anything but a vulgar and even criminal practice centered entirely on pecuniary gain. But for gentlemen, gambling could function as a forum for the display of honor, as long as it was carried out on an informal basis as a contest between friends rather than in any more official mode, such as bookmaking.[25] Under such circumstances, it allowed men to put their money where their mouths were, risking significant financial loss if their confidence in a particular horse or jockey turned out to be misplaced. If a rich and genteel racegoer could not resist the thrill of the wager, he could model his conduct on that of local eminences such as Adam Bingaman, a leader of the racing fancy not only in Natchez but at several Louisiana courses in the late antebellum era. According to the *Spirit of the Times*, "if [you are] beaten by him [Bingaman], you are consoled by the blandishment of his manners and made to forget you are the loser. When defeated, no sorrowing cloud hangs gloomily o'er his brow, but the past is soon lost in the amusing jest." If practiced in the wrong—that is, the financial—spirit, racetrack gambling was sordid, but among true gentlemen, it was an opportunity to display the excellence of one's character, to show that, in Rudyard Kipling's phrase, one could "meet with Triumph and Disaster / And treat these two impostors just the same."[26] Of course, a man as rich as Bingaman could survive even a heavy gambling loss, viewing it as an "amusing jest" rather than a crushing blow, whereas both professional gamblers and hapless poor men might sink beneath a "sorrowing cloud" under such circumstances. But to the Nabobs, and to respectable society more generally, such men deserved no sympathy; they had been justly punished for their avaricious behavior.

As a result of this distinction between the elite and the plebeian, the types of gaming that were especially popular under the Hill, such as roulette, were illegal, whereas wagering on races held at the track located in the upper town was not. On the Fourth of July 1835 in Vicksburg, a town of two thousand people located seventy miles upriver from Natchez, the local militia, augmented by a large number of civilians, launched an assault on the gamblers who habitually congregated in the riverfront area known as the Kangaroos. The attackers not only smashed the faro tables and roulette wheels that attracted these men to the neighborhood's saloons and gaming parlors but lynched five white men whom they identified as professional gamblers. By contrast, while some residents of and visitors to Natchez avoided Pharsalia for moral reasons, the course's habitues had no reason to fear for their safety or even, for the most part, their reputations, as no Nabob was likely to be viewed as comparable to those "confidence men" who generated so much anxiety not only along the Mississippi but throughout the antebellum United States. According to the Vicksburg clergyman Benjamin Houghton, what made blacklegs so repugnant to society was not the fact that they gambled, or even that they sometimes cheated, but that these activities constituted their livelihoods, whereas the same could certainly not be said of a leading planter such as a Minor or a Bingaman.[27]

The propensity of Pharsalia's patrons to engage in high-stakes wagers did not separate these men either from the ranks of the respectable or from the attendees of competitions at other elite-dominated tracks throughout the antebellum South. But their attitudes with regard to race, and specifically the behavior in which they permitted at least some men of color to engage at this course, went against common practice at many other tracks throughout the region. Textual and visual depictions of race days in Virginia, South Carolina, and Alabama, and even of the great North-South "match races" that were held at the Eclipse Course on Long Island, show these events to have been starkly segregated with respect to race.[28] As Katherine Mooney has shown, in the pre–Civil War United States nearly all of the men and boys who served as jockeys for blooded horses were Black, and the majority of them were enslaved.[29] The same was true of many horse trainers and nearly all grooms and stable hands. These individuals would be present at the track, as would other enslaved people, in their capacities as coachmen, ladies' maids, and nannies. Free Black women and men might also be in attendance as vendors of food and drink to the spectators. For these people of color, the time that they spent at the races was work, whether it involved contributing to the success of a running horse or to the convenience and comfort of white spectators. It was not unheard of for African Americans to enjoy the spectacle of the arrival of attendees at the track, to watch the races while seated atop the fences that surrounded the racing complexes, or to loiter on a track's outskirts to bet with one another or just to soak up the carnivalesque atmosphere. But interracial fellowship and gambling at a sporting event was more typical of crowds of enslaved people and poor whites at a cockfight outside a tavern in the countryside than at a top-class racetrack.[30] Yet at Pharsalia it was not unknown for men of color to participate fully in the proceedings, and even to form sporting friendships with men of the Nabob community.

Much of what we know about the experience of racing at the Pharsalia track comes not from the personal papers of the Nabobs or articles in the Natchez newspapers or in the national sporting press, but from the writings of William Johnson (1809–1851). Johnson was born near Natchez as the son of an enslaved woman and a white man who was probably his enslaver; the latter manumitted him when Johnson was ten years old. Such a turn of events was not uncommon in the plantation South, but Johnson attained a level of wealth and property ownership that was unusual among antebellum white southerners, let alone

William Johnson, ca. 1845.

people of color, especially those who had been born into slavery. At his death, he owned not only a large and comfortable house in a fashionable section of Natchez but also an eight-hundred-acre plantation on the town's outskirts, and he enslaved thirty-one people. His estate was valued at $25,000, which today would be worth approximately $850,000—not an impressive sum in comparison with the fortunes of the Nabobs, but a huge amount to the rest of Natchez's inhabitants. Johnson was notable not only for his financial success but also for his creation of an immense archive that documented his life in granular detail: more than two thousand pages of diary entries, daybooks, financial records, and miscellaneous jottings comprise "the most detailed personal chronicle maintained by an African American in the antebellum-period South." These records depict two further, and linked, aspects of Johnson's highly atypical experience as a man of color in the pre–Civil War South: his close relationships with men of the local white elite and his passionate involvement in horse racing.[31]

Throughout his adult life Johnson attended horse races around Natchez as often as he could, and he was always keen to hear the latest results from the tracks at New Orleans and elsewhere in Louisiana. He even subscribed to the *Spirit of the Times,* a choice that testified simultaneously to his literacy, his disposable income and leisure time, and his enthusiasm for the turf.[32] But unlike many of those who purchased or read the *Spirit,* he was a participant in rather than merely a spectator of the racing world. While he greatly enjoyed watching and wagering on the action at Pharsalia, he also owned several racehorses and employed several of his enslaved men as jockeys. Lacking the immense financial resources of the Nabobs, he could not purchase top-quality blooded horses, such as Adam Bingaman's Sarah Bladen, the "Champion of the Southwest," and as a result his animals raced either at the quarter-mile track at Natchez-under-the-Hill or in the secondary events at Pharsalia that followed the high-stakes competitions between the stables of the Nabobs and their friends. The latter were often quarter-mile sprints, as these horses were not physically capable of completing the longer, multiple-heat races run by better-bred and -trained horses, but they allowed the less privileged men of the area, "with their dirks and whisky flasks," "to feel that they too were participants in the royal pastime." But the fact that a man of color was permitted to be a subscriber to the ACJC, even if his stable did not meet the standard of most of its other supporters, and was thus able to race them on the same course as those of the region's most prominent turfmen, demonstrates how racial attitudes differed in Natchez from those of longer-established communities to the east.[33]

In 1860 Mississippi was home to approximately four hundred free people of color, and half of those lived in Natchez. Although Johnson was by some distance the wealthiest member of this community, the town was home to a number of other relatively affluent freedmen, most of whom were small businessmen who, like him, owned both slaves and land. They and their families sat at the top of the social hierarchy of the local free Black community, socializing and marrying almost entirely among themselves and making every effort to distinguish themselves not only from enslaved men and women but from the less privileged and sophisticated members of their small group. Although they avoided the area's frequent "darkey balls" and modeled their behavior on that of the local white bourgeoisie, they were all too aware that their economic success was not reflected in the spheres of politics or social life within Natchez; they were barred from voting, running for office, or participating in jury service or in the local militia. While a vast gap separated them from the slaves whom they saw every day, some of whom they owned, an equally broad fissure lay between them and even middle-class local whites, let alone the Nabobs.[34]

Other than his wealth, what factors allowed William Johnson to attain a social level far above that of any other free person of color in Natchez? His diaries show that, while he was literate, the level of his written expression was low in comparison with that of the Pharsalia grandees, several of whom had graduated from universities that would later be incorporated into the Ivy League, or even of less wealthy local whites. For example, on 24 March 1838, he wrote that "it is the Last Day of the Jocky Clubb Races Here and it was the most Splendid days raceing that I ever saw on this tract I think."[35] And although he owned land and slaves, Johnson met his day-to-day expenses through his ownership of several barber shops, one of which was located in Natchez-under-the-Hill, and a bathhouse, and made further profits as a moneylender. By the mid-1830s he had made enough money that he was able to outsource much of the work of shaving and cutting hair to his apprentices, but barbering was a low-status occupation in the late antebellum era; it was seen by most white men as a feminized form of labor and classed with other types of service work, such as the domestic occupations that employed so many free women of color, or the customer-focused responsibilities of male clerks in the dry goods stores of the urban Northeast. Under these circumstances, Johnson's apparently "dashing" style of self-presentation might have struck affluent white Natchezians as less redolent of aristocratic style than of that of the "extraordinarily dressed" young men whom Olmsted had encountered on his visit to the town, or, still more damningly, of the ludicrously overdressed African Americans whom Edward Williams Clay caricatured in his widely circulated *Life in Philadelphia* cartoon serial in the late 1820s.[36]

Portrait miniature of Adam Bingaman, by Benjamin Trott, ca. 1810. Decorative Arts of the Gulf South database, The Historic New Orleans Collection.

The main element that allowed William Johnson to "enjoy membership in the brotherhood of racing men" was his close friendship with Adam Bingaman, a relationship that developed from their mutual love of the sport. At first glance such a connection seems highly improbable, as Bingaman was not only one of the richest of the Nabobs but a man whose personal qualities earned him renown throughout the Lower Mississippi Valley. His passion for racing is evident from the fact that, from the mid-1820s to the early 1840s, he and William J. Minor took the lead in the Mississippi Association and were essential to the creation and flourishing of Pharsalia, and they also played a dominant role in the emerging racing culture of Louisiana, most notably in New Orleans and in St. Francisville, just across the state border in West Feliciana Parish. Toward the end of this period, Bingaman's Tennessee-bred mare Sarah Bladen became one of the nation's most celebrated racehorses, gaining six turf victories in 1840;

even after she was defeated by a younger horse in 1842, the *American Turf Register* declared that "to this day, the Turfmen of the Old Dominion and of the North will not concede that *any* performance made at New Orleans equals that of *Sarah Bladen*, who, at eight years old, *with her full weight up*, ran four mile heats in 7:37–7:40." Bingaman made a number of visits to tracks in England and continental Europe, in the course of which he purchased dozens of horses for export to Mississippi, and he employed Edward Troye, the leading equine portraitist of his day, to paint them. In his heyday Bingaman was so renowned for his ownership of "crack horses" that even the bowie-knife-toting rustics of the tiny village of Satartia, located to the northeast of Vicksburg in Yazoo County, urged a visiting journalist to place a bet on a local race whose entrants included "Adam Bingerman's best-blooded colt."[37]

But as impressive as Bingaman's racing career was, his personal interests extended far beyond the turf world. A graduate of Harvard University, he was an avid reader and a scholar of languages, building up an immense library at his Fatherland plantation a few miles to the northwest of Natchez and organizing literary soirees with his brother-in-law, fellow Nabob Stephen Duncan. At a dinner party hosted by the planter Samuel Davis, the brother of the future president of the Confederacy, in the course of a visit to Natchez by the Massachusetts politician and diplomat Edward Everett, Bingaman amazed the attendees by making a toast to the guest of honor, who was nationally renowned for his oratory, not in one of the half-dozen European tongues that Bingaman had mastered but in "the musical and resonant language of the Indian Choctaw." He was for several decades the leader of the Whig Party in Mississippi, and through his marriage to Julia Maria Murray, at whose family's home he was a lodger during his studies at Harvard, he was linked to the intellectual and cultural circles of early republican New England, as Julia was the daughter of the minister John Murray, the founder of the Universalist denomination in the United States, and of Judith Sargent Murray, the playwright, poet, and advocate of women's rights and the sister of Winthrop Sargent, the first governor of the Mississippi Territory.[38] In Natchez he was regarded as "an authentic *jeunesse doree* of the [Mississippi] river"; not only was he rich, handsome, clever, and charismatic, but he was the grandson of both the Frenchman Pierre Surget and the German Christian Bingaman, two of the first planters to settle in the area, making him the Mississippian equivalent of a member of the First Families of Virginia. Both those who had known him personally and others who had learned of him at secondhand rhapsodized about his qualities. The Georgia-born lawyer W. H. Sparks described him as "highly gifted by nature in mind and personal appearance, which was most splendid and commanding, with a polished education and fascinating manners, and by nature an orator," while the Mississippi planter-politician J. F. H. Claiborne claimed that he was "a man of very superior and highly cultivated intellect, one of the best classical scholars in the State, of fine person and imposing manners."[39]

Bingaman's fellow Nabobs were notorious throughout the Lower Mississippi Valley for their extreme cliquishness, even in their relationships with those whom Winthrop D. Jordan termed the "second planters" of the Natchez area, some of whom referred to them as the "Swell-heads" and resented what they considered their arrogance and ostentation. Why, then, would Bingaman choose to form a lasting friendship with a man of color, even if the two shared a passion for racing, particularly in a cultural context in which popular opposition to gambling reflected concerns about the formation of interracial bonds that might threaten white dominance? The two men's connection at least occasionally stretched beyond the confines of the Pharsalia course; after a day spent hunting on Johnson's property, they dined at his house, both the visit to the home and the sharing of the meal representing a highly unusual degree of connection between an elite planter and a free Black man. Bingaman's enjoyment of Johnson's company likely stemmed from his other relationships with people of color, which "began on the racetracks and fields of his plantations in Natchez and flourished in New Orleans." The most important of these was that which he maintained over several decades with Mary Ellen Williams, who had been among the many people Bingaman enslaved at Fatherland, and with whom he began a sexual relationship after his wife, Julia, died in 1822.

Sexual connections between white men and enslaved women were, of course, commonplace throughout the antebellum South, but that which developed between Bingaman and Williams did not follow the usual pattern of such liaisons. Not only did Bingaman free Williams soon after they became involved—presumably giving her the option to leave him—but after his mother died in 1841 he left Natchez and relocated to New Orleans with Williams and their three children, where they took up residence not in the elegant Garden District, the premier "American" neighborhood in which many of his fellow

Nabobs maintained homes, but in the midst of the city's large community of free people of color. He acknowledged his son and two daughters with Williams as his "natural Children," and upon his death in 1869 his entire estate, which by that point was greatly diminished as a result of both the depredations of the Civil War and his extravagant expenditures on horses, passed to their daughter Elenora, his children by Julia having predeceased him. Bingaman's relationship with Williams and their children offers evidence that his attitudes toward people of color differed significantly from those of the majority of white southern men of his era, to such a degree that he could form a lasting friendship with a free man of color, albeit one who was affluent and literate and who owned slaves himself, based upon their intense mutual interest in turf matters. The connection between the two families persisted for decades after Johnson's death in 1851; Bingaman helped to administer Johnson's estate and ensured that appropriate care was provided for his son, who had been committed to a mental institution, and when Johnson's daughters Anna and Catharine moved with their widowed mother to New Orleans, they became close friends with Bingaman's daughters Charlotte and Elenora.[40]

The story of Adam Bingaman and his social, sexual, and familial relations with men and women of color points up the highly exceptional nature not just of his attitudes but of those of his fellow Nabobs as well, in ways that were reflected in their turf activities. It would be logical to expect that Bingaman's reputation would have suffered greatly in the latter decades of his life. That a man of his lineage, wealth, education, and intellect would, having become a widower before the age of thirty, opt not to marry another high-status white woman but instead to enter openly into a relationship with an enslaved woman that appears to have resembled a marriage in all but the legal sense, to live openly with her and their children in a racially mixed urban community, and to not only publicly acknowledge these children but to leave his estate to them rather than to his white kin, would in many antebellum southern—or, indeed, northern—communities have been a source of shame and scandal, as was, for example, Thomas Jefferson's relationship with Sally Hemings. Moreover, while Bingaman had inherited enormous wealth from both sides of his family, he had depleted it by the time that he reached middle age, having incurred vast debts due to his neglect of his estates and his extravagant spending on blooded horses and his support of Pharsalia and other tracks in the Lower Mississippi

Valley. His relocation to New Orleans was motivated as much by the necessity to liquidate his Mississippi holdings as it was by his desire to live openly with Williams and their children.[41]

One might imagine that Bingaman's peers would have rejected him and savaged his reputation, viewing him as a man who was unwilling or unable to control his sexual and financial appetites, and who as a result allowed his family's name—Bingaman was his parents' only son—as well as their fortune to decay. But his white friends and neighbors in Natchez, many of whom were also his kin, did no such thing, and as a result Bingaman's posthumous reputation, well into the following century, remained that of a political leader in Mississippi, a leading light of horse racing in the Lower Mississippi Valley, and above all a man who displayed all of the virtues associated with the antebellum plantation aristocrat—hospitality, generosity, gracious manners, and a love of sport—but who, unlike most of them, was also renowned for his intellectual achievements. The Mississippi lawyer and politician Reuben Davis, in his 1891 memoirs, described Bingaman as "one of the best and noblest of men . . . [one] whose pure and beneficent life would adorn any place." Two generations later, Harnett T. Kane devoted a lengthy chapter of his popular history of Natchez to Bingaman's life, depicting him as a figure of tragic grandeur. In this book, which Kane based primarily upon anecdotes recounted by the elderly Natchezians he interviewed, and which is thus more valuable as a reflection on the nature of historical memory than as a work of historical scholarship, he claimed that, after Bingaman sold Fatherland and his other plantations and relocated to New Orleans, he found solace in his "embossed volumes," which, along with some "fine garments, badly laundered" and a few pictures, were all that remained to him of his fortune, and that he mourned the day when he was forced to sell these books, as they comforted him in his solitude—ignoring the fact that Bingaman had in fact moved to the city with Williams and their children, and that the family had found a community there among the *gens de couleur libres*. Describing Bingaman's final hours, Kane painted a sentimental picture of the turfman speaking "feverishly of his horses" and asking those who had gathered at his deathbed to ensure that "when it's over, will you lay me some place where I can hear hoofbeats, now and then?" Kane quoted an elderly Natchez woman whom he described as a "grand dame" as stating that Bingaman was "our Lord Byron," and he claimed that, when they heard Bingaman's name, other elderly members of the community "indulged a quick smile." Even the descendants of the enslaved, according to Kane, had the warmest recollections of Bingaman; the "yellowed eyes" of one "gnarled, moustachioed retainer" lit up at hearing his name, and he warned his interlocutor to ignore anyone who spoke negatively of the man whom his father had served as a groom: "'Mister A.L.? Don't you believe half the thing' you hear on 'im. Them that says it ain't *this* little to 'im!' He indicated the tip of his brown finger."[42]

It is difficult to imagine a member of the elite classes of mid-nineteenth-century Richmond or Charleston maintaining such a glorious reputation under similar circumstances. But the Nabobs were not a fading gentry attempting to hold on to their prestige in the face of a rapidly changing southern, and American, economy and culture to which they feared that they were becoming ever more marginal. They were not only enormously wealthy, in comparison not just with other plantation owners but with the nation's leading industrialists, merchants, and bankers, but they had good reason to consider themselves to be on the cutting edge of American capitalism. Even before Mississippi entered the Union in 1817 the combination of the end of Native American resistance in the region and the emergence of the steamboat opened the Lower Mississippi Valley to national and Atlantic commerce. Within two decades, the state produced more cotton each year than any other in the Union, and Natchez had emerged as one of the world's great cotton ports. The city in which the Nabobs lived and that they had done so much to develop boasted a "dynamic and sophisticated commercial culture" that connected it to St. Louis to the north and New Orleans and the Gulf of Mexico to the south. As the federal government poured funds into the Planters' Bank of Mississippi, Natchez attracted not only investors, many of them from the North, who were keen to enter the booming commerce in cotton and in the land on which it grew, but less privileged men and women—rivermen, sex workers, and tavern-keepers among them—who sought opportunities in the town "under the Hill."[43] In addition to serving as an entrepôt for captive Africans smuggled into the United States after the banning of the transatlantic slave trade in 1807, it was second only to New Orleans in the nation's domestic slave trade, containing eight slave markets by 1850 and functioning as the headquarters of Franklin, Armfield and Co., one of the nation's leading trading concerns in human property.[44] Although the plantations of the Nabobs were located some miles beyond the city limits, the wealth they generated was reflected in the urban landscape of this "cultural oasis"; even a visitor as censorious as the Philadelphia Quaker Thomas Taylor, who came to the city in 1847 as a representative of the Bank of the United States in Pennsylvania, and who was so disgusted by the "town under the hill," informed his brother that the upper town was "much the handsomest & the most agreeable looking place" south of Cincinnati, due to its "spacious mansions & gardens," "fine looking churches," and "large & stately" public buildings surrounded by "numerous tall & beautiful Locust trees."[45]

Moreover, the Nabobs, although their families had by the Civil War's outbreak lived in Natchez for decades, and some had relocated there from elsewhere in the South, were far more cosmopolitan than any other regional planter aristocracy of the antebellum era. A number of them had, like Adam Bingaman, attended northern universities: Stephen Duncan and William J. Minor, for example, both went to the University of Pennsylvania, and the latter's son graduated from Princeton, as did that of Mississippi governor John Quitman.[46] And, like Bingaman, they might select their spouses from prominent families from New England, New York, or the mid-Atlantic states. Pennsylvania-born Duncan's first wife was Adam Bingaman's sister Catharine, while Minor wed Duncan's niece, Rebecca Gustine of Carlisle, Pennsylvania. Rebecca's sisters Margaret and Matilda, who were raised in Natchez, married the brothers Charles and Henry Leverich, leading New York financiers; the Leveriches were passionate racing enthusiasts, and on his frequent visits to Natchez, Charles accompanied Minor to the races. When the heat of the summer rendered the Lower Mississippi Valley uncomfortable, the Duncans and Minors went north, visiting kin and friends in East Coast cities before heading to the resorts of Saratoga Springs or Newport.[47] Cory James Young's recent work has illuminated the specifically Pennsylvanian origins of some of Natchez's leading families; as the Quaker State moved toward the abolition of slavery at the end of the eighteenth century, the sons of a number of slaveholding families from Cumberland County relocated to the Mississippi frontier to reestablish their plantations. Nabobs who sought educational opportunities or found spouses in the North, rather than rejecting local options, were in some instances returning to their or their families' origins.[48]

Many Nabob families were linked to the North by commerce as well as kinship. Unlike the majority of Virginian and Carolinian planters, they tended to diversify their economic interests, investing extensively in real estate, securities, and railroads. Although the most obvious source of their wealth was their vast cotton plantations and the enslaved people who toiled on them, William K. Scarborough described them as "pre-eminently capitalists" rather than the "lords of the manor" upon whom slaveholders throughout the Upper South had long fashioned themselves.[49] Given their financial and familial links to the urban North, it is not surprising that many Nabobs supported the Union after the outbreak of the Civil War. Beyond their fears that their personal and financial relationships in the North would be strained or shattered by the outbreak of hostilities, they did not identify themselves as being exclusively Mississippian, or even southern, and they were thus unmoved by popular appeals to local and regional loyalties. Among the Minors, it was not only the Pennsylvania-born Rebecca and her Pennsylvania-educated husband but their Natchez-raised children who were "ardent opponent[s] of disruption of the Union"; their daughter Catherine stated that, although she and her husband were proud residents of the Lower Mississippi Valley and "had always felt the deepest sympathy for the southern people and marvelled at their perseverance, endurance, and courage, they were both anxious for the North to win the war." They had no desire to see the end of slaveholding, the source of much of their wealth and prestige, but they "believed disunion would be ruinous to the general good of the country," as well as to themselves in particular.[50]

In many ways, the Nabobs were nationally connected but locally disconnected. In their relationships with the "second planters" of the Natchez area, those who owned twenty or fewer slaves, they expected the latter to defer to them as their natural superiors, whether among the men who crowded around the track at Pharsalia or the women who watched the competitions from the ladies' stand, in which the Nabob women, according to Olmsted, sat "marble-eyed in propriety, looking stealthily from the corners of their eyes without turning their heads" at their fellow attendees.[51] They possessed the cultural authority to set the behavioral tone of the city's public venues, but unlike the elites of the Lower South, they did not develop traditions such as "treating" through which they offered patronage to middle-class and even poor whites in exchange for their political support; indeed, few of them participated in local or state politics, other than Adam Bingaman, whose career owed more to his connections to influential Whigs in other states than it did to his engagement with the men of his own community.[52] As noted earlier, some of Bingaman's peers considered him the local equivalent of Lord Byron, and William Brooks Taylor has suggested that their values resembled those of the aristocracy of later Georgian England more than they did those that typified other parts of the antebellum South. They were willing on occasion to accept breaches of conventional sexual morality, such as Bingaman's quasi-marriage to a formerly enslaved woman, but they rarely permitted outsiders to engage with them on an equal footing, and while they could boast no titles of nobility, they saw themselves as being by right of birth innately superior to their neighbors, even those who were affluent and well-educated. Although no Nabob family had resided for more than three generations in Natchez when the Civil War began, and their fortunes were of still more recent foundation, these men and women expressed tremendous confidence in themselves as individuals and as a group. Like the jockey club members and their families in Virginia and South Carolina, they prided themselves on their "discriminating taste" and were convinced that they constituted "a cultural island in a sea of mediocrity," but unlike them they faced the future with confidence that the ongoing development of industrial capitalism would enhance their wealth and influence rather than undermining it.[53]

This sense of security, even arrogance, among the Nabobs gave Natchez racing its distinctive tone. In this community, the racetrack was a site that demonstrated the absolute dominance of this small group of intermarried local families rather than one at which local grandees, ordinary citizens, and urban boosters alike attempted to uphold the continued political and cultural significance of their city or state. The ACJC's rules mandated that Pharsalia's attendees behave with decorum, but its members, unlike those who ran Tree Hill or the Washington Course, saw no need to create elaborate rituals, such as ceremonial dinners or glittering balls, with which to impress outsiders. Local men and women, including not only the "second planters" and their families but members of the city's substantial community of free people of color, were welcome to attend Pharsalia's races but not to participate other than as docile spectators; it was only after these competitions had ended and many of the Nabobs and their kin had departed the track that the lesser sorts might assert themselves. Indeed, the relaxed attitude toward the presence of freedpeople could be interpreted as contempt toward nonelite whites, whose support was so unimportant to the Nabobs that the former did not need to be placated by a strict observance of the color line at public events.

For the members of this elite, the less privileged elements of their community were neither wanted nor needed to uphold civic pride; the guests whom the Minors and Duncans, Surgets and Bingamans valued were their kinfolk, friends, and business associates from the North or Louisiana. But while these outsiders were welcome, the Nabobs made few attempts to attract racing enthusiasts from other parts of the state or the region, as they were both willing and able to cover Pharsalia's costs among themselves rather than relying upon tourists for revenue or journalists for publicity. And although Natchez's leading turfmen subscribed to and even on occasion wrote for the leading sporting periodicals of the era, they displayed little interest in the goings-on at other southern tracks, with the exception of those in and around New Orleans, which they might visit or at which their stables might compete, with Adam Bingaman even establishing a short-lived track at Algiers, across the Mississippi River from the city.[54]

Pharsalia and its Nabobs, then, provide a distinctive counterexample in ideology and practice from those that typified the Virginian and South Carolinian racetracks of the antebellum era. The turfmen of Natchez deployed horse racing to tell a story about themselves and their community that was very different from those that were emphasized in the venues for horse sport located in longer-settled sections of the South, which prided themselves on what they considered their glorious heritage but were with good reason apprehensive that their futures were far less promising. But although the racing enthusiasts of Adams County had strong familial and commercial connections to the New Orleans area, their narrative, and thus their racing practices, differed just as sharply from those that developed in the Crescent City in the second quarter of the nineteenth century, as the following chapter will illuminate.

4

New Orleans

SPEED IN A CITY OF LEISURE

"Yes, I believe Metairie was a race course, once." "Yer hed better belebe it . . . es I sat dar all cum befo' me like er pickchure—all de quality fokes in dar kerredges, an' day had dar own fine stock in dem days—dar as Marsa Kenner, an' young Marsa Slocum, Marsa Robinson, an Connell S'linski, an' ever so many udders."

—M. AGNES THOMPSON, "Metairie," 1892

Money gotten easily, and without labour, is easily lost. Betting and horse-racing are amusements eagerly pursued, and often times to the ruin of the parties. A Louisianian will forego any pleasure, to witness and bet at a horse-race.

—TIMOTHY FLINT, *Recollections of the Last Ten Years*, 1826

New Orleanian Nicholas J. Hoey had only one topic on his mind in early April 1855. Writing to his friend Dugregiy Dupuy, a planter in Iberville Parish near Baton Rouge, he worried about the possibility that rain "may spoil the race on the 14th between those two justly celebrated flyers *Lecomte*, & *Lexington*." Hoey believed that the Louisiana horse Lecomte, to whom he referred as "*our nag*," would be victorious, but he noted that both horses were "noble sons of that old hero *Boston*, and inherit all his grand qualities, untiring, unflinching, & game to the last." He was disappointed that Dupuy would not be able to attend the competition but promised that in a subsequent letter he would send a detailed account of the event, along with a copy of "every paper that notices it." In his next epistle, composed six days after the race, he backed off from this commitment, claiming that "the subject of the great race has been worn thread-bare by the newspapers, and t'would be worse than idle to attempt to portray a scene, to which they have all done justice." Hoey was deeply disappointed by Lecomte's defeat and aware that his friend might not share his fascination with the race, but he concluded his letter by admitting, "I suppose you are most heartily sick of it, but I can't help writing and talking of it."[1]

Hoey had plenty of company in his obsession with the Lexington–Lecomte race. The competition was so popular that it attracted both aristocratic women and formerly enslaved men, and representatives of both groups deemed it worthy of discussion in their memoirs. The Honorable Amelia Murray, a Scots gentlewoman and a lady-in-waiting to Queen Victoria, attended the event in the company of the British consul in New Orleans and several other elite Englishwomen; although she had visited a number of English courses, she reported that she "never before saw a horse more graceful, or more beautifully formed, with such apparent gentleness and good temper, and yet with such an air of conscious superiority as this Lexington." James P. Thomas, a formerly enslaved barber from Nashville, was also in attendance that day. Like Murray, he marveled at Lexington's beauty and grace, and that of his rival, but he emphasized the role of enslaved men in the horses' training. According to Thomas, "the Boys loved those [horses] and guarded them affectionately and it broke their hearts when they failed to win."[2]

This was the third time that Lexington and Lecomte had faced off against one another on the New Orleans turf. Their first encounter took place in April 1854, in a widely publicized competition that was termed the Great State Post Stake and that also involved Alabama's Highlander and Louisiana's Arrow. Lexington won both of this event's heats, with Lecomte coming second; "they swung into the homestretch side by side . . . each at the top of his speed . . . but the speed of 'Lexington' was superior, and he shot past the judges' stand about four lengths ahead, winning the [second] heat and the race." But a few days later Lecomte defeated his rival on the same course, for the Jockey Club purse, and in so doing set a record of 7:26 for four miles, more than forty seconds faster than Lexington's winning time in the Post Stake. Nonetheless Lexington's owner, Richard Ten Broeck, was convinced that his horse still had what it took to beat Lecomte and offered to race him either against Lecomte or alone against the new record time. General T. J. Wells, Lecomte's owner, was initially reluctant to accept this challenge, believing that his horse had nothing to prove, but he changed his mind after 2 April 1855, on which date Lexington, although carrying three extra pounds from his jockey, the Irishman Gilbert Watson Patrick (popularly known as Gilpatrick), ran against the clock and shaved more than six seconds off of Lecomte's record time. Three weeks later, Lexington decisively defeated Lecomte in the that year's Jockey Club purse race, of which Hoey wrote to Dupuy; he completed the first heat in 7:23 and was unchallenged in the second, as Wells withdrew his horse, who was suffering from colic and so clearly in distress that, in Hoey's words, he "should have had a Doctor nursing, instead of a Jockey riding him."[3]

The combination of a clear victory over his great rival and the setting of a competition record made Lexington into a figure of fascination not only in the turf world but across the nation. Writing a half century later, the sports journalist and race judge Charles Trevathan waxed lyrical on this topic, claiming that the horse's fame was not restricted to "the sunny South" but extended "far up into the North, even into parts where the race-horse was not known." Lexington, he asserted, "belonged not alone to the turfmen. He was the heritage of the nation," to such an extent that, for many years, "any little child of America could have told you the story of Lexington."[4] Trevathan overestimated the persistence of Lexington's renown, particularly beyond turf circles, and even in his own era the horse soon faded from public view. Following his triumph over Lecomte, his health declined to the point that he was no longer able to race, and Ten Broeck, who had paid $2,500 for him in 1853, in 1856 sold him for $15,000 to the leading breeder Colonel Robert Aitcheson Alexander of Woodburn Farm in Kentucky, where he stood at stud for a number of years and, despite his complete blindness, was the nation's leading sire for fourteen consecutive years. In 1870 Hamilton Busbey, the cofounder and editor of the recently established New York–based sporting journal *Turf, Field and Farm,* stated that "for the past six years the fields on our principal race-courses have largely been made up of the get of Lexington," especially the "great triumvirate" of Asteroid, Kentucky, and Norfolk.[5]

Although Lexington's turf primacy was short-lived, it reshaped the American racing world in the years just before the Civil War and helped to shape that world's rapid and dramatic metamorphosis after the end of the conflict. It made a celebrity of the Irish-born Gilbert Patrick at a time at which nearly all jockeys on the American turf were slaves or free men of color, a harbinger of the increased appreciation of the rider's role in racing and the resulting replacement

The champion horse Lexington; photograph by James Mullen. New York Public Library, The Miriam and Ira D. Wallach Division of Art, Prints, and Photographs: Photography Collection, Robert N. Dennis Collection of Stereoscopic Views.

of Black horsemen by supposedly more skilled white jockeys in the final decades of the nineteenth century. It was a result of a growing fascination with equine performance as a statistical rather than a purely experiential phenomenon; spectators flocked to Lexington's races in the hope that he would not simply defeat his opponents, however decisively, but would smash both their and his previous time records in doing so. And, finally, it occurred at a course that had been developed not as a venue in which to showcase and uphold the social order of a localized southern community but as a site of profit and pleasure for anyone who could pay for admission.

Trevathan's belief in the durability of Lexington's reputation might have been overly optimistic, but it would not be unwarranted to suggest that the horse's brief but brilliant career resulted in a thoroughgoing change in American racing practices, one that continues to resonate within the sport today. But although Lexington, who was a son of the famous Boston with whom William Ransom Johnson won many races, and whom racing commentators praised for his good disposition and his "bold, free, elastic" action, was a racer of considerable promise, it is questionable whether he would have reached his potential on the track had he not been purchased and trained by Richard Ten Broeck, a man whose name, like that of his equine protégé, was legendary in his own era but largely forgotten a few decades later.[6] Although Ten Broeck, a native of upstate New York, did not begin his turf career in New Orleans until just a decade before the outbreak of the Civil War closed the city's racetracks, he reconfigured horse sport not only in the Crescent City but throughout the postbellum United States.

As noted in chapter 3, Natchez had acquired its first racecourse, Fleetfield, when the town was a tiny settlement under Spanish rule. Richmond's earliest tracks opened as soon as the city replaced Williamsburg as Virginia's capital, and the advent of Charleston's York Course marked the city's rise as a major Atlantic port. By contrast, although New Orleans was founded in 1718, a century later it was still devoid of horse sport, although in the wake of the Louisiana Purchase it had very quickly become the fifth-largest city in the United States, a magnet for European migrants, and the site of the nation's largest slave market. Moreover, it had already begun to develop, and promote, its reputation as a place of both leisure and luxury, in which residents and visitors could partake of every sort of pleasure, from dancing with the city's famously alluring "quadroons" to viewing a suspenseful contest between a skilled matador and an aggressive bull.[7] But it was not until 1820 that New Orleans acquired its first racetrack, which the sugar planter Francois de Livaudais, one of the few French Creoles to own racehorses, laid out at his Live Oak estate, just above Canal Street. The competitions at Live Oak, which as a private track existed primarily for the enjoyment of Livaudais's friends and kin, and at times included nonpedigreed entrants, were soon augmented by those staged at the Jackson Course, located east of the city in Chalmette, which local businessman William C. Withers opened in 1826 and named in honor of his commander at the Battle of New Orleans, and the

New Orleans Course, founded two years later, both of which were open to the general public. But none of these tracks remained in operation for more than a few years—an English lawyer stated that, although the Jackson Course was "in excellent order" and "the ground was good," it did not attract much of a crowd, perhaps due to its distance from the city, and was primarily the site of "a day of sport for the coloured population"—and it was not until the end of the 1830s that the sport would begin to flourish in the city.[8]

It was the influx of the "Americans," particularly those who were the younger sons of planters from the Upper South, and who were keen to introduce into their new home what they viewed as a socially prestigious leisure pursuit, that rapidly transformed New Orleans into the mecca of horse racing in the United States just before the Civil War. Although the city's French and Spanish Creole inhabitants had long enjoyed a variety of public recreations, they were more inclined toward concerts, balls, and theatrical performances than to spectator sports. Whereas racing had been enthusiastically embraced by the upper classes in England from the 1660s, the elites of metropolitan Spain and France showed little interest in the sport until well into the nineteenth century, when bourgeois mores supplanted those of the nobility. France had no jockey club until 1833, when the members of the Societe d'Encouragement pour l'Amelioration des Races de Chevaux en France created it in self-conscious imitation of its English antecedent, and it was not until 1857 that the opening of the Longchamp track in Paris's Bois de Boulogne made the sport fashionable to a wider public. Although the Duke of Osuna organized races on his estate near Madrid in the 1830s, nothing comparable to a Spanish jockey club emerged until the following decade, and racing did not "mature as a form of commercialized leisure" in Spain until the late 1860s.[9] But as the locus of both economic and social authority in the Crescent City shifted from the Creoles to the Americans, the latter were eager to add the sport to the long list of pleasures that were available to both the inhabitants of New Orleans and the many domestic and international visitors it attracted, as the old French city was transformed not only into a "merchant's capital" but also into a "great Southern Babylon," a site of wealth and luxury, pleasure and vice.[10]

Within the single year of 1837–38, New Orleans acquired three new racetracks. The Eclipse Course, the first local track reserved for the use of Thoroughbreds and "offering the largest purses in the Union," was located uptown by

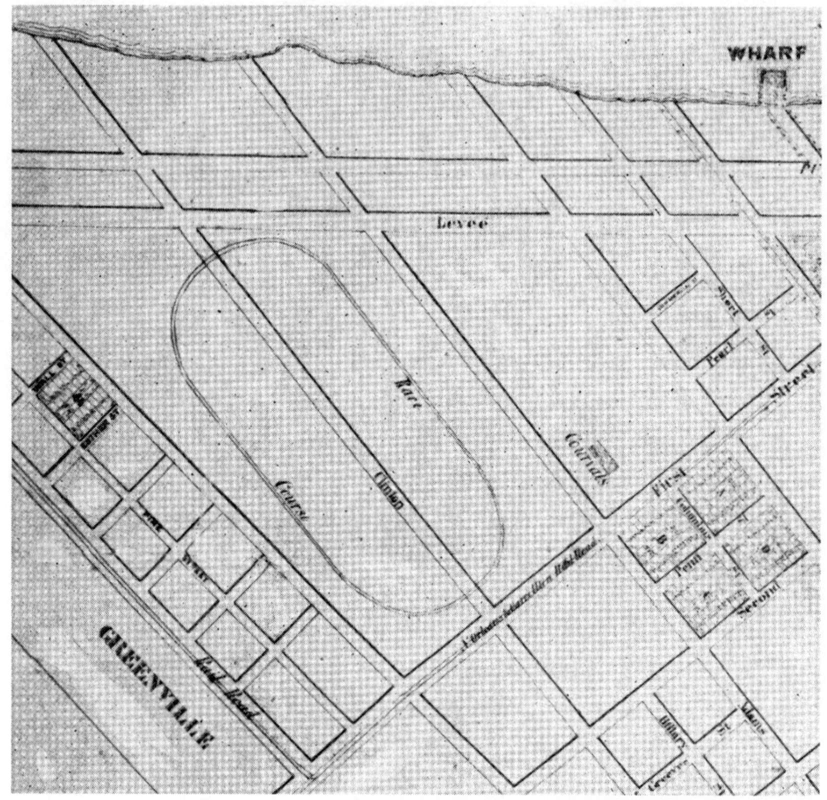

Eclipse Course, New Orleans, Louisiana, ca. 1845.
Map from Edgar A. Perilloux, *Carrollton Centennial, 1845–1945*, 5.
LSU Libraries, Louisiana and Lower Mississippi Valley Collections.

what is now Audubon Park and was accessible via the New Orleans & Carrollton Rail Road, whose cars also functioned as viewing stands for the races. There was also the Louisiana Course, situated on Gentilly Road where it met the Pontchartrain Railroad, and the Metairie course, outside the city limits in Jefferson Parish, at the junction of today's Metairie Road and Pontchartrain Boulevard. These courses, established by Virginia-bred turfmen, were not much more successful than their predecessors of the previous decade, due in large part to the coincidence of their founding with the Panic of 1837 and the onset in 1848 of a cholera epidemic, the effects of which caused both the Louisiana and the Eclipse tracks to close within a decade, and the Metairie to struggle to survive, despite the efforts of its jockey club. Greater success might have been expected from the Bingaman Course, which was opened in 1847 by the horse-breeder Adam Bingaman of Natchez, whose exploits as one of the leading turfmen of the Lower Mississippi Valley were described in chapter 3, and which was under the direction of the Virginian Colonel Yelverton N. Oliver, the former manager of the Eclipse Course, and also of Louisville, Kentucky's Oakland track. The site of twice-yearly six-day competitions sponsored by the Orleans Jockey Club, the Bingaman was located across the Mississippi River from the city, in the small town of Algiers.[11]

Despite the great esteem in which many local racing enthusiasts held both Oliver and Bingaman, the course failed to flourish. The location may have undermined the track's success, as it required city residents to travel to it by ferry, an unsatisfactory situation for those who preferred to arrive trackside on horseback or by carriage. The course's site was also less than ideal because, when the river rose, as it did frequently, the soil, including that of the racing surface, "remained, for a long period, as 'heavy' as the heaviest better on the best bottomed horse, on a stormy rainy day, could have desired." In the pages of the *Spirit of the Times,* correspondents made frequent comments about the Bingaman's problematic track conditions; in 1849 "Little 'Un," who claimed to speak for a group of turf fans who called themselves the "Fast Boys," complained that the track was "ancle-deep in mud, which I consider scarcely worth the trouble of going to see." This problem also afflicted the Orleans Jockey Club's meeting in April 1851; the races were initially postponed to the following month because heavy rainfall had made the course impassable, and for the same reason the final day's events had to be transferred to the Metairie track.[12] Although Bingaman's and Oliver's personal prestige encouraged the participation of some of the South's most celebrated horses, including Revenue and Peytona, large audiences were not guaranteed even under more favorable weather conditions; an account in the *Spirit* of a June 1850 event noted the "slender attendance" and reported that the proprietor had delayed the start of the day's activities in the hope that more spectators would arrive. The periodical was highly enthusiastic about the quality of the sport on offer at the December 1850 meeting, but its writer lamented that, although it "had afforded more real sport than any other [meeting] which has been held in this country for many years, we were constantly disappointed in not seeing a larger number in attendance to enjoy it." Due to both the paucity of spectators and Bingaman's belief that the course should provide entertainment for all, the managers varied the program of events, introducing pacing and trotting competitions. As a "people's track" with modest entry fees, the Bingaman hosted activities that were popular among the city's white working classes but scorned by its sophisticates, such as bull and bear fights and "Welsh Main" races, participation in which was open to "untrained horses of every quality of blood, all sizes and conditions, and ignorant of the ways of race tracks, with jockeys, too, not of the classic stamp—for some weighed 200 pounds who ought to have been only 100."[13]

In the end, even these activities could not generate prosperity for the Bingaman Course, and by the spring of 1852 its owners opted to dismantle its stables and grandstands and sell the land for town lots. But although the track was in operation for only a few years, it played a crucial role in the development of New Orleans as a racing center because it brought Richard Ten Broeck into the business; he was hired by Oliver and Bingaman in the spring of 1847 in the hope that he could make their new track run both smoothly and profitably. In this project, the most that could be said for Ten Broeck was that he may have succeeded in keeping the Bingaman going for longer than another track supervisor might have done. Rather, his contribution to the sport stemmed from his purchase of an interest in the struggling Metairie course, by which he worked to bring about a complete overhaul of that track's management and facilities. His decision to replace the Metairie Jockey Club with a joint-stock company, the Metairie Association, attracted controversy but generated the investment capital needed for a complete renovation of the course, transforming it into a glamorous showplace that would attract not just turf enthusiasts but the city's elite, as well as the tens of thousands who visited New Orleans each year in pursuit of all types of pleasure. These improvements, which were budgeted at ten thousand dollars, included a judge's stand that was to be "beautifully designed after the style of an oriental temple, with tall, graceful pillars, supporting a light and shining dome," while the ladies' stand would attract high-class female spectators by providing them with "costly and rich" accommodation, including parlors and retiring rooms that would be "furnished in the most sumptuous and tasteful manner."[14]

Richard Ten Broeck, by Joseph Brown, after Herbert Watkins, ca. 1870. Library of Congress, Prints and Photographs Division.

This building program was to be accompanied by a thoroughgoing review of the club's principles and procedures, to be remodeled in line with those of the South Carolina Jockey Club, which, as we have seen, was famed throughout the South for its gentility as well as for the high standard of its racing. As at the SCJC, for example, anyone who entered a horse in a competition at Metairie was required to select racing colors and dress his jockey in them, which had never been common practice in New Orleans but which was seen as improving both the aesthetics and the social tone of the trackside experience. The *Spirit*'s correspondent on this topic fairly glowed at the prospect that, finally, New Orleanian racing would be put "on a footing of permanence, respectability and fashion." After twenty-five years of false starts, "there shall hereafter be in the neighbourhood of this city, a race course where the sports shall be conducted on the highest and most honourable principles, and a Jockey Club that will command the confidence and respect of all classes of the community, as well as of the strangers who may visit us."[15]

In many ways Ten Broeck was an unlikely savior of the probity as well as the profitability of the New Orleans turf. He was not a native of the Crescent City, or even of the South, but had been born and raised in Albany, New York, the son of a family of "honourable standing" whose ancestors numbered among the earliest inhabitants of this Dutch settlement. Despite this highly respectable background, as soon as Ten Broeck reached adulthood he appears to have rejected the atmosphere in which he had grown up, being expelled from the military academy at West Point for indiscipline, and he soon "embarked upon the troubled waters of the turf, for which he had a predilection from boyhood." In order to finance his purchases of racing stock, he spent a number of years traveling up and down the Mississippi as a riverboat gambler, matching the stereotype of such men as combining a dandified style of self-presentation with an intimidatingly cold-eyed demeanor. The chronology of his life in the years between his expulsion from West Point and his arrival in New Orleans is unclear, with various sources presenting competing accounts, but at some point during the 1830s he fetched up in Virginia, where "he came out as the confederate of the well-known Colonel [William Ransom] Johnson, who may be styled the Napoleon of the American Racing World." Ten Broeck apparently impressed Johnson with his quickness of mind and his enthusiasm for and knowledge of horse sport, and the two made a tour of the leading tracks of the South, in the course of which the older man thoroughly schooled the younger in all aspects of horse training, track management, and bet setting.[16]

Having profited through his comprehensive turf education with Johnson, Ten Broeck struck out on his own, bringing stables of horses to race in Canada and Cuba, but he failed to profit in either locale, as the purses on offer in the former were far smaller than he had anticipated, and the inhabitants of the latter had little interest in competitions that involved American horses.[17] It would not be until his arrival in New Orleans that he succeeded in fashioning himself into a turfman *par excellence*, in the mode of his mentor Johnson and his employers Bingaman and Oliver. Without his involvement, it is difficult to imagine that the Metairie course would not only have remained in business but that it would have emerged by the middle of the 1850s as the most exciting racing venue in the United States. The track may have lacked the social cachet of Charleston's Washington Course, but it substituted for this atmosphere of grace and gentility "a distinctive New Orleans style," a "vulgar dash—the men [of the Metairie Association] wore green cutaways [coats] with brass buttons and flourished riding whips in the grandstand." The aristocratic English writer Matilda Houstoun, who visited the course around 1849, pronounced herself horrified by this "mockery . . . of Epsom and Newmarket," and especially by the costumes of the association members, which "they seemed, in the ignorance of their hearts, to consider a sort of racing costume . . . the 'correct thing' to wear on these *sporting* occasions," but this ambience was as well-suited to the social atmosphere promulgated by the new American elite of the Crescent City as the self-conscious restraint of the Washington Course was to that valorized by "old Charlestonians" of the late antebellum era. But given that Ten Broeck was not merely an outsider both to New Orleans and to the South but, still more damningly, had spent years as what the Alabama-born lawyer and social commentator Daniel Robinson Hundley described as "a peripatetical blackleg, gambling for a livelihood . . . [who] travels on the river steamboats mostly, and lives by plucking all such poor pigeons as remind him of his former[ly genteel] self," how did he rise to a position of such dominance over the racing world of New Orleans?[18]

Ten Broeck's mentor in turf matters, Johnson, was not merely a leading breeder and trainer of horses but also, according to the former jockey and horse trainer John H. Davis, "one of the greatest plungers of his time," a turfman who "made probably more matches than any man alive and wagered more money on the results." According to Davis, a "plunger" was a man "who [was] not afraid to take a chance and bet [his] money," and Johnson, the "leviathan of the betting ring," was known to wager as much as seventy-five thousand dollars on the performance of one of his horses in a single race. Such behavior might initially appear ungentlemanly in its recklessness and ostentation, but Davis claimed that nearly all of the "plungers" he had encountered prior to the Civil War had been genteel and well-educated. In Johnson's case, his immense wagers served as evidence of his status as "one of Nature's noblemen" and as "the grandest man [Davis] ever knew," as "whether he won or whether he lost it was not perceptible in his manner." Such calm in the face of both success and failure, also noted in the trackside conduct of Adam Bingaman, separated the blackleg, who cared only for financial gain, from the aristocratic "plunger." Although Ten

Broeck was the scion of an affluent and respectable family that had arrived in the American colonies in the seventeenth century, his background was not, at least in the opinion of many southern racing enthusiasts, as impressive as that of Johnson, whom Davis described as being "of one of the best families in the South," and who "towered as a giant amid a race of giants, for the men of the South were all big men in heart."[19]

More problematically, while Johnson was renowned as a racetrack "plunger," Ten Broeck had spent years as a professional gambler, a man who would likely have attracted scorn and even disgust from the members of the era's Virginian and South Carolinian jockey clubs. But his years of traveling across the South, whether at Johnson's side or on riverboats up and down the Mississippi, appear to have taught him some important lessons, including the increasing economic, political, and social power of the planters of the Southwest in comparison with those farther to the north and east, and the fact that many within this rising class were fond of ostentatiously flaunting their wealth and just as ostentatiously risking it. This understanding underpinned the event that brought Ten Broeck his first fame in New Orleans, the organization of the "Great Horse Race" of April 1854, which ignited the rivalry between Lexington and Lecomte. According to Mobile resident "John," the author of a letter to the *New York Times*, this competition, in which entrants were drawn from Alabama, Kentucky, Louisiana, and Mississippi, but not from Virginia or South Carolina, enthralled the public of the Gulf South; "people at the North have been troubling themselves about the Nebraska bill in Congress—it hardly elicits a remark here, or it has been swallowed up in the more attractive theme of horse-racing; for the last three months the qualities of the different horses have been canvassed." The prospect of this race not only generated constant discussion, but "bets have been placed upon bets"; when Kentucky's Lexington triumphed, those who had favored Alabama's Highlander lost one hundred thousand dollars, and partisans of Louisiana's Arrow, owned by the sugar planter Duncan Kenner, twice that amount.[20]

Ten Broeck had triumphed: he had arranged a race that generated immense excitement, not only among racing fans but among the wider publics of the states that had dispatched their equine representatives to this competition, and upon which huge amounts of money were wagered, whether by the millionaires of Natchez who risked thousands of dollars, seemingly without a care, or by the local newsboys who bet their hard-earned pennies in the hope of making a few more. The event had attracted an estimated twenty thousand spectators, including the former US president Millard Fillmore and several hundred women who "adorned the course and stand with their benignant presence," to the elegantly refurbished Metairie course, and public opinion was that "the whole affair was conducted on a plane so high that jobbery or foul play was not even hinted at by the most pessimistic."[21] Colonel Johnson had been the principal mover for the 1823 race at Long Island's Union Course between the southern equine champion Sir Henry and his northern rival American Eclipse; this event was the first of a series of "Great Match Races" between the leading horses of the two sections, and it is believed not merely to have created New York City's first traffic jam but to have generated nearly a quarter million dollars in bets. As the sports historian Nancy L. Struna observed, this series of intersectional competitions "launched a new era in the annals of American thoroughbred racing," one that involved huge crowds of spectators, immense wagers, and extensive coverage in the general newspapers as well as in the sporting press, becoming a truly national event rather than a local or regional one. By the mid-1840s, political hostilities between the southern and northern states had become so bitter that they could no longer be resolved, even temporarily, by the outcome of a horse race, but many southerners continued to enjoy intersectional competitions, and at the Metairie, Ten Broeck followed his mentor's example by arranging his own "Great Match Race," in which all of the competitors were southern, but that encouraged the inhabitants of four of the Union's most economically vibrant states to make considerable financial and emotional investment in the event.[22]

Johnson's half century at the apex of American horse racing was characterized by his unerring ability to spot and profit from changes within the turf world. Rather than clinging to a romanticized idea of the sport's past or maintaining an outdated loyalty to a particular locale or social system, he realized that the racing world of the Upper South was in decline in comparison to that of the Lower Mississippi Valley, and in his later years he relocated from Virginia to the newly vigorous Gulf South city of Mobile. Similarly, Ten Broeck gained advantage from his awareness that, in 1850s New Orleans, people—men and women; locals and visitors; Black, white, and of mixed heritage; rich and poor—were not attending the races primarily to uphold the social hierarchy, to recall a glorious but fading heritage, or even to transact business or politics, but simply to enjoy themselves. A major aspect of that enjoyment was the luxury of the facilities on offer—at least to those who could afford them—at the renovated Metairie track. Its elegant accommodation and lavish refreshments ensured that those visitors who became enraptured by what they saw as the romance and sensuality of New Orleans, a city that for North Americans was "the most exotic place to which one [could] travel without crossing an ocean or a border" and to Latin Americans was *el Paris hispano,* would incorporate the racecourse into their itineraries. He was also attuned to a significant alteration in not just *why* but *how* many spectators experienced races, and what they wanted from these events in a city in which the attractions were "so great and numerous."[23] All races were, of course, innately competitive, with each horse and jockey hoping to defeat their opponents, but increasingly the greatest appeal lay in those which centered around a sense of individual partisanship, whether based on a geographical loyalty, as with the various "Great Match Races," or, in the case of Lecomte and Lexington, in a fandom that had been encouraged by widespread media coverage and that was closer to that of the era's raucous boxing subculture than of the claims of many jockey club members that their sole goal was the improvement of the breeding of horses. Finally, Ten Broeck was well aware of the technological improvements in timekeeping, which made it possible to judge the performance of individual horses far more precisely than ever before, an innovation that encouraged a popular fascination with the setting and breaking of speed records. The immense success of the final face-off between Lexington and Lecomte in April 1855 was the logical outcome of these changes in the sport, and of Ten Broeck's innovative responses to them.[24]

As a former denizen of the Mississippi steamboat world, Ten Broeck was also mindful of changing attitudes toward gambling in the Lower Mississippi Valley. T. J. Jackson Lears has argued that it was not until the post–Civil War Gilded Age that the immense fortunes of the nation's *nouveaux riches* blurred societal boundaries to such an extent that professional gamblers and leading capitalists now "inhabited a common realm of sybaritic excess and theatrical display" in their attitudes toward financial risk, but, as the recent work of, among others, Edward Baptist, Sven Beckert, Walter Johnson, and Scott Marler has emphasized, by the 1850s much of the Valley had reached a stage of capitalist development well beyond that of the longer-settled sections of the plantation South and that rivaled that of New York and the industrial Northeast. In Virginia and South Carolina, a "plunger" could only gain societal approbation if, like William Johnson, he was an individual of undeniable gentility who behaved as if winning and losing was just a game, but as the Crescent City metamorphosed into both the Merchants' Capital and the City That Care Forgot, most visitors, and even many residents, felt that gambling was an acceptable recreation, as long as it was staged in an upmarket setting, and that it was a legitimate aspect of the pleasure inherent in the sport of racing.[25]

As central as Ten Broeck was to New Orleans's development into a racing mecca in the mid-nineteenth century, he did not achieve this transformation single-handedly. Much of the impetus behind the sport's rise to prestige and popularity came from the members of the Orleans Club on Canal Street, a social organization with approximately four hundred members, the majority of whom were younger men who enjoyed racing, gambling, and drinking, and who had rejected or been blackballed from participation in the city's more staid and business-oriented Pelican Club. The Orleans also presented a sharp contrast to the city's Boston Club, the third-oldest such organization in the country, which, although its ambience was less stuffy than that of the Pelican, prided itself on the "propriety of demeanor and proper courtesy" among its members; some young men of good family joined the Orleans for a few wild years, then moved on to the more sedate and prestigious milieu of the Boston. Members of the former club included the aforementioned Adam Bingaman, William J. Minor, and T. J. Wells, as well as Louisiana racing enthusiasts such as Minor's kinsman Duncan Kenner, Paul Hebert, of a family that claimed descent from the first French child born in North America, and "all the prominent turfmen of the South and Southwest . . . in fact the racing fraternity was strongly represented, and that the club soon became very 'horsey' goes without saying, and racing and merits of horses were topics well understood and knowingly discussed." Although the Orleans was in existence only between 1850 and 1856, its members played a dominant role in the establishment of the Metairie Jockey Club, and "on the occasion of great races in the grand days of the 'Old Metairie' the parlors, halls, lunch rooms, refreshment and card rooms of the Orleans Club were most lively and exciting places."[26]

The club closed in 1856, due to a combination of poor management and ever-more-virulent political disagreements among its members. Some of its adherents reconstituted themselves the following year into the Pickwick Club, named for the group at the center of Charles Dickens's *The Pickwick Papers* and primarily concerned with the recently established Mardi Gras festivities organized annually by the Krewe of Momus, but by this time the Metairie racetrack, now reorganized and renovated under Ten Broeck's aegis, had become sufficiently respectable that it attracted the support of the members of the Boston, to which Kenner also belonged, and that had become the principal social venue for the city's Anglo-American business elite. Scott Marler has observed that membership in institutions such as the Boston benefited these men not only through the personal contacts they made therein but because the local newspapers devoted considerable attention to the clubs' activities, which attracted the notice of a much wider public. In a society built upon enslaved labor, conspicuous leisure, whether in the form of membership in a social club or attendance at the race course, was in itself a form of luxury, and it is thus not surprising that by 1858 the Metairie races included a Boston Club Stake.[27]

As Richard Ten Broeck was neither a New Orleanian nor a southerner nor a plantation owner, it is unlikely that he would have made such an impact on the city's racing practices had he not found a confederate in Duncan Kenner. Kenner, the owner of Ashland plantation in Ascension Parish, was the son of a Virginian who had set himself up as a merchant in New Orleans when it was under Spanish rule, and had introduced his sons to the sport in which his antecedents had participated; their ancestor Captain Rodham Kenner had been a prominent turfman of the Old Dominion in the colonial era. Like William Ransom Johnson, Kenner gained from his peers the sobriquet of "Napoleon," in this instance, "of the Louisiana Turf," but unlike Johnson and other leading turfmen of the pre–Civil War South, he was familiar not only with American racing practices but with those of England and Europe, having embarked upon his "Grand Tour" after graduating from Miami University of Ohio in 1832. In the course of this trip, in which he also visited Paris, Vienna, Dresden, Prague, and Naples, he made a stop at Tattersall's, the London horse auction house located at Hyde Park Corner. Although English and Irish racing men regarded this venue as the holy of holies for the "sporting aristocracy," Kenner claimed to have found the establishment "quite common," especially in comparison with the royal stables, which he also visited. Nonetheless, upon his return to Ashland he instituted a number of innovations based on what he had observed in England, most notably focusing his training program on jockeys as well as on horses. He was one of the first southerners to do so, with the prominent exception of Colonel Johnson and his jockey Charles Stewart, as until the 1830s most turfmen believed that victory or defeat was predicated on the actions and character of the horse rather than those of its rider. Among the enslaved young men whom Kenner trained as jockeys were the celebrated Abe Hawkins and Henry Hammond, and his friends Bingaman, Wells, and Minor soon adopted his tactics. Turf fanciers competed for invitations to Ashland, at which they hoped to stand with Kenner on the mansion's second-floor balcony, the ideal vantage point from which to view the private track that surrounded the house and upon which he and his host of jockeys and grooms worked his stable of famed or emerging horses.[28]

The combination of Kenner's vast wealth and his enthusiasm for and knowledge of the breeding, training, and racing of blooded horses allowed him to emerge as the dominant figure of the Louisiana turf in the late antebellum era and to be recognized as such not only by New Orleanians, among whom "in the days of the glories of the American turf, Mr. Kenner's name ever ranked among the first," but also by visitors from England.[29] He was also unique in his ability to bridge the gap that continued to separate "Creoles" from "Americans" for decades following the Louisiana Purchase. William Kenner had died bankrupt, but his son's career in both law and politics flourished because his fluency in French and the social graces he had acquired during his European travels encouraged many among the city's Francophone elite to welcome him into their commercial and social lives. So successful was Kenner at ingratiating himself within this world that in 1839 he married Anne Guillemine ("Nanine") Bringier, whose family owned a string of sugar plantations along the River Road between New Orleans and Baton Rouge, one of very few instances in which a Creole heiress chose an American husband; it was Nanine's dowry that helped Kenner make Ashland into an exceptionally large and lavish plantation family home and a center of scientific innovation in sugar production as well a horse-breeding and -training ground.[30] But Kenner's kinship connections among the state's Anglo-American elite were also important to his success; his mother had been a member of the Minor family of Natchez, and his uncle was the renowned racing enthusiast William J. Minor, whom we encountered in the previous chapter.

When Ten Broeck purchased the Metairie Jockey Club's course in 1851 and created the Metairie Association, he held the largest number of the organization's shares, but of the other fourteen subscribers, Kenner and Minor were co-equals in second place. Like his nephew, Minor was a man whose love of high-stakes gambling was such that he could have been considered a "plunger," although he rarely engaged in games of chance, preferring to make wagers with his friends over political issues or questions of local interest. On a single day in 1847 he is reported to have bet his friend Adam Bingaman five hundred dollars on an aspect of the legal structure of the newly organized Commercial Bank of Natchez, while wagering two hundred dollars against John Nevitt of Natchez that General Zachary Taylor would win the upcoming presidential election. At the track, he might bet as much as two thousand dollars on the outcome of an individual race. For Minor and many of those who joined the Metairie Association or attended its events, it was not the presence of gamblers that sullied the atmosphere of a particular track, as many Virginians and Carolinians claimed, or that of the sport of racing more generally, as was the general sentiment throughout the urban North in the late antebellum era. What mattered most in terms of a track's reputation was the quality of the competition that it offered, and as the purses awarded to the winners rarely offset the costs of purchasing and training a top-quality Thoroughbred, without the large sums generated by successful wagers few turfmen could afford to participate in the sport.

Minor's withdrawal from racing at Natchez was sparked by his disgust that the Adams County Jockey Club permitted nonelite white men and free men of color, such as the barber William Johnson, to race their horses and mules on the Pharsalia track after the day's main races had ended; in his diary, he fumed that "the Pharsalia Course has been *desecrated* by this mule race." But no such fate would befall the Metairie course, no matter how many blacklegs might descend upon it, as long as it continued to host the nation's finest horses. The British journalist James Silk Buckingham alluded to this situation in his narrative of his travels through the southern states; he claimed that, among Americans, "the very term 'sportsmen' . . . means 'gamblers'; and not, as with us, persons fond of hunting and shooting, merely." "The 'black-legs' of Newmarket [England]," he asserted, "would be called 'sportsmen' here; and this is the term by which the 'gamblers' of New Orleans, who make that city their haunt in winter, and spread themselves over the watering-places in the summer, are always known." Buckingham might sneer at what struck him as the pretensions of the Louisiana turfmen, but to Minor, Kenner, and the others who constituted the business and planter elite of the state, and who included some of the richest men in the late antebellum United States, the combination of record-smashing horses and jockeys and the opportunity to win or lose a fortune on their performances not only made racing the sole established sport in pre–Civil War New Orleans but precipitated a national fascination with it that would dictate its fate in the post–Civil War era.[31]

William Head Coleman claimed that "the brightest episodes of the history of the turf in New Orleans occurred before 1855," as it was "in these good old antebellum days, when horse-racing was pursued purely as an amusement, and not as a means of accumulating fortunes." In his view, the Metairie course's golden era ended when the majority of its visitors became motivated at least in part by the hope of financial gain. But in reality it was the final Lexington–Lecomte race that was the beginning of that course's most successful years, allowing New Orleans to become, in popular opinion, the center of American racing. On race days, the shell road that led from the center of the city to the Metairie course became a "celebrated theatre for young men," attracting not only inhabitants of and tourists to the Crescent City but Louisianians from as far away as Rapides Parish, a distance of two hundred miles. The St. Charles Hotel, on St. Charles Avenue in the city's "American" Garden District, where the Metairie Jockey Club had held its meetings, and whose owners, Messrs. Hall and Hildreth, pronounced themselves dedicated to "the encouragement of the Sports of the Turf in the city," making frequent donations to the Metairie of both silver trophies and purse funding, not only accommodated visitors to the races but functioned as a clubhouse for the leading local turf enthusiasts, including Ten Broeck, Kenner, Minor, Bingaman, and Wells.[32] As post time drew near, the members of the association, their male kin, and their guests took their places in their stand, with their wives and daughters accommodated in the luxurious area reserved for female attendees, whose presence allowed the event to be "gemmed by the rich beauty of the sunny south." It was these men and women whom the New Orleans local-color author Grace King romanticized as "knights and their fair companions from all over the land of chivalry," despite the fact that few of the Anglo-American families from whom the association's members were drawn had been either rich or socially prominent for more than one generation, and they were far prouder of their current success than of any past glories. Meanwhile, the hoi polloi, including both professional gamblers and amateur bettors, middle- and working-class white men and women, free people of color, and at least a few enslaved individuals, milled around the track's edges, all awaiting the moment at which the tap of a drum would cause the crowd's chatter to cease, and the horses, carrying jockeys dressed in the silks that marked both them and their mounts as the property of a particular turfman, would approach the starting point. The most enthusiastic fans could see a race nearly every week of the year, but the great days of the Metairie came for six days each spring and a further six in the autumn, when twenty thousand spectators might be in attendance, including "people from all parts of the South and West."[33]

As was true in other racing centers of the United States throughout the nineteenth century, the sport received criticism on moral grounds from a variety of commentators. Henry Benjamin Whipple, later the first Episcopal bishop of Minnesota, visited New Orleans from upstate New York as a young man in the mid-1840s and decried racing on several counts. The fact that "thousands of dollars have been won & lost on the field" was evidence of the frivolity and wastefulness of such a pastime, but Whipple was also concerned about its effects on the animals, whom he described as "noble horses under whip & spur & perhaps killing themselves with exertion." Worse still, these contests were frequently held on Sundays, making the "holy & sacred" day a time of "dissipation and gaiety." A contributor to New England's *Christian Reflector* was still more disgusted by this "revolting desecration of the *Holy Sabbath,*" which provoked him to ask, "Where was all of this? Among barbarians or Papists?" The anonymous author of 1849's *Truth Is Stranger Than Fiction, or, New Orleans As It Is* similarly deplored the staging of races on the Sabbath, and went on to critique the personal morals of leading local turfmen, particularly "B———," clearly referring to Adam Bingaman, who "has had a mulatto woman as his bed companion for years" and had four children with her, yet was highly regarded as a sportsman and a gentleman within the New Orleanian racing world.

While residents of French Creole heritage were not morally opposed to racing in general, and some men of this community were frequent spectators thereof, they were skeptical about the attendance of women at the track, despite the existence of elegant accommodations for female visitors and the enthusiastic participation of many respectable Anglo-American women. Although the memoirist Eliza Ripley's family were of Anglo-American descent, the only race she attended, despite residing near New Orleans throughout the 1840s and 1850s, was that between Lexington and Lecomte; she claimed that "ladies had never been in evidence at a horse race in Louisiana" as "the bare idea was a shock to the Creole mind, that dominated and controlled all the fashionable, indeed, all the respectable minds in New Orleans at that day." We might attribute Ripley's claims to the fact that she spent little time in the city itself prior to the Civil War, and thus may have been unaware of the frequent presence of women trackside; as a woman of Kentuckian heritage and no doubt familiar with the Creole distaste for "Kaintucks," she may also have been attempting to separate herself from the "Kentucky belles" who attended this event in support of Lexington. Although Ripley was charmed to meet these "dashing, high-bred, blue-blooded Kentucky women," members of leading families such as the Breckenridges, the Flournoys, and the Johnsons, she was also convinced that, when they sped from the St. Charles Hotel to the Metairie course in a stagecoach, crammed full of spectators of both sexes as if in a "circus van," "many a cautious Creole mamma made her innocent mam'zelles repair to the backyard while she hastily closed the shutters." Once at the track, she asserted, the only other women present were "some *demi-mondaines* scattered here and there, in inconspicuous places," but the lack of other respectable female guests did not embarrass the visitors. As Lexington entered the final lap, one Kentucky woman jumped onto a bench and requested that her escort "hold me while I holler"; according to Ripley, "never did I hear the full compass of the female voice before, nor since."[34] For these observers, the New Orleans turf flew in the face of piety and decorum and was thus a dangerously corrupting influence on local morality, particularly that of girls and women.

If such complaints had little power to affect racetrack attendance in Virginia or South Carolina, in which the local jockey clubs were perpetually anxious about maintaining the respectability of their events, they had still less influence in New Orleans, many of whose inhabitants by the mid-nineteenth century either reveled in their city's reputation as a place of pleasure or at least accepted that the entertainments on offer attracted both commerce and tourism. As Kathryn Olivarius has noted, the city's public culture was heavily influenced by its challenging physical and immunological climate; it was a place in which white men "drank and gambled more and lived hedonistically," and where many "wishe[d] only to be rich, and to lead a short life and a merry one."[35] Such men were drawn to Metairie and the pleasures it promised, and the fact that so many of the course's attendees at any time were either short-term sojourners

Life on the Metairie, by Theodore Sidney Moise. Hodges Photography Collection. Courtesy of Fair Grounds Race Course and Slots.

or individuals whose intent to remain in New Orleans was undermined by the lurking presence of yellow fever and other tropical ailments presented a sharp contrast with the racing audiences of Richmond, Charleston, and Natchez. If the population of New Orleans was in perpetual flux, it could not develop and maintain a strictly delineated social structure within which residents were constantly anxious about their own gentility and others' perceived lack thereof. In the context of the racetrack, this situation relieved Ten Broeck and the Metairie Association of responsibility for upholding strict decorum, as long as visitors refrained from behavior that was obviously disruptive. Even the presence of the higher class of the city's "public women" was accepted at the course, although they were obligated to arrive there in carriages that their drivers would park in the inner oval, and they were forbidden to leave these vehicles. This arrangement allowed male guests to arrange rendezvouses with the glamorous courtesans who were among the city's attractions but prevented respectable women and censorious men from having to interact with them.[36]

The Metairie course continued to stage well-attended competitions up to the beginning of the Civil War, and although the track was soon transformed into Camp Walker, to which several thousand Confederate troops were sent to drill, the members of the association held their usual December meeting in 1861, with the profits to be donated to New Orleans's "gallant volunteers in the field, and their families at home." Although attendance was far lower than in "the piping times of peace," due to the limited number of blooded horses that remained available for sporting purposes as well as to the fact that many of the city's younger men were now serving in the Confederate army, the turfmen announced their plan to hold another meeting in the spring of 1862, but by that time the city was occupied by Union forces under the command of the much-detested General Benjamin Butler, and the course was closed for the rest of the conflict. It would never again host a gathering comparable to that depicted in English Victor Pierson and Charlestonian Theodore Sidney Moise's painting *Life on the Metairie*, which was created in 1867 but represented the track in its pre-war heyday, with Adam Bingaman and William J. Minor prominently featured among the attendees. The Bostonian journalist and travel writer Eleanor Early wrote of this work that "the forty-four well-known New Orleanians assembled at the track, all look[ed] prosperous and happy, and never dream[ed] that pretty soon a social climber was going to be as good as his word, and make a graveyard of their beautiful track."[37] Despite the heroic efforts of Duncan Kenner, who, although he had lost many of his best horses to a Union raid on his Ashland plantation, was determined to revive both the Metairie Association, now renamed the Metairie Jockey Club, and its course at the war's end, the other shareholders simply did not have the funds needed to do so, and by 1872 they reluctantly agreed to sell the property, whose location atop a natural ridge with good drainage encouraged its transformation into a cemetery. Local folklore states that its purchaser, Charles T. Howard, the director of the Louisiana State Lottery Company, had been unsuccessful in gaining membership in the association because the members considered him a "social climber," and swore that he would have his revenge by transforming the course into a graveyard. This claim is undermined by the fact that Kenner was appointed to the first board of the Cemetery Association, but the fact remains that, after the course closed,

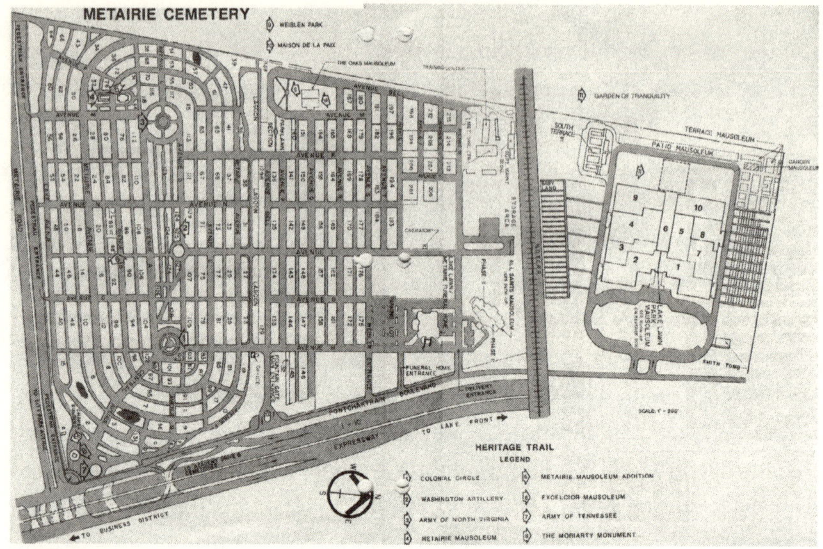

Map of Metairie Cemetery, showing the footprint of the track. US GenWeb Archives.

none of the city's new tracks, including that which opened at the Fair Grounds in 1872, and whose Louisiana Jockey Club included some of the younger members of the Metairie Association, ever attained a comparable level of social or sporting prestige. In Grace King's words, "the old Metairie is expiating its sins now as a cemetery, and its patrons, its beaus and its belles and its horses—they are expiating their sins too, in cemeterial ways."[38]

We might assume that the Metairie's postwar decline would have been a great blow to Richard Ten Broeck, but he had disassociated himself from active involvement in the course back in 1856, at which time he had sold his shares in the association and set out to "assert the progress of his country on the English turf." John Randolph of Roanoke, who had toured England's racecourses in 1830, was convinced that "the time would come sooner or later when the American Thoroughbred would be able to contest honors with the best that the English turf could present," and the possibility of bringing a stable of American-bred and -trained horses to compete in the most prestigious English races had been discussed among the turfmen of the Lower Mississippi Valley since at least 1851. William J. Minor, writing under the pseudonym "A Young Turfman," had urged the readers of the *Spirit of the Times* to support an idea that he believed would improve Anglo-American relations in general: "To make the English our fast friends we must go over and win the Goodwood Cup with an American-bred horse," as doing so would put paid to the English agricultural writer John Lawrence's assertion that, as of the early nineteenth century, American turfmen "do not yet appear to have made any progress in establishing a thorough racing breed."[39]

Presumably emboldened by his successful tenure at the Metairie, Ten Broeck assembled a string of horses, including Lecomte, whom he had purchased from General Wells for ten thousand dollars, and embarked for England on the steamer *Asia* in August 1856. At his departure, not only the sporting papers but the wider American press expressed a jingoistic sense of optimism about his prospects: "We should not be surprised were he to come off victorious . . . as we have beaten the English in many things, why should we not beat them in racing also?" was a typical comment. This confidence, it turned out, was misplaced; Lecomte, along with his sibling stablemates Prior and Prioress, was ill throughout the voyage and performed poorly on the English track, notably in the Goodwood Cup, a result that the jockey Gilpatrick blamed on Ten Broeck's alleged failure to keep his horses properly trained and in top condition during their travels, and encouraging London's *Racing Times* to ridicule Ten Broeck's horses as "all fudge," as "they don't know what a racehorse is in America."[40] For the most part, American racing enthusiasts rejected the claim of some British sporting journalists that Ten Broeck, rather than doing his utmost to win the competitions in which he entered his horses, was deliberately undermining the performances of Lecomte and the others and making a fortune by betting against them, but at his far from triumphal return to the United States in the autumn of 1858 they were forced to admit that his "American Invasion" had been troubled from its inception, as Lecomte and Prior "were noble horses, but they had already reaped their fields of glory, and should not have been pushed to conquests anew," while Prioress, "though a good racer, is said not to be first class," although she triumphed in at Newmarket, winning the Cesarewitch stakes as "the crowd cheered the American." The success of the "Invasion" had also been limited by the fact that British and American racetracks presented horses and their riders with very different conditions, and because in many instances Ten Broeck's jockeys were not sufficiently familiar with their mounts.[41] Apparently undaunted, Ten Broeck returned to England the following year with a new string of horses, but although he experienced a number of successes, "he had kept up a comparatively large and expensive establishment for some years, and . . . his success was not nearly enough to pay the charges of the concern." By the summer of 1861, the *Racing Times* reported that he was set to retire permanently from turf activities.[42]

But while the Metairie course's story had effectively reached an end at this time, its progenitor's was far from over. Returning to the United States at the war's end, the man whose life had led him from West Point to the steamboats of the Mississippi and from Metairie to Goodwood showed himself capable of further reinventions. As the locus of American racing moved from New Orleans to New York, and its leading turfmen were no longer southern planters but a new northern elite of financiers and industrialists, Ten Broeck drew upon his personal charisma and his decades of racing experience in both Britain and the Lower Mississippi Valley to make himself a trusted advisor to men who had great enthusiasm for, but little knowledge of, the sport, most notably James R. Keene, who was both "the greatest stock-gambler who ever lived"—like Colonel Johnson, he was the leading "plunger" of his era—and "a man of culture yet a crony of race-track habitues." In this role, Ten Broeck did as much to shape racing in this new venue as he had in the old. From New Orleans's turf world he imported the recent fascination with statistics and the setting and breaking of records and the belief that the popularity of trackside wagering, and even the presence of professional gamblers, was not incompatible with respectability and the attendance of women of good reputation. These convictions had only been strengthened during his English sojourn, to which was added the abandonment of the race made up of multiple heats in favor of a single short dash, which, as we will see, almost immediately became an integral element of post–Civil War northern racing. It would be most accurate to consider Richard Ten Broeck not as the last leader of the antebellum turf but as one of the creators of that of the postbellum era, and thus, in many ways, of the sport as it exists today.[43]

5

Saratoga

FROM SEDATE RESORT TO RACING MECCA

[Saratoga] is indeed by far the most varied and cosmopolitan of our watering-places . . . entertaining hundreds of coarse parvenus, but the summer home of much of that wealth which has acquired or inherited the grace of refinement.

—"Saratoga: The American Baden-Baden," 1871

We said "Saratoga is the place for [Henry] James. It's the only place that would reconcile him to America." I suppose we thought no other place could be so bad, even in America, and the whole country would profit by the contrast.

—WILLIAM DEAN HOWELLS, *Life in Letters of William Dean Howells,* 1928

For the majority of white southerners, the summer of 1865 was not a time of individual or communal pleasure. Several months after the end of the Civil War, many former Confederates were struggling to come to terms not only with the failure of their "Glorious Cause" but with the destruction of the social order that they had fought so tenaciously to preserve. Many men who had spent years in military service came home to find their businesses, farms, or plantations in ruins, and while they relished their reunions with loved ones, some found it difficult to reaccustom themselves to civilian life, particularly when their worlds had been overturned by the end of slavery and the physical and economic devastation of much of the region. Other men had yet to return, as they had been discharged from service or freed from Union prisoner-of-war camps hundreds of miles from their homes and were obliged to make their way back on foot, often hungry, ill-shod, and in poor health. Southern women rejoiced at the return of their husbands, fathers, brothers, and sons, but at the same time some were embittered by the privations they had suffered during the conflict, and by their feeling that the Confederate state had not rewarded or even acknowledged these sacrifices. Myrta Lockett Avary, a Virginia-born journalist whose childhood encompassed the war and its aftermath, depicted postwar southern women, at least those of the formerly elite classes, as having previously lived as "social queens, who had had everything the heart could wish," as "reduced to harder cases than their negroes had ever known," while life seemed to offer even fewer possibilities for their male kin, among whom "many seemed to feel that they no longer had a country." Younger people were often desperate for sociability amid the general gloom, but the best that most could hope for under the circumstances were "starvation parties," at which "the festal boards were thinly spread," and the guests wore their old uniforms or decades-old garments exhumed from musty trunks. Scenes such as these distressed even some northern visitors, such as the New York–based historian Benson J. Lossing, who, in the course of a postwar sojourn in Tidewater Virginia, mourned that "the sudden change wrought in the condition of the residents was lamentable . . . the wealthy and refined, the noble and gentle—men and women who had never experienced poverty nor the necessity for toiling—[were] instantly reduced from abundance and ease, to want and hardship."[1]

At a time that many who had been wealthy before the war were now adjusting to a life devoid of luxuries, and some were struggling to provide themselves and their dependents with necessities, the racetracks of the former Confederacy were also stripped of their antebellum glamour. We have seen in chapter 2 that Charleston's Washington Course had been transformed into a notoriously wretched prisoner-of-war camp for Union soldiers; soon after the conflict's end the federal government turned it over to the South Carolina district of the Freedmen's Bureau, and local African Americans inaugurated what would become the national tradition of Memorial Day by commemorating the sufferings of its inmates. In Virginia, the town of Petersburg and its environs had in June 1864 become the site of a siege that would last until the war's end ten months later, during which the Newmarket course became part of the no-man's-land separating the opposing armies, and the home of the renowned turfman Otway P. Hare, along with his huge collection of racing memorabilia and some "very elegant horse trappings and equipments," was destroyed. In Richmond, the Tree Hill plantation on which the eponymous track was located had been converted into pasturage for the livestock that supplied meat and dairy products to the enormous Chimborazo military hospital complex, and the nearby Fairfield course had been used for military drills. Meanwhile, the Pharsalia track, the pride of the Natchez Nabobs, had, like that of New Orleans's Metairie Association, been turned at the war's outbreak into a training facility for Confederate troops. In the autumn of 1861 Pharsalia was the site of both the trials and the executions of more than twenty enslaved men whom a self-appointed "Executive Committee" of the area's leading planters deemed guilty of participation in the Second Creek conspiracy, which was allegedly aimed at overthrowing the Nabobs and other Adams County plantation owners.[2]

But a very different atmosphere prevailed at Saratoga Springs, just under two hundred miles north of New York City. Of course, northerners were at this time flushed with victory, despite their shock and grief at Abraham Lincoln's assassination, and this community of seven thousand, like many other parts of the Union, had not been physically affected by the destruction of warfare. But it was not only men and women from the victors' side who made their way to the town's recently opened racetrack. Although before the war Saratoga had had no tradition of Thoroughbred racing, it had since the early nineteenth century been a popular spa and resort, particularly for affluent southerners who wanted to escape the summer heat. They stayed at town founder and promoter Gideon Putnam's luxurious Grand Union Hotel and enjoyed the fashionable social life that developed around the local mineral springs, although some were unnerved by the confidence and independence of the free Black men and women who worked at the town's hotels and restaurants, and alienated by what they considered the chilly reserve of elite northerners. Saratoga, which by the 1850s had become "the most celebrated watering place in the U.S.," continued to flourish throughout the war, although in those years few of its guests came from below the Mason-Dixon Line. But, as the *New York World* reported, by the summer of 1865, "Southern faces [were] reappearing" trackside; they apparently included at least one "prominent confederate general" and several Kentuckian horse breeders, as well as the noted Richmond turfman John Minor Botts. The presence of such individuals at the course, which testified to "the Southern interest in all that belongs to racing, to horses, and to sport," moved a northern spectator to describe the scene, particularly the apparently mutually comfortable proximity of the former Union general Joseph "Fighting Joe" Hooker, who had commanded the Army of the Potomac, and a group of southern racing fans as "the first palpable evidence I have had of peace and reconstruction."[3]

The presence of southern turf enthusiasts at Saratoga was not limited to the 1865 season. In the following year the attendees included a number of well-known New Orleanian turfmen, several of whom were honored by the organizers by being asked to serve as race-day officials: William Conner, who had been the Metairie Association's secretary, was a starter; the former Louisiana governor, Confederate general, and association president Paul Hebert was an official guest of the judges; and none other than Duncan Kenner was a timer. In 1871 Senator Thomas Bayard Jr. of Delaware asked Hebert and Kenner to be race-day judges. The latter's gentlemanly deportment, dapper self-presentation, and vast knowledge of turf matters so impressed the managers of the Saratoga track that in 1870 they named a new race for three-year-olds the Kenner Stakes in his honor. Although Kenner had lost most of his best horses when federal troops raided his Ashland plantation in 1862, and had found little success in his attempts to revive the Metairie Association and its course at the war's end, these setbacks did not prevent him from regaining his position as one of the nation's most respected turfmen after the war.[4]

We might wonder at the enthusiastic reception that Kenner and other southerners found at the Saratoga track. The years that immediately followed the war's end and Lincoln's assassination were not yet characterized by what Nina Silber termed "the romance of reunion" between North and South, a process that would come to fruition in the following decade. In the immediate prewar years, some southerners had curtailed their annual visits to Saratoga Springs in favor of sojourns at the Virginia Springs resorts because "the prevalence of anti-slavery doctrines" in the former made them feel unwelcome, and in the wake of the conflict northern public opinion tended to characterize white southerners, particularly those who had constituted the region's antebellum elite, as both unmanly and unwomanly. The men of the "chivalry" were depicted in the northern popular press as lacking the self-discipline that was the hallmark of true masculinity, while their wives and daughters were painted as embittered viragoes, far removed from the northern ideal of decorous womanhood.[5] However, some of the principal turfmen of the antebellum South, such as Kenner and many of the Natchez Nabobs, had made lengthy visits to the northern states, to Europe, or both in the decades before the war, and in so doing had formed strong connections with privileged northerners, as the elites of both sections "became more aware of the class-based qualities that transcended regional affiliations." The warm welcome that these southern "race horse men" received at Saratoga so soon after the war's end was also a response to the reappearance of a cross-sectional prewar racing fraternity that had been both created and reflected within the pages of such periodicals as *Spirit of the Times*. The amiable mingling of turf fans from across the newly reunited nation could indeed be viewed as a harbinger of "peace and reconciliation," but it also testified to the fact that, in its early years, and despite its success, the Saratoga racetrack was a liminal site, and the presence of distinguished turfmen such as Kenner was necessary to enforce both its social respectability and its sporting prestige.[6]

Throughout the antebellum South, the men associated with the foundation and flourishing of individual tracks were individuals of high social standing, such as Colonel William Ransom Johnson at Richmond's Tree Hill, Charles Cotesworth Pinckney at the Washington Course in Charleston, and the Natchez Nabobs at Pharsalia. Richard Ten Broeck's days as a riverboat gambler may have made him suspect to some members of New Orleans's sedate Pelican and Boston Clubs, but his genteel Dutch New York background and his apprenticeship with Colonel Johnson rescued him from being written off as an unprincipled blackleg, as did his evident knowledge of and passion for the sport. The same was true of Adam Bingaman, whose Harvard education, deep knowledge of literature and languages, and elegant manners outweighed his financial collapse and his openly acknowledged relationship with a woman of color. But the Saratoga track's creator, John Morrissey, was a far more problematic individual. He had immigrated with his parents from Ireland to Troy, New York, twenty-five miles from Saratoga, where the family scraped a meagre living. In his teens, Morrissey was an illiterate manual laborer who acquired "a checkered work record, a reputation for viciousness, and sundry indictments for burglary and assault." After moving to Manhattan, he became an enforcer and vote-getter for the Tammany Hall political machine, then a faro dealer in San Francisco in the aftermath of the Gold Rush, and finally a notoriously violent boxer nicknamed "Old Smoke." Enriched by his Tammany connections, his winnings in the ring, and his proprietorship of various gaming establishments, in 1861 he moved to Saratoga Springs, where he opened the Club House, an elegant gambling facility on Matilda Street (now Woodlawn Avenue), and replaced "exchang[ing] blows with a half-naked ruffian for the amusement of the mob" with running "a gilded and alluring pest house for the corruption of good society." Aware that success in this town required the approval of both local elites and affluent tourists, Morrissey kept his contacts in the underworld of brothels, taverns, and boxing rings at some distance; he "sugared the disreputable pill he had forced upon the community" by making substantial donations to local charities and cultivating friendships among the respectable. Having organized the town's first racing event in July 1863, the following year he established and underwrote the Saratoga Association for the Improvement of the Breed of Horses, whose founding members included the Wall Street financiers Leonard Jerome and William Travers, who were partners in a Manhattan investment firm. But to some people, his Irish heritage, lack of education, past as a boxer and a gambler, and involvement in a notoriously corrupt political machine placed him forever beyond the boundaries of social approval.[7]

Even if Morrissey had been a less controversial figure, his new track had to contend with the unusual nature of the relationship between the newly established association and the local community. The men who made up the former were individuals of considerable wealth and authority. In addition to Travers and Jerome, they included Erastus Corning Jr., a director of the New York Central Railroad and the leading citizen of the nearby state capital of Albany; the Westchester County sportsman John R. Hunter; and the stockbroker George Archer Osgood, who was the son-in-law of the renowned tycoon "Commodore" Cornelius Vanderbilt.[8] But the majority of these men were Manhattanites who, like most of the visitors to the new racecourse, came to Saratoga only for a few weeks each summer. From its colonial beginnings, the American concept of the jockey club, as distinct from that of England, had been rooted in locality; a club's members were drawn from the inhabitants of the city, town, or, in more rural areas, county in which the course with which it was associated was located. Of course, there were plenty of exceptions to this rule; for example, a number of the members of Charleston's South Carolina Jockey Club spent most of each year on their Lowcountry plantations and visited the city only for the few months that constituted the winter social season, and William J. Minor, who owned plantations in both Mississippi and Louisiana, was active in both Natchez's Adams County Jockey Club and New Orleans's Metairie Association. But although the Saratoga Association was not entirely devoid of locally based members—James Marvin, for example, had been born in nearby Ballston and was the proprietor of Saratoga's grandiose United States Hotel before his election to Congress—the majority of those involved with it lived almost two hundred miles away, and its most prominent Saratogian proponent, Morrissey, was so polarizing a figure that, although he had been the prime mover in the course's establishment as well as its initial financial supporter, his name was omitted from the documentation under which the association incorporated itself.[9] As has so often been true of resort towns, the majority of Saratoga's year-round residents were far less affluent than its summer sojourners; men who owned hotels or gambling houses might be able to afford to support horse racing, but those who worked in these venues generally could not do so.

Until 1863, horse sport in Saratoga was limited to the trotting track on Union Avenue, Horse Haven, which had opened in 1847. Many locals were aware that their southern summer visitors tended to be turf enthusiasts, and that the Virginia Springs resorts offered their guests not only pseudomedieval equestrian tournaments but races, so they opted to offer these tourists what many northerners of the era considered the only acceptable variety of horse-centered competition. Trotting, also known as harness racing, was a low-cost activity in which gambling did not factor prominently, and thus it lacked racing's associations with greed, waste, and other vices deplored by pious Christians, sober businessmen, and social reformers alike. It was also considered to be a far more democratic pastime, as the horses that participated in it were not high-bred and high-priced animals that performed no productive labor but were usually driving horses owned by ordinary people; one champion, Lady Suffolk, had pulled an oyster cart before being purchased for the trotting track. As the Bostonian physician and essayist Oliver Wendell Holmes opined, "horse-*racing* is not a republican institution; horse-*trotting* is," because "the racer is incidentally useful, but essentially something to bet upon," whereas "the trotter is essentially and daily useful, and only incidentally a tool for sporting men." A racing champion such as Lexington ran "like a locomotive," thrilling yet dangerous, while a trotter kept to a brisk but disciplined gait, steady and safe. The sharp contrast between these two sports caused some anxiety among Saratogians that the introduction of racing, promoted largely by enormously rich Manhattanites, might drag down the tone of the resort, alienating its usual visitors and encour-

Coming from the Trot, by Currier and Ives, 1869. Yale University Art Gallery, Whitney Collections of Sporting Art, given in memory of Harry Payne Whitney (B.A. 1894) and Payne Whitney (B.A. 1898) by Francis P. Garvan (B.A. 1897), 2 June 1932.

aging their replacement by professional gamblers and other undesirables. As the *Spirit of the Times* contributor "Druid" noted in 1857, "there is no love of the *race horse* in the free States; trotters are their fancy."[10]

That northern racing experienced its revival in upstate New York is in many ways quite surprising. As noted earlier, the first organized race between blooded horses to have been staged in England's North American colonies had taken place at the Newmarket course in Hempstead, Long Island, in 1666. Ten miles away in Douglaston, Queens, the Union Course, founded in 1821 in the wake of the state legislature's repeal of various strictures against racing, in addition to staging regular competitions became "the theatre of some of the grandest turf battles ever decided on American soil," hosting several of the match races between northern and southern champions that were staged at regular intervals between 1823 and 1845, and that, as "represent[ing] war by surrogate means," attracted immense crowds and widespread publicity. Colonial Manhattan had also had its racetracks, including one in Greenwich Village and another, established by the enormously rich DeLancey family, near the Bowery; according to Hamilton Busbey, the editor of the New York–based sporting journal *Turf, Field and Farm,* "the people of New York, like those of the more Southern states, indulged in racing before they even dreamed of going to war with Great Britain," but the Revolution brought these activities to a halt, as it did elsewhere in the colonies, and in Manhattan the sport did not revive until the 1820s, when it gained the support of some among the city's declining Knickerbocker elite. It collapsed again barely a decade later, due to the combination of the economic chaos unleashed by the Panic of 1837 and the rise throughout the Northeast of public opposition to both racing and gambling, sparked by the Second Great Awakening. Beyond the greater New York City area, the state had no tradition of racing; Richard Ten Broeck notwithstanding, it held little appeal for the Dutch-descended residents of the Hudson River Valley, nor did it attract the evangelical Christians of the "Burned-Over District" in the central and western parts of the state, although there is no evidence that the members of the latter group believed, as the reformer Thomas L. Nichols asserted, that "horse-racing is supposed to have been prohibited in the Decalogue." Had John Morrissey not possessed both the determination and the resources to open a new racetrack, and had he failed to attract the patronage of respected men such as Travers and Jerome, it is extremely unlikely that Saratoga would have become the racing mecca that it remains today.[11]

The Saratoga races generated tremendous public enthusiasm from their outset. On the track's opening day, 3 August 1863, newspapers estimated that anywhere between five and fifteen thousand people were in attendance, many of whom were wealthy, socially elite Manhattanites. Their ranks included a large number of fashionably dressed women who, mimicking female visitors to southern courses, watched the action from their carriages, which were parked next to the track. The meeting, which featured eight races and involved twenty-six horses, and which was held at the Horse Haven trotting course on Union Avenue, was pronounced a great success by both attendees and reporters, but it was clear to Morrissey and his backers that this course was not suitable for their ambitious plans; the site was too narrow, the grandstand was far too small for the number of spectators they hoped to attract, and trees blocked the view of much of the action. The well-capitalized Saratoga Association purchased a

125-acre tract of land across the street from Horse Haven, reserving the latter as an exercise ground for the horses, and worked quickly to ensure that the new one-mile course would be ready by the following summer. The wealth and influence of the association's members facilitated the rapid construction of the new course and its outbuildings and the beautification of its grounds in time to host Saratoga's first four-day race meeting, which opened on 2 August 1864.[12]

It is important to recall that at this time the Civil War was very far from over. While the Confederate war effort had been seriously, perhaps even fatally, damaged a year earlier by the Union victory at Gettysburg, Southern forces had in no way given up the fight. In the weeks that immediately preceded the 1864 Saratoga race meeting, Virginian Jubal Early's division reached the suburbs of Washington, DC, before it was repulsed by a much larger Union force hastily gathered from a number of commands. In Georgia, John Bell Hood's troops attempted to hold Atlanta, a crucial transport and supply hub for the entire Confederacy. In Virginia, the Siege of Petersburg, which was to destroy the Tree Hill track and Otway P. Hare's home, dragged on, and just over twenty-four hours before the Saratoga racetrack gates opened the Battle of the Crater would take the lives of nearly five thousand men, many of whom were African American volunteers for the Union. Union commander Ulysses Grant described this "disaster" as "the saddest affair I have witnessed in this war."[13]

Some Americans considered horse racing a form of frivolity that was entirely unsuitable during a time of national trial. The Unitarian minister Matthew Hale Smith, who wrote a column for the *Boston Journal* under the pseudonym "Burleigh," argued that "no man who has any respect for himself or regard for his country will revel at Saratoga when the times demand sobriety and economy." Since Thoroughbred racing was a new activity at the resort, rather than a long-established element of the northern social round or sporting calendar, one might assume that such reproaches would have shamed potential attendees into staying away. But in fact, as Smith was forced to admit, "the races [of August 1864] attracted nearly all the sporting community of the country," or at least those of the Union, although the military situation prevented the attendance of large numbers of young men; "shoulder straps and uniforms do not appear." It seems likely that some northerners were drawn to the event because of, rather than despite, the worrisome news they heard from the various battle fronts; after more than three years of warfare, plenty of Americans were eager for distraction and sociability wherever it might be found. Turf enthusiasts were keen to tour the new course, and followers of fashion, particularly young women from rural areas or small towns who aspired to regional celebrity as belles, hoped to mingle with the elite and attract mention in the newspapers for their stylish attire. To his relief, however, Smith noted that "dress is modest and subdued" among the female attendees, in comparison with the lavish styles of the late antebellum years; "few gorgeous ladies appear . . . few jewels are worn, and when a party appears with a profusion of diamonds they are at once voted snobs."[14]

Horse owners, jockeys, and gamblers all eagerly anticipated the inaugural running of the Travers Stakes, a mile-and-three-quarters dash for three-year-olds, with a stake of $2,500, or approximately $42,000 in modern money, provided by William Travers, the first president of the Saratoga Association. It was the first "feature race" to be established in the United States and is evidence of the increasing fascination among American turfmen, particularly those from the North, with English racing practices. The readers of sporting periodicals such as the *American Turf Register* and the *Spirit of the Times* had by this time, especially as a result of Richard Ten Broeck's "American Invasion" a few years earlier, become familiar with the most celebrated annual races at English tracks, and many were intrigued by sporting events that were known, reported upon, and discussed throughout Britain and its empire, such as the St. Leger, the Oaks, and, most famous of all, the Derby, which from the early nineteenth century onward routinely attracted crowds of one hundred thousand or more to the Epsom Downs course in Surrey, on the outskirts of London. The renown of these contests was so great that Lord Clifford of Chudleigh, making his maiden speech in the House of Lords in 1831 and having proposed that his fellow peers meet on a particular day to discuss a piece of legislation, "was met by a loud cry of 'Oaks! Oaks!"; when he suggested another date, they responded with "Derby! Derby!," indicating that the Lords never sat on the days of these events. Clifford, embarrassed by his ignorance, responded by noting that he had spent much of his life on the Continent, and was thus "painfully ignorant of the Saints' days of the English church." But although the United States Congress had been known in the early nineteenth century to recess for race days at the Alexandria, Virginia, track, only a widely publicized and long-scheduled competition between sectional champions, such as the Great Match Races of the 1820s through the 1840s, or one in which celebrated rivals faced off against one another, as with Lecomte and Lexington's duel in 1855, would be deemed newsworthy on a national level. Even a spectacular victory at Tree Hill, Pharsalia, or Metairie was unlikely to attract much notice outside of its local or, at best, regional context, other than among the most dedicated racing aficionados who read the sporting papers. The Travers Stakes was intended to mimic the prominence, and thus the media coverage, that the "classic" English races boasted, and its creation offers an early hint of the Anglophilia with which post–Civil War American racing would soon become imbued, due not least to the laying in 1866 of the Atlantic cable, which cut the time in which news could be transmitted between England and the United States from several weeks to a few minutes.[15]

The Travers Stakes was an immediate success; it fulfilled its founders' hopes that it would function in national culture as an American variant of the English "feature race," and it continues to hold a prominent place in the national racing calendar more than a century and a half later, and to attract the attention even of people who are otherwise not particularly interested in the sport. Frequently referred to within the turf world as the "fourth race of the Triple Crown," it represents what would become a dramatic and permanent change in American racing practices. When immense crowds flocked to the Metairie course in 1855 to watch Lexington race against Lecomte, the event consisted of three heats, each of four miles, as was common practice in the antebellum era, as it had been prior to the American Revolution; a top-class race nearly always involved three separate attempts at a distance of between two and four miles. This practice apparently dates back to Charles II's patronage of Suffolk's Newmarket course. Because his father's forces had been defeated by the superiority of Oliver Cromwell's cavalry, the monarch was determined to create an English breed of horses that combined speed with stamina, and the "King's Plate" races, three circuits of nearly four miles each, were used to evaluate the outcomes of experiments in breeding, first at Newmarket and then at the country's other major racetracks. Some of the most celebrated blooded horses of eighteenth-century England, including Herod, Matchem, and Eclipse, were renowned as "stayers" who triumphed over long distances, but the advent of champions such as Flying Childers, who is said to have run a mile in a minute, and Regulus caused turfmen to shift their preferences to shorter, "single dash" races between younger, lighter, and faster horses, and by the beginning of the nineteenth century, heat racing had essentially disappeared from English tracks.

American owners, breeders, trainers, and fans, however, "held shorter races in the utmost contempt," maintaining allegiance to the longer races with their "heroic distances" and spurning mere speed in favor of its integration with "bottom," or stamina, in "the glory of the four-mile horse." The British naval officer Frederick Marryat, who toured the East Coast in the late 1830s, expressed regret that his country had not retained this practice; he was impressed by what he saw as the superiority of American racing, in which "the distances run . . . are much longer than ours, and speed without bottom is useless." But as racing disappeared from southern venues in which it had flourished for a century or more and was reborn in northern locales, American practices came into closer alignment with those of England, and the new, highly publicized competitions such as the Travers and the Triple Crown races led the way. In the words of the turf historian John Hervey, the mid-1860s to the early 1870s witnessed "the abandonment of the old-established and sanctified Southern system, which placed the 4-mile horse upon the apex of the structure, glorified gameness and stamina above speed, per se, held fast by heat racing." "Ante-bellum racing and the ante-bellum Thoroughbred . . . had become old-fashioned"; the younger, smaller horse supplanted the older, larger one, raw speed became valorized over endurance, and the physiology of the Thoroughbred became closer to that of the American quarter horse.[16]

But it was not only the thrill of seeing horses run extremely fast over short distances that encouraged the decline of heat races and their replacement with short dashes; it was also the fact that this alteration allowed track managers to schedule a larger number of individual races on each day of a meeting. While some turf enthusiasts were disappointed by the disappearance from the American track of a tradition that they valued not only as an aspect of their nation's racing heritage but as the true test of a horse's abilities, numerous racecourse visitors considered this new practice to offer a far more exciting experience. Not only did it pack all of the drama of a race into just a few minutes, with the horses running flat out as soon as they came out of the starting gates rather than being constrained by their jockeys to pace themselves over a long distance, but it offered the spectators more chances to place wagers, as one race soon followed another. In its inaugural season the Saratoga course offered just two races per day; today, most days of its current six-week season feature ten.[17]

In August 1865, Saratoga's third racing season and its first in peacetime, the meeting was extended to six days and drew twelve thousand spectators, and two years later the number of races per day was increased from two to three; both figures indicate the track's success in attracting visitors. The association was also successful in ensuring that the right sort of people were encouraged to attend, and the wrong types kept away. In 1865 the *Milwaukee Daily Sentinel,* citing an account from the *New York Times,* reported that the races "were conducted in the most genteel and respectable manner. A large number of respectable families were in attendance, and no boisterous individual or rough expression was heard . . . [I]f there were any 'plug uglies' present they had to be on their good behaviour." This anonymous "Saratoga correspondent" concluded his or her statement by asking "who ever heard of such a race track scene in this country before?" and allotting the credit for this happy situation to Morrissey's adroit managerial tactics. Such words might well have irked southerners, particularly patrons of Charleston's Washington Course, who insisted that such problems as drunkenness, foul language, and pickpocketing had never afflicted their meetings, but they helped to reassure those northerners who remained skeptical about the sport's respectability.[18]

From this perspective, Morrissey and the Saratoga Association had triumphed in the challenging task of creating a new track that was simultaneously popular and respectable, particularly in a region that, in the words of a correspondent for the *London Daily News,* had until recently been governed by a "grave Puritan spirit . . . which objected to trivial amusements." Moreover, at this time the quality of the racing at Saratoga was unquestionably excellent, attracting the nation's best horses and jockeys and its most celebrated breeders, owners, and trainers. From its opening day, it had experienced no difficulty in attracting elegant women and girls of good family, and while the inadequacies of the Horse Haven trotting course had been evident in the inaugural season, the Saratoga Association's new track was in itself a powerful lure to visitors, who expressed themselves unanimously as favorably impressed both by the venue and by the speed with which it had been constructed. Each racing day attracted on average ten thousand spectators, and "everything is done to render the races

Saratoga Race Course, by Albert Berghaus, 1875, from *Frank Leslie's Illustrated Newspaper,* 14 August 1875, 400. Syracuse University Art Museum, The Rona and Martin Schneider Collection of Late 19th and Early 20th Century American Fine Art Prints. 2019.0123.

agreeable and acceptable to [those] who assemble to witness them." The land on which the course and its buildings sat, which the association had purchased for one hundred dollars per acre less than a decade earlier, was now valued at three times that price. Within a few years of its introduction, the Travers Stakes had not only fulfilled association members' hopes that it would become as widely known and discussed in the United States as the St. Leger and the Oaks were across the Atlantic, but, as will be described in subsequent chapters, it had encouraged the creation of other "feature races," such as those that would eventually constitute racing's "Triple Crown." Even the frequently skeptical *Harper's Weekly* magazine pronounced the 1865 race meeting to have been "a series of horse races the most splendid ever witnessed on the [American] continent." Why, then, did many turf fans soon come to feel that what was profitable for the town and the track was not necessarily in the best interests of the sport?[19]

Jockey clubs and track managers had since before the Revolution judged the success of their race meetings at least in part by their ability to attract female guests, as they believed that genteel women's beauty and elegance would draw men to the course, even if they had little desire to watch the competitions, and that the presence of such refined ladies would elevate the social tone of the gathering and discourage improper behavior. A course that failed to appeal to respectable women would soon lose its reputation for propriety and style, and would devolve into a haunt of gamblers, layabouts, and thugs. This particular issue was never a problem at Saratoga; the town's long history as a summer resort for the nation's wealthy and fashionable meant that there were plenty of women about each summer, whether wives with their husbands and children or daughters who had accompanied their parents. For them, the racetrack was just one of the town's many attractions, and was thus devoid of any implication of sordidness; as a sporting venue that appealed to the town's male guests, it was an ideal locale in which young unmarried women could display themselves in their best clothes, in the hope that catching a gentleman's eye across the grandstand would result in an invitation to sample the famous mineral waters at Congress Park or a signature on a dance card at one of the three grand balls that were held each week of the summer season at the town's most luxurious hotels, where newly popular European social dances such as the polka and the waltz were introduced into the United States. Like Newport, its rival northern resort, Saratoga was, in the words of the British consul George Towle, a "marriage bourse," and its balls functioned as "great matrimonial fairs, where the marriageable wares are shown off at their best." Even the fabulously rich "Commodore" Cornelius Vanderbilt participated in this commerce; in 1869, a year after his first wife's death, he eloped with and married Frank Armstrong Crawford, an Alabamian woman forty years his junior, whom he had met at Saratoga."[20]

Beautiful women of respectable backgrounds, fashionable clothes, glamorous social events, and elite marital possibilities—what could be problematic about these elements of the racing season? Had the Washington Course not helped to ensure both its financial and its social success for more than half a century by attracting elite young women of marriageable age and providing them with the opportunity to display themselves in their finery at the races and the Jockey Club ball? It is difficult to imagine that Morrissey, a man who had grown up in abject poverty and who craved both wealth and social status, would have been dismayed to read newspaper accounts of the Saratoga racing

Our Watering Places—Horse-Racing at Saratoga, by Winslow Homer, from *Harper's Weekly*, 26 August 1865, 533. The Met, Harris Brisbane Dick Fund, 1936, 36.13.11(2).

season that emphasized the "magnificent appearance" of the grandstand's "great display of fashionable ladies," and that noted that many of these ladies attended each day of the meeting in order "to put in an appearance in some ravishing change of costume."[21] But while the presence of stylishly dressed young women of demure aspect and unimpeachable respectability could only be an asset to any track event, the majority of bourgeois Americans of this era took exception to what they considered vulgar, ostentatious excess, which, according to journalists and visitors alike, was making itself increasingly evident at Saratoga. The *New Haven Daily Palladium* interviewed a woman who had arrived at the grandstand wearing diamond ornaments in her hair worth twenty eight thousand dollars—nearly a half million dollars in today's money—and whose husband had hired an off-duty police officer to stand behind her, "with nothing else to do but to see that her diamond head suffered no violation." Another New England newspaper asked its readers why female visitors to Saratoga who "pretend[ed] to have taste in dress [would] wear gold bracelets at the breakfast table," and why they would appear in the evening in "a dreadful horror of waterfalls and cascades and frizzles and tags and tails and long trains and low-tide dresses." The writer acknowledged that some of these "over-dressed creatures lounging this evening in the parlors of the Union [Hotel], have earned the right to do as they please" by indulging in elaborate clothing and hairstyles, as they may have been among those affluent northern women who had put aside luxuries during the war in order to raise funds for and even to volunteer as nurses with the United States Sanitary Commission. Nevertheless, he wished that they were "not so bound and hampered by fashion," which in some cases, he asserted, rendered them less rather than more elegant and attractive.[22]

It was not only in their sartorial choices that Saratoga's female guests struck some observers as considerably less appealing than they believed themselves to be. In William Dean Howells's 1889 novel *A Hazard of New Fortunes*, the affect of the *nouveau riche* Saratoga guest Mela Dryfoos, the daughter of a newly established natural-gas millionaire, is characterized by "too instant and hilarious good-fellowship, which expressed itself in hoarse laughter and in a flow of talk full of topical and syntactical freedom," attributes that soon alienate Mela's more sophisticated and genteel fellow tourists. Howells had made several visits to Saratoga; not only was his depiction of Mela based on his observations of social life at the resort, but the figure of the female parvenu was by this time easily recognizable to his readers.[23] But even women who dressed simply and displayed impeccable manners might succumb to temptation during their visits to Saratoga, in the form of gambling. Although women were not permitted to place bets at the Saratoga track until the 1890s and had to content themselves with making small wagers of items such as gloves or trinkets with their companions, John Morrissey allowed them to enter his luxurious Club House casino during "the more virtuous morning hours [of 10:00 a.m. to noon] . . . for the education of those who have but taken their first lesson in the art of poker, brag and roulette." At this time, aristocratic women were a frequent presence in the gaming rooms and casinos of some the most exclusive European resorts, but although Saratoga's promoters and its guests alike hoped that their social scene would replicate that of these famously glamorous and sophisticated spas, the general opinion among most Americans at this time was that playing cards for money, even for low stakes, was simply not an acceptable pastime for any female who wished to be considered a lady, and was one continental custom that the town should forebear to adopt. In the words of a contributor to the *Milwaukee Daily Sentinel*, "as affairs are now progressing, Saratoga is the 'Bad-'un' [a pun on the name of the German spa town of Baden-Baden] of America in more senses than one."[24]

By 1870, the novelist Henry James asserted that "the good old times of Saratoga . . . are rapidly passing away." Before the Civil War, and thus prior to the opening of the racetrack, the resort's amenities and activities were "simple and severe," and it was thus "the chosen resort of none but 'nice people.'" By contrast, as James claimed to have been informed again and again throughout his visit, and came to believe, by this time "the company is dreadfully mixed," and the town had become "dense, democratic, [and] vulgar." The male guests tended to be self-made men like the father of the fictional Mela Dryfoos, and while James admitted that he was impressed by their achievements—"it was not in lounging that they gained their hard wrinkles and the level impartial regard which they direct from beneath their hat-rims"—he considered them to be "hard nuts" rather than "the mellow fruit of a society which has walked hand-in-hand with tradition and culture," and in conversation with these men he claimed "to hear the cracking of the shells." Among the women James stated that he had encountered "the democratization of elegance," because few of the female visitors had experienced the type of upbringing of the women and girls whom he would have encountered had he attended an antebellum race at Tree Hill, Pharsalia, or the Washington Course; these "uninitiated nobodies" who appeared each day in a lavish new costume were "dressed beyond [their] life and opportunities." Although he described female visitors as bedecked with such fashionable items as "diamonds and laces," satin shoes, and "an uplifted volume of gauze and lace and flowers," he declared that the first impression that he and others received of these women was not of beauty or elegance but merely of an "abundance of petticoats."[25]

During his visit James paid little attention to Saratoga's sporting opportunities. On being informed that Morrissey's Club House was among those local attractions that were popularly considered to be "in their respective kinds . . . the finest in the world," he did not contradict his informant, "but privately I thought of the blue Mediterranean, and the little white promontory of Monaco, and the silver-gray verdure of olives, and the view across the outer sea to the bosky cliffs of Italy." He did not visit the track, but while observing the "festally-minded" people who of an evening entered the grand ballroom of the United States Hotel on Washington Street, he noted with distaste that the building's basement office was occupied by a loud, coatless man, "black in the face with heat and vociferation," taking racing wagers from "a dense group of frowsy betting-men." But in his opinion the real problem with Saratoga, the factor that would prevent it from becoming an American version of an aristocratic watering-place such as England's Cheltenham, let alone a truly glamorous Continental resort like Baden-Baden, was that, although over the past two decades the United States had seen the creation of a large number of substantial fortunes, including those that the "hard nuts" had hewn out of California or Alaska, as well as those that more refined individuals such as Travers and Jerome had accrued on Wall Street, it had yet to develop what James termed a "leisure-class." While he claimed that Saratoga's female visitors had too much time on their hands, the fact was that there were simply nowhere nearly enough men to go around. Few of these female guests lacked husbands, fathers, brothers, or sons, but these men spent far less time at leisure than their female kin did. During his time at Cheltenham, James had noted the presence of "a multitude of young men who had the whole day on their hands," a characteristic shared by the various "Saratogas of Europe." But at Saratoga itself, young men might spend a few days in the town in the company of their mothers, sisters, or wives, but they soon returned to Manhattan or other cities to get back to the business of "rolling up greenbacks in counting-houses and stores." Even men who had already earned or inherited large fortunes were expected to remain deeply engaged in their work, as American society was far less indulgent than that of contemporary England or western Europe regarding young men of conspicuous leisure; what seemed aristocratic in the Old World came across as indolent in the New. In their absence, girls and women at Saratoga were reduced to dancing with one another, or with young boys, devoting immense amounts of time and money to their appearance with little prospect of it being appreciated by a husband, a potential fiancé, or even a dance partner.[26]

In the hierarchy of the nation's resorts, Saratoga frequently suffered by comparison to Newport, the Rhode Island resort town that by the 1830s began to attract some of the southerners who no longer felt at ease in Saratoga. As early as 1866 the former was widely judged to be "the more fashionable," but its society was becoming excessively "mixed," with "less of the old grace,

Club House at the racetrack, Saratoga Springs, New York. Library of Congress, Prints and Photographs Division, Detroit Publishing Company Photograph Collection.

and elegance, and air of high-breeding" but with more "elaborate toilets" and "fine horses." Newport would by the end of the nineteenth century be radically transformed by the arrival of some of the nation's richest men and women, with their fifty-room summer "cottages," their two-hundred-foot yachts, and their wardrobes by Charles Worth of Paris, but in 1870, when James visited, "this catastrophe was still to come." At that time, young men were "far more numerous than at Saratoga, and of vastly superior quality," and young women displayed a blend of modesty and self-assurance that allowed them to develop into "delightful matrons." The resort's finest aspect, for James, was the fact that "nowhere else in this country . . . does business seem so remote," which gave the town "a faintly European expression, in so far as [it] suggest[s] the somewhat alien presence of leisure." Because Saratoga's guests, such as James's "hard nuts," had in many instances been born into poverty and had worked extremely hard to make their fortunes, they found it very difficult to "live for amusement simply, beyond the noise of commerce or of care"; these "busy money-makers" "scan[ned] the Wall Street reports posted daily in the hotel offices" until they could return to their places of business.[27] In 1870 Newport's summer visitors were on average as wealthy as those at Saratoga, but in many instances their fortunes were of longer standing, and they disapproved not only of ostentation but of the discussion of money itself. The latter community, by contrast, was in the eyes of a number of contemporary commentators entirely based around money; an English visitor of 1865 expressed his shock at the "fabulously high prices" that were attached to every aspect of life in this "ugly village," asserting that "Saratoga did not want poor people, and took a very effectual means to keep them away." Some members of the racing "fancy" apparently never paid their wash and board bills at the town's hotels and lodging houses but instead spent whatever funds they had on maintaining an appearance not merely of prosperity but of wealth, without which their prospects of success, whether at the track or the ballroom, were slim.[28]

A major challenge to the reputation of Saratoga racing was that its early years coincided with a moment in American history in which the nation held a deeply conflicted view of wealth, particularly that which had been recently acquired, and was displayed by its possessors through lavish lifestyles. Henry James was charmed by the summer residents of Newport, whose conduct reminded him of the leisured classes of contemporary England and Continental Europe, but his was a minority view among Americans in the years immediately after the Civil War. In his widely read novel *The Potiphar Papers* (1856), the New England–raised writer and journalist George William Curtis warned affluent young Americans that, if they attempted to model themselves on the aristocracy of Europe, they would become "foolish parvenus frenzied in the pursuit of an elegance which, in its nature, is inaccessible to them," with the result that "we should hear insipidity praised as good-humor, and nonchalance as ease." But he believed that "the sharp common sense of this people prevents so melancholy a spectacle," and that younger Americans, even those born in privileged circumstances, were imbued with "social independence" and "shrewd common-sense"; they were proud to establish their own fortunes, and they respected others for their characters and accomplishments rather than their social preeminence. These men were, or would develop, very much in the mold of "Brother Jonathan," the icon of American national identity that separated the Yankee Doodle of the Revolution from the Uncle Sam who emerged during the Gilded Age. Jonathan was a Yankee whose guileless manner masked his shrewdness, who made his own money through hard work, thrift, and an eye for opportunity, and who inevitably got the better of those who underestimated him, particularly city slickers and arrogant aristocrats. Although he might sometimes appear ingenuous, at base his character was quite similar to that displayed by those "hard nuts" whose presence, James claimed, so detracted from the atmosphere of Saratoga, and even if he became rich, he would be neither willing nor able to join that "leisure class" that the writer so esteemed.[29]

By the middle decades of the nineteenth century, affluent American urbanites, particularly those of the northeastern cities, had become increasingly embarrassed by the persistence of the Brother Jonathan archetype, seeing him as a relic of an unsophisticated recent past that they were keen to consign to history. Jonathan's humor struck them as vulgarity, his thrift as miserliness, and his lack of pretension as boorishness. As we will see in the following chapter, New Yorkers were particularly keen to raise their levels of wealth and refinement and to transform their city, or at least the sections thereof in which they lived, into a "monied metropolis," and their success in this endeavor brought them great pleasure, despite being satirized by writers such as Curtis and deplored by the long-established but no longer rich Knickerbockers.[30] No doubt some of this hostility was sparked by envy, but it is important to note that the greatest fortunes of the midcentury arose not from the traditional economic spheres of land ownership or mercantile activities but from the dramatic expansion of financial capitalism, epitomized by the rise of Wall Street as a financial hub, and from profiteering during the Civil War. The latter activity attracted particular hostility; there was no shame attached to making money by producing the goods without which the Union army could not function, but tales abounded of conscienceless manufacturers who fulfilled their lucrative government contracts by relentlessly cutting corners in production, making goods that they were knew were of inferior quality, such as rations so rotten as to be inedible by even the hungriest soldiers and blankets that were so thin and easily torn that they not only failed to keep the men warm but were "so remarkably fine, that many of our soldiers use them for fishing-nets." Such goods were widely referred during the war as "shoddy," and northern periodicals frequently personified such unprincipled, unpatriotic greed in the form of fictional characters bearing "Shoddy" as a surname, depicting them as vulgar in the extreme and obsessed not only with acquiring as much money as possible but with flaunting it at every turn, ignoring the sacrifices that their fellow Americans were making on the battlefield and the home front alike. Thus, when "Mrs Shoddy" ventured to the Manhattan luxury emporium of Tiffany & Company to purchase diamond jewelry, paid for by her husband's factory's production of poor-quality goods at inflated prices, she displayed not only her wealth but her lack of taste and grace: "There enters a woman, she's ugly and course [*sic*] / As stout as an ox and as tall as a horse / She's red in the face and amazing in dress / More vulgar by far than all words can express."[31]

It was this concept of "shoddiness" that played a significant role in undermining Saratoga's appeal to the possessors of older fortunes, and to those who admired them. Henry James expressed his distaste for the "hard nuts" whom he encountered on the porches of the town's hotels, as to him they seemed devoid of grace or culture and overly focused on business, but at least they had presumably made their fortunes through honest toil rather than by chicanery. But some of the town's other guests were considered far less deserving of respect; those lodgings that before the war had been occupied by members of the South's plantation gentry were now inhabited not only by those who had recently acquired immense fortunes in the newly established and seemingly mysterious and unsavory oil industry but by numerous examples of "Shoddy pere, Shoddy mere . . . Mesdemoiselles Shoddy . . . [and] the youthful masculine scions of the House of Shoddy," who now infested Saratoga, along with New York State's other leading resort towns, Lake George and Trenton Falls, and even Newport. The English journalist John Edwin Hilary Skinner, who visited Saratoga at the war's end, complained of the presence of individuals whom he did not dignify with either names or occupations but to whom he referred simply as "shoddy" and "petroleum." Skinner pronounced the 1865 race meeting to have been "unusually good" in terms of the quality of the competition, but although he was not a Confederate sympathizer, he lamented the absence of the elegant southerners whom he had observed at Saratoga on a prewar visit, whose ways, he claimed, were so appealing that they were often emulated by the town's more prosperous and sophisticated northern guests. Not only had many members of this former group been "killed or ruined" during the conflict, but "society had abhorred a vacuum, and their place was supplied by oil and shoddy." In Skinner's opinion, this change was clearly very much for the worse with regard to the atmosphere of the races and of the town in general, but "what did it matter to Saratoga," as long as "there was no falling off of custom at the hotels; no abatement in the demand for carriages"?

As a visiting female journalist wrote in 1868, although she considered the Saratoga track probably the finest in the country, its female spectators displayed "more money than refinement," and whereas before the war the elites of the South, as well as those of Philadelphia and New York, had set a tone of taste and dignity, "now, the *crème de la crème* is a bad quality of skimmed milk, and Saratoga is a huge caldron, bubbling over with vice and frivolity." Jennie E. Hicks, a columnist for the *New York Mail* who wrote under the name "Sophie Sparkle," lamented that the resort now attracted "shoddy people who endeavor to conceal their ignorance with thick layers of gold," and the Scottish-born cattleman John Clay Jr. complained that "the shoddy throng these gay rooms," epitomized by "a vulgar man with a more vulgar wife, clad in gay garments and studded with costly jewels, who boast much and talk large." By 1874 even the author of a guidebook promoting the resorts of the Northeast was forced to admit that, among the "wonderfully variegated collection of people" who came to Saratoga each summer, "here, undoubtedly, comes more or less shoddy, and in shoddy fashion," as many a "Miss McFlimsey or a Mrs. O'Shoddy" would arrive with her purse containing "plenty of greenbacks." The yawning social gap that separated the genteel southerners of the antebellum years from the Shoddys who supplanted them after the war was similarly apparent to Saratoga's African American hospitality workers. George Augustus Sala, a frequent contributor to the *Illustrated London News*, described his conversation with the "courtly head-waiter" at the Clarendon Hotel on Broadway, a venue popular among "a class of visitors who do not desire to mingle with the somewhat promiscuous company which fills the larger hotels." He reported the man as opining that "ver Souf was ver real fashion . . . now vere's nuffin but Shoddy folks . . . ver ruination of real style."[32]

The advent of such "Shoddy folks" was not the only threat to Saratoga's social status; the town, and specifically its racetrack, also became a flashpoint for new anxieties about gambling. As we have seen, the presence of blacklegs had long been a source of concern among American turfmen, but in the first season at Saratoga, Morrissey and his backers introduced a new form of wagering:

pool-selling, also known as "Calcutta pools," which was the only form of gambling permitted at the new racecourse, with the exception of informal wagers between friends. Under this arrangement, a designated pool-seller would hold an auction in the evening before each day of the racing season, during which he would raffle off the individual horses in each competition, with the highest bidder having his first choice and usually opting for the animal that had been designated the favorite. At the day's conclusion, the "owners" of the winning horses would collect all of the money in their respective "pools," which consisted of the sums wagered by those whose horses had come up short, minus the 3 to 5 percent that the pool-seller received for his facilitation of these transactions. The pools were sold in the basement of the town's United States Hotel, as described a few years later by Henry James, and were run by the Irish-born Kentuckian Robert Underwood, a veterinarian, breeder, and seller of horses and "the founding father of modern bookies." The *New York World* described Underwood as a man "of a pleasant, lively and facetious disposition, always good humoured, and ready to crack a joke, even when getting off a $5,000 pool," and his right to call himself "Dr. Underwood" endowed him with a degree of respectability that concealed the fact that it was John Morrissey who actually controlled the auctions. By 1872 Morrissey had opened a "Pool-Room" behind his Club House casino on Putnam Street, which the *Spirit of the Times* described as "a great improvement on the dives where pools used to be sold," and praised the opportunity for those "outside the ring of large speculators [to stand] a chance of making their investments on favourable terms."[33]

The crowds that Underwood and his successor, the "mellifluous" Robert Cathcart Jr., attracted to their auctions reflected the enthusiasm for betting among many of those who came to Saratoga for the races, but pool-selling soon sparked controversy, notably in relation to the presidential election of 1876, during which Morrissey organized bets that amounted to more than a third of a million dollars. Due to allegations of voter fraud in several states, the announcement of the new chief executive was delayed, and Morrissey felt obliged to return the gathered funds, to numerous complaints from the bettors involved. New York legislators fastened upon this discontent and the chicanery they claimed that it represented to pass a bill early in 1877 that banned pool-selling in all venues throughout the state, in the face of energetic lobbying for exemption on the part of the Saratoga Association, whose leaders claimed that the sport could not survive without this revenue stream. The result, however, was not an immediate cessation of wagering on the outcomes of races; instead, it permitted the practice of bookmaking to flourish, as it had long done at the English turf as well as at a number of antebellum American courses. The difference was that those who wished to place bets no longer needed to go to Saratoga, or any other racetrack, in order to do so; they could consult the odds that were posted in public spaces throughout cities and towns and place their bets with a local "bookie," who usually operated out of a masculine space such as a saloon or barbershop, and who would receive almost immediate results of every race via the Western Union Telegraph Company, whose racing department soon became the most profitable part of the firm. But this increase in convenience was a disaster for Saratoga, as those whose main interest in racing was in gambling no longer needed to visit either the track or the town to transact their business. This was good news for turf purists, who shed no tears at the absence of those who were more interested in the odds than in the horses, but it precipitated a sharp economic decline for the town and its turf activities.[34]

Both the resort and the racetrack continued to attract visitors throughout the 1880s, but the prestige of the latter was clearly on the wane within the turf world. The number of horses entered in its stakes races declined, and the men who headed the country's premier stables came to view the Saratoga track as a resting ground for their horses rather than as a racing mecca at which they hoped to set records. After 1878 a number of these turfmen were lured to the newly renovated track at Monmouth Park, in Oceanport, New Jersey, at which the purses on offer were significantly larger, and where pool-selling remained legal. Another challenge was the loss to death or ill health of many of the founding members of the Saratoga Association, including Morrissey, Vanderbilt, Travers, and Jerome, as well as the retirement of James Marvin and of Saratoga Association secretary Charles Wheatly, who had designed the course. After "Old Smoke's" death in 1878, the ownership of his Club House casino and of his controlling interest in the racetrack passed to his partners in his Manhattan gambling house, Charles Reed and Albert Spencer, who were not the type of men who could attract high-status new members to the association. But their successor, Gottfried Walbaum, who gained control over the course starting with the 1892 season, was still more problematic, and it was under his management that the Saratoga track faced the greatest crisis in its existence.[35]

In the track's early years, Saratoga's more straitlaced guests had considered John Morrissey an unsuitable racing entrepreneur, but "Dutch Fred" made "Old Smoke" appear almost respectable by comparison. Walbaum, who had previously been the proprietor of a gambling house, a brothel, and a poolroom, had begun his career in track management at the Guttenberg course in North Bergen, New Jersey, which opened in 1886 and which was considered an "outlaw" track because it allowed the participation of jockeys, owners, and bookmakers who had been blacklisted at other venues. Few people attended this racetrack's events based on their interest in the sport, as the horses in competition there were not just mediocre but frequently decrepit; owned by bookmakers known as "undertakers," they were entered in races simply to encourage betting. Still more disreputable was the practice of winter racing, which had been unproblematic at southern tracks, but in the Northeast the turf was often frozen, leading to injuries of both horses and riders and causing the Humane Society to issue a call to ban such events. The *New York Times* described the Guttenberg's visitors as "people who dared not show their faces in New York City during the daytime for fear of police recognition and arrest"; although this claim is hyperbolic, the clientele was by most standards unsavory. Nonetheless, it was an extremely profitable business, and it provided Walbaum with the quarter-million dollars he used to purchase a 90 percent interest in the Saratoga racecourse in 1891.[36]

Just a few months later Walbaum and three of his associates, known in the greater New York metropolitan area as the "Big Four," were arrested at the Guttenberg and charged with "running a disorderly house" with respect to betting practices at the track. All four pled guilty, and each was sentenced to a year in jail and a fine of four hundred dollars for having run the course "in season and out of season as a gambling merry-go-round pure and simple," but New Jersey's Board of Pardons remitted the custodial sentence after each man paid his fine. Any turf enthusiast who hoped that Walbaum would mend his ways when he took control at Saratoga was bound to be disappointed. Because he was a night owl, he put back the daily post time at the track from 11:30 a.m. to 2:30 p.m., angering both the hoteliers and the bookmakers. A number of owners and trainers who had long been associated with the course took their horses elsewhere, to such an extent that several of the most popular annual events, such as the Alabama Stakes and the Spinaway Stakes, both for fillies, and the Saratoga Cup, second in prestige only to the Travers Stakes, had to be canceled because they failed to attract a sufficient field of top-quality competitors, and even the nationally renowned Travers saw its purse cut to just $1,125, less than half of what it had been at its inauguration fewer than three decades earlier.[37] Worst of all, to many observers, was Walbaum's expansion of both the venues and the audiences for gambling, in the face of the nation's increasing distaste for wagers and the popular social reformer Anthony Comstock's contention that "the morals of the community are not to be measured by the gambler's pocket nor the integrity of our young men sacrificed for the jockey's interests." Walbaum established "retiring rooms" in the track's grandstand; such facilities were normally spaces in which guests, especially women, could refresh themselves and relax in an atmosphere of quiet respectability, but Walbaum allowed the entrance therein of bookmakers who accepted wagers not only from male customers but from women and even children. It was this practice that encouraged the celebrated muckraking journalist Nellie Bly, in a lengthy front-page article for the *New York World*, to refer to Saratoga in general, and its racecourse in particular, as not merely "our wickedest summer resort" but "the wickedest spot in the United States," a "wild vortex of gambling and betting" filled with "race-track riff-raff," among many other disreputable and even criminal types.[38]

Bly's widely read exposé, though almost laughably sensationalist, precipitated a crisis at Saratoga; the following year, just a few weeks before the opening of the racing season, the newly elected president of Saratoga village, the lawyer Charles Sturges, "gave notice that the laws relative to gambling should be carried out to the letter," which resulted in the closure of the Club House casino and the rest of the town's gaming venues. This decision was a disaster for both the track and the resort, as visitor numbers dropped dramatically, not least among guests from the South and the West; without "the sporting crowd which goes there to play the bank and the races," "there is little life or business in the town," and the receipts at the track fell to just over thirty thousand dollars, in a season at which each of the New York City tracks netted more than a half million dollars. Saratogians, even some of those who execrated what they viewed as the evils of gambling, complained bitterly when their community suddenly became "as quiet and respectable as Chelsea, Mass.," a sedate Boston suburb, and they were left "wondering whether respectability is going to pay." Their fears were stoked by reports such as that made by the journalist Eliza Putnam Heaton, that "five times as many people watch the 'purely agricultural hoss trot' at a county fair, as the name and fame of Saratoga have this year called together" at the course. Walbaum claimed that, as a result of the gambling ban, the Saratoga Association had that year incurred a deficit of between forty and fifty thousand dollars, and thus he would be unable to open the track for the next season unless these restrictions were relaxed, but the legal authorities were unmoved either by his pleas or those of local business owners, and in 1896 the racecourse indeed failed to open for its usual season. It did so in 1897, but it did not stage the much-anticipated feature races of the Spinaway Stakes or the Saratoga Cup, and attendance was low and receipts poor.[39]

In its first incarnation, then, the Saratoga track had lasted just over thirty years, an unimpressive span in comparison with the longevity of some of its antebellum predecessors, and, still more embarrassingly, it had expired largely because of an excess of money rather than a lack thereof, as with the southern courses. The Saratoga Association became moribund, as did the celebrated Travers Stakes, and it appeared that the town's hope for the return of its earlier prosperity rested upon its transformation into a cottage resort for sedate families. But several of the nation's richest and most influential turfmen were determined to forestall this possibility by gaining control of the course from Walbaum and transforming it under the aegis of the Manhattan-based American Jockey Club. August Belmont II and James R. Keene, the club's leaders, were aware of Saratoga's increasing popularity as a summer resort, and they were confident that, as long as race days there were arranged to avoid clashes with those at the downstate tracks, its course would face no obstacles to renown and prosperity alike. Keene and Belmont charged the lawyer William Collins Whitney, Keene's business associate, a former secretary of the navy and the founder of the great Westbury racing stable on Long Island, with purchasing the track and placing it under the control of the reconstituted Saratoga Association for the Improvement of the Breed of Horses, whose members pledged to devote 95 percent of each year's profits to the improvement of the track complex's facilities and the establishment of additional stakes races. The Travers Stakes was revived for the 1901 season, which also marked the inauguration of the Saratoga Special, a winner-take-all race for two-year-olds, and although the track closed for the 1911 and 1912 race meetings, due to a dispute with Governor Charles Hughes and the New York State legislature over the legalities of bookmaking, it was soon regaled as both the "Camelot" and the "dowager queen of the American turf" and was patronized by such Gilded Age luminaries as "Diamond Jim" Brady and the Vanderbilt and Morgan families, as well as celebrities including the composer Victor Herbert, the singer Chauncey Olcott, and the actress Lillian Russell. The Saratoga course retains this reputation today.[40]

Had Whitney, Belmont, Keene, and their fellow American Jockey Club members been unwilling or unable to revive the Saratoga racecourse, it is unlikely that the sport would have persisted in the upstate New York community. Hagiographic accounts of these men and of the club offer the impression that sharp-elbowed but honorable New Yorkers had galloped to the rescue of this failing venture, armed for success with their superior ideals and practices of track management and the promotion of the sport. But in the decades that preceded this takeover of the Saratoga track, despite the numerous problems described above, its founders had played a crucial role in reviving horse racing in the North as it disappeared from many parts of the South. The efforts of Morrissey, Travers, and Jerome bore fruit not only in financial terms but in proving that northerners indeed had an appetite for this pastime, even while the nation was at war, and that in peacetime those southern turfmen who could afford to do so were happy to travel to a track located deep into formerly enemy territory in order to enjoy top-class sport. They imported from the English turf the tradition of feature races and predicted correctly that these events would soon acquire the popularity and media coverage long reaped by those across the Atlantic. More significantly, they brought American racing into line with English practices by replacing heat races with much shorter dashes, to the distaste of traditionalists but to the profit of those who were financially involved with the turf and the pleasure of the majority of spectators. What eventually doomed the Saratoga Association was the loss of its founders, specifically Morrissey's entrepreneurial genius and Jerome's and Travers' social prestige; in their absence, the association soon foundered, as it was not designed as a locally grounded jockey club such as those of the antebellum South, which could rely on the logistical, financial, and emotional support of an urban or regional elite. Nor did it, prior to Belmont's and Whitney's intervention, benefit from the leadership of an intensely ambitious, and extremely deep-pocketed, new class of turf enthusiasts who were determined to establish their hegemony not over a single track, or even those of a region, but across the sport itself. Their story is the subject of the following chapter.

6

New York City

CREATING A NATIONAL TURF ELITE

"The opening of Central Park saved horseflesh in New York," said an old jockey. Few who knew the truth would gainsay this assertion. The opening of Jerome Park did as much for "horseflesh" by rescuing the sport of horse racing from the blackguards and thieves, into whose hands it had fallen, and placing it upon a respectable footing.

—JAMES D. MCCABE JR., *Lights and Shadows of New York Life; or, the Sights and Sensations of the Great City*, 1872

At none of our race-courses is there the exclusiveness of old Jerome; there is no place provided where a gentleman can repair without being cross-questioned as he could at Jerome. It may be that the times demand the change, but whether it is for the better I shall not undertake to say.

—W. S. VOSBURGH, "The Passing of Jerome Park," 1901

In 1872 the affluent Manhattan lawyer and socialite Ward McAllister decided to create a social institution in his city that would be comparable to Almack's Assembly Rooms, the notoriously exclusive London club that his father had visited in the 1820s, at the invitation of the Duke of Wellington.[1] This group, which one of McAllister's friends dubbed the Patriarchs, would function as an arbiter of social prestige in a rapidly expanding and ever-more-diverse metropolis; its members, twenty-five of "the leading representative men of the city," would organize balls and dinners during New York's annual winter social season. The alphabetical listing of the founding Patriarchs was headed by the names of John Jacob Astor III and his brother William Backhouse Astor Jr., whose surname was nationally synonymous with great wealth, but most of the others reflected the age rather than the size of their owners' fortunes, and included men from such Knickerbocker clans as the DeLanceys, the Livingstons, the Rhinelanders, the Schermerhorns, and the Van Rensselaers. The Astors owed their inclusion largely to William's having married Caroline "Lina" Schermerhorn, who had succeeded her aunt Ann Cottenet (Mrs. William) Schermerhorn as New York society's leading hostess; it was she who became responsible for the organization of the Patriarchs' events. Astor's grandfather, a German fur trader turned real estate magnate who became the United States' first multimillionaire, had decades earlier been admitted to the exclusive Saint Nicholas Society on the basis of having lived in New York before 1785, and thus the younger John Jacob and his brother, who had further shifted the family's business endeavors from commerce to finance, escaped the scorn of the Knickerbockers for the *nouveaux riches*, despite the comparatively recent founding of the family's fortune.[2]

McAllister emphasized that, while he was willing to include among his Patriarchs some male Manhattanites whom he associated with the "money power," he was determined that the group would "not in any way be controlled by it," convinced as he was that, in an organization that held the power to give "a passport to society to all worthy of it," "a handful of men having royal fortunes" should not wield "a sovereign's prerogative, i.e. to say whom society shall receive, and whom society shall shut out." Such authority, McAllister claimed, was reserved for those whom he termed "representative men," particularly "the old Colonial New Yorkers," those descended from "the old Dutch settlers" and "the British families of long standing in the city," whom he described as having gone "quiet" at a time that a number of "colossally rich men" had come to dominate Gotham's economic and cultural life. Each Patriarch would invite a few men and women to an event, on the basis that they were "such people as would do credit to the ball," and those deemed worthy of repeated invitations would acquire a "secure social position" and "a stepping-stone to the best New York society." Just as "city fathers" traditionally dominated a metropolis's politics, the Patriarchs would play the leading role in their community's social life and ensure that it reflected their values and practices.[3]

From their inauguration, the Patriarchs' balls received extensive coverage both in the city's newspapers and in those based elsewhere in the United States, as a new breed of journalists known as "society reporters" were keen to depict for their readers the gatherings of local and national elites.[4] The *New York Times*, the paper of record for middle- and upper-class Manhattanites throughout the Gilded Age, described these events in considerable detail and with a discernible air of approval, while William Randolph Hearst's *Sunday Journal*, a "yellow" periodical aimed at a far less elite readership, offered its readers a "beautiful ten color art supplement" in commemoration of the 1896 ball.[5] While the former paper's contributors penned elaborate textual depictions of these events' guests, décor, refreshments, and activities, it was the latter that, through its commission of a collectible image by the well-known illustrator Walter Granville-Smith, immortalized these balls in the public imagination. The painting emphasized the refined elegance of the venue and the guests—the women's gowns being simultaneously stylish and modest, and the décor of Delmonico's Hall centering on displays of fresh flowers rather than on elaborate fixtures—and encouraged its working-class viewers to imagine their city's social leaders as individuals not only of wealth and lineage but of taste and grace. A columnist for the *San Francisco Daily Evening Bulletin* expressed his amazement that McAllister, a man of "no previous importance and no standing now in financial, literary or artistic circles," could become a "society boss," but the women and men of Manhattan's upper bourgeoisie waited impatiently to be welcomed into the social world that he ruled.[6]

For those New Yorkers who could not hope to receive an invitation to a Patriarchs' ball, nor to gain admission to the city's other exclusive venues, such as the Academy of Music and its successor, the Metropolitan Opera House, yet wished to see the metropolis's grandees at play, the ideal venue at which to do so was the Jerome Park racetrack. This course, established at a cost of more than $250,000 by the Wall Street speculator Leonard K. Jerome, who had made his fortune in the Panic of 1857, opened on 25 September 1866, and Jerome modeled it not on the English or the antebellum southern turf but on that which he had observed in Paris. It occupied two hundred acres of the old Bathgate estate in what was then Westchester County, but which in less than a decade would become part of the Bronx, and which in 1898 would join the consolidated city of New York. Those who could not afford to keep or rent a carriage and horses, such as the "dashing four-in-hands, filled with beautiful women and their attending cavaliers" that passed through Central Park en route to the course, could travel from Manhattan on the New York and New Haven Railroad, alighting at Fordham Station, or board one of the "got up vehicles of all kinds

Coaches at Jerome Park on a Race Day, from *Harper's Weekly*, 19 June 1886, 389. Library of Congress, Prints and Photographs Division.

. . . farmer wagons, market wagons, butcher carts, express wagons . . . fitted up with temporary seats, and passengers taken at so much per head." If they could not meet the cost of entry to Jerome Park, they could watch the contests from atop the overlooking "Dead-head hill," where working-class spectators, primarily Irish or African American, could purchase sandwiches, lemonade, and beer. But if they joined those "more favored spectators" inside the grounds, they could enjoy the spectacle not only of the nation's finest horses and its most celebrated jockeys but also that of Gotham's elites and national celebrities. General Grant was the guest of honor at the inaugural competition, but some other attendees were both wealthier and less respectable, including John Morrissey, the former boxer who, as we saw in the previous chapter, had recently established the Saratoga track; the stockbroker "Diamond Jim" Fisk; and Josephine Woods, who operated New York's most expensive and exclusive brothel.[7] The source of her prosperity notwithstanding, Woods was widely known for her elegance, as was Jerome himself, who was almost as devoted to his role as a stylish man-about-town, particularly at the theater and the opera, as he was to his financial and sporting endeavors. The Duke of Marlborough sniffed that Jerome was a "vulgar kind of man" who "drives about six and eight horses in New York (one may take this as a kind of indication of what the man is)," but his conspicuous consumption was not only viewed with admiration by many of his fellow New Yorkers but failed to dissuade Marlborough's younger son, Lord Randolph Churchill, from marrying Jerome's eldest daughter Jeanette ("Jennie"), or to prevent her two younger sisters from also finding husbands among the English elite.

Although the working classes could congregate atop the nearby hill, and the middling sort might pass through the imposing iron gates at Jerome Avenue and 198th Street, the Grand Stand, which offered the best views of the races' beginning and end, and the Club House, which was sited in "the most retired and elevated portion of the grounds" and boasted a spacious dining room decorated with paintings of American and English equine celebrities, were initially reserved for the members of the course's parent organization, Jerome's newly established American Jockey Club, and their families. The *New York Clipper,* a trade paper serving the sporting and theatrical industries, noted sarcastically that "none but the sweet scented and kid glove subscribers can enter" these structures. Thus protected from proximity to the hoi polloi, the city's elite, especially its women, felt comfortable attending the competitions; the audience dressed as if they were attending "the opera or an evening reception," and each race day "was marked by a display of female beauty, wealth and fashion that amazed the country." The ladies' escorts, their husbands, fathers, and brothers, were less notable for their style, but they too attracted considerable attention because they numbered among the city's, and the nation's, richest and most influential men, many of them, like the "hard nuts" that Henry James encountered at Saratoga, self-made.[8]

During the Civil War, New York had rapidly transformed itself from a primarily mercantile city into the financial center of the nation, symbolized by the opening in 1865 of the imposing Stock Exchange building on Wall Street. By the conflict's end it had become the home of "a class of Gothamites who seemed to wear their net worth on their ostentatious sleeves." In the stinging words of May King Van Rensselaer, a "member of one of the oldest Knickerbocker families" and a doyenne of Manhattan society, "all at once [society] was assailed from every side by persons who sought to climb boldly over the walls of social exclusiveness," just as the Patriarchs feared. These *nouveaux riches* were popu-

The First Meeting, Jerome Park, N.Y, by H. Schile, 1873. Yale University Art Gallery, Whitney Collections of Sporting Art, given in memory of Harry Payne Whitney (B.A. 1894) and Payne Whitney (B.A. 1898) by Francis P. Garvan (B.A. 1897), 2 June 1932.

larly referred to as "swells," in contrast to the "nobs" of the Patriarchs and the "Knickerbocracy," and the final third of the nineteenth century saw these two factions compete for dominance over New York society in a number of cultural and leisure venues. The Jerome Park course and its successors, Morris Park in the Bronx and Belmont Park, located on the boundary between Queens and Long Island, were central sites in this competition, as were the meetings of the American Jockey Club and its successors, the Board of Control and The Jockey Club (TJC), the last of these doing more than any previous turf organization in the history of American racing to reshape the sport's practices and values. Although the "swells" eventually claimed victory over the "nobs" in terms of both their wealth and their social preeminence, much of the ethos of the latter infused the club, and thus American racing more generally.[9]

The history of racing in the New York area began in the 1660s, when the English, having recently taken over the colony from the Dutch who had settled it a half century earlier, established the first racetrack in British North America at Long Island's Salisbury Plain, approximately thirty miles from Manhattan. However, the sport soon waned in popularity throughout the colony, as it did across the Northeast for most of the next two hundred years; as the physician and writer Thomas L. Nichols observed in 1864, "in New England and most of the North, horse-racing is supposed to have been prohibited in the Decalogue, and the races are not very reputably attended."[10] Prior to the opening of Jerome Park, top-class racing in the New York City area was limited to the "Great Match Races" that were held intermittently between 1823 and 1845 and were staged at the Union Course, the first in the nation designed specifically for Thoroughbred horses, which opened in 1821 near the site of the seventeenth-century track. These competitions, head-to-head races between equine champions representing the northern and southern states, attracted enormous crowds and considerable attention from general-interest newspapers as well as from the sporting press; of the first one, between Eclipse and Sir Henry, the English man of letters William Newnham Blane reported that "it was really amusing to see the interest this race excited; indeed an election for a President would not have excited greater.'" En route from Washington to New York, Blane found that "all the steam-boats and carriages were crowded with Southerners who were going to see this great contest ultimately decided," and he estimated that "about 20,000 people, chiefly Virginians and Southerners," had made the journey. In 1836, when the North's Post Boy faced off against John Bascomb, the English aristocrat Sir Charles Augustus Murray claimed that the whole city "was on the *qui vive,* owing to the approach of the races; on the second day of which was to be decided the great match between the North and the South. I do not remember ever to have seen such excitement at a Derby or St. Leger: stocks, companies, land and house speculations, politics, cotton, in short, all the ordinary New York topics of interest were forgotten in the one absorbing subject." But these were intermittent and irregularly scheduled events, and their popularity did not result in the formation of a jockey club or the opening of a nearby racetrack with a regular program of events.[11]

New York was not subject to the lingering influence of Puritanism with which much of the Northeast remained imbued well into the nineteenth century, but the city's inhabitants, although they enthusiastically patronized taverns, theaters, dance halls, boxing rings, gambling venues, and even an occasional cockfight, did not share their southern contemporaries' passion for racing.[12] Associating the sport with English aristocratic practices that allegedly undermined republican virtue and lured spectators into irresponsible wagering, the state legislature formally outlawed racing in 1802, although the ban appears not to have been aggressively enforced prior to its reversal two decades later. At least as importantly, before the advent of the railroads it would have been very difficult to attract large numbers of spectators to racetracks located at some distance beyond the city limits, as New Yorkers were far less likely than southern urbanites to keep horses and carriages. Manhattanites were clearly willing to make their way on occasion to the Union Course for the match races—an estimated sixty thousand attended in 1823, creating what may have been the first "traffic jam" in Gotham's history, and between seventy and one hundred thousand were at the final competition in 1845—but few would have been willing to undertake this arduous trip on a regular basis.[13] Within the city, whose population increased from sixty thousand at the beginning of the nineteenth century to more than a million just before the outbreak of the Civil War, landowners and developers were reluctant to assign dozens or even hundreds of the acres they controlled to the creation of a racetrack complex that would be in use for only part of each year if they had the option to make far greater profits by building desperately needed residences, warehouses, and business premises within the narrow strip of land between the East and Hudson Rivers.[14]

This situation, however, altered dramatically after the first sections of Central Park opened to the public in 1858. In the words of an "old jockey" whom the writer James D. McCabe Jr. interviewed in the early 1870s, it was this site that "saved horseflesh in New York." Affluent New Yorkers developed almost overnight a passion for riding on horseback or in carriages along the park's miles of scenic drives, which were closed to public transportation, to such an extent that the daily "carriage parade" became an essential ritual for the genteel and a source of fascination for the city's tourists and its less privileged inhabitants alike. Between four and five each afternoon the park's eastern carriage drive, which ran parallel to Fifth Avenue between Fifty-Ninth Street and the entrance to the pedestrianized Mall seven blocks to the north, was taken over by the horses and vehicles of "everyone who counted: the aristocracy, the new smart set, the parvenus, the celebrities, [and] the deplorably notorious," the last of which included the aforementioned brothel-keeper Josephine Woods. Autumn

Saturdays were especially glamorous, as they featured "more of the fashionable classes of our citizens," who, along with their "prancing steeds and gilded carriages," had returned from their summer sojourns at Newport, Saratoga, and "other famous resorts."[15]

Some of the participants, particularly the sedate Knickerbockers, favored broughams, light and compact closed vehicles whose passengers were invisible to onlookers, but the more exhibitionistic opted for the low-sided landau or the open-fronted victoria, which allowed them to be seen with ease. The former were typified by modestly attired women whose vehicles were "pulled by one horse in a handsome but quiet harness," while the latter were epitomized by "a lady [who] drove by in an open victoria wearing a feathered bonnet and a dress with velvet panels and cascading fringes and flounces."[16] In a city in which the immediate postbellum era saw both established and emerging elites becoming more Anglophile in their lifestyles in the face of the metropolis's increasingly diverse population, this promenade was modeled on that of Rotten Row and the South Carriage Drive in Hyde Park, which had since the previous century been a leading site of sociability for wealthy Londoners and those who enjoyed observing them. Even Walt Whitman, who was neither a member nor an admirer of the Manhattan plutocracy, found himself fascinated by what he termed an "impressive, rich, interminable circus on a grand scale, full of action and color," though he also claimed that the faces of the carriages' passengers tended to be "ashy and listless." In his opinion, the rich were "far from happy," and thus they in no way merited the envy of the "poor and plain."[17]

Although Thoroughbred racing had long been absent from the metropolis prior to the opening of Jerome Park, trotting, or harness racing, was by the 1850s extremely popular in New York, perhaps more so than anywhere else in the nation, and by midcentury the city was home to at least seven trotting courses. Given the park's popularity among carriage owners, it is not surprising that this sport soon became part of its program. Trotting enthusiasts drove through the park to show off their vehicles and horses en route to "the road," their term for Harlem Lane (now St. Nicholas Avenue) on its northern edge, which was the starting point for competitions that attracted the participation or spectatorship of politicians, lawyers, and bankers, as well as of grandees such as "Commodore" Cornelius Vanderbilt, at that time the richest man in the world, and ineluctably respectable figures such as Dr. Henry Ward Beecher,

Trotting Cracks on the Road: Scene—Harlem Lane, by Thomas Kelly, 1870. Yale University Art Gallery, Whitney Collections of Sporting Art, given in memory of Harry Payne Whitney (B.A. 1894) and Payne Whitney (B.A. 1898) by Francis P. Garvan (B.A. 1897), 2 June 1932.

the renowned clergyman and social reformer. Like General Grant, who when visiting the city in 1865 was keen to see the Lane, the financier August Belmont and the Wall Street lawyer and cofounder of the Saratoga track William Travers were trotting enthusiasts, but their interests would soon shift toward a different mode of horse sport.[18]

Many Americans of the mid- to late nineteenth century considered trotting to be quite distinct from racing; although it was not uncommon for spectators to place wagers on the outcome of the former contests, and the sport was adopted by some of the East Coast's richest men, it lacked the aristocratic overtones and the association with gambling and other types of vice that frequently clouded racing's reputation. But in the immediate postbellum era New York was a city filled with young men of all social ranks, some of whom found civilian life dull after their service in the Union army, and who craved forms of leisure that were faster-paced and more thrilling than the stately "circus" of the carriage parade or the comparatively slow "pacing" that typified harness races; in their opinion, "these days, to have money and not own fast horses . . . is to be nobody."[19] But it was their elders, particularly those who had made vast fortunes during the Civil War, who gratified these desires by promoting a sport that would not merely allow them to show off their stables—the finest Thoroughbreds being significantly more expensive and difficult to acquire than even the best carriage horses or trotters—but would facilitate the eventual eclipse of the Knickerbockers and their own emergence, both locally and nationally, as not just *a* but *the* new American elite.

According to Donald Mrozek, newly rich urban Americans of the final third of the nineteenth century "conducted [sport] as a mode of consumption and a fashion," and this claim was particularly true, in the words of the Unitarian clergyman Price Collier, of those who "having been recently poor, are trying to appear rich." These elite men, and increasingly their female kin, embraced forms of recreation, such as tennis, golf, swimming, and archery, in which they could participate at the country estates that they were acquiring on Long Island or in Westchester County, or at a new type of leisure site, the country club, whose facilities mimicked those of the British country house, and which first appeared in the United States in 1880, selecting its members based upon not only their wealth but their religion, ethnicity, and personal reputation. Among this class, sport was becoming increasingly privatized, practiced away from the eyes and ears of journalists and plebeians alike. Meanwhile, ordinary Americans were increasingly drawn to the emerging "city games," team sports, especially baseball, that were played in public at both the amateur and the professional level.[20]

Racing, however, occupied a space that lay between these competing imperatives. August Belmont notoriously asserted that "racing is for the rich," referring to racetrack audiences as well as to the owners of the horses whose competitions they watched, to justify the high admission prices at Jerome Park and the practice of segregating even affluent spectators according to whether or not they were members of the American Jockey Club. Both sporting periodicals and the general-interest press criticized this practice, noting that at the English turf, which was increasingly admired throughout the United States as the ideal of racing excellence, track admission was usually either free of charge or priced to be accessible even to the working classes, and, other than in the grandstand, racegoers were free to wander the grounds as they chose, a scene depicted by William Powell Frith in his widely exhibited painting *The Derby Day* (1858). Indeed, according to Frith, Charles Dickens, and many other observers of the English turf, the pleasure of attending a race lay as much in observing the great variety of one's fellow spectators as in the sport on offer; as a *Times* of London contributor wrote of the Epsom Downs track on a Derby day, "every part of the course and hill swarmed with a restless crowd of thousands upon thousands . . . card sharpers, organ grinders, n——r melodists—genuine and counterfeit—dancers upon stilts, acrobats, German bands, gentlemen, ladies, thieves, and policemen, all mixed into that indescribable crowd that goes to form a Derby racecourse." By contrast, from its opening day "the Bluff," as the Jerome Park course was popularly known, was noted for its "orderly and good-humored" spectators, and "the occasion is rarely marred by any act of rowdyism or lawlessness." It was not intended to be a venue dominated by "the common herd" or by "the blackguards and reckless gamblers who disgrace the American turf" but instead reflected the "aristocratic" variant of racing, marked by an atmosphere of deference to the elite. This atmosphere attracted the attendance of "ladies who are 'in society,'" as "the every day mob cannot get within 1,000 feet of them and must content themselves with gazing at the beauties from afar."[21]

Belmont and Jerome could be dismissed as *nouveaux riches* from New York's "fast set" who lacked the English aristocracy's confidence, and thus the latter's willingness to mingle with their perceived inferiors, but their motivation for restricting audiences at the track to the affluent, and for banning the sale of alcoholic beverages other than at the clubhouse, also reflected their desire, like that of their antebellum southern predecessors, "to make the turf respectable, to render racing a refined and dignified recreation among gentlemen." The Epsom Derby had begun in 1780, and as a long-established and wildly popular fixture of the English turf calendar it could afford to be associated with a carnivalesque atmosphere, but in the years immediately following the Civil War many New Yorkers and other northerners continued to view the sport as disreputable, and its popularity before the war throughout the southern states as indicative of the cultural immaturity of those whom the Knickerbocker civic leader George Templeton Strong described, in an impressively alliterative phrase, as "a race of lazy, ignorant, coarse, sensual, swaggering, sordid, beggarly barbarians." "The Broadway merchant and Beaver street importer, the Broad street broker and

Exchange place banker, the Nassau street journalist and Fifth avenue dandy, the club-lounger and Tenth street artist, the belle of Madison avenue and the leader of Twenty-third street fashion, the majestic entertainer of Fifth avenue and the charming coquette of Stuyvesant square" were all welcome at Jerome Park, and their variety added spice for the spectators and attracted those who wished to see "the brilliant crowd in attendance," but the presence of members of the working classes, regardless of their race or ethnicity, was considered to seriously detract from both the glamour and the reputation of the venue and its competitions.[22] Wealthy Americans of the Gilded Age, particularly those who lived on the East Coast, admired and imitated many aspects of contemporary English culture, but rather than sharing Dickens's affection for the festive chaos that marked some of its turf's most celebrated gatherings, they considered such events "nothing but carnivals of drunkenness, crime and misery," indulged in simultaneously by "the idle rich and the idle poor," and thus constituting an unacceptable model for the sport's revival in the northern states. Class-mixing was not a major problem upstate at Saratoga, long a summer resort for the wealthy, but Jerome Park, like Epsom Downs, was located at the edge of its nation's great metropolis. If it were to model itself on an English track, its managers would have preferred that it be Newmarket, which was sited in the eponymous small Suffolk town nearly seventy miles from London, and which was patronized primarily by wealthy turfmen rather than by those seeking interclass conviviality.[23]

New Yorkers who had some familiarity with English racing traditions feared that the strictly hierarchical atmosphere that typified Jerome Park boded ill for the course's long-term prospects. Whereas *Harper's Weekly* had opined shortly after the track's opening day that Jerome and his American Jockey Club had succeeded in "giving [racing] dignity and remov[ing] from it many of its degrading associations," due to "the arrangement which has been made for the presence of ladies, and which secures them from all intrusion as effectively as if they were at a matinee in their own drawing-rooms," just a year later it adopted a far more critical stance.[24] Its correspondent admitted that "fashionable people have taken up the sport, and sanction the club meetings with their august presence," and that "to call a race-course a park was an adroit move to render horse-racing respectable." But without the "holiday, picnic character" and the "picturesque, open-air aspects of the great English races," Jerome Park's events had a sterile atmosphere. They were devoid of the "enjoyment or holiday hilarity . . . [of] an English race, with its carriages covering the field, the open-air eating, drinking, and merry-making, [and] the sports that fill up the time," and were thus of limited appeal. "If we must have the race," this writer urged, "let us give it this out-of-door character, the people assembling on the field, where the sun, the air, and their own good spirits may conduce both to health and pleasure."[25] A more plebeian commentator, the itinerant gambler John Morris, writing as John O'Connor, pointed out that in England, home to a monarchy and a long-established landed aristocracy, "the same price carries the peasant as well as the prince to any part of the course where spectators are allowed," whereas the "shoddy aristocracy comprising the Jerome Park Racing Association . . . seized on half the grand stand, which was splendidly fitted up, for the exclusive use of the lords of wealth." Noting that "they also had a fancy castle built on a knoll nearly opposite the grand stand, with coffee-houses, restaurants, etc., attached," but that "within this hallowed precinct, none but the shoddyites and their invited guests might venture," he wondered "what are we coming to in this free Republic!"[26]

The social atmosphere of Jerome Park, modeled upon the French Jockey Club's Longchamp on the western outskirts of Paris, was distinct not only from that of Epsom Downs and other English courses of the era but also from that of antebellum southern racing venues, and this difference stemmed primarily from the recent establishment and urban sources of the fortunes of those "fashionable people"—industrialists and financiers and their families—who patronized it. The English aristocracy of the mid-Victorian period retained both an affinity for rural life and a paternalistic attitude toward ordinary men and women; its members were sufficiently secure in their social position that they were willing to mingle at public events with those of lower socioeconomic status, whereas the "*parvenus* of New York society [who] form[ed] its 'codfish aristocracy'" feared that such mixing could undermine their claims to gentility. And whether or not one agrees with George Fredrickson's much-debated assertion that the pre–Civil War South was a "*herrenvolk* democracy" within whose social structure race was a more significant factor than class, the fact remains that the region's elite men often felt it necessary to make at least token gestures of equality toward poorer whites in order to uphold the principle of racial supremacy in a society whose economy, politics, and culture were built upon Black slavery, but in which a significant number of whites owned no slaves.

Even at Charleston's Washington Course, which was renowned throughout the South for its genteel ambience, nonelite whites were normally welcome guests even during Racing Week, provided that they behaved decorously and did not attempt to enter the spaces reserved for the members of the South Carolina Jockey Club and their guests. Even "crowds of the most promiscuous character," one Charlestonian journalist claimed, could be improved through studying the behavior of their social superiors at the track, as long as the former accepted that their "mental inferiority [should] naturally submit itself to the guidance of education and talents . . . [T]he language of manners of the polite are closely imitated, and decorum and elegance succeed vulgarity and impertinence."[27] By contrast, in post–Civil War New York, as the sociologist Shamus Khan has observed, "as access to elite status became less limited through family ties and more open to men of new wealth, New Yorkers found a new mechanism of social closure. They created an exclusive culture distinct from that of the common American, the result of which was something far more elitist"—and racing was a particularly visible representation of that culture.[28]

If nonelite white men and women were notably less present on the grounds of Jerome Park than they had been at southern tracks prior to the Civil War, spectators of color were still rarer. Although New York City was home to nearly ten thousand African Americans in 1865, and that number doubled by 1880, few passed through the complex's gates.[29] Both custom and cost barred many Black men and women from the antebellum South's racing venues; just as Black New Yorkers were normally limited to watching the Jerome Park races from "Dead-head Hill," most of those who lived in Richmond, Charleston, Natchez, or New Orleans saw only what was visible when they seated themselves atop the fences that surrounded these cities' tracks. But many African Americans passed through the gates as enslaved or free working people, driving carriages, attending white women or children, selling refreshments or souvenirs, or tending to the equine competitors as grooms or stable hands. Most significantly, nearly all pre–Civil War jockeys were boys or men of color; although the majority remained enslaved, some of the most successful succeeded in gaining their freedom as long as they promised to continue riding—and winning—for their former owners.[30] As will be discussed in the following chapter, white riders began to replace Black ones almost immediately after the Civil War, and within a half century African American jockeys were as rare a sight on the American turf as white ones had been throughout the antebellum era. Both native New Yorkers and the majority of the city's visitors during Jerome Park's heyday tended to employ white men or women, often Irish or Irish American, as their carriage drivers, ladies' maids, and nannies, and thus the servants who accompanied their employers on outings to the track contributed little to the venue's racial diversity. Although the African-descended population of London in the later nineteenth century was considerably smaller and even poorer than that of New York, a visitor to Epsom Downs in this era was far more likely either to be or to encounter a person of color, who would be appreciated by many white attendees as an aspect of the event's carnival atmosphere rather than scorned as an interloper.[31]

Throughout most of its years of operation, and even as new tracks opened elsewhere in the Northeast and in more recently settled parts of the United States, such as California, Jerome Park's policies and atmosphere continued to reflect August Belmont's assertion that racing was and should remain a pastime for the wealthy, as both participants and spectators. It remained a site at which Thorstein Veblen's "leisure class" enjoyed its leisure and took pleasure in the admiration and envy it evoked among both the spectators atop "Deadhead Hill" and the readers of New York's newspapers—in the society pages as well as the sporting news. At the park, according to the *Spirit of the Times*, one might encounter "all that was cultured, refined, and fashionable in New York society," and even the most refined woman could attend the races "without any departure from those proprieties of life which render her sex estimable."[32] But any hopes that its patrons had that the course might have as long a life as Charleston's Washington Course, which operated for more than a century, were frustrated by the infrastructural requirements of the expanding metropolis. In order to provide additional water storage capacity for the Central Park Reservoir, the "famous old racecourse, on which so many celebrated horses have been ridden to defeat or victory," was annexed by the city's aqueduct commissioners as the site of an additional reservoir, and the track's final competitions were held on 24 August 1894. A few years later Walter S. Vosburgh, a journalist who would become the leading American turf historian of the first half of the twentieth century, mourned that "the 'bluff,' with its assemblage of beau and belles, is fast yielding to shovel, pick, and dynamite; the course over which Glenelg, Hanover and Kingfisher strode in triumph is a drear waste," and "the 'lawn,' where thousands have cheered the Withers and Belmont winners, is now occupied by the brown-skinned sons of Italy," immigrant laborers employed in creating the reservoir, and "who perhaps scoff at its racing memories as they recall their ancestors' feats in the chariot races of the emperors."[33]

Still more damaging to Jerome Park's ambitions than the decisions of municipal officials were the actions of gambling men, the newest variant of that figure that had been the source of such consternation at southern tracks for the past century. Even in comparison with those of other *nouveaux riches* of later nineteenth-century New York, Leonard Jerome's fortune was of very recent vintage, and he had gained it not through industrial production, banking, or real estate development but via financial speculation, an activity that remained mysterious and often suspect to many Americans of this era.[34] Although he was renowned for his glamorous lifestyle and was one of the first rich Americans to marry his "dollar princess" daughters into the English aristocracy, he occupied a liminal position within the ranks of the nation's Gilded Age turf leaders. As John Dizikes has observed, two distinct factions soon developed within this group. One consisted of "those plutocrats who emulated the British racing aristocracy," the most prominent of whom were August Belmont Sr., William Collins Whitney, and Pierre and George Lorillard.[35] Although Belmont was an immigrant and had been raised as a Jew, and would be satirized by Edith Wharton in her novel *The Age of Innocence* as Julius Beaufort, a vaguely sinister plutocrat of obscure origins, he had secured his fortune a generation before the Civil War and had served as President Franklin Pierce's ambassador to the Netherlands and as the chair of the Democratic National Committee. His determination to "stand by the Government at any sacrifice" during the Civil War, in conjunction with his influence with his employers, the London-based Rothschild banking dynasty, encouraged the Lincoln administration to deploy him as "an unofficial financial and diplomatic agent" for Anglo-American relations during the conflict. Although Ward McAllister and his Patriarchs considered him "a representative man of new money in the metropolis," upon his marriage to Caroline Slidell Perry he not only converted to his wife's Episcopal faith but linked himself to a family of *Mayflower* descendants and distinguished naval officers, including his father-in-law, Commodore Matthew Perry, who in 1853 had opened long-isolated Japan to American commerce. While Jerome's personal style was, to some observers, lavish to the point of vulgarity, Belmont, an art collector, an ardent supporter of the opera, and the first New Yorker to employ a French chef in his home, was considered to be "an artist in his household . . . everything is to him an object of sincere artistic solicitude," a richer version of the American aesthete Gilbert Osmond of Henry James's *The Portrait of a Lady* (1881). In 1877 the *New York Sun* wrote of him that "he taught New Yorkers how to eat, how to drink, how to dress, how to drive four-in-hands, how to furnish their houses, how to live generally according to the rules of the possibly somewhat effete, but unquestionably refined, society of the Old World." Manhattan gentlemen who emulated Belmont could be confident that they did not resemble the unsophisticated "Brother Jonathans" of the early republic or the self-made "hard nuts" whom James observed at Saratoga, but were as refined as the men of the English and Continental *haute bourgeoisie* and aristocracy.[36] Such men included the turfman William Collins Whitney, who was also of *Mayflower* stock, had been initiated into the self-consciously elite Skull and Bones society while a student at Yale, and married Flora Payne, a Standard Oil Company heiress, and the Lorillard brothers, who were the heirs to a century-old tobacco fortune and the sons of the owner of more than a half million acres of undeveloped land to the north of Manhattan.[37]

In sharp contrast to these gentlemen stood those whom Dizikes termed the "buccaneers," "social outsiders" typified by the English-born James R. Keene, the patron of Richard Ten Broeck, who later became an open enemy of Whitney and the Lorillards on track matters, and who was notorious throughout the United States as the Gilded Age's greatest "plunger," one of those "men who were not afraid to take a chance and bet their money" and who "must be a bundle of nerves and filled with discrimination to the utmost degree." Playing up rather than attempting to mask his rise from poverty and obscurity to immense wealth, Keene was willing to speculate wildly "in everything that came along—wheat, lard, opium, and fast horses." "The intrinsic value of the properties in whose shares he dealt, as bear or bull, as the mood suited his fancy, never concerned him in the least," and he took pride in his ability to accept a tremendous loss in the stock market or at the racetrack with a calm that verged upon indifference, as William Ransom Johnson and Adam Bingaman had done decades earlier.[38] Along with the "copper man" Jesse Lewisohn (whose wife had been a showgirl and a mistress of the flamboyant financier "Diamond Jim" Brady), the Irish immigrant and former "pick-and-shovel man" Marcus Daly, and the onetime

Brooklyn butcher Michael Dwyer, Keene was a tremendous racetrack gambler. Self-consciously aristocratic racing men such as Belmont, Whitney, and the Lorillards shared this passion but were more restrained in their activities. Jerome, who admired the men of the latter group and imitated their self-presentation, but whose life experiences were far closer to those of the former, welcomed both to his course; although he was determined to prevent racketeering from gaining a foothold within his "untarnished sportsman's dream," he was far less concerned about the social origins of its guests, provided that they were wealthy and appropriately dressed and behaved in accordance with the venue's rules.[39]

It was this lack of sympathy between the two factions that constituted its principal supporters that resulted in something of a social eclipse of Jerome Park some years prior to its closure by city authorities. August Belmont's conviction that racing should be reserved for the wealthy also applied to trackside gambling, with betting at Jerome Park initially available only to members and their guests in the clubhouse. He and some other members of the American Jockey Club were thus dismayed when Jerome, having returned from a visit to Europe, in 1871 introduced French pari-mutuel gambling machines at the course, offering an opportunity for "the masses" to place small wagers. These masses indeed flocked to the course; the *Spirit of the Times* reported that "there was such a rush to buy tickets that not half of those who wanted them could be supplied," but this boost to the track's finances, if not its social éclat, was short-lived, as the New York State legislature became increasingly determined to limit gambling opportunities. Saratoga's John Morrissey inadvertently inflamed this hostility; he had taken approximately $350,000 in wagers on the 1876 presidential race, and when it became clear that the election results would not be known for weeks or months, he called off all of the bets and returned the funds to the bettors, but retained 2 percent of the total as his commission. Many other pool-sellers followed his example, engendering complaints from numerous bettors who believed that Morrissey and others of his ilk had cheated them. This controversy, in combination with long-standing moral objections to gambling, encouraged the legislators to pass a bill in March 1877 that barred the existence of facilities for registering wagers and selling pools. Jerome Park was particularly vulnerable to this change, as the law was supposed to apply throughout New York State but was not enforced outside the New York metropolitan area, making Saratoga a more appealing venue for many turf fans. Between 1876 and

Morris Park Races. Library of Congress, Prints and Photographs Division.

1877 the latter venue's receipts declined dramatically; although they rebounded in the next decade, some of Jerome Park's longtime supporters lost interest in the course, and before they could be won back the city announced its plan to transform the area into a reservoir.[40]

With the announcement of the impending closure of Jerome Park came two opportunities for "the men who considered racing a sport rather than merely a means for gambling."[41] The first, and the more obvious, was the establishment of a new racecourse in the New York area that would not only replace Jerome Park but would boast the spotless reputation that the latter had forfeited through its introduction of facilities for lower-stakes gambling. This was Morris Park, located in what is now the Bronx neighborhood of the same name and bounded by Sackett Avenue, Pelham Parkway, Williamsbridge Road, and Bronxdale Avenue. It was hailed on its opening day, 20 August 1889, as "the finest racetrack in the world," and its inaugural races were covered by newspapers in Chicago, Milwaukee, St. Paul, Los Angeles, and Portland, Oregon. In 1901 the turfman and Jockey Club historian Walter Vosburgh asserted that "probably the fashionable display is as great to-day at the club-house and paddock at Morris Park as it ever was at Jerome," due largely to the complex's "palatial clubhouse and excellent facilities." Yet it would operate for just fifteen years, at which time the locus of Gotham's racing moved to the new Belmont Park course on Long Island, which would be the recipient and new home of the Washington Course's famous gates.[42]

Although Morris Park hosted the Triple Crown Belmont Stakes race between 1890 and 1904, its existence is largely a footnote to New York City's history of horse sport, an interval between the decline of Jerome Park and the opening of the Belmont course. But the second innovation, the formation in 1894 of The Jockey Club, was perhaps the most significant event in the history of the sport in the period from the end of the Civil War to the present day.

As described previously, from the beginnings of Thoroughbred racing in the American colonies it was a local jockey club that controlled every aspect of the sport at an individual course; the members managed the venue's finances and operations or hired a professional to do so, organized and publicized the annual sporting program, approved the horses, jockeys, and owners who competed in these events, and to the best of their ability monitored the behavior of the attendees. Sporting publications such as the *American Turf Register* and the *Spirit of the Times* facilitated the sharing of information across the nation, encouraging clubs' practices to become more similar throughout the middle decades of the nineteenth century, but members nonetheless passionately upheld their group's right to establish its own rules for its competitions. But the proliferation of tracks in the greater New York area, some of which were perceived as seedy and lawless, in combination with ongoing public anxiety about various forms of gambling, risked bringing the sport as a whole into disrepute, and both the sporting press and the leading turfmen of New York and its environs became anxious about racing's future.

In 1891 Pierre Lorillard expressed to a group of horse owners and track managers his fear that "unless some control were exercised[,] growing abuses would soon, and seriously, affect the popularity of racing." The result was the creation of the Board of Control for New York State's courses, a body of seven representatives of horse owners and track administrators with the authority to license jockeys, update the rules of racing, and outlaw courses whose management failed to abide by its rules. Although the board acted on a number of occasions to suspend jockeys whom it believed had acted dishonestly, and barred from its tracks owners and trainers whose horses competed at the notorious Guttenberg course, the group struggled to cope with the number and variety of instances of cheating, doping, and miscellaneous "tricks on the turf."[43] In less than three years, and despite the involvement of August Belmont Jr., a man renowned for both his wealth and his integrity, a combination of economic upheaval (from the Panic of 1893) and the perception among both turfmen and journalists that the Board of Control was not so much a force for restoring racing's reputation as a clique dedicated to advancing its own interests brought its moment of dominance to a quick end. In February 1894 Keene, whose stable was at that time the most profitable in the world, with the support of the most elite among Manhattan's breeders and owners of Thoroughbred horses—men of the Belmont, Whitney, and Vanderbilt families, among other leading industrialists and financiers—initiated the greatest alteration in the history of American racing, proposing the formation of a single national group, known simply as The Jockey Club (TJC) and modeled on its English namesake. It aimed to imitate its transatlantic counterpart, being made up of "men more interested in the turf than in particular meets" and claiming the authority to schedule competitions, license turf personnel, namely jockeys, trainers, and bookmakers, and set rules and regulations for both racing and betting that every venue of any repute would be obliged to follow. It would also "constitute a court of final appeal in the interpretation of rules, with power to discipline all persons under its jurisdiction." The laws of the individual states would still technically supersede those of The Jockey Club, but state racing commissions would accept TJC as the ultimate arbiter of the sport. The foundation of TJC and the concentration of power in the hands of its members would, many turfmen hoped, bring an end to scheduling disputes between neighboring jockey clubs and, more importantly, would curb the growing power of both legal and illegal gambling and bookmaking interests, a pressing issue at a time when the legislature of neighboring New Jersey had closed the state's tracks in response to these concerns. In doing so, it would encourage the public to "respect and have confidence in racing" and would

August Belmont Jr., ca. 1910. Library of Congress, Prints and Photographs Division, George Grantham Bain Collection.

therefore convince them to "support [it] more fully," as it would be cleansed of its association with shady individuals and equally shady practices.[44]

TJC's predecessor, the American Jockey Club, had lacked the prestige of organizations such as the New York Yacht Club and the Academy of Music, owing to its "principles of purchased inclusion" (admission of the majority of those who were able to afford its dues, including controversial New York figures such as "Boss" Tweed); the Anglophile Yacht Club, founded in 1844, restricted membership to those whom its founders considered socially impeccable. It served primarily as "an integrating organization of horse fanciers and bettors" whose intent was the promotion of racing in a state that up to the Civil War had shown little interest in the sport, and although most of its members numbered among the city's richest inhabitants, it was scorned by many reformers and Knickerbockers alike; the vast wealth of these *nouveaux riches* could not compensate for their moral and behavioral failings.[45] But as the nineteenth century drew toward its close, the approbation of "Old New York" mattered less and less to men such as August Belmont and his namesake son. Their ever-expanding wealth encouraged them to consider themselves the peers not of the Knickerbockers, with their relatively small fortunes and austere style of life, but of the aristocracy of Europe, especially that of England. Manhattan's trading concerns had shipped cotton to English factories for decades before the Civil War, and many of the commercial magnates whom that war had enriched began to follow Belmont's lead and seek "a cultural repertoire appropriate to a rising elite" among the aristocracy of the "Old World."[46] Although many titled families' fortunes were in decline by the late nineteenth century, their heritage and the trappings thereof that they retained allowed them to maintain their sense of legitimacy among themselves and within their nations, and to engage in a way of living that seemed both older and more appealing to men of new fortunes than that of New York's "Upper Ten." For their part, impecunious English aristocrats who would have scorned the daughters of their own country's industrialists and bankers welcomed their much wealthier American counterparts; Pauline Whitney married the grandson of the Marquess of Anglesey, and Maude Lorillard, the son of Baron Revelstoke. And although Commodore Vanderbilt, the world's richest man at his death in 1877, was generally considered insufficiently refined for the society of "Old New York," within two decades his great-granddaughter Consuelo made the most prestigious match of all the "dollar princesses" when she married Charles Spencer-Churchill, the ninth Duke of Marlborough and the first cousin of Winston Churchill, who was the grandson of Leonard Jerome.[47]

Belmont had lived in Germany until he was in his mid-twenties, but as a man of Jewish background and a financier he had no possibility of gaining a foothold in the aristocracy of his native land, which was dominated by the "Junker" agrarian and military families of Prussia. But in England the richest Jewish families, including Belmont's early employers the Rothschilds, mixed socially with the nobility and adopted their country estate lifestyle; by the 1870s the Vale of Aylesbury in Buckinghamshire was often referred to as "Rothschildshire" because members of the clan owned so many estates in the area. As a columnist for the London *Times* observed, "when an American has made a fortune he finds it almost impossible to live quietly in his own country. The chief attraction is England."[48] And in England, for turfmen such as Belmont, the chief attraction was the racing world.

The last quarter of the nineteenth century was of course not the first time that American racing enthusiasts had been fascinated by English racing. Although in the early republican era they were keen to contrast what they claimed were the democratic practices of their variant of the sport with the undesirably aristocratic ones of their former mother country, by the 1830s the pages of the United States' sporting papers included accounts not only of feature races such as the Epsom Derby and the St. Leger but of more quotidian English turf events, and of that nation's leading horses and their breeders. Contributors debated the superiority of breeding, training, and racing methods on both sides of the Atlantic and expressed their opinions regarding imported Thoroughbreds and their American progeny. As growing political tensions between the North and the South prevented the continuation of sectional match races, racing enthusiasts throughout the country urged leading turfmen to organize an "American Invasion" of the English turf, and in 1856 Richard Ten Broeck took up this challenge, bringing three American horses, including the celebrated Lecomte, to "test the powers of the English race horse on English ground by actual experiment with those bred in America."[49]

As discussed in chapter 4, Ten Broeck's "Invasion" had little success in terms of winning races. But his English sojourn nonetheless had a major impact on the American turf world when he returned to the United States after the Civil War to find southern racing moribund and the sport in the process of reforming itself in previously inhospitable northern venues. Although his horses had not performed well in England, he had ingratiated himself with the leaders of the turf there as a man whom they saw as "typical of the shrewd, dry, humorous American that one reads of in the novels of Mark Twain," a more sophisticated and self-aware version of the long-standing stereotype of "Brother Jonathan."[50] In so doing, he paved the way for far richer men such as August Belmont to be welcomed by the members of The (English) Jockey Club and to consider not only creating a version thereof in America that would parallel the English club's "incipient bureaucratization of the entire sport" but jettisoning long-standing American racing practices and replacing them with English ones.[51] The late nineteenth century saw a revival of "Anglophobia" in some aspects of American political culture but not in the sporting world or that of the New York society with which it intersected. Some Americans might deplore the persistence of the aristocracy and "institutions of class rule" in Britain, but the leaders of post–Civil War racing found English sporting practices attractive and wielded the cultural authority to embed them within the American turf.[52]

Although antebellum southern jockey clubs were concerned, even obsessed, with ensuring that their members were men of good character, the participants in and even the progenitors of pre–Civil War turf societies might be flamboyant characters such as William Ransom Johnson or Richard Ten Broeck. The twenty-seven men who founded the new Jockey Club, by contrast, "reflected a certain social consistency," and the club's meetings "had an austere air which helped build its reputation of firmness and justice."[53] But how did this club, the creation of a small number of self-consciously genteel but newly rich New Yorkers, so rapidly become "the most prestigious organization in American racing"?[54] On a macro level, this development stemmed from its members' status as national rather than regional economic and social leaders, men whose names were synonymous with vast wealth and power to Americans across the nation, just as those of Rockefeller and Ford would be a few decades later. As Christopher McGrath observed, by the end of the nineteenth century "a stable of thoroughbreds had become the hallmark of a new, international plutocracy," and it was difficult to challenge the claim that America's plutocrats, like those of Europe, should hold sway over racing in their country.[55] These individuals' fortunes could in themselves be interpreted as evidence that they possessed the judgment needed to manage a sport that required significant financial investment, while also suggesting that they would not be tempted to cut corners or engage in illegal practices, as less deep-pocketed turfmen had so frequently done. They were also politically well-connected, a particularly important attribute at a time at which state legislatures throughout the nation threatened to criminalize gambling and thus undermine racing's financial basis.[56]

Within the sport itself, TJC's dominance was facilitated by its encouragement of practices that had begun to emerge in the United States just before the Civil War and were themselves imitative of English traditions, the most important of which was the rapid and complete replacement of "the old-established and sanctified Southern system" of four-mile heats with the dashes that had been popular across the Atlantic since the beginning of the century, and that emphasized raw speed over the long-vaunted concept of "bottom," or stamina. With younger horses sprinting over shorter distances, a track could stage more contests per day and thus attract attendees who were at least as interested in gambling opportunities as they were in equine sport; even the celebrated feature races that were created in the last third of the century, including those of the Triple Crown, were single dashes of less than two miles.[57] Technological innovations of the era also encouraged popular acceptance of the club's practices: the invention of the stopwatch and the camera permitted a horse's speed to be measured ever more precisely and allowed judges to discern the victor in a contest in which two or more contenders passed the finish line in an apparent dead heat; hence the term "photo finish." As a result, racing audiences increasingly adopted a more national perspective, favoring particular horses not for their place of birth or training but for their record of achievements, which the ever-more-efficient wire networks spread across the United States, "show[ing] how speed was becoming a major element of an emerging mass press."[58] The club's decision in 1897 to add to its statutes a prohibition on the doping of horses frustrated some jockeys and trainers but was welcomed by the nation's animal-lovers; it both supported fair practice within the sport and expressed compassion toward the animals upon which its success rested.[59] Finally, in 1896 August Belmont Jr. acquired on the club's behalf the rights to the *American Stud-Book*, the ultimate source of authority regarding which horses could, by virtue of their descent, be classed as Thoroughbreds, and therefore be eligible to race at any track recognized by the club.[60]

In fact, TJC was not completely successful in establishing dominion over American racing to the same extent as the English Jockey Club had across the Atlantic. It dominated the sport in the greater New York City area, due to the wealth and renown of its leaders and the strength of their political connections; almost immediately after TJC's founding, the New York legislature created a racing commission to manage the state's turf business, in which TJC members played a dominant role. These attributes cemented New York's dominance within American racing, but as the sport expanded all the way to the West Coast, even the financial and political clout of TJC did not empower it to maintain complete control over every course in the United States. Racing entrepreneurs who felt that they needed TJC's approval sought to gain it by abiding by all of the club's regulations, but those who were less concerned with winning its favor often ignored its diktats, and the organization had limited ability to exert its authority beyond New York. The club might designate nonconforming racing venues as "outlaw" tracks and prevent men who were employed or sent their horses to these courses from accessing those that TJC controlled, but this rule was not a universal concern of American turfmen. The men of TJC were a national elite, in contrast to the Knickerbockers, who had little interest in the world beyond "little old New York," but their wealth and political influence did not necessarily translate into cultural dominance in the way that, for example, the antebellum South Carolina Jockey Club held sway over both racing and elite social life both in Charleston and throughout the state. As racing shifted from a diversion that occupied a few days two or three times a year to a business with a significantly longer season, or even one that existed throughout the year, and as gambling was formalized and was openly acknowledged as central to the sport's allure, a track's success was based almost entirely on the number of visitors it could attract and the amount of money it could make from them. TJC members and their associates would not have welcomed the hoi polloi into their trackside clubhouses, let alone into TJC, but they were happy for people of all classes, races, ethnicities, and religions to pay their admission fees and crowd into the lower-priced areas of their racing complexes. As long as the "lesser sorts" refrained from overtly disruptive or criminal activities, even the most self-consciously aristocratic turfmen were unconcerned about their appearance or behavior. The link between a jockey club and the residence of its members had begun to break in Saratoga; with TJC's advent it disappeared.[61]

Allen Guttmann asserted that the noteworthy characteristics of modern sports are, in alphabetical order: bureaucracy; equality; quantification; rationalization; records; secularism; and specialization, and his fellow sports historian John Gleaves contends that, according to these standards, horse racing was one of the first to modernize.[62] By the end of the nineteenth century American racing was far more similar to that of contemporary England than to that of the antebellum South; one can imagine that a "Napoleon of the Turf" such as William Ransom Johnson would have been both puzzled and alarmed had he lived long enough to compare the turf world of his prime with that of a half century later. TJCs success was at once a cause and a result of many of these changes, and although it never attained the level of control its members craved, its innovations shaped the sport into what it largely remains today. In the following chapter, the example of Louisville's Churchill Downs shows how a combination of northern and English practices with seemingly traditional yet actually recently emerged aspects of southern leisure resulted in the creation of a venue whose success remains as persistent as it is paradoxical.

7

Churchill Downs

THE NEW SOUTH'S OLD SOUTH

> The races commence to day and the city is crowded. Mr Bullogh said it reminded him of what Louisville was some four or five years since. A great many strangers have been refused at the Galt House and all the other hotels are crowded. What is something new there are a great many Southerners. There must be a rise in the cotton or some such thing.
>
> —ANN J. PEARCE to her brother Judge William S. Bodley, 1843

> I have been to the races once since I came, & I do not care to go again, it was a grand, large, elegant aft[ernoon]. About 15000 people, it was Derby day, & of course an extra crowd. Pappa & Hugh have been every day so far, they last all of next week but I hardly think Hugh will stay, as he is not getting rich betting, he is a little like me his horses come in last as a general thing . . . Mamma says you would of enjoyed the races last thursday, as they were extra good, the track was in good condition, & weather grand.
>
> —"DAISY L" to "Friend Will," 1882

Meriwether Lewis "Lutie" Clark Jr. was probably extremely anxious on the morning of 17 May 1875. He had devoted the past three years to conceiving, financing, and developing a new racetrack for his hometown of Louisville, and the day had finally arrived on which this new course would see the first running of what Clark, his fellow members of the recently reconstituted Louisville Jockey Club, and the city's political and commercial elite hoped would be not just an exciting and well-attended competition but a "feature race" that would soon command national and perhaps even global attention comparable to that accorded the classics of the English turf. The weather broke in Clark's favor, as the day was warm and cloudless but breezy, and he was no doubt relieved to see that "the course was in splendid order, and all the appurtenances requisite for the comfort and convenience of racing was ready to hand." The competitors were fifteen "youngsters" and included Henry Price McGrath's Chesapeake, whose sire was the famed Lexington, but it was another of McGrath's horses, Aristides, who triumphed in what one observer claimed was "the best race at the weights ever run by three-year-olds in this country." Clark would have been still more gratified by the size and composition of the crowd; "the Grand Stand presented one solid mass of human faces, while the quarter-stretch, the public stand, and a portion of the field was covered with people." This audience was "composed of all grades of society," from butchers to bankers, all manifesting their excitement but refraining from uncouth behavior, and the ladies' section of the Grand Stand was "one grand bouquet of beauty, refinement and intelligence." This attendee opined that "today will ever be historic in the turf annals of Kentucky, as the first 'Derby Day,' of what I hope to see a long series of turf festivities," and his prediction was accurate.[1] Although Clark would suffer financial reverses during the Panic of 1893 that, in combination with his history of depression, would cause him to commit suicide in 1899, he lived long enough to see his ambitions for the Derby fulfilled. By 1881 the Derby winner was worth more than the farm on which he had been raised, and the race was more famous than the Belmont or Travers Stakes.[2] But its triumph was not a foregone conclusion, and a deeper delve into its history illuminates the contradictions that lie at the heart of its success.

Those who intend to attend the Preakness Stakes, in chronological terms the second of the Triple Crown races, will find the website of the competition's venue, Baltimore's Pimlico Race Course, of little help in choosing their outfits for the event. It offers no fashion tips, and its online gift shop sells only such functional items as T-shirts, jackets, and baseball caps, most of them black with flashes of yellow, the competition's official colors.[3] For the Belmont Stakes, the eponymous Long Island course's e-boutique offers similar types of casual wear; although the Longines watch company gives an annual "Prize for Elegance" to the most stylish attendee, the announcement of the prize offers no advice about how "elegance" is defined in this context.[4] But attendees of the Kentucky Derby can access not only dozens of newspaper and magazine articles and blog posts each year that comment in detail on Derby Day style, but the event's official website discusses this topic under the headings of "Visitor Information," "Party Planning," and "Derby Traditions," emphasizing the innately southern nature of the day and of racegoers' sartorial choices. Women are encouraged to "express their inner Southern Belle" by wearing colorful dresses and wide-brimmed hats, and men are requested to avoid stodgy business suits or sloppy sportswear in favor of the seersucker jackets, bow ties, and sockless loafers favored by the modern southern gentleman. Those who plan to watch the race at an off-site Derby party rather than at Louisville's Churchill Downs can imitate in-person watchers' style and feast on an "ultimate down-home spread with fun regional recipes" such as succotash, fried okra, and pecan pie, accompanied by the race's iconic drink, the mint julep, served in a commemorative glass.[5]

Derby fans might be surprised to discover that the race's official fashion partner is not a southern designer or shop but Vineyard Vines, a Connecticut-based clothing company whose founders were inspired by their childhood summers on Martha's Vineyard, in Massachusetts, or that the "down-home spread's" "regional recipes" were created by another national chain, Williams-Sonoma, based in the San Francisco Bay area.[6] But any complaints about a lack of southern authenticity would in reality be irrelevant. Although the Derby is promoted by its organizers and adored by many of its attendees as "an ultimate Southern tradition," an event that "celebrates Southern culture and . . . its rich traditions" and is marked by its host city of Louisville's "particular brand of Southern hospitality," the race and the festivities surrounding it do not actually represent the final flourish of antebellum southern racing culture. Instead, they originated as a post–Civil War initiative to bring the English-style racing that was becoming so popular in the North to a border state that prior to the conflict was renowned in the turf world as "a great horse-breeding State" but not as a site of top-level sport. Clark and his supporters had some success in attracting spectators to their track, but their financial resources were far inferior to those of New York, and Louisville was much smaller in terms of population than New York City and not comparable as a site of tourism or commerce. Within a few decades it became clear to Churchill Downs' promoters that they needed to offer something that would appeal not only to turf aficionados but to a broader audience, particularly of northern tourists, and by the early decades of the twentieth century they chose to promote an ideal of "southern charm" and hospitality that was a contemporary creation rather than a deeply rooted tradition.[7]

Antebellum Kentucky was not devoid of horse sport, unsurprisingly for a state that was not only geographically southern but drew many of its early settlers from Virginia, some of whom brought their bloodstock with them. By 1800 it was the home of ninety thousand horses, the highest number per capita of any state in the new nation, and the rapid transformation of central Kentucky's leaders from backwoodsmen such as the celebrated Daniel Boone to descendants and emulators of the Tidewater gentry encouraged a dedication to horse sport, especially after "that fine horse-flesh which came with early gentry from Virginia yielded foals with yet finer points and greater speed." As one commentator rhapsodized, "a true daughter of Virginia, Kentucky had racing from the earliest days, even when hostile savages still roamed her splendid forests," and another asserted that, following the influx of white settlers just after the Revolution, "the history of the State has almost been the history of the horse."[8] By the 1840s it boasted more tracks than any other state, even Virginia. A number of resorts, including Montgomery County's Olympian Springs and Spring Hill near Crab Orchard, included racing as a "daily amusement" in their round of leisure activities (hydropathic physician J. J. Moorman noted that "gaming is carried to a great excess" at these spas but that "good sport may be confidently expected" there), and the sport existed at least intermittently at Georgetown, Hickman, Hopkinsville, Madison, and Versailles.[9] By 1830 Louisville, whose jockey club was founded in 1823 after four decades of intermittent competitions around the city, sponsored regularly scheduled three-day spring and fall meetings at the Oakland course, located at today's Seventh Street and Magnolia Avenue, which boasted a large clubhouse and hotel, an elegant pavilion, and stabling facilities for a hundred horses, although the proposed "Chinese Pagoda . . . for ladies who many take an interest in the turf" was never built.[10] Locals described the Oakland races as attracting impressive fields of competitors and filling the city's hotels, particularly the luxurious Galt House, although one Louisvillian complained in 1839 that the spring races had attracted "all the Scoundrels between New Orleans and Pittsburgh," no doubt drawn by the scheduled match race between Gray Eagle and Wagner, the champions respectively of Kentucky and Louisiana, and a visitor from Shelby County deplored the necessity of sharing

Oakland House and Race Course, by Robert Brammer and Augustus A. Von Smith, ca. 1840. Speed Art Museum. Museum Art Fund Conservation supported in part by a grant from the National Endowment for the Arts. 1956.19.

his stagecoach with a number of "dirty mechanics . . . all anxious to get to the Louisville races."[11]

The state's second-largest city, Lexington, located eighty miles from Louisville, was its other principal site for racing throughout the antebellum era. Its first jockey club emerged in 1797 and its second in 1809, and after the latter folded in 1825, racing was organized the following year under the aegis of the Kentucky Association for the Improvement of the Breed of Horses. In 1842 the members hired Colonel Yelverton Oliver, renowned for his successes both in Virginia and at Oakland, to manage the Association Course, located at Fifth and Race Streets, which was the United States' second one-mile fenced dirt track, and replaced the circular Old William Track. Lexington racing benefited from its location in what had already become renowned as the Bluegrass Region, in which the soil, filled with phosphate and calcium, and the water, with a high mineral content, built strong equine bones and ensured the animals' overall hardiness; "about nine tenths of the horses trained in Kentucky are within a few miles" of the city.[12] Although one Lexingtonian echoed the plaints of many other southern turf fans by decrying the presence of "blacklegs and gamblers, collected by the races" in the autumn of 1851, and another thundered to an audience of students at the city's Transylvania University that the jockey club was one "to which no good citizen can . . . belong; and from which men of honour should turn, as from a thing that degrades them," on the whole the association's endeavors, combined with Oliver's "long experience and standing as a manager" and his renown for "spirit, liberality, and courtesy," resulted in the "embracing amongst its members [of] some of our best and most respected citizens," thus keeping racing on a respectable footing.

But most of the local turfmen among these "respected citizens" were also breeders, and "foreign horses," meaning those from outside the state, rarely competed at the Lexington track, a situation that both reflected and reinforced Kentucky's marginal place in the pre–Civil War racing world. The Scots aristocrat Sir Charles Augustus Murray, who visited Louisville in the mid-1830s, was impressed to see "one or two heats run in very good time," but he was scathing in his evaluation of the race's attendees as "common folk and non-members [who] were welcome as spectators and not required to pay admission." Murray asserted that the women were devoid of "beauty or fashion," and he deplored the presence of "the more rough and unpolished portion of society" among the men, among whom "the swearing of some of the lower orders . . . especially among the horse-traders and gamblers, would shock ears accustomed to the language of Billingsgate or a London gin-shop, so full is it of blasphemy." Even sophisticated Kentuckians such as Henry Clay were observed at the Lexington races "talking as loudly, betting as freely, drinking as deeply, and swearing as excessively as the jockeys themselves."[13] Most damningly, on occasion a shortage of entrants for a specific race resulted in the inclusion of an unpedigreed horse, as at Louisville in October 1822, when an aged mount named Boots was permitted to compete in order to make up the numbers, despite his having "neither scutcheon nor ancestry."[14]

These anecdotes indicate the gap that separated antebellum racing in Louisville and Lexington from the type that existed in Richmond, Charleston, Natchez, and New Orleans. Although many nineteenth-century Kentuckians prided themselves on their actual or embellished Old Dominion ancestry, "the world of Henry Clay was not simply a duplication of the world of George Washington and Thomas Jefferson." Neither the jockey club members of Louisville nor those of Lexington had any grounds upon which to imagine their race meetings as representing the gentility with which Virginian racing had long been associated, at least up to the early decades of that century, nor could they convince themselves, let alone others, that these gatherings were, like Race Week in Charleston, a social event capable of attracting the leading families of the entire South.[15] Henry Clay was both a wealthy planter and a leading politician who gained national renown as the "father of the American System" of internal improvements, but neither he nor his fellow Kentucky turfmen possessed either the vast riches or the impeccable hauteur of the Natchez Nabobs, nor could any city in their state offer domestic or foreign visitors the glamour and luxury with which racing and other forms of leisure were imbued in the emerging tourist mecca of New Orleans.[16] By the middle of the nineteenth century, American racing enthusiasts had no doubts as to the quality of Kentucky horses—was Lexington, named for his Kentucky birthplace, not the brightest star of the antebellum firmament?—but few were impressed by the social tone of its turf sport, which an Alabamian visitor described as attracting "a most ungentlemanly crowd of ringtailed roarers, gamblers, and loafers."[17] This situation resulted in a vicious cycle by which other southerners opted against bringing their horses to the state's tracks and simultaneously deplored the provincial nature of the competitions.

But the end of the Civil War dramatically altered the status of racing in the Bluegrass State. The conflict's end saw most of the antebellum South's most celebrated and prestigious courses damaged to the point that they were beyond repair, particularly at a time when the majority of prewar turf enthusiasts had little money to spare for such pursuits. The only leading track to revive the sport was Charleston's Washington Course, but the combination of a lack of funds among the members of the South Carolina Jockey Club and a paucity of top-quality horses in the area prevented these endeavors from matching those for which it had been renowned before the war. Kentucky, however, as a border state that had not seceded from the Union, had not experienced the same degree of wartime destruction; both Louisville and Lexington continued to hold meetings throughout the conflict, making Kentucky the only state in the nation to hold races in each year of the war. Its antebellum grandees had in many cases retained their fortunes, and their lauded horse-breeding operations had remained largely intact, with much of their bloodstock avoiding being commandeered by the Confederate forces or confiscated by those of the Union.[18] If racing on a scale and of a style redolent of the pre–Civil War South was to be revived below the Mason-Dixon Line, and the sport was not to be dominated entirely by the New York financiers and industrialists who had created and patronized Saratoga and Jerome Park and its successors, the Bluegrass State was the obvious site for such a rebirth.

In chapter 5, we saw that some leading southern turfmen who had the financial resources to travel to the North were willing to do so, especially to the Saratoga Springs racetrack, and that men such as Duncan Kenner were welcomed by northern racing aficionados as old friends rather than as wartime enemies. It might, however, seem more surprising that, just a few years after the Civil War's end, many southerners were eagerly promoting their states as tourist destinations for northern visitors and that significant numbers of the latter showed themselves equally eager to take up this offer. Tourism was not just a source of much-needed capital for the postwar South but an important aspect of the "romance of reunion" between North and South, a cultural development by which the more affluent white inhabitants of both regions soon came not only to forgive one another's wartime transgressions but to forge ties of friendship and romantic love across the sectional divide.[19] Travelogues abounded that rhapsodized over the natural beauty of southern landscapes, from the mountains and "hollers" of Appalachia to the moss-hung swamps of Louisiana, and many guidebooks emphasized not only the charms of the region's cities and resort areas but the appeal of its human resources, particularly its young white women, such as those who simultaneously "frown[ed] their defiance" and "twirl[ed] their fans" when they encountered the "Northern Beaux" who were their fellow guests at Virginia's White Sulphur Springs. The rustic, even shabby accommodations found at "the White" and other resorts, like the simple attire of its young female guests, struck some northern guests as pathetic, symbolic of the well-deserved humbling of a formerly arrogant slaveholding class. Mark Twain and some other northern commentators ridiculed the pseudomedieval ring tournaments that were held at a number of southern watering places, in which young men termed themselves "disinherited knights" and "pretend[ed] to worship a young woman from a modest wooden house in the neighborhood."[20] But these aspects appeared to others as reflective of pre-industrial ideals of authenticity and gentility that offered a refreshing change from the ostentatious display that soon characterized Saratoga and other sites of leisure in the former Union states.[21] Many of the men who less than a decade earlier had marched south as soldiers of "Father Abraham" were ready to consider returning as vacationers, some accompanied by their wives and children and others hoping to meet a "southern belle" of good family if little money who, according to the plotlines of a number of the era's popular romantic novels, might come north as a conqueror, not of the Union military but of the heart of one of its former officers, with whom she and their future offspring would play their small role in binding up the nation's wounds and reuniting its white citizens across regional lines.[22]

Kentucky faced greater challenges than most of the other southern states in fashioning itself into a popular destination for northerners. Although it had been a slave state from the time of its founding until the end of the war, it had remained neutral throughout the conflict, and slavery had never been as central to its economic, social, or political life as it had been in much of the Confederacy. Moreover, although it had for decades been home to a coterie of wealthy planters, these families had not emerged in the nation's imagination as an American aristocracy comparable to those of the states to its east and south, lacking the centuries-long pedigrees of the Tidewater Virginians and the Lowcountry South Carolinians or the glamour of the Natchez Nabobs and the "Creoles" and "Americans" of New Orleans. To the average post–Civil War American, northern or southern, Kentucky was as much associated with rough-and-ready frontiersman like Daniel Boone or the brawling flatboatmen whom Francophone New Orleanians sneeringly termed "Kaintucks" as it was with plantation beaux and belles; it was widely considered by outsiders to be a place characterized by lawlessness and violence among its white inhabitants, epitomized by the legendary feud between the Hatfield and McCoy clans on the Kentucky–West Virginia border.[23] It lacked the evocative landscapes of the Atlantic coast and the Appalachian Mountains, and its cities could not boast the European flavor of Charleston or New Orleans. Indeed, only the presence until 1865 of enslaved labor rendered the state culturally distinct from its Union-supporting neighbors Ohio and Indiana. Finally, its largest and most prosperous city, Louisville, had since its founding during the American Revolution been tightly connected to northern business interests, functioning more as a "midwestern commercial city" than as a "planters' city" such as Charleston, and was linked to the North by an extensive network of canals and railroads.[24]

On the other hand, Louisville had the advantage of geographical proximity to major population centers, especially those of the burgeoning Midwest. The city's postbellum boosters, its political and business leaders, were determined to reshape their city into the "Gateway to the South," a sobriquet still in use today, and a revival of Kentuckian Thoroughbred racing on a far grander level than that which had existed in the antebellum era was a major aspect of this endeavor. Considering the expertise that many Kentuckians possessed in the breeding, training, and racing of blooded horses, one might have expected that some of the members of the pre–Civil War turf elite would have taken a leading role in this task, but it was largely the initiative of Colonel Meriwether Louis Clark Jr., one of Louisville's leading citizens but not a passionate turfman. However, one of his grandfathers was William Clark, of the celebrated expedition to the Pacific, and the other, Samuel Churchill, was a founder and the first president of the Louisville Jockey Club and its Oakland track. Moreover, "Lutie" had briefly been a classmate of Richard Ten Broeck at West Point, and his marriage to the latter's wife's niece, Mary Martin Anderson, gave him a point of contact with the elite English racing men that Ten Broeck had met a decade earlier during his "American Invasion." Clark had not evinced a great interest in racing before 1872, but when a number of local horse breeders asked him to help them revive the sport, he traveled to France and England and drew upon Ten Broeck's acquaintanceship and familial social connections "with the intention of learning as much about racing in Europe as possible" and attended the annual Derby at Epsom Downs as the guest of Admiral Rous, the son of the Earl of Stradbroke, who was known as the "Dictator" of the English turf and was for decades the president of the English Jockey Club. There Clark, like some men of the New York racing fraternity, became fascinated by the English concept of the "feature race," a competition that would not only attract fans of horse sport or inhabitants of a specific locality or region but would assume a significant place in the national calendar of events and captivate the country's news media. If his native Louisville could host such an event, publicize it throughout the United States, and surround it with subsidiary activities that would appeal to those less interested in the competition itself, the city would profit in both financial and cultural terms.[25]

Louisville's Oakland course had closed before the outbreak of the Civil War and had been used as a training ground and accommodation for Kentucky's Union volunteers, and it had never entirely recovered from the exigencies of the Panic of 1837. Its replacement, Woodlawn, which opened in 1860 and was located to the northeast of the city, was initially able to lure "an immense crowd of sportsmen" and "the fashionable, in crowds," but it soon struggled to draw visitors, due to its inconvenient location, lack of facilities for guests, and difficult track surface. It finally shut in 1870, with the result that the Bluegrass State's most populous city was now without a racecourse.[26] Clark took advantage of this lacuna by setting out to build support among his fellow elite Louisvillians for the creation of a new, world-class track that could rival those that had opened in New York City during the past few years. On 22 June 1874 Louisville's leading politicians and businessmen assembled at the recently rebuilt Galt House, the city's most prestigious hotel, and voted in favor of the incorporation of a new Louisville Jockey Club that would build and manage such a track, with each of the Club's 320 members pledging one hundred dollars toward this goal. Clark leased eighty acres of land on Louisville's southern border from his uncles, Henry and John Churchill, and commissioned the construction of what soon became known as the nation's safest racetrack in terms of avoiding injury to horses, yet also boasted a very fast surface. The name to which it was referred by journalists from its opening and that became official a half century later, Churchill Downs, paid homage to the landowners and their enterprising nephew, and was also imitative of that of Surrey's Epsom Downs, the course that had hosted the English Derby since its inception almost a century earlier.[27]

Clark and his fellow Louisville boosters hoped that the city's new racecourse would succeed by drawing upon not only the area's renown as the breeding ground of fine horses but as a site of lavish hospitality, epitomized in the words of Margaretta Brown, the wife of one of Kentucky's first senators: "The profusion and display at our entertainments has ever been a matter of astonishment to strangers. For fear of being thought mean . . . we could not invite a friend to dinner, but the table must groan with costly piles of food." In 1871 these civic business and social leaders had deployed what they depicted as Kentucky's

Finish of the one-mile race at Churchill Downs in Louisville, Kentucky, Derby Day, 1901. Library of Congress, Prints and Photographs Division, Detroit Publishing Company Photograph Collection.

unique brand of sociability in convincing the city's and the state's politicians to invite the Russian Grand Duke Alexis, a son of Tsar Alexander II who was touring the United States, to make a stop in Louisville. Although the prince, tired from almost three months of constant travel, implied in a letter to his mother that he found the visit wearing, the local newspapers assured their readers that he had been delighted by his sojourn, and that the combination of the magnificence of his reception and his pleasure in it showed that the city was both highly sophisticated and warmly welcoming.[28]

Churchill Downs opened on 17 May 1875, and for its inaugural meeting Clark included three races, all of the "feature" variety: the Kentucky Derby, the Kentucky Oaks, and the eponymous Clark Handicap, which were modeled upon, respectively, the Epsom Derby, the Epsom Oaks, and the St. Leger Stakes. In line with both English precedent and the postwar American replacement of multiple heats with shorter dashes, the Derby was run over a mile and a half; the Oaks, for fillies, a mile and a quarter; and the Clark, a mere mile and an eighth.[29] The Kentucky Derby is actually a quarter mile shorter than its Epsom equivalent, reflecting "the emphasis on speed that would dominate the United States" from this time onward.[30]

On the eve of the track's opening, the *Louisville Courier-Journal* opined hopefully that the inaugural race meeting would bring "thousands of visitors from distant cities" and that Kentucky would gain renown as "the home of the finest horses in the world," and this optimism was not misplaced.[31] Not only were ten thousand people in attendance, but the crowd was impressively varied, including not only politicians and financiers but actresses, peddlers, and "the butcher, the baker [and] the ashcart driver." Women of color, often referred to as "mammies," sold country ham, fried fish, and fried chicken from beneath the stands, and visitors had their choice of gambling options. "Excitable gentlemen throng the new-fangled [pari-mutuel] betting machines to back their judgment on horse flesh, while 'carpet-bag' bookies take bets as low as a nickel [and] craps, chuck-a-luck, spindle and shell games flourish everywhere." Those visitors who were old enough to recall the 1839 match race between Wagner and Gray Eagle at Oakland gained "another event from which to date and by which to compare great gatherings of the wealth, fashion, and general elements of the population."[32]

If Clark and the men of the Louisville Jockey Club feared that the success of this inaugural season would be a one-off, their anxieties were assuaged the following year. The *Courier-Journal*'s correspondent at the "Great Race" crowed with delight about all aspects of the event, in which New Yorker (and "Patriarch") William Backhouse Astor's horse Vagrant triumphed. This competition attracted "the largest crowd I ever saw on any race track," and the attendees included former Kentucky governors James Fisher Robinson and Beriah McGoffin, their presence attesting to the course having already acquired an aura of respectability. And while the Kentucky turf had not experienced much success in luring out-of-staters to its races prior to the Civil War, in this second year of competition Churchill Downs was already attracting spectators from St. Louis, Cincinnati, Memphis, Detroit, Chicago, New Orleans, New York (including Saratoga's John Morrissey and the Manhattan turf leader Pierre Lorillard, whose horse Parole was a contender), and even California. "The ladies' stand was a bower of beauty," and the "beaux" in attendance were as stylish as the "belles," both "add[ing] color to the spectacle in elegant white vests, glossy boots, broad cravats, linen dusters, Shetland shawls, belt-bottomed skirts, ruffles, Leghorn straw hats and ten-button gloves." Importantly, the female spectators were ladies deemed to be of the utmost respectability; the *Courier-Journal*'s reporter closed his account with a list of the women present, including Miss Hattie Carr of Cambridge, Massachusetts, and Miss Mollie Bruce of New York City.[33]

Churchill Downs continued both to attract large crowds and to appeal to fashionable young women. In 1877 every seat in the ladies' stand was filled, "as it has become quite fashionable to attend the Derby and wager small amounts," as female guests had done at the Richmond and Charleston courses before the war. Sallie Downs, renowned as a "famous beauty of the South," was reported to have staked a pair of kid gloves on the Derby's outcome. An eighteen-piece orchestra was engaged to serenade the ladies, and although the jockey club did not follow antebellum practice by organizing a postrace ball for its members and their female guests, racegoers could attend a "hop" at the Galt House or D'Arcy's Bal de l'Opera at Woodland Gardens, a German beer garden. In 1879 a young man from St. Louis wrote to Lizzie Haldeman, the daughter of the founder and publisher of the *Courier-Journal,* of his disappointment that he was unable to visit her during Race Week, during which he assumed that she would be "in a great state of excitement." "Louisville is a little Paris during the Races," he stated, "everybody seeming to abandon themselves to pleasure and betting." By 1882 Derby Day attracted fifteen thousand guests, and a local young woman reported that her father and brother went to the Downs every day that week, despite the latter's "not getting rich betting . . . his horses come in last as a general thing."[34]

At antebellum southern racetracks, as at Jerome Park, both pleasure and betting were considerably more restrained than they were at Churchill Downs from its inception. If Clark's goal was that the Kentucky Derby would become as celebrated a national event in the United States as the Epsom competition was in Britain, it was acceptable, even desirable, that the former take on something of the social atmosphere of the latter. As one journalist commented in 1881, "caste is forgotten" at the Louisville course, and "the street gamin jostles the aristocrat"; the following year another reported that "gypsies, street singers, dancing Negroes, grandes dames, charlatans, high-hatted cavaliers, cabs, barouches and four-in-hands distinguish this crowd from any other in the world," and in 1883 a journalist claimed that "everybody was there, without regard to age, race, color, sex or previous condition of servitude." Such descriptions could as easily be applied to the activities at Epsom; indeed, an observer in 1886 stated that at Churchill Downs, "the crowd and venue resemble an English hunting print," perhaps a reference to William Powell Frith's internationally renowned painting *The Derby Day*. By the end of the 1880s Churchill Downs' racegoers included individuals as picturesque as the former outlaw Frank James and the flamboyant financier James Buchanan "Diamond Jim" Brady.[35]

Men such as James and Brady would not have been welcome at most antebellum racetracks. As a leader of a violent gang of robbers, the former would have been shunned by jockey club members and genteel audiences alike, and while the latter was not associated with criminality, he was also not a man who could be considered a gentleman, famed as he was for a lifestyle that was ostentatious even by the standards of the Gilded Age and for his extramarital relationship with the actress and singer Lillian Russell. Even among the *nouveaux riches* of 1860s New York, Leonard Jerome's combination of new money and conspicuous consumption and John Morrissey's involvement in disreputable forms of sport and commerce rendered these turf leaders controversial, not least to August Belmont, who despite his vast fortune despised excessive wagers and believed that they tainted the sport's reputation. Yet the presence of these men, along with carnivalesque personalities such as the widely exhibited dwarves Francis Joseph "General Mite" Flynn and Lucia Zarate, was generally viewed as evidence that Churchill Downs and its Derby had succeeded in attracting figures of fame and fascination, as continues today with the appearance at the Derby by figures of notoriety such as porn star Stormy Daniels and reality television personalities Kim Kardashian and NeNe Leakes.[36]

Churchill Downs also from the outset defied the conventional wisdom behind decades of racing by not merely permitting but facilitating the presence of various types of organized betting at the course. Clark opposed such activity on the part of track officials and reporters, believing that it represented a conflict of interest, but like his mentor Admiral Rous he realized that the sport could not survive without the financial support and the audiences generated by wagering opportunities, as the entry fees and gate receipts yielded from racing seasons that were only a few weeks long were unlikely to cover a course's annual operating expenses. Rous was alarmed by the prospect of heavy betting, or what Americans termed "plunging," and Clark, a man who was renowned for his integrity, disliked bookmaking and felt that pari-mutuel machines offered a more ethical option for placing bets. The "Paris Mutual" system allocated funds to the backers of the top three horses in each race, reserving a percentage of the sums wagered as a contribution to the track's management expenses, thus helping to stabilize its finances. But many turf visitors found this system slow to operate and felt that its mechanical nature detracted from the convivial ambience of the event that was central to their experience, choosing instead to place their wagers at betting parlors or with pool-sellers located trackside or at the Galt House. Matters came to a head in 1882, when the Brooklyn-based brothers Michael and Philip Dwyer, former butchers and meat wholesalers who had recently become the owners of New York's leading stable, and whose horse Hindoo had won the 1881 Derby, stated that they would not enter their much-heralded colt Runnymede in the Derby unless Clark allowed their friends to provide bookmaking services at Churchill Downs on the day of the race. So keen was "Lutie" to ensure the participation of this "star eastern 3 year old" that he grudgingly assented to the brothers' request. Having done so, he felt that he had no option but to open up the track to general bookmaking from then onward; by 1889 he acceded to bookmakers' demands for the removal of the pari-mutuel machines that they claimed were undermining their profits.[37] The significant growth in the final third of the century in the influence throughout the South of evangelical Christianity, like that of the Second Great Awakening decades earlier, generated considerable hostility toward all forms of gambling among its adherents, but Clark's reputation as a man of impeccable personal morality forestalled such anxieties from bringing the Downs into disrepute. As the *Courier-Journal* declared in 1891, he had "done all in his power to protect the unsuspecting from that curse of every race-course, the tout; he has disciplined jockeys, owners and trainers until crooked racing is unknown on the track," and he had followed his friend Admiral Rous's example by creating a uniform system of jockey weights and devising a corpus of racing rules of which some remain in use today.[38]

By 1886 many American turfmen would have concurred with the *Courier-Journal*'s claim that "the widespread interest in the [Kentucky Derby] meeting has attracted people from all over the country" and that the race was now, just a decade after its creation, "almost a national institution."[39] This outcome is remarkable when one considers that prior to the Civil War, Kentucky was far less significant as a site of racing than it was of horse breeding, that the state occupied a geographically and culturally liminal space between the North and the South, and that even the famously upright "Lutie" Clark accepted from Churchill Downs' opening the necessity of offering betting opportunities to its visitors. In the absence of this Louisville track, top-class southern racing would probably have remained as moribund for the rest of the nineteenth century as it had been immediately after Appomattox. But this regional triumph rested upon the incorporation of Kentucky's horses and their breeders and owners into the new world of postbellum racing that by 1875 was centered on New York. Although Clark and his fellow jockey club members were in far better financial shape after 1865 than most other members of the southern gentry, their fortunes were modest in comparison with those of the Lorillards, Astors, Whitneys, and Belmonts who now dominated American racing. Their state had avoided the extremes of wartime destruction, but Kentucky's many breeders of blooded horses had lost their antebellum clientele of turfmen from the Lower South, particularly the Lower Mississippi Valley, and they were therefore in desperate need of a new group of purchasers for their bloodstock. A northern "capitalistic aristocracy which had both leisure and cash" was eager to acquire the finest products of the Bluegrass region, but these horses were usually taken north to compete at the New York courses. Kentucky's "native nurserymen were essentially suppliers of that larger racing market," occupying the position of tradesmen rather than participants in post–Civil War horse sport.[40]

Breeding fine racehorses and selling them to some of the nation's richest men generated profits for a small number of Kentucky residents but could not on their own transform Louisville into a magnet for tourism and commerce, and urban boosters feared that the state's racing would be of interest largely to its inhabitants and on the margins of the sport in the broader national context, as it had been before the war. Yet, as we have seen, Clark and the Louisville Jockey Club were able from the opening of Churchill Downs to attract not only an affluent and respectable crowd that included many women but one that drew visitors from far beyond the borders of the state, and this success only increased over the next few years. The term "Triple Crown" was not in use until the 1920s, but from its inauguration the Kentucky Derby assumed the status of a great sporting occasion among the general public as well as within the racing fraternity.[41] Throughout the final third of the nineteenth century New York State, particularly New York City, was beyond any doubt the cynosure of Thoroughbred racing within the United States, and while some new courses opened in the formerly Confederate states, they lacked both top-class competition and social preeminence, rendering the South as marginal within the sport during this era as it had been dominant in the century before the Civil War. What factors allowed Kentucky, and Louisville and Churchill Downs in particular, to so rapidly rise to such an important position in the turf world of the late nineteenth century?

Beyond the outstanding quality of many of the horses bred and trained in the Bluegrass region, what Louisville and its track had to offer to northern turfmen was its southernness, or what Maryjean Wall termed its "neo-Southern identity," one centered upon a highly romanticized view of antebellum plantation life that was becoming increasingly popular throughout the United States as the Civil War moved from lived experience into the historical past. Generations of scholars have discussed the rise of the "Lost Cause" myth as a source of emotional comfort to white southerners in the face of crushing human and economic devastation and unwelcome societal upheaval, and central to this mythology was an image of the antebellum plantation that owed more to Sir Walter Scott's medievalist romances than it did to the reality of even the most elite slaveholders. This conception of southerners as gallant knights and fair ladies, of the plantation as an organic community comparable to a medieval fiefdom, and of enslaved people as loyal and contented retainers was a form of psychic compensation for men and women who were struggling to cope with many types of loss. It assured them that their values had been worth fighting for, that they could retain these principles even without the wealth and human property that had underpinned them, and that they could transmit them to a younger generation that had never known this society as it had existed before the war. As with the "romance of reunion," white women played a crucial role in support of this ideology, both as symbols of the allegedly superior virtues of the antebellum South and as participants in formal and informal groups dedicated to the commemoration and memorialization of Confederate soldiers.[42]

If it is easy to appreciate why this mythology was appealing to so many white southerners, it is not obvious why it was alluring to their northern neighbors, many of whom had resented and feared the plantation gentry of the "Slave Power" before the war and rejoiced in their marginalization at the end of the conflict. But the very successes of the northern states in the decades after the war's end, epitomized by the interlinked processes of industrialization, financialization, and urbanization, generated considerable anxiety among those who stood to benefit the most from these changes. Inhabitants of the Northeast had since the early republican period feared that their region's burgeoning cities, although their commercial prospects offered opportunities for domestic and foreign migrants and symbolized the new nation's rapid rise in international esteem, were places in which even wholesome youths from good rural or small-town stock could fall into corruption. The sensational Helen Jewett murder case of 1836, in which a prostitute was murdered in her bed in a high-class Manhattan brothel and one of her regular clients, a young clerk of respectable background, was accused of the crime, epitomized these concerns; many newspapers' readers were fascinated by this tale of sex and violence but were simultaneously horrified to discover that seemingly virtuous young people could fall into lives of vice and crime just a few months after arrival in a city.[43] Of course, cases such as this one were highly unusual, but "confidence men and painted women" apparently lurked everywhere in the United States' cities, even inveigling their way into unimpeachably respectable settings in order to lure innocent young men and women into all sorts of immorality.[44] The transformation of Manhattan into a "monied metropolis" immediately after the Civil War inflamed these anxieties. At the elite level, the Knickerbockers were socially and economically eclipsed by *nouveau riche* bankers and industrialists of humble or shady—or "shoddy"—origins. At the same time the city, like many others in the North and the Midwest, saw an influx of immigrants, the majority of whom were not "old stock" northern Europeans or even Irish, but Catholics and Jews from southern and eastern Europe who were widely viewed as unassimilable to American ways of life and thought to be destined to become criminals, subversives, or beggars.[45]

These rapid social changes encouraged some inhabitants of the northern states to feel a greater sympathy with the former Confederacy than would have been imaginable even a few decades earlier. Before the war, the image of the South as a society that was hidebound by tradition and unable or unwilling to engage with most aspects of modernity aroused the scorn of many northerners, but the social changes that accompanied the United States' emergence as a global economic and diplomatic power after the Civil War encouraged some to reevaluate their assessments of southern society. The sight of young southern men of genteel backgrounds donning homemade "armor," giving themselves knightly titles, and crowning as their "Queen of Love and Beauty" a young woman from a once wealthy but now impoverished family appeared ludicrous to some outsiders, a sign that southerners were unable to cope with their diminished circumstances and had retreated into childish fantasies; one southern clergyman even described these individuals as resembling "a sett of maniacks dancing in their chains."[46] But such pastimes could appear charmingly innocent in comparison with the ostentation that characterized the lifestyles of the emerging *haute bourgeoisie* of the era, such as the young women who came to breakfast at Saratoga's hotels sporting gold bracelets and attended the resort's evening events in an "excess of Paris fashion." In comparison with Saratoga and Newport, the facilities at southern resorts such as Virginia's White Sulphur Springs were rustic and even shabby, but their dilapidation charmed northern guests in its apparent authenticity. Whereas Saratoga's African American workers, most of whom had been born free in the North, were noticed for their confidence, those at "the White" were "old household or body servants" who had until recently been enslaved, and were praised for their courtesy. Even Robert E. Lee's presence in the years immediately after the war contributed to some northern guests' enjoyment of a visit to the springs, as "he does not talk politics, but he is ready to talk pleasantly and affably on any other topic," and he appeared to them not as an enemy commander but as a perfect example of "the old-fashioned Virginia gentleman" whose genial politeness made him "a welcome addition to every group."[47]

While many southern locales began their attempts to attract northern tourists through a partly invented tradition of "southern hospitality" within a few years of the Civil War's end, several decades would pass before Churchill Downs' management would adopt this strategy. The course was initially highly successful in attracting an audience, and its attendees came largely for the same reasons that others patronized the New York City racing venues: the allure of the sport itself or the appeal of the track as a place of fashionable leisure and sociability. But creating *ex nihilo* a course whose facilities for participants and guests alike were state-of-the-art was an expensive proposition, and despite the Downs' popularity, its income did not match its expenses, although Clark not only forewent his salary but contributed thousands of dollars from his own funds in its support. As a result, the purses on offer, even at the Derby, were small compared to those at the New York tracks and especially at Chicago's American Derby, established in 1884. Larger rewards attracted better and more famous horses and encouraged some midwesterners to abandon Churchill Downs in favor of the Windy City.[48] The situation was made worse by the onset of the Panic of 1893, probably the nation's worst financial crisis prior to the Great Depression of the 1930s. In 1894 the debt-laden complex was purchased by a group of investors led by the Louisville turfman and bookmaker William F. Schulte, incorporating it as the New Louisville Jockey Club. Clark, a man whose name was synonymous with integrity and possessed far greater social cachet than Schulte, was retained as the course's presiding judge, but in 1899 he committed suicide, having suffered "melancholia" for years as well as distress at his financial situation and what he considered unwelcome if necessary changes to the track to which he had devoted the latter half of his life.[49]

The Schulte regime made a number of vital alterations to Churchill Downs' physical fabric, dramatically upgrading the stables and replacing the increasingly dilapidated grandstand with a new structure "adorned with the now-iconic twin spires." But the 1890s were a difficult decade for racing and for Kentucky alike. The shady practices of "outlaw" tracks such as the aforementioned Guttenberg, including the drugging of horses and the bribery of jockeys, became linked in public opinion with the sport as a whole, causing a number of state authorities to ban it and respectable folk to stay away from the surviving venues. The nation as a whole felt the effects of the 1893 economic crisis for several years thereafter, but in Kentucky they were combined with vigilante violence that affected not only the state's African American population but its political leaders; in 1900 Kentucky gained the unwelcome distinction of seeing the first murder of a sitting governor when William Goebel was shot on his way into the State Capitol building in Frankfort. Daniel Boone had been in his grave for nearly a century, but his homeland appeared to have regressed to the frontier mentality of his lifetime.[50]

Under such circumstances Schulte and his associates found it as difficult as their predecessors had to ensure the course's prosperity and reputation, and in 1902 they relinquished operational control to a group of socially esteemed

Louisvillians, including the city's mayor, Charles Granger, but more importantly to Martin J. Winn, widely known as "Matt" and eventually accorded the cognomen "Mr. Derby." Winn's father was an Irish-born grocer, and Matt was first a traveling salesman and then a partner in a local clothing business. Although he lacked an impressive pedigree, he was both a smart businessman and a gregarious city booster famed for his love of fine bourbon and cigars. Perhaps more importantly, in 1904 Governor John C. W. Beckham gave him the honorary title of "Colonel" in recognition of his services to Louisville and to Kentucky in general. That Winn had never served in the military was insignificant; he had been recognized as a person of merit, and the title was the final element in the persona he deployed in the service of Churchill Downs.

Like Schulte, Winn and his associates made a number of reforms at the track, but on a wider scale: expelling the bookmakers and reintroducing pari-mutuel machines in order to fend off the most aggressive antigambling sentiment and taking advantage of New York's harsh new laws against wagers to convince the state's, and nation's, leading turfmen to participate in the Derby and other feature races. Winn claimed to have watched the inaugural Derby from his father's grocery wagon and to have attended each one since then; he was "appalled" by the possibility that the Downs might close and its famous competition come to an end, and he devoted the rest of his long life to ensuring that the track would not just survive but flourish. And the Derby did become, as Clark had hoped, as famous and beloved a national event as its English equivalent. Winn was aided in this goal by what one scholar has termed the "creation of a Confederate Kentucky" as "a place full of colored people, pretty girls, and polite men," replacing the state's image of frontier violence with one of the southern gentility upon which other locales in the region had capitalized for a generation.[51]

The 1890s witnessed the birth of "plantation literature," a genre of fiction that offered readers, particularly northern and midwestern city-dwellers, an escape into "a more pleasant past depicted in the lifestyle of the antebellum South." Thomas Nelson Page is today the most widely known of these authors; as the son of a planter and the descendant of several of the First Families of Virginia, his work, epitomized by the story collection *In Ole Virginia,* portrayed the Old Dominion as a land of cavaliers and their ladies fair, surrounded by "good old darkies" who were happy to work for masters they loved.[52] Although much of Kentucky was more similar to either the urban Midwest or rural Appalachia, the immensely popular work of Annie Fellows Johnston incorporated the Bluegrass region into this mythology. Her twelve-volume "Little Colonel" series of novels for children began with the premise of the earlier genre of romances of reunion: a Kentucky colonel had disowned his daughter after she married a Yankee and moved with him to the North, but father and daughter were reconciled by the latter's five-year-old daughter, born and raised in New York but immediately at home in the town of Lloydsboro, "one of the prettiest places in all Kentucky." Grandfather and granddaughter become so close that the latter rejoices in gaining the nickname "the Little Colonel." A generation later F. Scott Fitzgerald ridiculed "the warm milk of Annie Fellows Johnston," but her books sold more than a million copies and retained their popularity among (white) American children for decades; in 1934 Shirley Temple, Hollywood's top box-office draw, starred in a film of *The Little Colonel.* Although not as widely read as Johnston's novels, those written for adults by James Lane Allen and John Fox Jr. similarly focused on the charm and gentility of the Bluegrass region, personified in the figure of the Kentucky colonel and his faithful Black retainers. These fantasies of a simpler, more stable, yet also more romantic society than that of a North or a Midwest marked by mass immigration and increasing social inequality encouraged nonsouthern readers to believe that the Civil War had been fought to preserve a distinctive way of life rather than to defend the institution of slavery, and thus a "Kentucky colonel" could be transformed from an enemy combatant to a charming representative of chivalry.[53]

At Churchill Downs, Winn capitalized on the counterfactual co-optation of Kentucky into a sentimentalized version of the Confederacy by incorporating old and new traditions into Churchill Downs' rituals. In his first year at the Downs, he decreed that the mint julep, made with Kentucky bourbon and served in a new souvenir glass each year, was the Derby's official drink, honoring both the state's century-long production of fine whiskey and the legend of Clark's having served the famous Polish actress Helena Modjeska a julep at a pre-Derby breakfast. That same year he decreed that the Derby winner should be draped in a garland of red roses, and in 1924 he made official the vernacular practice by which attendees sang Stephen Foster's "My Old Kentucky Home" as the horses made their way to the starting line.[54]

Paradoxically, the performance of supposedly timeless southern authenticity that attracted northern and midwestern visitors to the region influenced Churchill Downs' management to jettison some of the longest-standing traditions of the southern turf. The most obvious of these changes was the replacement of African American jockeys by white riders. From the end of the American Revolution until the outbreak of the Civil War, white jockeys were a rarity at the American track; indeed, jockeying was widely stigmatized as "n——r work," other than on the rare occasions in which a leading turfman chose to ride his own horse or a celebrated white jockey, usually English- or Irish-born, was selected to ride a champion. The overwhelming majority of jockeys were enslaved boys and men who were the property of the breeders, trainers, and owners of racing stock, and who were initially selected to be trained to ride because they possessed or could be forced to develop and maintain a "trim figure" and a weight of less than a hundred pounds, in line with rules shared across the region's jockey clubs. They were "brought up in the stables," and although they were "subjected to the regular training process and preparation for riding," it was their "familiarity with their master's thoroughbreds," along with their inability to leave the plantation or to choose an alternate occupation, that made them ideal jockeys.[55] A small number of these individuals were able to parlay their triumphs at the track into manumission, albeit usually with the proviso that they continued to ride exclusively for their former owners. A few became famous even beyond the turf world, such as Charles Stewart, who was first a groom, then an exercise rider, and then the top jockey for William Ransom Johnson before becoming the latter's principal horse trainer.[56] For some spectators, Black riders were an integral part not only of the sport but of its spectacle; to southerners their presence was simply the normal order of things, whereas to English or European guests it provided a piquant and picturesque difference to their turf practices. But northern visitors did not favor this indubitably southern practice; most had little familiarity with people of African descent, and just as their female relatives preferred to hire white women or girls as housekeepers, cooks, maids, and nannies, turfmen from the North were reluctant to entrust the health and turf success of their fabulously expensive stock to boys or men of color. It was primarily Irish migrants or their American-born sons whom New Yorkers preferred in the saddle, just as they did in the kitchen or the nursery.

At the inaugural Derby, fourteen of the fifteen jockeys were African American, and the winning horse, Aristides, was ridden by Oliver Lewis and trained by Ansel Williams, both of whom were men of color. Another Black jockey, Isaac Burns Murphy, was victorious in the Derby in 1884, 1890, and 1891, as were Willie Simms in 1896 and 1898 and Jimmy Winkfield in 1901 and 1902. But Winkfield would be one of the last Black jockeys to compete in a Triple Crown race for more than a century, and Simms remains the only one to have won each of the races that would later constitute the Triple Crown. Although their victories and those of Lewis and Murphy, and the fact that Black jockeys rode the winning horses in more than half of the first twenty-eight Derbies, proved that African Americans were as able to succeed in the postbellum short dash races as they had in the earlier system of heats, the prejudices of northern owners and, soon thereafter, of the increasing number of white riders essentially forced horsemen of color out of the top class of American racing for most of the twentieth century.[57]

Foster's song "My Old Kentucky Home" remains an integral aspect of Kentucky Derby tradition. The Derby's website asserts that "in the world of sports, there is not a more moving moment than when the horses step onto the track for the Kentucky Derby post parade and the band strikes up 'My Old Kentucky Home' and 160,000+ people sing along."[58] The song, published in 1853, is narrated in the voice of an enslaved person who speaks of "the time when the darkies have to part," when the bondspeople of a Kentucky plantation are put up for sale and dispersed to slave traders who will sell them to planters in the Lower Mississippi Valley, but who continue to long "for the old Kentucky home far away." Beyond the irony inherent in these words being sung by a mostly white crowd, some of whose members are the descendants of slaveholders, lies another: that just as enslaved people were forced to leave the Bluegrass State for "the field where the sugar-canes grow" in Louisiana, Black jockeys were pushed off the track at Churchill Downs, and, still more ironically, this change was accepted and encouraged by northern turfmen and spectators who were lured to Kentucky by its inhabitants' performance of an "authentic" form of southernness.

For this performance to succeed, it was necessary that Kentucky, or at least its Derby, represent "a land of benevolent white masters, genteel white mistresses, and simple and loyal blacks pining for the comforts and certainty of a land before the traumas of the war and Reconstruction." Free men of color, who were central to the competition as a whole and to the success or failure of a top-class Thoroughbred, with the possibility of gaining acclaim and money should their mount win, were not part of this imaginary, even if for generations the southern racetrack had been "a place run on the labor and skill of black men." Kentuckians and northerners alike were happy to purchase trackside snacks from Black women to whom they referred as "mammies," or to observe African Americans perform domestic or manual labor at the course, but they were not pleased to see them in roles in which they displayed expertise and gained money and acclaim.[59] Winn encouraged this "quasi-theme park version of a bygone era" by employing a "long line of colored boys," who of course were actually adult men, to wait upon him in public as his valets, and during his reign at the Downs the author of the Works Progress Administration's Kentucky guidebook reflected this attitude, describing Black stable hands and exercise riders as "carefully selected for their tact, skill, and disposition" and caring for horses with "an attitude . . . of a colored mammy toward the 'white chile' in her care."[60]

While contemporary Derby attendees can, and are encouraged to, believe that what they are experiencing represents treasured antebellum traditions, the greatest difference between the pre–Civil War southern turf and its replacement lies not with racing regulations or communal rituals but with the apparent indifference of Churchill Downs' management to spectators' behavior. Not only were various forms of wagering accepted from Churchill Downs' opening, but the "masses" were encouraged to attend, watching the race not from atop a nearby hill, as at Jerome Park, or at a respectful distance from jockey club members and other men and women of genteel background, but from what became known as the infield, the circle of grass situated within the oval of the track. These spectators could not observe the full panorama of the race, but they were literally at the center of the action, and were liberated from the behavioral constraints associated with the grandstands. This practice was inaugurated in 1883, at which time more than ten thousand people attended the Derby, and this central space was "filled with a crowd that reached from stretch turn to finish point"; the number of spectators doubled just two years later, and by 1900 reached thirty thousand.[61] Moreover, Clark mandated that admission to the infield should be free of charge, a practice that was suspended after his death but reinstated a few years later and remained in force until 1920, by which time "demand for tickets was too high to justify free admission." The policy of the "free field" gave the Derby a "country fair" atmosphere, with some spectators driving their wagons and buggies to the middle of the course. This "Fifteenth-Amendment crowd," which included men, women, and children of all races, resembled that which so many visitors found intriguing at Epsom, and its behavior was sedate in comparison with that of Triple Crown racing audiences from the 1960s onward. Nonetheless, it would have horrified the men of the prewar jockey clubs of Richmond, Charleston, and Natchez, as well as August Belmont, who was unapologetic in his conviction that racing was a sport not just by but for the rich, and that the only reputable type of track was one that could function as their playground, with people outside this charmed circle to be at most seen and not heard.[62]

What accounts for this dramatic departure from antebellum racing's near obsession with spectatorial decorum? The most significant factor is the original motivation for the creation of the new Louisville Jockey Club and its racecourse. As we have seen, although its predecessors, particularly those located in the Upper South, hoped to attract favorable attention to their locales, and to encourage out-of-towners to spend money there, their primary goal was to showcase the excellence of their racing, in terms of both sport and sociability, as a way to retain or regain hegemony in and on behalf of their community. As long as each season's revenues covered its expenses, profit was not of great concern, and success was measured not by the size of the crowds but by their composition and behavior, and thus the impression they made upon outside observers. The postbellum situation in Louisville, though, was very different. Although the city had offered horse sport before the war, and its environs were celebrated for the outstanding quality of the horses they produced, its tracks were not as renowned as those elsewhere in the South. "Lutie" Clark was a municipal booster more than he was a turfman, and his desire to create a new jockey club and track stemmed from his and other municipal leaders' concerns about Louisville's prosperity and its ability to attract commerce and investment from outside Kentucky, particularly from the North and the Midwest, with which it had long been connected. Both the city and the state had emerged after the American Revolution, and for decades thereafter were associated primarily with riotous frontier-dwellers and roistering riverboat men rather than planter-aristocrats who valorized a strict code of public conduct. And, perhaps most significantly, the tourists that Clark and his successors, especially Winn, hoped to lure to their Derby were drawn there by a sense of this competition as a national occasion, and by its venue's successful presentation of a version of "authentic" southern identity that preserved what they considered the most appealing aspects of antebellum life while allowing them to ignore the issues that had precipitated the Civil War and have continued to trouble the nation ever since.

Conclusion

For most contemporary Americans, horse racing is a subject of interest for a single day in early May, on which the Kentucky Derby takes place at Louisville's Churchill Downs racetrack. A minority are either personally involved in or deeply passionate about the sport, but for the rest, Derby Day offers the opportunity to place a bet in the hope of picking the winner, to gather in a bar to watch the event on a big-screen television, or to hold a social event at which the guests can dress in seersucker suits and flamboyant hats, sip mint juleps, and play at being southern gentry. But for those who, like me, grew up in the Albany, New York, area, racing has a different and more intense meaning, due to our city's proximity to the town of Saratoga Springs, just thirty miles away. The Saratoga Race Course is famous for its age—founded in 1863, it is widely, if inaccurately, renowned as the oldest currently operating track in the United States—and for its hosting of the Travers Stakes, a competition that predates the establishment of the three Triple Crown races and that is often referred to by racing fans as the "Midsummer Derby."[1] To residents of the area, however, with the exception of the small population of serious turf enthusiasts and trackside gamblers, it is the social milieu that surrounds the sport that provides most of the excitement. Every August, the usually sleepy town of Saratoga, best known for the other eleven months of the year as the home of Skidmore College, overflows with visitors, and those who attract the greatest attention from local media are not the jockeys and trainers who are responsible for the winning of races or the setting of records, or even the various celebrities who make their way to the track each summer, but the members of the long-established New York families whose names are redolent of the novels of Edith Wharton, and who have been patrons of the Saratoga Race Course for more than a century.[2] Chief among these for more than fifty years were Cornelius Vanderbilt ("Sonny")

Whitney and his wife, Marie Louise ("Marylou"); his family has owned more winning Thoroughbred horses than any other in the history of the sport in America, and she was known as the "Queen of Saratoga" for her social and philanthropic endeavors. In terms of media coverage and public interest, Mrs. Whitney's annual ball, held every year between 1960 and 2012 at the town's Canfield Casino pavilion, eclipsed all but the most dramatic racetrack doings.[3] Neither I nor anyone of my acquaintance ever attended the Whitney Ball, but we nonetheless consumed media coverage of the event, which Mrs. Whitney might attend costumed as Little Bo-Peep or Glinda the Good Witch from *The Wizard of Oz*. We might snicker at the sight of this increasingly elderly woman dressed in pink from her enormous hat to her stiletto-heeled shoes, or wearing a hoop skirt and a powdered wig, but at the same time we respected her, because she was someone who might be considered an American aristocrat rather than a person of fleeting celebrity, and although she clearly loved the spotlight, she used her social capital to raise large amounts of money for charities, including those that benefited the essential but often poorly paid Latino and African American grooms and exercise riders employed at the Saratoga track.

The ongoing involvement of old-money families such as the Whitneys, who epitomize both glamour and community spirit, has helped the Saratoga Race Course maintain its reputation as a venue that not only attracts the nation's leading Thoroughbred horses and jockeys but offers its guests, whether they are long-standing club members or first-time visitors who have paid a few dollars for general admission, an atmosphere of old-fashioned elegance and decorum. Although patrons are allowed both to bring their own alcoholic beverages and to purchase them at bars located throughout the complex, security staff are vigilant in policing drinking behavior, preventing the occurrence of the notorious scenes of communal excess that occur each year among the infield attendees at the Kentucky Derby, and still more so at Baltimore's Preakness Stakes. Those seated in the grandstand may dress casually, as long as they wear shirts and shoes, but all of the other viewing areas have strict dress codes that are subject to "management's discretion," and the track's website states that "even when not required, many choose to honor these cherished traditions [of elegant attire for both men and women] when heading to the track." This atmosphere of self-conscious graciousness and formality has been, and remains, so prevalent at this racecourse that in 2007, when Saratoga was selected as the theme for the newest and largest of the resort complexes at Florida's Walt Disney World, it was chosen not only for the fame of the track and of the nearby mineral springs and spa that were the original source of the town's success, but because of its appeal to "adult nostalgia for a genteel past."[4]

The most coveted summer job in the area, for those who had reached New York State's then legal drinking age of eighteen, was waiting tables at the Saratoga Race Course clubhouse. Many of us had held similar jobs at other local restaurants and had not particularly enjoyed this line of work, and our parents would probably have frowned on our seeking employment in bars or at betting parlors, but to us, and to them, Saratoga racing represented a very different atmosphere, one devoid of seediness or danger. The clubhouse was a physically attractive environment, and we heard tales of patrons whose wagers had paid off leaving lavish tips for their servers, but beyond that appeal we were attracted by what we considered the romance of the track, regardless of the level of our knowledge of or interest in the sport. The members of the New York Racing Association (NYRA), the course's operators, are entirely aware of the fact that, for many visitors, the excitement of seeing "a dynamite collection of the best horses from throughout the country" is merely the icing on the cake that is "the gorgeous and leisurely pleasures of the track itself." The late sportswriter Walter Wellesley ("Red") Smith's directions for traveling to Saratoga from New York City read, "drive north for about 175 miles, turn left on Union Avenue, then go back 100 years in time," and when the NYRA drew up its plans for a major redevelopment of the entire complex in commemoration of its 2013 sesquicentennial, its stated aim was not to modernize the facilities beyond the changes needed for safety and access but "to preserve and restore the historic character of the Race Course as a whole."[5]

In contrast to Churchill Downs' performance of an "authentic" southernness based in a plantation myth that developed after the Civil War and that the track's boosters marketed to northern and foreign visitors as invoking the romance of the Old South without the discomfort of references to slavery and conflict, Saratoga has no need to rewrite its history; it has merely to emphasize elements thereof, such as dressing formally to attend a sporting event, that have become unusual in modern American culture. Although neither the Travers Stakes nor any other day of the eight-week season gains the attention accorded the Derby, Saratoga is significantly more successful than Churchill Downs in attracting large audiences every day that it is open. In the summer of 2021, despite the ongoing threat of the COVID-19 virus, the course attracted more than a million spectators, with an average of twenty-six thousand per day. Not only did those numbers increase in 2022, but the average daily wager total was the highest in the track's 150-plus-year history.[6] Clearly, many people are keen to buy what Saratoga's management is selling.

This book has examined tracks in six states, from the beginnings of Thoroughbred racing in the American colonies through the end of the nineteenth century, and it has illuminated the transition in American racing from a local to a national sport, and from one in which jockey clubs that represented urban or regional elites deployed racing in order to maintain their and their locale's importance to one in which profit is central and management is the bailiwick of professionals. We might conclude that the current situation at Baltimore's Pimlico Race Course is the logical outcome of the changes discussed throughout the book, that today very few people are interested in racing other than on a couple of days each year on which particularly famous races are scheduled, and that even then their interest is piqued more by a desire to participate in a nationally renowned and publicized event, especially one associated with festive excess, than by a real engagement with the sport. But Saratoga's trajectory implies that racing's decline in the United States is not irreversible and that people will come to a racetrack not just because they want to be part of a famous feature competition or spend a day engaged in the bacchanalian pleasures of the infield, but because they seek, and find, a type of organic fellowship, even if this community is imagined, at a course whose management is keen to emphasize every aspect of its history, and at which at least a few families have over generations maintained their commitment to it in a manner that is simultaneously philanthropic and glamorous. This study has argued that, over centuries and across regions, American racing has always offered something more to its participants and audiences than the aesthetic enjoyment of horses in motion, the thrill of high-quality competition, or the possibility of a successful wager. The question remains whether this "something more" can be identified and marketed to today's audiences, and if they will respond as eagerly as Americans of the past did to this sport as both entertainment and ethos.

NOTES

INTRODUCTION

1. "Maryland Jockey Club Reports Record Preakness Weekend," *Bloodhorse*, 19 May 2019, www.bloodhorse.com/horse-racing/articles/233774/maryland-jockey-club-reports-record-preakness-weekend.

2. Frank Vespe, "Pimlico to Run 12 Days of Racing in 2017," *Bloodhorse*, 21 December 2016, www.bloodhorse.com/horse-racing/articles/218545/pimlico-to-run-12-days-of-racing-in-2017; Judith Weinraub, "Sure Bet for the Preakness: 32,000 Baked Crab Cakes," *Washington Post*, 18 May 2005.

3. Other aspects of the plan were similarly unwelcome to racing fans: the turf and dirt tracks would be realigned from their long-established sites to make room for a private development that would include a hotel, shops, and a supermarket.

4. "Horse-Racing: Pimlico Track Should Be Demolished and Rebuilt, Study Says," www.reuters.com/article/us-horseracing-pimlico-idUSKBN10E0RM; Maryland Stadium Authority homepage, www.mdstad.com/; Andrew Beyer, "Wrinkled Old Pimlico Is in Need of a Facelift," *Washington Post*, 13 May 1999; Bill Ordine, "Slots Money Could Fund Racetrack Improvements," Maryland Department of Agriculture, 15 February 2013, https://news.maryland.gov/mda/news-clippings/2013/02/15/slots-money-could-fund-racetrack-improvements/.

5. Jace Evans and Sam Schmieder, "At Pimlico, Racing Fans Remember When Tracks, Not Casinos, Drew Crowds," *Capital News Service*, https://cnsmaryland.org/gambling/community/pimlico.html.

6. The Jockey Club, *22nd Annual Roundtable Conference on Matters Relating to Racing* (New York: The Jockey Club, 1974), 9.

7. William Norman Thompson, "The Interstate Horseracing Act of 1978," in *Gambling in America: An Encyclopedia of History, Issues, and Society*, by Thompson (Santa Barbara, CA: ABC-CLIO, 2001), 199.

8. See Iris Bergmann, "He Loves to Race—or Does He? Ethics and Welfare in Racing," in *Equine Cultures in Transition: Ethical Questions*, ed. Jonna Bornemark et al. (New York: Routledge, 2019), 117–33; Tanya McGuane et al., "'You Wanna Ride, Then You Waste': The Psychological Impact of Wasting in National Hunt Jockeys," *Human Kinetics Journal* 33 (2018): 129–36; and Adam Nelson, "Hot to Trot: Why Dressage Is Yielding Such Interest from Fans and Sponsors," *Sport Business*, 28 September 2017, www.sportbusiness.com/2017/09/hot-to-trot-why-dressage-is-yielding-such-interest-from-fans-and-sponsors/.

9. Patrick Battuello, "Shuttered U.S. Racetracks (since 2000)," *Horseracing Wrongs*, https://horseracingwrongs.org/shuttered-u-s-tracks-since-2000/; Hadley Meares, "The Glitz and Glamour of Hollywood Park," *Curbed Los Angeles*, 20 September 2018, https://la.curbed.com/2018/9/20/17691686/hollywood-park-inglewood-race-track-history.

10. William Parker Cutler and Julia Perkins Cutler, eds., *Life, Journals, and Correspondence of Rev. Manasseh Cutler, LL.D* (Cincinnati: Robert Clarke, 1888), vol. 2, 143; Clay McShane and Joel A. Tarr, "The Centrality of the Horse in the Nineteenth-Century American City," in *The Making of Urban America*, ed. Raymond A. Mohl, 2nd ed. (Lanham, MD: SR, 1997), 118.

11. *New York Times*, quoted in Kimberly Gatto, *Belmont Park: The Championship Track* (Charleston, SC: History Press, 2013). In the late nineteenth century, the Bowery was the home of the poorest New Yorkers, and Fifth Avenue that of the richest.

12. Charles E. Trevathan, *The American Thoroughbred* (New York: Macmillan, 1905), 294, 304–5.

13. Robert Cantwell, *Bluegrass Breakdown: The Making of the Old Southern Sound* (Urbana: University of Illinois Press, 1984), 144, 232.

14. Joseph Roach, *Cities of the Dead: Circum-Atlantic Performance* (New York: Columbia University Press, 1996), 122.

15. Daniel Sergeant, "Place Bonding, Fan Identification, and Nostalgia and Fenway's Future: Observations about Red Sox Nation" (PhD diss., University of Florida, 2012), 132.

16. The Derby, the most popular annual race in the United States, attracts 150,000 to 160,000 spectators, whereas an average racing day draws only a few thousand to Churchill Downs (Maggie McGrath, "Kentucky Derby Special: How 143-Year-Old Churchill Downs Keeps Betting—and Winning—on a Dying Sport," *Forbes.com*, 3 May 2018, www.forbes.com/sites/maggiemcgrath/2018/05/03/churchill-downs-doubles-down-on-the-success-of-the-kentucky-derby/#4b94cc3f1c80). See also Sarah Bray, "Inside the Kentucky Derby's Exclusive, Secret Clubhouse," *Town & Country*, 12 May 2016, www.townandcountrymag.com/leisure/sporting/news/a6127/kentucky-derby-the-mansion/.

17. Anthony Szczesiul, *The Southern Hospitality Myth: Politics, Race, and American Memory* (Athens: University of Georgia Press, 2017), 2; Drew Whitelegg, "From Smiles to Miles: Delta Air Lines Flight Attendants and Southern Hospitality," *Southern Cultures* 11 (2005): 7–27; *Southern Hospitality Natural Foot Care*, www.sohofeet.com/.

18. Mark McKee, "A Day at the Races: How to Dress for the Kentucky Derby," *The Manual*, 4 May 2023, www.themanual.com/fashion/best-kentucky-derby-mens-outfits/.

19. "Derby Traditions," *Kentucky Derby*, www.kentuckyderby.com/history.

20. "Kentucky Derby to Allow Spectators in September," *New York Times*, 25 June 2020.

21. Heather Braga, "35 Things You Can Wear to Watch the Kentucky Derby," *BuzzFeed*, 22 April 2019, www.buzzfeed.com/hbraga/things-to-wear-to-a-kentucky-derby-party; *Kentucky Derby Store*, https://store.kentuckyderby.com/?pk_vid=fcb771c79b84bc001595539037aa1e03; Churchill Downs Annual Report 2019, https://ir.churchilldownsincorporated.com/static-files/0526f0e6-66ee-4363-8cf3-c758657a48db; "How the Kentucky Derby Makes a Business Impact Each Year," *Business First Family*, https://businessfirstfamily.com/business-impact-kentucky-derby/.

22. "Kentucky Derby Museum Celebrates Best Year Ever," *Kentucky Derby Museum*, 8 October 2019, www.derbymuseum.org/Media-And-Press/Article/323/Kentucky-Derby-Museum-celebrates-Best-Year-Ever.

23. On boxing in the nineteenth-century United States, see Elliott J. Gorn, *The Manly Art: Bare-Knuckle Fighting in America*, updated ed. (1986; Ithaca, NY: Cornell University Press, 2012), esp. 129–36, 273.

24. "The South Carolina Jockey Club. Its Prospects—The General Prevalence of Racing, &c," *Charleston Mercury*, 14 February 1846. Richard Stott defines blacklegs as "nomads, traveling from town to town with their gambling paraphernalia and running games in taverns or rented houses" (Stott, *Jolly Fellows: Male Milieus in Nineteenth-Century America* [Baltimore, MD: Johns Hopkins University Press, 2009], 120); Hunt Boulware, "'Unworthy of Modern Refinement': The Evolution of Sport and Recreation in the Early South Carolina and Georgia Lowcountry," *Journal of Sport History* 35 (2008): 440.

25. J. Milton Mackie, *From Cape Cod to Dixie and the Tropics* (New York: G. P. Putnam, 1864), 95; *Charleston Courier*, 23 February 1830.

26. An 1830 list of the nation's racetracks enumerated forty-seven such facilities, of which just six were located north of the Mason-Dixon Line: one in Ohio, one in New Jersey, and two each in New York and Pennsylvania ("Sporting Intelligence: List of Race Courses in the United States," *American Turf Register and Sporting Magazine* 2, no. 2 [October 1830]: 93). Between 1830 and 1861 a number of additional tracks opened in the South, particularly throughout the Lower Mississippi Valley, but none in the North.

27. Of particular influence in this debate is the "herrenvolk thesis," first promulgated by the American historian George M. Frederickson and influenced by the Belgian sociologist Pierre van den Berghe, which stated that the existence of Black slavery was the foundation of white unity throughout the antebellum South (Frederickson, *The Black Image in the White Mind: The Debate on Afro-American Character and Destiny, 1817–1914* [Middletown, CT: Wesleyan University Press, 1971], 61, 62). More recent interventions include Jeff Forret, *Race Relations at the Margins: Slaves and Poor Whites in the Antebellum Southern Countryside* (Baton Rouge: Louisiana State University Press, 1996); David Brown, "A Vagabond's Tale: Poor Whites, Herrenvolk Democracy, and the Value of Whiteness in the Late Antebellum South," *Journal of Southern History* 79 (2013): 799–840; and Keri Leigh Merritt, *Masterless Men: Poor Whites and Slavery in the Antebellum South* (New York: Cambridge University Press, 2017).

28. The work of Peter Burke, although focused on early modern Europe, was central to the development of a deeper understanding of the significance of sport and leisure in daily life; see Burke, *Popular Culture in Early Modern Europe* (New York: Harper & Row, 1978); and Peter Burke, "Viewpoint: The Invention of Leisure in Early Modern Europe," *Past & Present* 146 (1995): 136–50.

29. For a useful overview of the historiography of American sport, see Steven A. Riess, "The New Sports History," *Reviews in American History* 18 (1990): 311–25. Thanks to Andrew Fearnley for this reference.

30. Rebecca Cassidy, *Horse People: Thoroughbred Culture in Lexington and Newmarket* (Baltimore, MD: Johns Hopkins University Press, 2007), 54, 56–57. The English Jockey Club was established in 1750.

31. Click, *The Spirit of the Times: Amusements in Nineteenth-Century Baltimore, Norfolk, and Richmond* (Charlottesville: University Press of Virginia, 1989); Jeter, "A Racing Heritage," *Louisiana History* 30 (1989): 5–22; Otis, "Washington's Lost Racetracks: Horseracing from the 1760s to the 1930s," *Washington History* 24 (2012): 136–54; Sparks, "Gentleman's Sport: Horseracing in Antebellum Charleston," *South Carolina Historical Magazine* 93 (1992): 15–30; Struna, "The North-South Races: American Thoroughbred Racing in Transition, 1823–1850," *Journal of Sport History* 8 (1981): 28–57; Wall, *How Kentucky Became Southern* (Lexington: University Press of Kentucky, 2010); Katherine C. Mooney, *Race Horse Men: How Slavery and Freedom Were Made at the Racetrack* (Cambridge, MA: Harvard University Press, 2014); Kenneth Cohen, *They Will Have Their Game: Sporting Culture and the Making of the Early American Republic* (Ithaca, NY: Cornell University Press, 2017); Harrison, *The John's Island Stud* (Richmond, VA: Old Dominion Press, 1931); Hervey, *Racing in America, 1665–1865*, 2 vols. (New York: The Jockey Club, 1944); Osborne, *The Thoroughbred World* (New York: World, 1971); Robertson, *The History of Thoroughbred Racing in America* (Englewood Cliffs, NJ: Prentice-Hall, 1964); Weeks, *An Historical Account of Racing in the United States* (New York: Historical Company, 1898). Mooney offers a helpful overview of recent scholarship in "'I Got the Horse Right Here': New Directions in Sporting History," *Register of the Kentucky Historical Society* 115 (2017): 645–60.

32. Breen, "Horses and Gentlemen," *William and Mary Quarterly*, 3rd ser., vol. 34, no. 2 (April 1997): 239–57; quotation on 257. Geertz first set out his concept of "thick description," a term that he borrowed from the British philosopher Gilbert Ryle, in his seminal article "Deep Play: Notes on the Balinese Cockfight," *Daedalus* 101 (1972): 1–37.

33. Beckert, *The Monied Metropolis: New York City and the Consolidation of the American Bourgeoisie, 1850–1896* (New York: Cambridge University Press, 2001).

34. Isaac, *The Transformation of Virginia, 1740–1790* (Chapel Hill: University of North Carolina Press, 1982), xxvi, 81. Although Isaac does not cite the work of the French sociologist Pierre Bourdieu, the latter's concept of the "habitus" is in many ways comparable to Isaac's ideas regarding "statements" (see Bourdieu, *Outline of a Theory of Practice*, trans. Richard Nice [Cambridge, UK: Cambridge University Press, 1977]).

35. Levine, *Highbrow/Lowbrow: The Emergence of Cultural Hierarchy in America* (Cambridge, MA: Harvard University Press, 1990). Levine was influenced by Peter Burke's concept of the "great" and "little" traditions of western European culture, as described in the latter's *Popular Culture in Early Modern Europe*.

36. Walter Johnson, *River of Dark Dreams: Slavery and Empire in the Cotton Kingdom* (Cambridge, MA: Harvard University Press, 2013), 5.

37. Steven A. Riess, *The Sport of Kings and the Kings of Crime: Horse Racing, Politics, and Organized Crime in New York, 1865–1913* (Syracuse, NY: Syracuse University Press, 2011), 34, 32.

38. See Raymond Boyle, "'We Are Celtic Supporters. . . .': Questions of Football and Identity in Modern Scotland," in *Game Without Frontiers: Football, Identity and Modernity*, ed. Richard Giulianotti and John Williams (London: Routledge, 2017).

39. "The 20th Century Awards: *Sports Illustrated* Honors World's Greatest Athletes," *Sports Illustrated*, 3 December 1999.

40. On sports venues as physical spaces, see Robert W. Lewis, *The Stadium Century: Sport, Spectatorship and Mass Society in Modern France* (Manchester, UK: Manchester University Press, 2017); Robert C. Trumpbour, *The New Cathedrals: Politics and Media in the History of Stadium Construction* (Syracuse, NY: Syracuse University Press, 2007); Sean Dinces, "The Attrition of the Common Fan: Class, Spectatorship, and Major League Stadiums in Postwar America," *Social Science History* 40 (2016): 339–65. Thanks to Andrew Fearnley for these references.

41. Levi-Strauss, *Le totemisme aujourd'hui* (Paris: Presses Universitaires de France, 1962), 128.

1. VIRGINIA: GENTILITY AND DECLINE

First epigraph: "The Races," *Niles' Weekly Register,* 7 June 1823.

Second epigraph: James B. Ransom, "The Charleston Races," *American Turf Register and Sporting Magazine* 9, no. 5 (May 1838): 217; italics in original. "Old Virginia Never Tire" was "a time-honoured expression applied to the Old Dominion State, or the Mother of Presidents. It is generally heard, however, as a negro expression" (Albert Barrere and Charles G. Leland, eds., *A Dictionary of Slang, Jargon & Cant* [Edinburgh: Ballantyne, 1890], vol. 2, 99). Frequently sung by coffles of enslaved people as they were forced to walk hundreds of miles from their Virginia homes to be sold to planters in the Lower Mississippi Valley, it became the basis first of a minstrel song and then of a boast regarding the quality of Virginia-bred horses (G. W. Featherstonehaugh, *Excursion to the Slave States* [New York: Harper & Brothers, 1844], 37).

1. John Beaufain Irving, *The South Carolina Jockey Club* (Charleston: Russell & Jones, 1857), 25; italics in original. On Sir Archy (sometimes spelled "Archie"), see Elizabeth Amis Cameron Blanchard and Manly Wade Wellman, *The Life and Times of Sir Archie: The Story of America's Greatest Thoroughbred, 1805–1833* (Chapel Hill: University of North Carolina Press, 1958); and Alexander Mackay-Smith, *The Thoroughbred in the Lower Shenandoah Valley, 1785–1842* (Winchester, VA: Pifer Printing, 1948), 5. Archy was sometimes referred to as the "Godolphin of America" in tribute to both his descent from the Godolphin Arabian, one of the three Arabian horses in England from whom all Thoroughbreds must claim descent, and his status within American racing as the founder of a dynasty of equine champions (Jessica Dallow, *Race, Gender and Identity in American Equine Art: 1832 to the Present* [New York: Routledge, 2022], 27).

2. A. Levasseur, *Lafayette in America in 1824 and 1825; or, Journal of a Voyage to the United States,* trans. John D. Godman (Philadelphia: Carey & Lea, 1829), 196, 197; Richmond Jockey Club, Records, 1824–1838, Mss. 4 R 41531, p. 3, Virginia Historical Society, Richmond.

3. "Richmond Races, Fall Meeting," *Alexandria Gazette & Advertiser,* 26 October 1824; Marie Tyler-McGraw, *At the Falls: Richmond, Virginia, and Its People* (Chapel Hill: University of North Carolina Press, 1994), 99. On the Seldens and Tree Hill, see Mary Selden Kennedy, *Seldens of Virginia and Allied Families, vol. 1* (New York: Frank Allaben Genealogical Company, 1911).

4. W. G. Stanard, "Racing in Colonial Virginia," *Virginia Magazine of History and Biography* 2 (1895): 305; Mary Newton Stanard, *Richmond, Its People and Its Story* (Philadelphia: J. B. Lippincott, 1938), 55; *Fourteenth Annual Report of the Board of Public Works, to the General Assembly of*

Virginia (Richmond: Samuel Shepherd, 1830), 49; Harry M. Wood, *Richmond: An Illustrated History* (Northridge, CA: Windsor, 1985), 67.

5. Cynthia A. Kierner, "'The Dark and Dense Cloud Perpetually Lowering over Us': Gender and the Decline of the Gentry in Postrevolutionary Virginia," *Journal of the Early Republic* 20 (2000): 185, 191, 193.

6. "Chronology," in *Sports in America from Colonial Times to the Twenty-First Century: An Encyclopedia*, ed. Steven A. Riess (London: Routledge, 2011), vol. 3, 985; Graham Budd, *Racing Art and Memorabilia* (London: Philip Wilson, 1997), 121; Daniel Denton, *A Brief Description of New-York, formerly called New-Netherlands*, ed. Gabriel Furman (New York: William Gowans, 1845), 6.

7. York County Order Book, 1672–1694, 85, reprinted in Warren M. Billings, ed., *The Old Dominion in the Seventeenth Century: A Documentary History of Virginia, 1606–1700*, rev. ed. (Chapel Hill: University of North Carolina Press, 2007), vol. 2, 387; Nancy L. Struna, "The Formalizing of Sport and the Formation of an Elite: The Chesapeake Gentry, 1650s–1720s," *Journal of Sport History* 13 (1986): 218; John Hervey, *Racing in America, 1665–1865* (New York: The Jockey Club, 1941), vol. 1, 18, 19; Stanard, "Racing in Colonial Virginia," 294, 298; Bruce Bennett, "Sports in the South up to 1865," *Quest* 28 (1977), 5; Fairfax Harrison, "The Equine FFVs: A Study of the Evidence for the English Horses Imported into Virginia before the Revolution," *Virginia Magazine of History and Biography* 35 (1927): 334. The acronym "FFV" stands for "First Families of Virginia," a term that refers to a self-defined group of descendants of the leading families of colonial Virginia.

8. John H. Wallace, *The Horse of America, in His Derivation, History, and Development* (New York: privately printed, 1897), 117; Tollie Jean Banker, "A Peculiar Diversion: The Social Ramifications of Quarter-Racing in the Eighteenth-Century Tidewater Virginia" (master's thesis, University of Tennessee–Knoxville, 2006), 53; Nancy L. Struna, "Sport and Society in Early America," *International Journal of the History of Sport* 5 (1988): 299; Michal J. Rozbicki, *The Complete Colonial Gentleman: Cultural Legitimacy in Plantation America* (Charlottesville: University Press of Virginia, 1998), 163; Thomas Anburey, *Travels through the Interior Parts of America* (London: William Lane, 1789), vol. 2, 395; Herbert Manchester, *Four Centuries of Sport in America* (1931; New York: Benjamin Blom, 1968), 44; Emory G. Evans, *A "Topping People": The Rise and Decline of Virginia's Old Political Elite, 1680–1790* (Charlottesville: University Press of Virginia, 2009), 151; Albert H. Tillson Jr., *Accommodating Revolution: Virginia's Northern Neck in an Era of Transformations, 1760–1810* (Charlottesville: University Press of Virginia, 2010), 22; Jane Carson, *Colonial Virginians at Play* (Williamsburg, VA: Colonial Williamsburg, 1965), 115.

9. "Turf Register—Pedigrees," *American Turf Register and Sporting Magazine* 4, no. 8 (April 1833): 426; Brian Patrick Tyrrell, "Bred for the Race: Thoroughbred Horses and the Politics of Pedigree" (PhD diss., University of California-Santa Barbara, 2019), 61–62. The Darley Arabian, the Byerley Turk, and the Godolphin Arabian were the "Big Three foundation sires" (Donna Landry, *Noble Brutes: How Eastern Horses Transformed English Culture* [Baltimore, MD: Johns Hopkins University Press, 2009], 95) from whom all modern Thoroughbred horses descend. See also Harold B. Gill Jr., "A Sport Only for Gentlemen," *Colonial Williamsburg* 20 (1997): 52.

10. John Rogers Williams, ed., *Philip Vickers Fithian: Journal and Letters, 1767–1774* (Princeton, NJ: University Library, 1900), 54; Rev. William Henry Foote, D.D., *Sketches of Virginia, Historical*

and Biographical (Philadelphia: William S. Martien, 1849), 203–4; Zbigniew Mazur, *The Power of Play: Leisure, Recreation and Cultural Hegemony in Colonial Virginia* (Lublin, Poland: Wydawnictwo Uniwersytetu Marii Curie Sklodowskiej, 2010), 180. By contrast, Fithian's employer, Landon Carter, was unusual among the planters of Tidewater Virginia in execrating racing as a waste of time and a spur to gambling, and was enraged that his son Robert enjoyed both practices (Aram Goudsouzian, "House of Cards: Leisure, Freedom, Authority, Revolution, and the Diary of Landon Carter," *Journal of Sport History* 49 [2022]: 8–9). Virginia's Baptists also opposed racing, considering it both ungodly and avaricious (Fairfax Harrison, *The Roanoke Stud, 1795–1833* [Richmond: Old Dominion, 1930], 205).

11. See A. G. Roeber, "Authority, Law, and Custom: The Rituals of Court Day in Tidewater Virginia, 1720 to 1750," *William and Mary Quarterly*, 3rd ser., vol. 37, no. 1 (1980): 29–52; and Rhys Isaac, *The Transformation of Virginia, 1740–1790* (Chapel Hill: University of North Carolina Press, 1982), 317.

12. *Virginia Gazette* (Parks), 7 October 1737, 3; Fairfax Harrison, *The Belair Stud, 1747–1761* (Richmond, VA: Old Dominion, 1929), 76. The *Gazette* was published weekly in Williamsburg between 1736 and 1780, and was printed in succession by William Parks, William Hunter, Joseph Royle, Alexander Purdie, Alexander Purdie and John Dixon, John Dixon and William Hunter, Jr., and John Dixon and Thomas Nicholson (www.accessible-archives.com/collections/the-virginia-gazette/).

13. Philip G. Smucker, *Riding with George: Sportsmanship and Chivalry in the Making of America's First President* (Chicago: Chicago Review Press, 2017), 316. Throughout the eighteenth century, items of clothing and personal decoration increasingly came to differentiate Virginians of various social ranks (see Anthony S. Parent, Jr., *Foul Means: The Formation of a Slave Society in Virginia, 1660–1740* [Chapel Hill: University of North Carolina Press, 2003], 210, 212).

14. Cynthia A. Kierner, *Beyond the Household: Women's Place in the Early South, 1700–1835* (Ithaca, NY: Cornell University Press, 1998), 46; Kenneth Cohen, "Well Calculated for the Farmer: Thoroughbreds in the Early National Chesapeake, 1790–1850," *Virginia Magazine of History and Biography* 115 (2007): 373, 385. In the eighteenth century, the term "jockey" applied to a man who owned a horse rather than to one who rode it in a race.

15. Isaac, *Transformation*, 101; Fred Shelley, ed., "The Journal of Ebenezer Hazard in Virginia, 1777," *Virginia Magazine of History and Biography* 62 (1954): 400, 403.

16. *Virginia Gazette* (Rind) 23 August 1770, 3; Moncure Daniel Conway, *Barons of the Potomack and the Rappahannock* (New York: Grolier Club, 1892), 120; John Harrower, "Diary of John Harrower, 1773–1776," *American Historical Review* 6 (1900): 87. The *Virginia Gazette*, published by Clementina Rind, was the rival of the more widely known paper of the same name (Martha J. King, "Clementina Rind (d. 1774)," *Encyclopedia Virginia*, https://encyclopediavirginia.org/entries/rind-clementina-d-1774/).

17. *Virginia Gazette* (Purdie and Dixon), 30 August 1770, 4; *Virginia Gazette* (Purdie and Dixon), 20 October 1774, 3; Francis Barnum Culver, *Blooded Horses of Colonial Days* (Baltimore: privately published, 1922), 119, 120; *Virginia Gazette* (Purdie and Dixon), 28 April 1774, 2; *Virginia Gazette* (Purdie and Dixon), 10 February 1774, 2; "Diary of John Harrower," 78; Dora Chinn Jett, *In Tidewater*

Virginia (Richmond: Whittet & Shepperson, 1924), 156. While it is difficult to draw precise comparisons between historical and contemporary currency values, a hundred guineas in 1770 would be worth approximately £9,000 today (estimated via the National Archives of the United Kingdom's Currency Converter, 1270–2017, www.nationalarchives.gov.uk/currency-converter).

18. Hugh Jones, *The Present State of Virginia* (New York: Joseph Sabin, 1865), 32.

19. *Virginia Gazette* (Parks), 1 July 1737, 4; *Virginia Gazette* (Parks), 30 November 1739, 3; *Virginia Gazette* (Parks), 14 December 1739, 3; William H. P. Robertson, *The History of Thoroughbred Racing in America* (Englewood Cliffs, NJ: Prentice-Hall, 1964), 16; "The Cocke Family of Virginia," *Virginia Historical Magazine* 4 (1896): 216; *Virginia Gazette* (Purdie and Dixon), 25 April 1766, 3. It is not clear precisely when the Williamsburg Jockey Club came into existence; some authors claim that it did so by 1732 (John Hervey, *Racing in America*, vol. 1, 64).

20. J. F. D. Smyth, *A Tour in the United States of America* (London: G. Robinson, 1784), vol. 1, 21, 20; *Virginia Gazette* (Purdie and Dixon), 24 October 1766, 2; A. J. Morrison, ed., *Travels in Virginia in Revolutionary Times* (Lynchburg, VA: J. P. Bell, 1922), 9; *Virginia Gazette* (Purdie and Dixon), 23 April 1767, 2. See also Laura Croghan Kamoie, *Irons in the Fire: The Business History of the Tayloe Family and Virginia's Gentry, 1700–1860* (Charlottesville: University Press of Virginia, 2007).

21. Nancy L. Struna, *People of Prowess: Sport, Leisure, and Labor in Early Anglo-America* (Urbana: University of Illinois Press, 1996), 139; James Douglas Anderson, *Making the American Thoroughbred* (Norwood, MA: Plimpton, 1916), 5.

22. *Extracts from the Votes and Proceedings of the American Continental Congress* (London: J. Almon, 1774), 18–19; italics mine.

23. Blanchard and Wellman, *Sir Archie*, 12; *Virginia Gazette* (Dixon and Hunter), 30 October 1778, 3.

24. Quoted in Odai Johnson, *London in a Box: Englishness and Theatre in Revolutionary America* (Iowa City: University of Iowa Press, 2017), 126. Although the Congress's strictures against racing were lifted in 1789, popular opinion above the Mason-Dixon Line remained largely hostile to the sport as a pastime that was not only ungodly but also ill-suited to a new republic. An 1802 address signed by nearly three thousand Philadelphia manufacturers and mechanics, for example, referred to the sport as an "English dissipation" for "idle landed gentlemen" (Jennie Holliman, *American Sports [1785–1835]* [Durham, NC: Seeman, 1931], 111; Elliott J. Gorn and Warren Goldstein, *A Brief History of American Sports* [Urbana: University of Illinois Press, 1993], 50).

25. Bonnie S. Ledbetter, "Sports and Games of the American Revolution," *Journal of Sport History* 6 (1979): 34; John Hervey, *Racing in America*, vol. 1, 120.

26. *Virginia Gazette* (Dixon and Nicolson), 28 August 1779, 1; *Virginia Gazette* (Dixon and Nicolson), 25 September 1779, 3; *Virginia Gazette* (Purdie), 19 April 1776, 4; Lyman Horace Weeks, *The American Turf: An Historical Account of Racing in the United States, with Biographical Sketches of Turf Celebrities* (New York: Historical Company, 1898), 18.

27. Johann David Schopf, *Travels in the Confederation, 1783–1784*, ed. and trans. Alfred J. Morrison (Philadelphia: William J. Campbell, 1911), 52, 55, 65–66.

28. Emily Ellsworth Fowler Ford Skeel, *Notes on the Life of Noah Webster* (New York: privately printed, 1912), vol. 1, 141; Fairfax Harrison, *Early American Turf Stock, 1730–1830* (Richmond,

VA: Old Dominion, 1934), 28; Patrick Nisbett Edgar, *The American Race-Turf Register, Sportsman's Herald, and General Stud Book* (New York: Henry Mason, 1838), vol. 1, 446; "Memoir of Shark," *American Turf Register and Sporting Magazine* 3, no. 1 (September 1831): 1. "Election" in this context refers to the day each year on which the legislatures of New England first convened, an event marked by a ministerial sermon (see Mark A. Noll, "The Election Sermon: Situating Religion and the Constitutional in the Eighteenth Century," *DePaul Law Review* 59 [2010]: 1225).

29. Skeel, *Notes*, vol. 1, 143; Tappahannock Jockey Club Minute Book, 1796–1801, Marion du Pont Scott Papers, Mss. 11092d, p. 6, Albert and Shirley Small Special Collections Library, University of Virginia, Charlottesville; John Bernard, *Retrospections of America, 1797–1811*, ed. Mrs. Bayle Bernard (New York: Harper & Brothers, 1887), 153; Tayloe Family Papers, Mss1 T2118 d994–995, Virginia Historical Society; Kamoie, *Irons in the Fire*, 119. An earlier jockey club had briefly existed at Tappahannock in the mid-1780s (see Louis B. Wright and Marion Tinling, eds., *Quebec to Carolina in 1785–1786: Being the Travel Diary of Robert Hunter, Jr., a Young Merchant of London* [San Marino, CA: Huntington Library, 1943], 219, 251–52).

30. "Sporting Intelligence of 1795," *American Turf Register and Sporting Magazine* 4, no. 3 (November 1832): 148; Jacques-Pierre Brissot de Warville, *New Travels in the United States of America, Performed in 1788* (Dublin: W. Corbet, 1792), 434. The Alexandria racecourse appears to have revived soon after Brissot de Warville's visit, and it remained in use until around 1810. Tayloe established the Washington [DC] Jockey Club in 1798 and founded the city's National Course, which operated between 1802 and 1845 (Lara Otis, "Washington's Lost Racetracks: Horse Racing from the 1760s to the 1930s," *Washington History* 24 [2012]: 139, 141; Kamoie, *Irons in the Fire*, 119).

31. "Petersburg Jocky Club Book, 1785," *William and Mary Quarterly*, 2nd ser., vol. 18 (1938): 210; Cohen, "Well Calculated for the Farmer," 385; Edward A. Wyatt, "Petersburg Plans a Turf Museum," *Commonwealth* 6, no. 1 (January 1939): 13; Lee W. Formwalt, "An English Immigrant Views American Society: Benjamin Henry Latrobe's Virginia Years, 1796–1798," *Virginia Magazine of History and Biography* 85 (1977): 388; Benjamin Henry Latrobe, *The Journal of Latrobe: The Notes and Sketches of an Architect, Naturalist and Traveler in the United States from 1796 to 1820* (New York: D. Appleton, 1905), 22, 23; Isaac Weld Jr., *Weld's Travels through the States of North America, and the Provinces of Upper and Lower Canada During the Years 1795, 1796, and 1797*, 4th ed. (London: John Stockdale, 1807), vol. 1, 185. Lamplighter was the get of Medley, who like Shark, a famed sire of fillies, was imported to Virginia in 1784 (Henry William Herbert, *Frank Forester's Horses and Horsemanship of the United States and British Provinces of North America* [New York: Stringer & Townsend, 1857], vol. 1, 136).

32. Morris Birkbeck, *Notes on a Journey to America* (London: James Ridgeway, 1818), 11; John Eisenberg, *The Great Match Race: When North Met South in America's First Sports Spectacle* (Boston: Houghton Mifflin, 2006), 113, 115.

33. "Newmarket (Va.) Fall Races," *Spirit of the Times*, 28 October 1854; Dr. George H. Conn, *The Arabian Horse in America* (Woodstock, VT: Countryman, 1957), 91.

34. "William R. Johnson," McIntosh Family Papers, Mss1 M1898 a7-a12, pp. 2, 4–5, Virginia Historical Society; Katherine C. Mooney, *Race Horse Men: How Slavery and Freedom Were Made at the Racetrack* (Cambridge, MA: Harvard University Press, 2014), 20; Charles Stewart, "My Life

as a Slave," *Harper's New Monthly Magazine* 69 (October 1884): 732; Blanchard and Wellman, *Sir Archie*, 32, 33.

35. David Hackett Fischer and James C. Kelly, *Bound Away: Virginia and the Westward Movement* (Charlottesville: University Press of Virginia, 2000), xiii; "Foreign Spectator," *Independent Gazetteer*, 28 August 1787 (thanks to Max Edling for this reference); Joan S. Howland, "Let's Not 'Spit the Bit' in Defense of 'The Law of the Horse': The Historical and Legal Development of American Thoroughbred Racing," *Marquette Sports Law Review* 14 (2004): 488; Robertson, *The History of Thoroughbred Racing*, 27; Kierner, *Beyond the Household*, 146; Smucker, *Riding with George*, 312; Harrison, *The Belair Stud*, 92. There is some debate among historians regarding the extent of Jefferson's involvement in racing. Edwin Morris Betts asserted that "there is no record to show that Jefferson raced his studs," but he noted that, when Jefferson purchased the Thoroughbred Tarquin from his and Washington's friend William Fitzhugh in 1790, the former wrote in his account book that the horse excelled in two-mile heats (Betts, *Thomas Jefferson's Farm Book* [Princeton, NJ: Princeton University Press, 1953], 88). There is no doubt, however, that Jefferson greatly enjoyed attending races and that he "was a good rider, and rode a fine horse," including the one upon which he traveled to his 1801 presidential inauguration ("Letter from 'Senex,'" *Wilkes' Spirit of the Times*, 23 January 1864, 336; John Hervey, *Racing & Breeding in America and the Colonies* [London: London & Counties Press Association, 1931], 22).

36. Hervey, *Racing in America*, 144; Cohen, "Well Calculated for the Farmer," 385.

37. "Virginia Races," *American Turf Register and Sporting Magazine* 1, no. 3 (November 1829): 152. On "treating," see Isaac, *Transformation*, 104–14; and Charles S. Sydnor, *Gentlemen Freeholders: Political Practices in Washington's Virginia* (Chapel Hill: University of North Carolina Press, 1952), 39–59. In 1796 George Washington wrote in his diary that most of his "People," meaning his enslaved laborers, "had gone to the races," probably those held at nearby Alexandria (quoted in Philip D. Morgan, *Slave Counterpoint: Black Culture in the Eighteenth-Century Chesapeake and Lowcountry* [Chapel Hill: University of North Carolina Press, 1998], 417).

38. Scott Peeples, *The Man of the Crowd: Edgar Allan Poe and the City* (Princeton, NJ: Princeton University Press, 2020), 48; Wirt Armistead Cate, "History of Richmond," unpublished typescript (ca. 1943), vol. 1, 213, Valentine Richmond History Center, Richmond, Virginia. My thanks to Kelly Kerney for helping me access this latter work.

39. David Alexander, *The History and Romance of the Horse, Told with Pictures* (New York: Cooper Square, 1965), 122; James Parton, *Life of Andrew Jackson* (New York: Mason Brothers, 1859), 267; Alan Macey, *The Romance of the Derby Stakes* (London: Hutchinson, 1930), 25. When asked if he had ever experienced failure, Jackson allegedly responded, "nothing that I can remember, except Haynie's Maria. I could not beat her" (Margaret Lindsley Warden, "The Fine Horse Industry in Tennessee," *Tennessee Historical Quarterly* 6 [1947]: 143).

40. Mary Newton Stanard, *Richmond*, 55; William M. S. Rasmussen and Robert S. Tilton, *Old Virginia: The Pursuit of a Pastoral Ideal* (Charlottesville, VA: Howell, 2003), 103; Hamilton Bushey, "The Running Turf in America [Second Paper]," *Harper's New Monthly Magazine* 41 (1870): 249; Jessica Dallow, "Antebellum Sports Illustrated: Representing African Americans in Edward Troye's Equine Paintings," *Nineteenth-Century Art Worldwide* 12 (2013), www.19thc-artworldwide.org

/autumn13/dallow-on-edward-troye-s-equine-paintings; Mackay-Smith, *Thoroughbred,* 25; Jane Louise Mesick, *The English Traveller in America, 1785–1835* (New York: Columbia University Press, 1922), 68.

41. Virginius Dabney, *Richmond: The Story of a City* (Charlottesville: University Press of Virginia, 1976), 86; Louis H. Manarin and Clifford Dowdey, *The History of Henrico County* (Charlottesville: University Press of Virginia, 1984), 215; T. J. Macon, *Life Gleanings* (Richmond: W. H. Adams, 1913), 40; Hervey, *Racing in America,* vol. 2, 15; announcement by John Randolph of Roanoke of a match race between Miles Selden's colt and Randolph's filly, 8 June 1805, Brock Collection, Box 7, Item 14, Henry E. Huntington Library, San Marino, California; Blanchard and Wellman, *Sir Archie,* 22, 42–43.

42. Patricia C. Click, *The Spirit of the Times: Amusements in Nineteenth-Century Baltimore, Norfolk, and Richmond* (Charlottesville: University Press of Virginia, 1989), 60; John H. Davis, *The American Turf with Personal Reminiscences* (New York: John Polhemus Printing, 1907), 128; Cate, "History of Richmond," vol. 1, 214; "E. H.," "'Observer' on Flora Temple, &c," *Porter's Spirit of the Times* 2, no. 3 (21 March 1857): 43; "Doc" of Richmond, Virginia, "Racing Reforms," *Charleston Courier,* 20 August 1858; "Richmond (Va.) Fall Meeting: Fairfield Course," *Spirit of the Times,* 1 November 1851; "The Virginia Turf," *Spirit of the Times,* 29 November 1856 (originally published in the *Richmond Daily Dispatch*); Hervey, *Racing in America,* vol. 2, 228; *Rules and Regulations of the Fairfield Jockey Club* (Richmond: C. H. Wynne's Steam-Power Presses, 1853), 3.

43. Alexander Wilbourne Weddell, *Portraiture in the Virginia Historical Society* (Richmond: Virginia Historical Society, 1945), 115; "Hamlintonian—Pedigree and Performances," *American Turf Register and Sporting Magazine* 6, no. 3 (November 1834), 111–12; "Reminiscences of Balie Peyton," in Anderson, *Making the American Thoroughbred,* 236; Benjamin Ogle Tayloe, "Synopsis of American Turf History," *Wallace's Monthly* 3, no. 5 (June 1877): 400; "Florizel," "History of the Great Race-Horse, Boston," *Wallace's Monthly* 3, no. 9 (October 1877): 771, 776; Robert Bailey, *The Life and Adventures of Robert Bailey* (Richmond, VA: J. & G. Cochran, 1822), 156; T. J. Jackson Lears, *Something for Nothing: Luck in America* (New York: Viking, 2003), 105; Richard Stott, *Jolly Fellows: Male Milieus in Nineteenth-Century America* (Baltimore, MD: Johns Hopkins University Press, 2009), 242. English-born Henry William Herbert, who published extensively on the history of sports in the nineteenth-century United States under the pseudonym Frank Forester, described Florizel as a horse who "knew nothing of whip or spur, frequently distancing renowned competitors, and retiring from the turf [after the race against Peacemaker] when no other opponent would meet him" (Herbert, *Frank Forester,* vol. 1, 402).

44. Richmond Jockey Club, Records, 14, 20; Gerald Hammond, *The Language of Horse Racing* (London: Routledge, 2016), 49; Hervey, *Racing in America,* vol. 2, 15. The Newmarket rules were also adopted as the basis for those of the Norfolk Jockey Club, which was briefly celebrated for its "high class" racing, but which failed to recover from the severe damage it sustained during the War of 1812 (Norfolk Jockey Club Book, Mss 4 N 7676 a1 [unpaginated], Virginia Historical Society; Hervey, *Racing in America,* vol. 2, 21). On African American jockeys in the antebellum United States, see Mooney, *Race Horse Men.* It was acceptable for respectable women in late colonial and early national Virginia to engage in gambling by playing cards and entering lotteries, but the

placing of bets at sporting events was deemed unladylike. Michael Gretter, a wealthy real estate speculator and an elder of Richmond's Shockoe Hill Presbyterian Church, complained that any type of game of chance in which women might engage at the racetrack could have a damaging effect on both their morals and their health: "in the years of 1806 & 1807 the Ladies of Richmond were in the habit of frequenting the Racefield & playing *cards for money*. When they lost, they often exhibited unbecoming signs of their disappointment. A Lady of high standing lost her life caused by her devoting too much of her nights in this gambling" (Loose Items: Notes of Michael Gretter, Michael Gretter Papers, Mss 1 G8688 a13–32, Virginia Historical Society; italics in original). See also Linda L. Sturtz, "The Ladies and the Lottery: Elite Women's Gambling in Eighteenth-Century Virginia," *Virginia Magazine of History and Biography* 104 (1996): 165–84.

45. "A New York Turf Editor Discovers a Richmond Race Track," *Richmond Literature and History Quarterly* 2 (1979): 39, 40; Click, *The Spirit of the Times*, 60; Manarin and Dowdey, *Henrico County*, 214; Hervey, *Racing in America*, vol. 2, 15.

46. Pegram Johnson III, "The *American Turf Register and Sporting Magazine:* A 'Quaint and Curious Volume of Forgotten Lore,'" *Maryland Historical Magazine* 89 (1994): 6, 8; "Virginia Races,"158. The clubmen's love of champagne may have encouraged them to establish the Chateau Margaux stake race in 1832, the winner of which was obligated to pay the club for his victory with six dozen bottles of this wine, introduced to Virginia by Thomas Jefferson, who had developed a taste for it as minister to France from 1785 to 1789 (Richmond Jockey Club, Records, 73; "Chateau Margaux Stakes," *American Turf Register and Sporting Magazine* 3, no. 11 [July 1832]: 563).

47. "Philander," "Horse Racing Delineated," *Virginia Religious Magazine*, 1 May 1807; italics in original. On the Second Great Awakening in Virginia, see Mark A. Beliles, "The Christian Communities, Religious Revivals, and Political Culture of the Central Virginia Piedmont, 1737–1813," in *Religion and Political Culture in Jefferson's Virginia*, ed. Garrett Ward Sheldon and Daniel L. Dreisbach (Lanham, MD: Rowman & Littlefield, 2000). Philander's critique of racing echoes the attitudes of many early republican Americans toward gambling, that its sinfulness lay in the fact that it was innately unproductive: "property is shifted from one individual to another, and here and there one probably gains more than he loses; but nothing is actually *made*, or *produced*" (William Alexander Alcott, *The Young Man's Guide*, 2nd ed. [Boston: Lilly, Wait, Colman, and Holden, 1834], 145; italics in original).

48. Blanchard and Wellman, *Sir Archie*, 10; "Opinion of the Protestant Episcopal Church on the Subject of Fashionable Amusements," *Easton Gazette*, 20 May 1819; "Bellefonte (NOT-57)," Virginia Landscape Surveys, Virginia Historical Society; "Doc," "Racing Prospects in Virginia," *Spirit of the Times*, 10 October 1857. Philander was probably the Reverend Conrad Speece, the editor of the *Virginia Religious Magazine* (James Waddell Alexander, *The Life of Archibald Alexander, D.D.* [New York: Charles Scribner, 1854], 199).

49. Henry Adams, *History of the United States during Thomas Jefferson's Administration* (New York: Charles Scribner's Sons, 1891), vol. 1, 51; "A Virginia Turfman," "Reflections on the Present State of the Turf in Virginia," *American Turf Register and Sporting Magazine* 5 (September 1833): 11.

50. Harrison, *The Roanoke Stud*, 39, 206; "The Racing Stock of the Late Edmund Irby, Esq. of Nottoway County, Virginia," *American Turf Register and Sporting Magazine* 2, no. 9 (May 1831): 455;

italics in original; Samuel Mordecai, *Richmond in By-Gone Days: Reminiscences of an Old Citizen* (Richmond: George M. West, 1856), 177, 180; italics in original; Mordecai, *Virginia, Especially Richmond, in By-Gone Days; with a Glance at the Present: Being Reminiscences of an Old Citizen*, 2nd ed. (Richmond: West and Johnston, 1860), 252. See also Alexander Wilbourne Weddell, "Samuel Mordecai: Chronicler of Richmond, 1786–1865," *Virginia Magazine of History and Biography* 53 (1945): 265–87.

51. "A Virginia Turfman," "Reflections," 11, 12; italics in original; Irving, *The South Carolina Jockey Club*, 26.

52. Hervey, *Racing & Breeding*, 33; untitled article, *Richmond Examiner*, 2 June 1863.

53. "Proposition to Form a 'Virginia Jockey Club,'" *Richmond Whig*, 31 July 1857.

54. Susan Dunn, *Dominion of Memories: Jefferson, Madison, and the Decline of Virginia* (New York: Basic, 2007), 41. It is worth noting that, though Virginia's total population was declining at this time, Richmond's was growing; it was home to fewer than six thousand people in 1800, but more than twenty thousand in 1840 (Peeples, *The Man of the Crowd*, 15).

55. Trevor Burnard, *Planters, Merchants, and Slaves: Plantation Societies in British America, 1650–1820* (Chicago: University of Chicago Press, 2013), 134, 11; Evans, *A "Topping People,"* 168, 178, 199; Hervey, *Racing in America*, vol. 1, 122; "Things in Virginia," *Boston Evening Transcript*, 19 September 1843; Hugh A. Garland, *The Life of John Randolph of Roanoke* (New York: D. Appleton, 1856), vol. 1, 225; "Virginia Races," 149–50; William Byrd II to Charles Boyle, Earl of Orrery, 5 July 1726, in *The Correspondence of the Three William Byrds of Westover*, ed. Marion Tinling (Charlottesville: University Press of Virginia, 1977), vol. 1, 355; Cyril Connolly, *Enemies of Promise*, rev. ed. (1948; Chicago: University of Chicago Press, 2008), 116.

56. Dunn, *Dominion*, 42; Fischer and Kelly, *Bound Away*, 221, 189, xiii; Peter Wallenstein, *Cradle of America: A History of Virginia*, 2nd ed. (Lawrence: University Press of Kansas, 2014), 121; Cohen, "Well Calculated for the Farmer," 397, 401; Robert P. Sutton, "Nostalgia, Pessimism, and Malaise: The Doomed Aristocrat in Late-Jeffersonian Virginia," *Virginia Magazine of History and Biography* 76 (1968): 47; Gregg Kimball, *American City, Southern Place: A Cultural History of Antebellum Richmond* (Athens: University of Georgia Press, 2000), 9.

57. "S.W.M.," "Demand for Horses in South Carolina," *American Turf Register and Sporting Magazine* 2, no. 7 (March 1831): 327; Johnson, "The *American Turf Register and Sporting Magazine*," 17; Hervey, *Racing*, vol. 2, 154.

58. William R. Taylor, *Cavalier and Yankee: The Old South and National Character* (New York: Oxford University Press, 1957), 15; Francois Weil, *Family Trees: A History of Genealogy in America* (Cambridge, MA: Harvard University Press, 2013), 92.

59. Elizabeth Fox-Genovese and Eugene D. Genovese, *The Mind of the Master Class: History and Faith in the Southern Slaveholder's Worldview* (New York: Cambridge University Press, 2005), 199; Ritchie Devon Watson Jr., *The Cavalier in Virginia Fiction* (Baton Rouge: Louisiana State University Press, 1985), 59, 66; Weil, *Family Trees*, 92; John Esten Cooke, *Henry St. John, Gentleman, of "Flower of Hundreds," in the County of Prince George, Virginia: A Tale of 1774–'75* (New York: Harper & Brothers, 1860), 41; Cooke, *The Virginia Comedians: or, Old Days in the Old Dominion* (New York: D. Appleton, 1854), vol. 2, 148. Cooke's listing of "Selim, Fair Anna, and Sir Archy" is puzzling;

Selim, who was born in Maryland in 1759 and was described by Henry William Herbert as "the best race-horse of his day," may well have competed at the Williamsburg track, but as Sir Archy was born in 1805, he neither raced against Selim nor appeared at Williamsburg; Fair Anna appears to have been fictional (Herbert, *Frank Forester*, vol. 1, 199).

60. Mark Twain, *Life on the Mississippi* (New York: Harper & Brothers, 1903), 347; Kelley N. Seay, "Jousting and the Evolution of Southernness in Maryland," *Maryland Historical Magazine* 99 (2004): 53.

61. Esther J. Crooks and Ruth W. Crooks, *The Ring Tournament in the United States* (Richmond: Garrett and Massie, 1936), 2. Brian de Bois-Guilbert was a Norman knight character in Scott's *Ivanhoe*. On the culture of the Virginia Springs resorts, see Charlene M. Boyer Lewis, *Ladies and Gentlemen on Display: Planter Society at the Virginia Springs, 1790–1860* (Charlottesville: University Press of Virginia, 2001).

2. CHARLESTON: THE CARNIVAL OF THE SOUTH

First epigraph: J. Hector St. John de Crevecoeur, *Letters from an American Farmer*, ed. Susan Manning (1782; Oxford: Oxford University Press, 1997), 151.

Second epigraph: Johann David Schopf, *Travels in the Confederation, 1783–1784* (1911; New York: Burt Franklin, 1968).

1. DuBose Heyward to Henry Ravenel Dwight, 4 January 1931, Ms. 43–375, South Carolina Historical Society, Charleston (hereafter SCHS); Katherine C. Mooney, *Race Horse Men: How Slavery and Freedom Were Made at the Racetrack* (Cambridge, MA: Harvard University Press, 2014), 119, 121; Douglas W. Bostick, *The Union Is Dissolved!: Charleston and Fort Sumter in the Civil War* (Charleston, SC: History Press, 2009), unpaginated. Hercules was enslaved by the famed turfman William Sinkler of Eutaw Plantation in St. John's Parish (Anne Sinkler Whaley LeClercq, ed., *Between North and South: The Letters of Emily Wharton Sinkler, 1842–1865* [Columbia: University of South Carolina Press, 2001], 10). On the Canteys, see Joseph S. Ames, "Cantey Family," *South Carolina Historical and Genealogical Magazine* (hereafter *SCHGM*) 11 (1910): 203–58.

2. "The Charleston (S.C.) Races," *New York Herald*, 17 February 1861. Albine's time of seven minutes and thirty-six and a half seconds for a four-mile heat set a record not only for the Washington Course but for the nation, and it still stands today (Randy Sparks, "Gentleman's Sport: Horse Racing in Antebellum Charleston," *South Carolina Historical Magazine* [hereafter *SCHM*] 93 [1992], 27).

3. Whitelaw Reid, *After the War: A Tour of the Southern States, 1865–1866*, ed. C. Vann Woodward (1866; New York: Harper & Row, 1965), iii, 69; Jack Thompson, *Charleston at War: The Photographic Record, 1860–1865* (Gettysburg, PA: Thomas, 2000), 207; Kevin R. Eberle, *A History of Charleston's Hampton Park* (Charleston, SC: History Press, 2012), 40; "The Martyrs of the Race Course," *Harper's Weekly*, 18 May 1867.

4. Henry O. Marcy, "Dr. Marcy's Recollections," *Cambridge (MA) Chronicle*, 4 June 1910; David W. Blight, *Race and Reunion: The Civil War in American Memory* (Cambridge, MA: Harvard University Press, 2001), 68–70. Free people of color made up just under 8 percent of Charleston's

population, according to the 1860 federal census (*Census of Charleston, South Carolina, for 1861* [Charleston, SC: Steam-Power Presses of Evans and Cogswell, 1861], 9).

5. "Charleston under Arms," *The Atlantic Monthly: A Magazine of Literature, Art, and Politics* 7 (1861): 505.

6. "Proposition to Form a 'Virginia Jockey Club,'" *Richmond Whig*, 31 July 1857; John Beaufain Irving, *The South Carolina Jockey Club* (Charleston, SC: Russell & Jones, 1857), 26; "The Virginia Turf," *Spirit of the Times*, 29 November 1856.

7. Mike Huggins, "The Proto-Globalisation of Horseracing, 1730–1900: Anglo-American Interconnections," in *Sport as History: Essays in Honour of Wray Vamplew*, ed. Tony Collins (Abingdon, UK: Routledge, 2011), 47.

8. George C. Rogers Jr., *The History of Georgetown, South Carolina* (1970; Spartanburg, SC: Reprint Company, 1990), 95, 222; "The St. George's Club," *SCHGM* 8 (1907): 88, 92; Langdon Cheves, "Izard of South Carolina," *SCHGM* 2 (1901): 216; Lacy K. Ford Jr., *Origins of Southern Radicalism: The South Carolina Upcountry, 1800–1860* (New York: Oxford University Press, 1988), 8; Walter Edgar, *South Carolina: A History* (Columbia: University of South Carolina Press, 1998), 171; Rules of the Santee Jockey Club, 1791, typescript, p. 1, SCHS; Norman Sinkler Walsh, *Plantations, Pineland Villages, Pinopolis and Its People* (Virginia Beach: Donning, 2006), 27; Thomas P. Ravenel Diary, 1855–1865 (unpaginated), Thomas P. Ravenel Collection, 12/314/5, SCHS; Richard N. Cote, *Mary's World: Love, War, and Family Ties in Nineteenth-Century Charleston* (Mount Pleasant, SC: Corinthian, 2001), 35.

9. Pineville Jockey Club bills and receipts, 1852–1854, Gaillard Family Papers, 11/49/20, SCHS; W. H. Mills, "The Thoroughbred in South Carolina," *Proceedings of the South Carolina Historical Association* (1937): 19. On the role and appeal of ritual in nineteenth-century American social clubs, see Mark C. Carnes, "Middle-Class Men and the Solace of Fraternal Ritual," in *Meanings for Manhood: Constructions of Masculinity in Victorian America*, ed. Carnes and Clyde Griffen (Chicago: University of Chicago Press, 1990), 37–52.

10. South Carolina Jockey Club Rules, 1828, p. 11, microfilm 45/4142/2, SCHS.

11. Hayden R. Smith, "Reserving Water: Environmental and Technological Relationships with South Carolina Inland Rice Plantations," in *Rice: Global Networks and New Histories*, ed. Francesca Bray et al. (Cambridge, UK: Cambridge University Press, 2015), 191; Randy J. Sparks, "Mary Fisher, Sophia Hume, and the Quakers of Colonial Charleston," in *South Carolina Women: Their Lives and Times*, ed. Marjorie J. Spruill et al. (Athens: University of Georgia Press, 2009), vol. 1, 40; Sophia Hume, *An Exhortation to the Inhabitants of the Province of South-Carolina, to bring their deeds to the light of Christ, in their own consciences* (London: Luke Hinde, 1752), 51; italics in original; Irving, *The South Carolina Jockey Club*, 33; Carl Bridenbaugh, *Myths and Realities: Societies of the Colonial South* (Baton Rouge: Louisiana State University Press, 1952), 81; Hunt Boulware, "'Unworthy of Modern Refinement': The Evolution of Sport and Recreation in the Early South Carolina and Georgia Lowcountry," *Journal of Sport History* 35 (2008): 439; Hennig Cohen, ed., *The South Carolina Gazette, 1732–1775* (Columbia: University of South Carolina Press, 1953), 78.

12. Bridenbaugh, *Myths*, 81; "Spectator," "Horse Races," *Charleston News and Courier*, 28 January 1912; Mary C. Ferrari, "Charity, Folly, and Politics: Charles Town's Social Clubs on the Eve of the Revolution," *SCHM* 112 (2001): 74; "The South Carolina Jockey Club: An Ancient Organization of

Historic Interest," *The Exposition*, March 1901, 126; Christina Rae Butler, *Charleston Horse Power: Equine Culture in the Palmetto City* (Columbia: University of South Carolina Press, 2023), 55. In 1768 the planter and lawyer William Henry Drayton's roan colt Partner won a match race at Newmarket against William Cattell's Havanna, for which achievement Drayton was rewarded with a silver plate valued at one thousand pounds (Keith Krawczynski, *William Henry Drayton: South Carolina Revolutionary Patriot* [Baton Rouge: Louisiana State University Press, 2001], 34).

13. Robert N. Rosen, *A Short History of Charleston* (San Francisco: Lexikos, 1982), 32; Emma Hart, *Building Charleston: Town and Society in the Eighteenth Century* (Charlottesville: University Press of Virginia, 2010), 138, 139; Amrita Chakrabarti Myers, *Forging Freedom: Black Women and the Pursuit of Liberty in Antebellum Charleston* (Chapel Hill: University of North Carolina Press, 2011), 25; Edward Pearson, "'Planters Full of Money': The Self-Fashioning of the Eighteenth-Century South Carolina Elite," in *Money, Trade, and Power: The Evolution of Colonial South Carolina's Plantation Society*, ed. Jack P. Greene et al. (Columbia: University of South Carolina Press, 2001), 307; Cara Anzilotti, *In the Affairs of the World: Women, Patriarchy, and Power in Colonial South Carolina* (Westport, CT: Greenwood, 2002), 43; William Cabell Bruce, *John Randolph of Roanoke, 1773–1833* (New York: G. P. Putnam's Sons, 1922), vol. 1, 138; M. A. DeWolfe Howe, ed., "Journal of Josiah Quincy, Junior, 1773," *Proceedings of the Massachusetts Historical Society* 50 (1916): 451, 467.

14. Jerome J. Nadelhaft, *The Disorders of War: The Revolution in South Carolina* (Orono: University of Maine Press, 1981), 144; Fairfax Harrison, *The John's Island Stud, 1750–1788* (Richmond, VA: Old Dominion, 1931), 131, 133, 145, 153; Louis B. Wright and Marion Tinling, eds., *Quebec to Carolina in 1785–1786: Being the Travel Diary and Observations of Robert Hunter Jr., a Young Merchant of London* (San Marino, CA: Huntington Library, 1943), 294; Eberle, *Hampton Park*, 31; Irving, *The South Carolina Jockey Club*, 11, 12, 14.

15. Tiya Miles, *All That She Carried: The Journey of Ashley's Sack, a Black Family Keepsake* (New York: Random House, 2021), 168; Rosemarie Zagarri, *The Politics of Size: Representation in the United States, 1776–1850* (Ithaca, NY: Cornell University Press, 1987), 48; Matthew Lockhart, "'Under the Wings of Columbia': John Lewis Gervais as Architect of South Carolina's 1786 Capital Relocation Legislation," *SCHM* 104 (2003): 176; Charles Carleton Coffin, *The Boys of '61; or, Four Years of Fighting* (Boston: Estes and Lauriat, 1884), 444; Lawrence T. McDonnell, *Performing Disunion: The Coming of the Civil War in Charleston, South Carolina* (Cambridge, UK: Cambridge University Press, 2018), 24; Kenneth Severens, *Charleston: Antebellum Architecture and Civic Destiny* (Knoxville: University of Tennessee Press, 1988), 17; Enrico Dal Lago, "The City as Social Display: Landed Elites and Urban Images in Charleston and Palermo," *Journal of Historical Sociology* 14 (2001): 384, 385; Terry W. Lipscomb, *South Carolina in 1791: George Washington's Southern Tour* (Columbia: South Carolina Department of Archives and History, 1993), 65; Myers, *Forging Freedom*, 30.The term "soft power" was coined by the political scientist Joseph S. Nye Jr. to describe the methods by which a polity tries to attain its goals through "the power of attractive ideas" and "intangible power resources such as culture, ideology, and institutions" (Nye, "Soft Power," *Foreign Policy* 80 [1990]: 166–67).

16. "An Ancient Organization of Historic Interest,"125; "Horses Were Run for Honor, Not Money," *Charleston News and Courier*, 23 March 1966; Boulware, "'Unworthy of Modern Refine-

ment,'"440; Richard Bodek, "Racing in Charleston," unpublished manuscript in author's possession. According to the Measuring Worth website, the value of this purse translates to approximately twenty-five thousand dollars in modern currency (www.measuringworth.com/calculators/uscompare/).

17. Marvin R. Zahniser, *Charles Cotesworth Pinckney: Founding Father* (Chapel Hill: University of North Carolina Press, 1967), 264; Rosen, *Short History*, 81; Dorothy Middleton Anderson and Margaret Middleton Rivers Eastman, *St. Philip's Church of Charleston: An Early History of the Oldest Parish in South Carolina* (Charleston, SC: History Press, 2014), unpaginated; Wylma Wates, "Precursor to the Victorian Age: The Concept of Marriage and Family as Revealed in the Correspondence of the Izard Family of South Carolina," in *In Joy and in Sorrow: Women, Family, and Marriage in the Victorian South, 1830–1900*, ed. Carol Bleser (New York: Oxford University Press, 1991), 12, 13; Maurie D. McInnis, *The Politics of Taste in Antebellum Charleston* (Chapel Hill: University of North Carolina Press, 2005), 313. See also Daniel Kilbride, "Cultivation, Conservatism, and the Early National Gentry: The Manigault Family and Their Circle," *Journal of the Early Republic* 19 (1999): 221–56.

18. Nicholas Michael Butler, *Votaries of Apollo: The St. Cecilia Society and the Patronage of Concert Music in Charleston, South Carolina, 1766–1820* (Columbia: University of South Carolina Press, 2007), 68–69; Eric Homberger, *Mrs. Astor's New York: Money and Social Power in a Gilded Age* (New Haven, CT: Yale University Press, 2002), 189; "Thomas's Reminiscences," *United States Magazine and Democratic Review* 8, no. 33 (September 1840): 232; Irving, *The South Carolina Jockey Club*, 152.

19. For example, during Race Week in 1828, "public amusements" beyond the races and the Jockey Club and St. Cecilia balls included plays, circus performances, and an exhibition of the French artist Jacques-Louis David's "splendid Painting of the Coronation of Bonaparte"; in addition, "for the lovers of music, [there is] a treat in the Panharmonican . . . a combination of 206 wind Instruments of 13 different kinds forming a complete Band," and "the paper-cutting gallery of Master Hankes, or more learnedly speaking the Papyrotomia," at which "the visitor may have a likeness of his own Phiz." (Margaret M. Adger to Thomas Smyth, 27 February 1828, in *Autobiographical Notes, Letters and Reflections, by Thomas Smyth, D.D.*, ed. Louisa Cheves Stanley [Charleston: Walker, Evans & Cogswell, 1914], 77). Hankes, who advertised his Papyrotomia in the *Charleston Courier* as presenting "Striking Likenesses . . . without the least aid from any drawing or machine," teamed up in March 1828 with Mr. Smith, the proprietor of the Panharmonican, offering the public combined tickets to the exhibition and the concert (Anna Wells Rutledge, *Artists in the Life of Charleston: Through Colony and State from Restoration to Reconstruction* [Philadelphia: American Philosophical Society, 1949], 200).

20. Adam Hodgson, *Letters from North America, Written during a Tour in the United States and Canada* (London: Hurst, Robinson, 1824), vol. 1, 50; "The South Carolina Jockey Club. Its Prospects—The General Prevalence of Racing, &c.," *Charleston Mercury*, 14 February 1846; italics in original; G. M., "South Carolina," *New England Magazine* 1, no. 4 (October 1831): 250. The Greek tribes' meeting at Olympia is a reference to the ancient Olympic Games.

21. John Drayton, *A View of South-Carolina, as Respects Her Natural and Civil Concerns* (Charleston, SC: W. P. Young, 1802), 226; Adger to Smyth, 23 February 1832, in *Autobiographical Notes*, ed.

Stanley, 77; James Stuart, *Three Years in North America* (Edinburgh: R. Cadell, 1833), vol. 2, 131; Bernard E. Powers Jr., *Black Charlestonians: A Social History, 1822–1885* (Fayetteville: University of Arkansas Press, 1994), 43; Jennie Holton Fant, ed., *The Travelers' Charleston: Accounts of Charleston and Lowcountry South Carolina, 1666–1861* (Columbia: University of South Carolina Press, 2016), unpaginated.

22. Nell S. Graydon, "Some Letters from John Christopher Schulz, 1829–1833," *SCHM* 56 (1955): 5; William M. Mathew, ed., *Agriculture, Geology, and Society in Antebellum South Carolina: The Private Diary of Edmund Ruffin, 1843* (Athens: University of Georgia Press, 1992), 103; Robert M. Cahusac to William Porcher, 17 February 1822, 43/568, SCHS; Joel Myerson and Michael C. Weisenburg, "'I Liked the Town No Better at Our Second Interview': A New Emerson Letter from Charleston in 1827," *New England Quarterly* 89 (2016): 500.

23. Rollin G. Osterweis, *Romanticism and Nationalism in the Old South* (New Haven, CT: Yale University Press, 1949), 129; Mildred Cram, *Old Seaport Towns of the South* (New York: Dodd, Mead, 1917), 116–17; David Ramsay, *The History of South-Carolina, from Its First Settlement in 1670, to the Year 1808* (Charleston, SC: David Longworth, 1809), vol. 2, 403–4; Rosser Howard Taylor, "The Gentry of Ante-Bellum South Carolina," *North Carolina Historical Review* 17 (1940): 125; John Lambert, *Lambert's Travels through Lower Canada and the United States* (London: Richard Phillips, 1810), vol. 2, 153. Although the SCJC ball was the most anticipated event of Race Week, elite Charlestonians also hosted their own celebrations; for two decades "Mrs King's ball took place on Tuesday in Race week, as regularly as the Jockey Ball on Friday" (Mrs. St. Julien Ravenel, *Charleston: The Place and the People* [New York: Macmillan, 1906], 474). The hostess was the wife of the jurist Mitchell King, the owner of a famous mansion at the corner of George and Meeting Streets.

24. James Shoolbred to John Shoolbred, 8 March 1791, James Shoolbred Letterbooks and Journals, 1786–1796, SCHS. My thanks to Sally Hadden for bringing this letter to my attention.

25. *Ordinances of the City Council of Charleston* (Charleston, SC: A. Timothy, 1789), 12.

26. Thornwell Jacobs, ed., *Diary of William Plumer Jacobs* (Brookhaven, GA: Oglethorpe University Press, 1937), 35.

27. Ford, *Origins of Southern Radicalism*, 5, 24; Charles Fraser, *Reminiscences of Charleston* (1854; Charleston, SC: Garnier, 1969), 62; Margaret L. Coit, "Moses Waddel: A Light in the Wilderness," *Georgia Review* 5 (1951): 34.

28. Francis Asbury, *The Journal of the Rev. Francis Asbury* (New York: N. Bangs and T. Mason, 1821), vol. 2, 185; William Read to Jacob Read, 14 February 1800, Read Family Papers, 11/342/1, SCHS; Larry H. Ingle, "Joseph Wharton Goes South," *SCHM* 96 (1995): 323; Drayton Mayrant, "Race Week in Charleston," *Charleston News and Courier*, 7 June 1964; Arney R. Childs, ed., *Rice Planter and Sportsman: The Recollections of J. Motte Alston, 1821–1909* (Columbia: University of South Carolina Press, 1953), 19; "Theodore," untitled article, *Charleston Courier*, 13 September 1842; Louise Haskell Day, *Alexander Cheves Haskell: The Portrait of a Man* (Norwood, MA.: privately printed, 1934), 28.

29. Raymond A. Mohl, "'The Grand Fabric of Republicanism': A Scotsman Describes South Carolina, 1810–1811," *SCHM* 71 (1970): 186; Marise Bachand, "Gendered Mobility and the Geography of Respectability in Charleston and New Orleans, 1790–1861," *Journal of Southern History*

81 (2015): 59; Marise Bachand, "A Season in Town: Plantation Women and the Urban South, 1790–1877" (PhD diss., University of Western Ontario, 2011), 180; Cahusac to Porcher, 17 February 1822; Caroline Gilman, *Recollections of a Southern Matron* (New York: Harper & Brothers, 1838), 111, 112; Cynthia M. Kennedy, *Braided Lives, Entwined Relations: The Women of Charleston's Urban Slave Society* (Bloomington: Indiana University Press, 2005), 162.

30. Childs, *J. Motte Alston*, 19; Richard Campbell, "Family Practices and Domestic Problems in a Transatlantic World: Reconstructing the Curious Case of Maria Alston," *SCHM* 113 (2012): 315; D. E. Huger Smith, "Nisbett of Dean and Dean Hall," *SCHGM* 24 (1923): 26; Sally Baxter Hampton to Lucy Baxter, 23 December 1855, in *A Divided Heart: Letters of Sally Baxter Hampton, 1853–1862*, ed. Ann Fripp Hampton (Columbia, SC: Phantom, 1994), 28.

31. Richard Mills to Eliza Mills, 21 March 1817, in Richard Xavier Evans, "Letters from Robert Mills," *SCHGM* 39 (1938), 118; Henry Wharton to Frank Wharton, 1 March 1848, in *Between North and South*, ed. LeClercq, 215.

32. J. Milton Mackie, *From Cape Cod to Dixie and the Tropics* (New York: G. P. Putnam, 1864), 94, 95; italics in original; Gilman, *Recollections*, 112. At midcentury a black satin vest was a popular garment for men "in elegant and fashionable society," but many observers considered it vulgar (Thomas J. Schoonover, *The Life and Times of Gen. John A. Sutter* [1895; Sacramento: Bullock-Carpenter Printing Co., 1907], 15).

33. Gilman, *Recollections*, 113; Irving, *The South Carolina Jockey Club*, 154; Mayrant, "Race Week"; McInnis, *The Politics of Taste*, 62; "Tracing the Tracks of Time," *Charleston Stagebill* 1, no. 9 (February 1993): 56; "Sports of the Turf in America," *American Turf Register and Sporting Magazine* [hereafter *ATR*] 3, no. 9 (May 1837), 423; "Charleston (S.C.) Races," *Spirit of the Times*, 4 March 1848, 19; "The Jockey Club at Charleston," *ATR* 2, no. 11 (July 1831): 564; David S. Shields, *Southern Provisions: The Creation and Revival of a Cuisine* (Chicago: University of Chicago Press, 2015), 129; Henry Wharton to Frank Wharton, 1 March 1848, in *Elizabeth Sinkler Coxe's Tales from the Grand Tour, 1890–1910*, ed. Anne Sinkler Whaley LeClercq (Columbia: University of South Carolina Press, 2006), xiii; Charles Dibdin, *The Songs of Charles Dibdin* (London: G. H. Davidson, 1848), vol. 1, 165; "The South Carolina Jockey Club: An Ancient Organization of Historic Interest," *The Exposition* 1, no. 4 (March 1901): 126. "The High-Mettled Racer" was originally composed for Dibdin's comic opera *Liberty-Hall; or, A Test of Good Fellowship*, which premiered at London's Drury Lane in 1785 (Diana Donald, *Picturing Animals in Britain, 1750–1850* [New Haven, CT: Yale University Press, 2007], 219, 352).

34. Kennedy, *Braided Lives*, 162; "E.J.," "Love at the Jockey Club Ball," *Saturday Evening Post* 1, no. 31 (2 March 1822): 1; originally printed in the *Charleston Courier*.

35. Rodger Stroup, "Up-Country Patrons: Wade Hampton II and His Family," in *Art in the Lives of South Carolinians: Nineteenth-Century Chapters*, ed. David Moltke-Hansen (Charleston, SC: Carolina Art Association, 1979), 2; Edward G. Longacre, *Gentleman and Soldier: A Biography of Wade Hampton III* (Nashville, TN: Rutledge Hill, 2003), 15; LeClercq, *Between North and South*, 88; Drew Gilpin Faust, *James Henry Hammond and the Old South: A Design for Mastery* (Baton Rouge: Louisiana State University Press, 1985), 159.

36. "A National Jockey Club," *Charleston Mercury*, 11 November 1859. This was not the first time that the SCJC had been held up to the turf world as an ideal to which all should aspire; in

1842 an anonymous contributor to the *American Turf Register* described it as "a model of what our Clubs, every where, should be," as "its members comprise the most eminent citizens of the State," and they managed to spend liberally on "the entertainment of its guests and the brilliancy of its meetings" while maintaining a healthy financial surplus ("Race Courses and Jockey Clubs," *ATR* [July 1842]: 404, 405).

37. Lillian Foster, *Wayside Glimpses North and South* (New York: Rudd and Carleton, 1860), 80.

38. Basil Hall, *Travels in North America in the Years 1827 and 1828* (Edinburgh: Cadell, 1829), vol. 2, 146–47.

39. Daniel R. Mandell, *The Lost Tradition of Economic Equality in America* (Baltimore, MD: Johns Hopkins University Press, 2020), 96.

40. Gregory E. O'Malley, "Slavery's Converging Ground: Charleston's Slave Trade as the Black Heart of the Lowcountry," *William and Mary Quarterly*, 3rd ser., vol. 74, no. 2 (April 2017): 276, 273, 280; italics in original.

41. Captain Willard Glazier, *Peculiarities of Great American Cities* (Philadelphia: Hubbard Brothers, 1884), 115; Charles Dickens, "Charleston City," *All the Year Round* 96 (23 February 1861): 462; Dal Lago, "The City as Social Display," 384; William H. Pease and Jane H. Pease, *The Web of Progress: Private Values and Public Styles in Boston and Charleston, 1828–1843* (New York: Oxford University Press, 1985), 9, 10; Kathleen Hilliard, "'In the Days of Her Power and Glory': Visions of Venice in Antebellum Charleston," in *The U.S. South and Europe: Transatlantic Relations in the Nineteenth and Twentieth Centuries*, ed. Cornelis A. van Minnen and Manfred Berg (Lexington: University Press of Kentucky, 2013), 75, 76; Barbara L. Bellows, "Of Time and the City: Charleston in 1860," *SCHM* 112 (2011): 157; W. F. G. Peck, "Four Years under Fire at Charleston," *Harper's New Monthly Magazine* 31 (August 1865): 358; Michael O' Brien, "Italy and the Southern Romantics," in *Rethinking the South: Essays in Intellectual History*, by O'Brien (Baltimore, MD: Johns Hopkins University Press, 1988), 110; Francois Weil, *Family Trees: A History of Genealogy in America* (Cambridge, MA: Harvard University Press, 2013), 83; Frances Anne Kemble, *Journal of a Residence on a Georgia Plantation in 1838–1839*, ed. John Anthony Scott (Athens: University of Georgia Press, 1984), 37.

42. McInnis, *The Politics of Taste*, 10; Weil, *Family Trees*, 82–83; Ford, *Origins of Southern Radicalism*, 137; William W. Freehling, *Prelude to Civil War: The Nullification Crisis in South Carolina, 1816–1836* (1965; New York: Oxford University Press, 1992), 40; Severens, *Charleston*, 27, 63; Blain Roberts and Ethan J. Kytle, "Looking the Thing in the Face: Slavery, Race, and the Commemorative Landscape in Charleston, South Carolina, 1865–2010," *Journal of Southern History* 78 (2012): 641n4.

43. Mathew, *Agriculture, Geology, and Society*, 103; Thompson, *Charleston at War*, 207; "The South Carolina Jockey Club," 126; Lambert, *Lambert's Travels*, vol. 2, 153. Gin sling was a cocktail consisting of gin, lemon juice, sugar, and bitters, and sangaree was made by adding lemon, sugar syrup, and nutmeg to a base of beer or wine.

44. Eliza Cope Harrison, ed., *Best Companions: Letters of Eliza Middleton Fisher and Her Mother, Mary Hering Middleton, from Charleston, Philadelphia, and Newport, 1839–1846* (Columbia: University of South Carolina Press, 2001), 77, 168, 234, 246, 251; italics in original; Catherine Clinton, *Fanny Kemble's Civil Wars* (New York: Oxford University Press, 2001), 65; Robert F. Dalzell Jr., *Enterprising Elite: The Boston Associates and the World They Made* (Cambridge, MA: Harvard University Press,

1987), 45. See also Daniel Kilbride, "Class, Region, and Memory in a South Carolina–Philadelphia Marriage," *Journal of Family History* 28 (2003): 540–60.

45. Irving, *The South Carolina Jockey Club*, 203; italics in original; "Sports of the Turf in America," *Southern Literary Messenger*, reprinted in *ATR* 3, no. 9 (15 April 1837): 424; Tyrone Power, *Impressions of America: during the Years 1833, 1834, and 1835* (Philadelphia: Carey, Lea & Blanchard, 1836), vol. 2, 62.

46. In the early months of the war, it was not a given that the SCJC would cancel Race Week for the duration of the conflict. In August 1861 the club's leaders announced that the event would take place the following February, and that such prominent turfmen as John Cantey and the Virginians Thomas Doswell and Otway Hare had entered horses for it ("ATTENTION TURFMEN!," *Charleston Mercury*, 16 September 1861). Due to the exigencies of the war, the event was canceled.

47. SCJC to the Assistant Commissioner, Bureau of Refugees, Freedmen, and Abandoned Lands, South Carolina, 30 August 1866, South Carolina Jockey Club Records, 1842–1900, Charleston Library Society, Charleston; Roberts and Kytle, "Looking the Thing in the Face," 652; "Charleston's Jockey Club," *The Argonaut*, 26 March 1900.

48. Sallie Doscher, "Art Exhibitions in Nineteenth-Century Charleston," in *Art in the Lives of South Carolinians*, ed. Moltke-Hansen,10; R. Arnold to SCJC, 12 October 1870, South Carolina Jockey Club Records; "The Charleston Races," *New York Times*, 21 January 1875; Thompson, *Charleston at War*, 208.

49. Elizabeth B. Pharo, ed., *Reminiscences of William Hasell Wilson (1811–1902)* (Philadelphia: Patterson and White, 1937), 14; "Spectator," "Horse Races," *Charleston News and Courier*, 28 January 1912; "Tracing the Tracks of Time," 56; "No Better Monument: The Charleston Library Endowed at Last," *Charleston News and Courier*, 3 February 1900; David S. Shields, "Madeira When Charleston Was Madeira Mad," paper presented at the Madeira Dinner, Gadsden House, Charleston, South Carolina, 25 September 2015, www.facebook.com/SlowFoodSouthern/posts/954654747926114; W. M. Hutchinson to Major Theodore G. Barker, 12 December 1892, South Carolina Jockey Club Records; Resolution of the South Carolina Jockey Club, 29 December 1900.

50. "Charleston's Jockey Club"; "Spectator," "Horse Races"; Major Theodore G. Barker to the Charleston Library Society, undated, in "No Better Monument"; Richard Wendorf, *America's Membership Libraries* (New Castle, DE: Oak Knoll, 2007), 54. According to the "Measuring Worth" calculator, $100,000 in 1900 would be worth more than three million dollars today.

51. "Historic Posts for Belmont Park," *New York Times*, 20 April 1903.

52. "Historic Posts for Belmont Park."

53. "Gave Them to Mr. Belmont," *Charleston News and Courier*, 18 April 1903; *The Works of Horace*, trans. C. Smart (New York: Harper & Brothers, 1863), 284.

3. NATCHEZ: NABOBS AT PLAY

First epigraph: Tyrone Power, *Impressions of America; during the Years 1833, 1834, and 1835*, vol. 2 (Philadelphia: Carey, Lea and Blanchard, 1836), 112.

Second epigraph: "The Fourth of July in Natchez," *Mississippi Free Trader*, 20 July 1850.

1. Frederick Law Olmsted, *A Journey in the Seaboard Slave States; with Remarks on Their Economy* (London: Sampson, Low, Son, 1856), 244, 411.

2. Olmsted, *A Journey in the Back Country in the Winter of 1853–4* (New York: Mason Brothers, 1860), 36–37. In 1850 Natchez was the largest town in Mississippi, with a population of just under 4,500 (J. Thomas and T. Baldwin, eds., *A Complete Pronouncing Gazetteer, or Geographical Dictionary of the World* [Philadelphia: J. B. Lippincott, 1859], 1210). In the mid-nineteenth century, clerks in New York and other northeastern cities were renowned, and often ridiculed by those of higher socioeconomic rank, for their dandyish attire and elaborate hair styles (Brian Luskey, *On the Make: Clerks and the Quest for Capital in Nineteenth-Century America* [New York: New York University Press, 2010], 85–86).

3. Joseph Holt Ingraham, *The South-West by a Yankee* (New York: Harper & Brothers, 1835), vol. 2, 29, 219.

4. Taylor to Mary Ann Phillips Taylor, 15 June 1847, in Edwin B. Bronner, ed., "Notes and Documents: A Philadelphia Quaker Visits Natchez," *Journal of Southern History* 27 (1961): 516; Gaines, quoted in Ella Hutchison Ellwanger, "Famous Steamboats and their Captains on Western and Southern Waters," part 2, *Register of the Kentucky State Historical Society* 18 (1920): 25; James R. Creecy, *Scenes in the South* (Washington, DC: Thomas McGill, 1860], 59; Jacob Young, *Autobiography of a Pioneer: On the Nativity, Experience, Travels, and Ministerial Labors of Rev. Jacob Young; with Incidents, Observations, and Recollections* (Cincinnati: Cranston & Curtis, 1857), 222–23.

5. Thomas Barker and Marjie Britz, *Jokers Wild: Legalized Gambling in the Twenty-First Century* (Westport, CT: Praeger, 2000), 22, 23; D. Clayton James, *Antebellum Natchez* (Baton Rouge: Louisiana State University Press, 1968), 254; David Sansing et al., *Natchez: An Illustrated History* (Natchez, MS: Plantation Publishing, 1992), 56. For firsthand accounts of Mississippi riverboat gamblers, see Thomas Ruys Smith, ed., *Blacklegs, Card Sharps, and Confidence Men: Nineteenth-Century Mississippi River Gambling Stories* (Baton Rouge: Louisiana State University Press, 2010).

6. Eugene D. Genovese, *The Sweetness of Life: Southern Planters at Home* (Cambridge, UK: Cambridge University Press, 2017), 237; Harnett T. Kane, *Natchez on the Mississippi* (New York: William Morrow, 1947), 7.

7. Robert E. May, *John A. Quitman: Old South Crusader* (Baton Rouge: Louisiana State University Press, 1985), 19; Matthew S. Berry, "Evangelical Religion and Benevolent Reform in the Antebellum Urban Southwest: Natchez and Vicksburg, Mississippi, 1800–1860" (master's thesis, Eastern Illinois University, 2008), 30.

8. The name of the second of these tracks is also spelled as "St Catharine's."

9. William Ransom Hogan and Edwin Adams Davis, eds., *William Johnson's Natchez: The Ante-Bellum Diary of a Free Negro* (Baton Rouge: Louisiana State University Press, 1979), 4; James, *Antebellum Natchez,* 136; Sven Beckert, *Empire of Cotton: A Global History* (New York: Knopf, 2014), 104, 117; Chad Vanderford, "Peter Little and the Pennsylvania Connection in Antebellum Natchez," *Journal of Mississippi History* 71 (2009): 321; William K. Scarborough, "Lords or Capitalists? The Natchez Nabobs in Comparative Perspective," *Journal of Mississippi History* 54 (1992): 242. The term "nabob" was first used to describe Englishmen who reaped immense fortunes from their involvement in the East India Company in the latter half of the eighteenth century (Margot Finn

and Kate Smith, introduction to *The East India Company at Home, 1757–1857,* ed. Finn and Smith [London: UCL, 2018], 19), and soon became a term to denote an individual of conspicuous wealth, usually acquired recently and probably in unethical or exploitative ways. One million dollars in 1860 is worth approximately $31,700,000 today (www.measuringworth.com/index.php).

10. Beckert, *Empire of Cotton,* 113; Stefan Link and Noam Maggor, "The United States as a Developing Nation: Revisiting the Peculiarities of American History," *Past & Present* 246 (2020): 269.

11. Christopher J. Olsen, *Political Culture and Secession in Mississippi* (New York: Oxford University Press, 2000), 30–31; Robert V. Haynes, *The Mississippi Territory and the Southwest Frontier, 1795–1817* (Lexington: University Press of Kentucky, 2010), 205; Federal Writers' Project, *Mississippi: A Guide to the Magnolia State* (New York: Viking, 1938), 240; "Natchez (Miss.) Jockey Club Races," *Spirit of the Times* (hereafter *Spirit*), 30 November 1850, 486; "Natchez (Miss.) Races," *Spirit,* 20 December 1851, 523.

12. The association transformed itself into the ACJC in 1845, which reconstituted itself in 1850 ("New Jockey Club at Natchez," *Spirit,* 23 August 1845, 432; "The New Jockey Club," *Mississippi Free Trader and Natchez Gazette,* 31 August 1850).

13. Randy J. Sparks, *Religion in Mississippi* (Jackson: University Press of Mississippi, 2001), 33.

14. Deanne Stephens Nuwer and Greg O'Brien, "Mississippi's Oldest Pastime," in *Resorting to Casinos: The Mississippi Gambling Industry,* ed. Denise von Herrmann (Jackson: University Press of Mississippi, 2006), 13; May Wilson McBee, comp., *The Natchez Court Records, 1767–1805: Abstracts of Early Records* (1953; Baltimore, MD: Genealogical Publishing Group, 1994), 1.

15. Richard Aubrey McLemore, *A History of Mississippi* (Jackson: University Press of Mississippi, 1973), vol. 1, 170; James, *Antebellum Natchez,* 32, 35, 37; Sparks, *Religion in Mississippi,* 33; Arthur H. DeRosier Jr., *William Dunbar: Scientific Pioneer of the Old Southwest* (Lexington: University Press of Kentucky, 2007), 60; Hugh Roberts, "Territorial Politics: Formative Identities and Networks in the Mississippi Territory, 1798–1817" (PhD diss., University of Kent, 2020), 120; Federal Writers' Project, *Mississippi,* 252; May, *John A. Quitman,* 20; J. Carlyle Sitterson, "The William J. Minor Plantations: A Study in Ante-Bellum Absentee Ownership," *Journal of Southern History* 9 (1943): 59.

16. Sansing et al., *Natchez,* 56; "Mississippi Jockey Club," *Misissippi* [*sic*] *Herald & Natchez Gazette* 41 (21 October 1807); "Proceedings of the State Legislature," *Mississippi State Gazette* 20 (20 March 1819); "Mississippi Association," *American Turf Register & Sporting Magazine* (hereafter *ATR*) 1, no. 2 (October 1829): 103.

17. "St Catherine's Course," *ATR* 1, no. 7 (March 1830): 360; italics in original; "Sporting Intelligence," *ATR* 4, no. 7 (March 1835): 361; "The Sporting Chronicle," *Traveller and Spirit of the Times,* 9 February 1833; Justin Behrend, "Rebellious Talk and Conspiratorial Plots: The Making of a Slave Insurrection in Civil War Natchez," *Journal of Southern History* 77 (2011): 27; Ingraham, *The South-West,* vol. 2, 219; United States Department of the Interior, *Final Environmental Statement for the Natchez Trace Parkway* (Washington, DC: United States Department of the Interior, 1978), vol. 1, 44; Laura D. S. Harrell, "Horse Racing in the Old Natchez District, 1783–1830," *Journal of Mississippi History* 13 (1951): 123; Franklin L. Riley, "Extinct Towns and Villages of Mississippi," in *Publications of the Mississippi Historical Society,* ed. Riley (Oxford: Mississippi Historical Society,

1902), vol. 5, 370–71; Lynn A. Nelson, *Pharsalia: An Environmental Biography of a Southern Plantation, 1780–1880* (Athens: University of Georgia Press, 2010); James H. Smith, *History of Madison and Chenango Counties* (Syracuse, NY: D. Mason., 1880), vol. 2, 422.

18. "Natchez (Miss.) Jockey Club Races," *Spirit*, 30 November 1850, 486; "Natchez (Miss.) Fall Races," *Spirit*, 11 December 1852, 570; "Jockey Club Rules and Regulations," *Spirit*, 24 January 1846, 566.

19. "Races—Pharsalia Course," *Mississippi Free Trader*, 17 November 1852.

20. "St. Catherine's Course," *ATR* 1, no. 7 (March 1830): 360; "Natchez (Miss.) Fall Races," *Spirit*, 2 December 1854, 409; "Natchez (Miss.) Races," *ATR* 8, no. 2 (October 1836): 92; Hogan and Davis, *William Johnson's Natchez*, 223.

21. "St Catharine's Course," *ATR* 2:12 (August 1831): 620; "Natchez (Miss.) Fall Races," *Spirit*, 1 December 1855, 498; Joseph A. Groves, *The Alstons and Allstons of North and South Carolina* (Atlanta: Franklin Printing, 1901), 339; "Natchez (Miss.) Fall Races," *Spirit*, 1 January 1859, 559; John H. Davis, *The American Turf* (New York: John Polhemus Printing, 1907), 132; "Racing Prospects in Mississippi," *Spirit*, 16 October 1858, 426.

22. "A Turfman," "Col. A. L. Bingaman—The Louisiana Turf," *Spirit*, 27 December 1856, 546.

23. "Natchez (Miss.) Jockey Club Races," *Spirit*, 1 April 1837; James, *Natchez*, 99; Margaret Bisland, "On Horseback over Byways near Natchez," *Outing: An Illustrated Monthly Magazine of Recreation* 15, no. 6 (March 1890): 475; Winthrop D. Jordan, *Tumult and Silence at Second Creek: An Inquiry into a Civil War Slave Conspiracy* (Baton Rouge: Louisiana State University Press, 1999), 35.

24. May, *John A. Quitman*, 212, 348; James, *Natchez*, 260; Charles S. Sydnor, *A Gentleman of the Old Natchez Region: Benjamin L. C. Wailes* (Durham, NC: Duke University Press, 1938), 164, 288; italics in original. Nevitt was apparently untroubled by religious strictures against gambling, as in 1832 he wagered nearly a thousand dollars on Andrew Jackson's reelection (Paul W. Rhode and Koleman Strumpf, "Historical Political Futures Markets: An International Perspective," National Bureau of Economic Research Working Paper 14377, October 2008, 9).

25. McLemore, *A History of Mississippi*, vol. 1, 416.

26. "A Turfman," "Col. A. L. Bingaman," 546; Rudyard Kipling, "If," in Kipling, *Selected Poetry* (London: Penguin, 1992), 243.

27. McLemore, *A History of Mississippi*, 414, 416; Timothy R. Buckner, "Vicksburg's War on Vice: Drinking, Gambling, and Race in the Antebellum South," *Journal of Mississippi History* 67 (2005): 311, 323–24; James, *Natchez*, 260, 89; Smith, *Blacklegs, Card Sharps, and Confidence Men*, 13; Joshua D. Rothman, "The Hazards of the Flush Times: Gambling, Mob Violence, and the Anxieties of America's Market Revolution," *Journal of American History* 95 (2008): 670; Thomas D. Clark and John D. W. Guice, *The Old Southwest, 1795–1830: Frontiers in Conflict* (1989; Norman: University of Oklahoma Press, 1995), 198. On the figure of the "confidence man" more generally, the classic study is Karen Halttunen, *Confidence Men and Painted Women: A Study of Middle-Class Culture in America, 1830–1870* (New Haven, CT: Yale University Press, 1982).

28. See Natalie A. Zacek, "Spectacle and Spectatorship at the Nineteenth-Century American Racetrack," *European Journal of American Studies* 14 (2020): 1–15.

29. See Katherine C. Mooney, *Race Horse Men: How Slavery and Freedom Were Made at the Racetrack* (Cambridge, MA: Harvard University Press, 2014), esp. chap. 1. As Mooney observed, "the entire performance of Thoroughbred racing in the South depended on black labor," as "from conception through foaling, training, competition, and retirement, the champions of the South were in the hands of slave horsemen" (38, 40).

30. Jeff Forret, *Race Relations at the Margins: Slaves and Poor Whites in the Antebellum Southern Countryside* (Baton Rouge: Louisiana State University Press, 2006), 61.

31. Dale Cockrell, "William Johnson: Barber, Musician, Parable," *American Music* 32 (2014): 1, 2; Kimberly Welch, "Black Litigiousness and White Accountability: Free Blacks and the Rhetoric of Reputation in the Antebellum Natchez District," *Journal of the Civil War Era* 5 (2015): 380. The financial comparison was made using the Measuring Worth website and contradicts John Stauffer's claim that Johnson's wealth at his death was nearly two million dollars in modern money (Stauffer, "Interspatialism in the Nineteenth-Century South: The Natchez of Henry Norman," *Slavery and Abolition* 29 [2008]: 250).

32. In 1836, the year in which Johnson first "subscribed to [a] paper called The Sperrits of Times," the magazine cost five dollars per year, as much as a high-quality literary journal such as the *Southern Literary Messenger*, and comparable to approximately $150 today. At the height of its popularity, the *Spirit* boasted forty thousand subscribers across the United States (Hogan and Davis, *William Johnson's Natchez*, 107; Elliott J. Gorn and Warren Goldstein, *A Brief History of American Sports* [Urbana: University of Illinois Press, 1993], 67).

33. Timothy R. Buckner, "A Crucible of Masculinity: William Johnson's Barbershop and the Making of Free Black Men in the Antebellum South," in *Fathers, Preachers, Rebels, Men: Black Masculinity in U.S. History and Literature, 1820–1945*, ed. Buckner and Peter Caster (Columbus: Ohio State University Press, 2011), 49; James, *Natchez*, 255; Norris W. Yates, *William T. Porter and the "Spirit of the Times": A Study of the Big Bear School of Humor* (Baton Rouge: Louisiana State University Press, 1957), 16; Hogan and Davis, *William Johnson's Natchez*, 41–42.

34. Stauffer, "Interspatialism in the Nineteenth-Century South," 250; John Hebron Moore, *The Emergence of the Cotton Kingdom in the Old Southwest: Mississippi, 1770–1860* (Baton Rouge: Louisiana State University Press, 1988), 260; Jordan, *Tumult and Silence*, 36. "Darkey balls," which were held in cities and towns throughout the antebellum South, were social events that were organized by slaveholders as rewards for good behavior among their bondspeople and were also attended by some free people of color. Johnson not only avoided these events but forbade his apprentices from attending them (Richard M. Raichelson, "Black Religious Folksong: A Study in Generic and Social Change" [PhD diss., University of Pennsylvania, 1975], 91).

35. Hogan and Davis, *William Johnson's Natchez*, 225.

36. Quincy T. Mills, *Cutting along the Color Line: Black Barbers and Barber Shops in America* (Philadelphia: University of Pennsylvania Press, 2013), 10, 24; Virginia Meacham Gould, preface to *Chained to the Rock of Adversity: To Be Free, Black, and Female in the Old South*, by Gould (Athens: University of Georgia Press, 1998), xi; Jasmine Nichole Cobb, *Picture Freedom: Remaking Black Visuality in the Early Nineteenth Century* (New York: New York University Press, 2015), 113.

37. Mooney, *Race Horse Men*, 36; Douglas Walter Bristol Jr., *Knights of the Razor: Black Barbers in Slavery and Freedom* (Baltimore, MD: Johns Hopkins University Press, 2009), 82; James, *Natchez*, 254; Edwin Adams Davis and William Ransom Hogan, *The Barber of Natchez* (Baton Rouge: Louisiana State University Press, 1954), 212; italics in original; Patti Carr Black, *Art in Mississippi, 1720–1980* (Jackson: University Press of Mississippi, 1998), 93; Creecy, *Scenes of the South*, 108, 111, 115.

38. Kane, *Natchez on the Mississippi*, 207; Jordan, *Tumult and Silence*, 124; Sansing et al., *Natchez*, 89; Thomas Reber, *Proud Old Natchez: History and Romance* (Natchez: privately published, 1909), 71; Zella Armstrong, comp., *Notable Southern Families* (Chattanooga: Lookout, 1922), 77, 78; "Graduates," *Harvard Register* 1 (1880): 72; Sharon M. Harris, introduction to *Selected Writings of Judith Sargent Murray*, ed. Harris (New York: Oxford University Press, 1995), xlii.

39. Kane, *Natchez on the Mississippi*, 146, 150; McBee, *The Natchez Court Records*, 593; W. H. Sparks, *The Memories of Fifty Years* (Philadelphia: Claxton, Remsen, & Haffelfinger, 1870), chap. 24; J. F. H. Claiborne, *Life and Times of Gen. Sam Dale, the Mississippi Partisan* (New York: Harper & Brothers, 1860), 223.

40. Moore, *The Emergence of the Cotton Kingdom*, 261; Buckner, "Vicksburg's War on Vice," 311; William Banks Taylor, "Southern Yankees: Wealth, High Society, and Political Economy in the Late Antebellum Natchez Region," *Journal of Mississippi History* 59 (1997): 115; Cecilia M. Shulman, "The Bingamans of Natchez," *Journal of Mississippi History* 63 (2001): 301: Joyce L. Broussard, "Stepping Lively in Place: The Free Black Women of Antebellum Natchez," in *Mississippi Women: Their Histories, Their Lives*, ed. Elizabeth Ann Payne et al., vol. 2 (Athens: University of Georgia Press, 2010), 33; J. Hawkins, *Reports of Cases Argued and Determined in the Supreme Court of Louisiana*, vol. 21 (New Orleans: Office of the *Daily Republican*, 1869), 435; Bristol, *Knights of the Razor*, 82–83; Gould, *Chained to the Rock of Adversity*, xi. On slaveholders' acknowledgment of their mixed-race children, see Daniel Livesay, *Children of Uncertain Fortune: Mixed-Race Jamaicans in Britain and the Atlantic Family, 1733–1833* (Chapel Hill: University of North Carolina Press, 2018). Elenora's name is also recorded as Elenore in some sources.

41. Kane, *Natchez on the Mississippi*, 156, 157. As Joshua D. Rothman has observed, in the antebellum South "a man might reasonably believe he could act toward black women sexually as he chose. So long as he kept his affairs quiet . . . no legal or public repercussions were likely to follow" (Rothman, *Notorious in the Neighborhood; Sex and Families across the Color Line in Virginia, 1787–1861* [Chapel Hill: University of North Carolina Press, 2003], 133–134). Bingaman, by contrast, was apparently unwilling to follow such a policy.

42. Morton Rothstein, "The Changing Social Networks and Investment Behavior of a Slaveholding Elite in the Ante-Bellum South: Some Natchez 'Nabobs,' 1800–1860," in *Entrepreneurs in Cultural Context*, ed. Sidney M. Greenfield et al. (Albuquerque: University of New Mexico Press, 1978), 83; Reuben Davis, *Recollections of Mississippi and Mississippians* (Boston: Houghton, Mifflin, 1891), 21; Kane, *Natchez on the Mississippi*, 157, 158, 155. Bingaman, ironically, was interred at New Orleans's Metairie Cemetery, which just a few years before his death had been the site of the Metairie Association course, which is discussed in the following chapter (Kane, *Natchez on the Mississippi*, 158).

43. Morton J. Rothstein, "'The Remotest Corner': Natchez on the American Frontier," in *Natchez before 1830*, ed. Noel Polk (Jackson: University Press of Mississippi, 1989), 96; Beckert, *Empire of Cotton*, 104; Federal Writers' Project, *Mississippi*, 240; Olsen, *Political Culture and Secession in Mississippi*, 30–31; Kimberly Welch, "Arteries of Capital: William Johnson and the Practice of Black Moneylending in the Antebellum U.S. South," *Slavery and Abolition* 41 (2020): 308; Joshua Rothman, "The Contours of Cotton Capitalism: Speculation, Slavery, and Economic Panic in Mississippi, 1832–1841," in *Slavery's Capitalism: A New History of American Economic Development*, ed. Sven Beckert and Seth Rockman (Philadelphia: University of Pennsylvania Press, 2016), 128. See also Thomas C. Buchanan, *Black Life on the Mississippi: Slaves, Free Blacks, and the Western Steamboat World* (Chapel Hill: University of North Carolina Press, 2004).

44. Stauffer, "Interspatialism in the Nineteenth-Century South," 249, 250. Franklin and Armfield's activities are described in detail in Joshua Rothman, *The Ledger and the Chain: How Domestic Slave Traders Shaped America* (New York: Basic, 2021); and Edward E. Baptist, "'Cuffy,' 'Fancy Maids,' and 'One-Eyed Men': Rape, Commodification, and the Domestic Slave Trade in the United States," *American Historical Review* 106 (2001): 1619–50.

45. Bronner, "A Philadelphia Quaker Visits Natchez," 518; Rebecca M. Dresser, "Kate and John Minor: Confederate Unionists of Natchez," *Journal of Mississippi History* 64 (2002): 192.

46. Martha Jane Brazy, *An American Planter: Stephen Duncan of Antebellum Natchez and New York* (Baton Rouge: Louisiana State University Press, 2006), 6; Sitterson, "The William J. Minor Plantations," 60; Jason T. Busch, "'Such a Paradise Can Be Made on Earth': Furniture Patronage and Consumption in Antebellum Natchez, Mississippi, 1828–1863" (master's thesis, University of Delaware, 1998), 35.

47. Alana K. Bevan, "'We Are the Same People': The Leverich Family of New York and Their Antebellum American Inter-Regional Network of Elites" (PhD diss., Johns Hopkins University, 2010), 9, 12, 149; Vanderford, "Peter Little and the Pennsylvania Connection in Antebellum Natchez," 325; William K. Scarborough, "Lords or Capitalists?," 256; Morton Rothstein, "The Changing Social Networks," 81. Thanks to Ronald Walters for bringing Bevan's work to my attention.

48. Cory James Young, "From North to Natchez during the Age of Gradual Abolition," *Pennsylvania Magazine of History and Biography* 143 (2019): 130.

49. Brazy, *An American Planter*, 188n26; Scarborough, "Lords or Capitalists?," 263, 268.

50. Frank Wysor Klingberg, "The Case of the Minors: A Unionist Family within the Confederacy," *Journal of Southern History* 13 (1947): 31, 38; Dresser, "Kate and John Minor," 191, 197.

51. Jordan, *Tumult and Silence at Second Creek*, 54; Taylor, "Southern Yankees," 107.

52. Haynes, *The Mississippi Territory and the Southwest Frontier*, 206.

53. Taylor, "Southern Yankees," 98, 107, 108, 109.

54. Shulman, "The Bingamans of Natchez," 310.

4. NEW ORLEANS: SPEED IN A CITY OF LEISURE

First epigraph: M. Agnes Thompson, "Metairie," in *Metairie and Other Aunt Tilda of New Orleans Sketches* (New Orleans: privately printed, 1892), 62.

Second epigraph: Timothy Flint, *Recollections of the Last Ten Years* (Boston: Cummings, Hilliard, 1826), 337.

1. Hoey to Dupuy, 3 April 1855; Hoey to Dupuy, 20 April 1855, Dugregiy Dupuy and Family Papers, 1852–1910, Mss. 3816, Louisiana and Lower Mississippi Valley Collection, Hill Library, Louisiana State University, Baton Rouge (hereafter LLMVC); emphasis in original. Boston, the get of Sir Archy, was "the king of Southern tracks in the 1830s and 1840s" and was widely regarded as the United States' first great race horse (Katherine C. Mooney, *Race Horse Men: How Slavery and Freedom Were Made at the Racetrack* [Cambridge, MA: Harvard University Press, 2014], 65; Francis Marion Bush, *Colonial Downs and More* [Bloomington, IN: iUniverse, 2011], 130).

2. Hon. Amelia M. Murray, *Letters from the United States, Cuba and Canada* (New York: G. P. Putnam, 1856), 284; Loren Schweninger, "A Negro Sojourner in Antebellum New Orleans," *Louisiana History* 20 (1979): 310. "Rambler," a contributor to the *Spirit of the Times,* reported similar emotional investment on the part of enslaved stable hands at an 1844 race at the Louisiana Course: "The enthusiasm displayed by the *darkies* in Gallwey's stable, when he won the first heat, I have never seen exceeded; but it only heralded the *overflow* when he was victor in the third. Mr. PORTER, of the 'Picayune,' very graphically describes them as 'jumping higher, throwing up caps oftener, and swearing *wusser,* than blackies ever did, so that when the race was won, they had nothing left to do, but to roll and tumble'" ("Rambler," "Review of the Louisiana Course Races," *Spirit of the Times,* 20 January 1844; italics in original).

3. George W. Ranck, *History of Lexington, Kentucky: Its Early Annals and Recent Progress* (Cincinnati: Robert Clarke, 1872), 137; Kent Hollingsworth, *The Kentucky Thoroughbred* (Lexington: University Press of Kentucky, 2009), 30; Mooney, *Race Horse Men,* 94; Hoey to Dupuy, 20 April 1855.

4. Charles E. Trevathan, *The American Thoroughbred* (New York: Macmillan, 1905), 305. Trevathan's claims regarding Lexington's renown in the North were hyperbolic; as John Rickards Betts noted, the region's newspapers in the weeks surrounding the famous race were less concerned with that event than they were with the conflict in "Bleeding Kansas," the formation of the new Republican Party, and the murder of the prizefighter William Poole (Betts, "The Technological Revolution and the Rise of Sport, 1850–1900," *Mississippi Valley Historical Review* 40 [1953]: 239).

5. Ranck, *History of Lexington, Kentucky,* 137; Rebecca Cassidy, *Horse People: Thoroughbred Culture in Lexington and Newmarket* (Baltimore, MD: Johns Hopkins University Press, 2007), 66; Hamilton Busbey, "The Running Turf in America: Second Paper," *Harper's New Monthly Magazine* 41 (July 1870): 248. According to Measuring Worth, the former price is comparable to $85,000 and the latter to $467,000 (www.measuringworth.com/calculators/uscompare/).

6. Henry William Herbert, *Frank Forester's Horse and Horsemanship of the United States and British Provinces of North America* (New York: Stringer & Townsend, 1857), vol. 1, 306.

7. Rashauna Johnson, *Slavery's Metropolis: Unfree Labor in New Orleans during the Age of Revolutions* (New York: Cambridge University Press, 2016), 1; Kenneth Aslakson, "The 'Quadroon-*Placage*' Myth of Antebellum New Orleans: Anglo-American (Mis)Interpretations of a French-Caribbean Phenomenon," *Journal of Social History* 45 (2012): 713; Hans C. Rasmussen, "The Culture of Bullfighting in Antebellum New Orleans," *Louisiana History* 55 (2014): 133; Louis J. Hennessey, "The Fair Grounds Race Course: A Time-Honored American Institution," in *Diamond Jubilee: The Fair*

Grounds, New Orleans, by Hennessey (New Orleans: New Orleans Fair Ground Corporation, 1947), 4; Harold D. Moser and J. Clint Clift, eds., *The Papers of Andrew Jackson*, vol. 6 (Knoxville: University of Tennessee Press, 2002), 528.

8. Nathan Burman, "Two Histories, One Future: Louisiana Sugar Planters and the Anglo-Creole Schism, 1815–1865 (PhD diss., Louisiana State University, 2013), 84; Dale A. Somers, *The Rise of Sports in New Orleans, 1850–1900* (Baton Rouge: Louisiana State University Press, 1972), 25; Crozet J. Duplantier, "A Sportsman's Town," in *The Past as Prelude: New Orleans, 1718–1968*, ed. Hodding Carter (New Orleans: Pelican, 1968), 189; James Stuart, *Three Years in North America*, 3rd ed. (Edinburgh: Robert Cadell, 1833), vol. 2, 226; Madelyn Hannan, "Horseracing in New Orleans: The Eclipse Course as a Case Study, 1837–1849" (master's thesis, University of New Orleans, 2002), 9–11. Very little information exists regarding the Live Oak races, but an unattributed newspaper notice from 1822 stated that the following January would see a four-day meeting there and expressed the hope that newspaper editors in Natchez, Huntsville, Lexington, and Nashville "who are friendly disposed towards the Turf, will please give publicity to the above notice" (New Orleans Scrap-Book, 1813–1865, p. 18, LLMVC).

9. Somers, *The Rise of Sports in New Orleans*, 24; Craig Anthony Bauer, "A Leader among Peers: The Life and Times of Duncan Farrar Kenner" (PhD diss., University of Southern Mississippi, 1989), 154; Robert Black, *Horse-Racing in France: A History* (London: Sampson Low, Marston, Searle, & Rivington, 1886), 2; Robert L. Herbert, *Impressionism: Art, Leisure, and Parisian Society* (New Haven, CT: Yale University Press, 1988), 152, 154; Jesus Cruz, *The Rise of Middle-Class Culture in Nineteenth-Century Spain* (Baton Rouge: Louisiana State University Press, 2011), 217. Daniel Roche wrote extensively on the role of the horse in the display of royal and aristocratic power in *ancien régime* France, but neither at home nor in *la Nouvelle France* did the members of the prerevolutionary elite deploy racing to bolster their hegemony (see Roche, *France in the Enlightenment*, trans. Arthur Goldhammer [Cambridge, MA: Harvard University Press, 1998], 275–77; and Roche, "Equestrian Culture in France from the Sixteenth to the Nineteenth Century," *Past and Present* 199 [2008]: 141).

10. Scott P. Marler, *The Merchants' Capital: New Orleans and the Political Economy of the Nineteenth-Century South* (New York: Cambridge University Press, 2013); 1; Thomas Ruys Smith, *Southern Queen: New Orleans in the Nineteenth Century* (London: Continuum, 2011), 62; Alecia P. Long, *The Great Southern Babylon: Sex, Race, and Respectability in New Orleans, 1865–1920* (Baton Rouge: Louisiana State University Press, 2004), 2.

11. Hannan, "Horseracing," 31, 40–41, 42.

12. "Southern Racing," *Spirit of the Times*, 9 June 1838; Somers, *The Rise of Sports in New Orleans*, 25, 26; James Guilbeau, *The Saint Charles Streetcar, or, the History of the New Orleans and Carrollton Railroad* (New Orleans: Louisiana Landmarks Society, 1975), 22; Duplantier, "A Sportsman's Town," 190; Henry Rightor, *Standard History of New Orleans* (New Orleans: Lewis, 1900), 472; Harnett T. Kane, *Queen New Orleans* (New York: William Morrow, 1949), 304; Jessica M. Lepler, *The Many Panics of 1837: People, Politics, and the Creation of a Transatlantic Financial Crisis* (New York: Cambridge University Press, 2013), *passim;* Alexander Mackay-Smith, *The Race-Horses of America, 1832–1872: Portraits and Other Paintings by Edward Troye* (Saratoga Springs, NY: National Museum of Racing, 1981), 113; Arthur F. Jones and Bruce Weber, *The Kentucky Painter: From the*

Frontier Era to the Great War (Lexington: University of Kentucky Art Museum, 1981), 42; A. Oakey Hall, *The Manhattaner in New Orleans; or, Phases of Crescent City Life* (New York: J. S. Redfield, 1851), 133; "Little 'Un," "The 'Fast Boys' at New Orleans," *Spirit of the Times*, 28 July 1849; "On Dits in Sporting Circles," *Spirit of the Times*, 26 April 1851; "Orleans Jockey Club Races," *Spirit of the Times*, 10 May 1851. The "best bottomed" horse was that of the greatest stamina.

13. "Bingaman Course, New Orleans," *Spirit of the Times*, 17 July 1847; "A Novel Race at New Orleans," *Spirit of the Times*, 8 June 1850; "Orleans Jockey Club Fall Meeting, Bingaman Course," *Spirit of the Times*, 21 December 1850; Steven A. Riess, ed., *Sports in America from Colonial Times to the Twenty-First Century: An Encyclopedia* (Abingdon, UK: Taylor & Francis, 2015), 454; "The Welsh Main Race at New Orleans," *Spirit of the Times*, 20 March 1852. The Bingaman was not the only New Orleanian course that resorted to staging popular recreations of the type disdained by turfmen in order to attract spectators; the Louisiana Course also featured greased pig races, gander pulling, and a greased pole exhibition ("Mark," "American Turf Statistics," *Spirit of the Times*, 17 July 1852). Peytona, owned by the South Carolinian turfman Wade Hampton II, had defeated Fashion in the North-South match race of 1845 (Herbert, *Frank Forester*, 165), and Revenue was the pride of the stable of the leading Virginian horse breeder John Minor Botts (Busbey, "The Running Turf in America: Second Paper," 249).

14. Sandra Frink has estimated that twenty thousand to thirty thousand people visited the city each year throughout the 1840s and 1850s, primarily during the "winter" season (November to May), when both the business and leisure scenes were at their height (Frink, "'Strangers Are Flocking Here': Identity and Anonymity in New Orleans, 1810–1860," *American Nineteenth Century History* 11 [2010]: 156, 159).

15. Somers, *The Rise of Sports in New Orleans*, 26, 27; "Mark," "American Turf Statistics"; John Dizikes, *Sportsmen and Gamesmen* (Columbia: University of Missouri Press, 2002), 145; "The Louisiana Turf," *Spirit of the Times*, 1 March 1851. In 1851, $10,000 was worth approximately $345,000 today (www.measuringworth.com/calculators/uscompare/relativevalue.php).

16. "Richard Ten Broeck Dead," *San Francisco Morning Call*, 2 August 1892; Dizikes, *Sportsmen and Gamesmen*, 142–43, 156; "Mr. Richard Ten Broeck," *Baily's Magazine of Sports and Pastimes* 8, no. 51 (1864): 55; "One of the Old School," *Illustrated American* 11, no. 130 (13 August 1892): 623.

17. Dizikes, *Sportsmen and Gamesmen*, 143; John H. Davis, *The American Turf* (New York: John Polhemus Printing, 1907), 50.

18. Dizikes, *Sportsmen and Gamesmen*, 145; D. R. Hundley, Esq., *Social Relations in Our Southern States* (New York: Henry B. Price, 1860), 246–47; Mrs. [Matilda C. F.] Houstoun, *Hesperos; or, Travels in the West* (London: John W. Parker, 1850), vol. 2, 70; italics in original.

19. John H. Davis, *The American Turf*, 28, 108, 109, 126; Peter S. Carmichael, *Lee's Young Artillerist: William R. J. Pegram* (Charlottesville: University Press of Virginia, 1995), 8. The famed calm of the "plunger" under all circumstances paralleled that of the man who engaged in high-stakes card games; "it is proverbial among the 'craft' [of card-playing] that a man who has the nerve to gamble extensively, as a rule, is possessed of the courage to stand under the ruin he has wrought. In fact, you rarely see more philosophic calmness than is exhibited at the gaming-table" ("Gambling at Saratoga," *San Francisco Daily Evening Bulletin*, 6 September 1866).

20. "John," "From Alabama," *New York Times*, 12 April 1854; "The Turf: Racing Prospects in New Orleans," *New Orleans Times-Picayune*, 12 December 1853. The "Nebraska bill" was the Kansas-Nebraska Act, which advocated the repeal of the Missouri Compromise of 1820 on the issue of the expansion of slavery into newly acquired United States territories, and was under impassioned debate in Congress in the early months of 1854 (see Alice Elizabeth Malavesec, *The F Street Mess: How Southern Senators Rewrote the Kansas-Nebraska Act* [Chapel Hill: University of North Carolina Press, 2017], 5). Measuring Worth compares $100,000 in 1854 to $3.1 million in 2020 (www.measuringworth.com/calculators/uscompare/).

21. W. H. Coleman, *Historical Sketch Book and Guide to New Orleans and Environs* (New York: William H. Coleman, 1885), 242, 243; Rightor, *Standard History of New Orleans*, 472; "Metairie Course Great Post State Stake," *Daily True Delta*, 2 April 1854; Robert Wickliffe Woolley, "Famous Old-Time Races," *Munsey's Magazine* 32 (November 1904): 290.

22. Nancy L. Struna, "The North-South Races: American Thoroughbred Racing in Transition, 1823–1850," *Journal of Sport History* 8 (1981): 28; see also John Eisenberg, *The Great Match Race: When North Met South in America's First Sports Spectacle* (Boston: Houghton Mifflin, 2006); and Paul Johnson, "Northern Horse: American Eclipse as a Representative New Yorker," *Journal of the Early Republic* 33 (2013): 701–76.

23. Kirsten Silva Gruesz, "Delta *Desterrados:* Antebellum New Orleans and New World Print Culture," in *Look Away! The U.S. South in New World Studies*, ed. Jon Smith and Deborah Cohn (Durham, NC: Duke University Press, 2004), 52; Frink, "'Strangers are Flocking Here,'" 160.

24. Betts, "The Technological Revolution and the Rise of Sport," 243. For mid-nineteenth-century Americans who considered themselves refined, even reading about "the loathsome details of prize fights . . . and the personal history and adventures of bullies" was anathema (see John Rickards Betts, "Sporting Journalism in Nineteenth-Century America," *American Quarterly* 5 [1953]: 45).

25. T. J. Jackson Lears, *Something for Nothing: Luck in America* (New York: Viking, 2003), 152, 153; Edward E. Baptist, *The Half Has Never Been Told: Slavery and the Making of American Capitalism* (New York: Basic, 2014); Walter Johnson, *River of Dark Dreams: Slavery and Empire in the Cotton Kingdom* (Cambridge, MA: Belknap Press of Harvard University Press, 2013); Scott P. Marler, *The Merchants' Capital;* Sven Beckert, *Empire of Cotton: A Global History* (New York: Knopf, 2014). The phrase "The City That Care Forgot" was first used about New Orleans in 1938, but the city had boasted such a reputation for at least a century (Louise McKinney, *New Orleans: A Cultural History* [New York: Oxford University Press, 2006], 24).

26. T. Michael Parrish, *Richard Taylor: Soldier Prince of Dixie* (Chapel Hill: University of North Carolina Press, 1992), 66; W. H. Coleman, *Historical Sketch Book and Guide to New Orleans* (New York: W. H. Coleman, 1885), 94, 95; Robert Tallant, *The Romantic New Orleanians* (New York: E. P. Dutton, 1950), 218; Lillian C. Bourgeois, *Cabanocey: The History, Customs and Folklore of St. James Parish* (1957; Gretna, LA: Pelican, 1998), 72.

27. Stuart D. Landry, *History of the Boston Club* (New Orleans: Pelican, 1938), 23, 27, 57, 59; Marler, *The Merchants' Capital*, 73, 75; Somers, *The Rise of Sports*, 28.

28. Bauer, "A Leader among Peers," 154, 156, 157, 158; Bauer, *A Leader among Peers: The Life and Times of Duncan Farrar Kenner* (Lafayette, LA: Center for Louisiana Studies, 1993), 65, 288; Garner

Ranney, ed., *A Man of Pleasure, and a Man of Business: The European Travel Diaries of Duncan Farrar Kenner, 1833–4* (Lafayette, LA: Center for Louisiana Studies, 1991), xiv; John Timbs, *Curiosities of London* (London: David Bogue, 1855), 704; Christopher Benfey, *Degas in New Orleans: Encounters in the Creole World of Kate Chopin and George Washington Cable* (Berkeley: University of California Press, 1997), 22, 23; Nathan Burman, "Two Histories, One Future," 88; Allie B. Windham Webb, ed., *Mistress of Evergreen Plantation: Rachel O'Connor's Legacy of Letters, 1823–1845* (Albany: State University of New York Press, 1983), 93–94.

29. Edwin L. Jewell, *Crescent City Illustrated: The Commercial, Social, Political and General History of New Orleans* (New Orleans: privately printed, 1873), 137; William Howard Russell, *My Diary North and South* (London: Bradbury and Evans, 1863), vol. 1, 413.

30. Harnett T. Kane, *Plantation Parade: The Grand Manner in Louisiana* (New York: William Morrow, 1945), 187, 189, 190–91; Stanley Clisby Arthur and George Campbell Huchet de Kernion, *Old Families of Louisiana* (1931; Baltimore, MD: Genealogical Publishing, 2009), 160; Grace Elizabeth King, *Creole Families of New Orleans* (New York: Macmillan, 1921), 414.

31. Bauer, "A Leader among Peers," 163; Charles L. Wingfield, "The Sugar Plantations of William J. Minor, 1830–1860" (master's thesis, Louisiana State University, 1950), 22, 25; Alana Bevan, "We Are the Same People: The Leverich Family of New York and Their Antebellum American Inter-Regional Network of Elites" (PhD diss., Johns Hopkins University, 2009), 149; diary of William J. Minor, 22 March 1857, quoted in D. Clayton James, *Antebellum Natchez* (Baton Rouge: Louisiana State University Press, 1968), 255; italics in original; James Silk Buckingham, *The Slave States of America* (London: Fischer, 1842), vol. 2, 213; Burman, "Two Histories, One Future," 85; Duplantier, "A Sportsman's Town," 90.

32. Coleman, *Historical Sketch-Book*, 241; Sarah Searight, *New Orleans* (New York: Stein and Day, 1973), 85; Mrs. Thomas Sibley to Thom Sibley, 4 April 1856, Morris-Sibley Papers, LLMVC; Martha Ann Peters, "The St. Charles Hotel: New Orleans Social Center, 1837–1860," *Louisiana History* 1 (1960): 199; Eliza Ripley, *Social Life in Old New Orleans: Being Recollections of My Girlhood* (New York: D. Appleton, 1912), 245; "The Racing Season," *New Orleans Times-Picayune*, 7 November 1850. Northerners were equally impressed by the hotel; Lillian Foster, a wealthy New Yorker who visited New Orleans in the 1840s, described it as "a magnificent establishment" and "one of the finest hotels in America" (Foster, *Wayside Glimpses North and South* [New York: Rudd and Carleton, 1860], 152, 153).

33. Robert C. Reinders, *End of an Era: New Orleans, 1850–1860* (New Orleans: Pelican, 1964), 160; Benjamin Moore Norman, *Norman's New Orleans and Environs* (New Orleans: B. M. Norman, 1845), 196; Rollin G. Osterweis, *Romanticism and Nationalism in the Old South* (New Haven, CT: Yale University Press, 1949), 130; Parrish, *Richard Taylor*, 66; Coleman, *Historical Sketch-Book*, 241.

34. Lester B. Shippee, ed., *Bishop Whipple's Southern Diary, 1843–1844* (New York: Da Capo, 1968), 116–17; "Revolting," *Christian Reflector*, 12 June 1839; italics in original; *Truth Is Stranger Than Fiction, or, New Orleans As It Is* (Utica, NY: DeWitt C. Grove, 1849), 33, 42, 45; Lura Robinson, *It's an Old New Orleans Custom* (New York: Vanguard, 1948), 111; Ripley, *Social Life in Old New Orleans*, 246–48; Hennessey, "The Fair Grounds Race Course," 5. On female attendance, see, for example, "Rambler," "Review of the Louisiana Course Races." Luke E. Harlow names Robert L.

Stanton, a Connecticut-born Presbyterian minister who spent thirty years in the South, as this pamphlet's probable author (see Harlow, *Religion, Race, and the Making of Confederate Kentucky, 1830–1880* [New York: Cambridge University Press, 2014], 178). The Congregationalist minister Timothy Flint, who visited New Orleans in the early 1820s, when the Creole-centered Live Oak course was the city's sole racetrack, claimed that "even the ladies visit these amusements, and bet with the gentlemen" (Flint, *Recollections of the Last Ten Years* [Boston: Cummings, Hilliard, 1826], 337).

35. Kathryn Olivarius, *Necropolis: Disease, Power, and Capitalism in the Cotton Kingdom* (Cambridge, MA: Harvard University Press, 2022), 98.

36. John O'Connor, *Wanderings of a Vagabond: An Autobiography* (New York: privately published, 1873), 136.

37. Dale A. Somers, "War and Play: The Civil War in New Orleans," *Mississippi Quarterly* 26 (1972): 13; W. H. Tunnard, *A Southern Record: The History of the Third Regiment Louisiana Infantry* (Baton Rouge: privately printed, 1866), 25; Duplantier, "A Sportsman's Town," 192; Carrie Meitzner Akard, "Southern Genre Painting and Illustration from 1830 to 1890" (master's thesis, University of North Texas, 1997), 105; Patti Carr Black, *Art in Mississippi, 1720–1980* (Jackson: University Press of Mississippi, 1998), 69; Eleanor Early, *New Orleans Holiday* (New York: Rhinehart, 1947), 219. New Orleans was not entirely devoid of racing during the Metairie's wartime closure; the riverboat gambler George H. Devol ran a lakeside entertainment venue whose offerings included racing, trotting, and pacing (Devol, *Forty Years a Gambler on the Mississippi*, 2nd ed. [New York: George H. Devol, 1926], 221).

38. Kane, *Queen New Orleans*, 304; Rosella Kenner Brent, "The Federal Raid upon Ashland Plantation in July 1862," Rosella Kenner Brent Recollections, LLMVC; Walter G. Cowan et al., *New Orleans Yesterday and Today* (Baton Rouge: Louisiana State University Press, 1983), 71; Henri A. Gandolfo, *Metairie Cemetery: An Historical Memoir* (New Orleans; Stewart Enterprises, 1981), 15; Early, *New Orleans Holiday*, 219; Leonard V. Huber et al., *New Orleans Architecture*, vol. 3: *The Cemeteries* (Gretna, LA: Pelican, 2004), 51, 52; Joy J. Jackson, *New Orleans in the Gilded Age: Politics and Urban Progress, 1880–1896* (Baton Rouge: Louisiana State University Press, 1969), 269; King, *New Orleans: The Place and the People*, 290. The Ashland raid reflected the Union army's practice of "taking all the negro men and horses they can find in the country" (John C. Rodrigue, *Freedom's Crescent: The Civil War and the Destruction of Slavery in the Lower Mississippi Valley* [Cambridge, UK: Cambridge University Press, 2023], 75).

39. Note by Lewis A. Walter, 1938, Louis Allahwyn Walker Additional Papers, Mss. A W232b 9, p. 2, Filson Historical Society, Louisville, Kentucky; Lyman Horace Weeks, *The American Turf* (New York: Historical Company, 1898) 119; "A Young Turfman, "Racing Prospects in Louisiana and Mississippi," *Spirit of the Times*, 8 November 1851; John Lawrence, *The History and Delineation of the Horse, in All His Varieties* (1809; New York: Olms, 1979), 215.

40. Somers, *The Rise of Sports in New Orleans*, 32; "American Race Horses Going to Europe," *New York Herald*, reprinted in the *Pittsfield Sun*, 21 August 1856; "Sporting Notions of the American Press," *Racing Times*, 19 January 1857; "The American Horses and the Goodwood Cup," *Bell's Life in London and Sporting Chronicle*, 13 September 1857. The Goodwood Cup, inaugurated in 1808 at

the eponymous course in Sussex, had by midcentury emerged as a highlight of the English racing season.

41. Sarah Agnes Wallace and Frances Elma Gillespie, eds., *The Journal of Benjamin Moran, 1857–1865* (Chicago: University of Chicago Press, 1948), vol. 1, 183; "The American Horses in England," *Racing Times*, 19 October 1857; "Mr. Ten Broeck's Return," *New York Evening Post*, 11 November 1858; John Dizikes, "Richard Ten Broeck," *American National Biography Online*, https://doi.org/10.1093/anb/9780198606697.article.1900217. Throughout the nineteenth century, the majority of Americans believed that relocating animals, including horses, from one part of the world to another was likely to result in significant physical changes, and even in degeneration (Ann Norton Greene, *Horses at Work: Harnessing Power in Industrial America* [Cambridge, MA: Harvard University Press, 2008], 87).

42. "Rumoured Retirement of Mr. Ten Broeck," *Racing Times*, 5 August 1861.

43. Dizikes, "Richard Ten Broeck"; Edwin Lefevre, "James Robert Keene," *Cosmopolitan: A Monthly Outing Magazine*, November 1902.

5. SARATOGA: FROM SEDATE RESORT TO RACING MECCA

First epigraph: "Saratoga: The American Baden-Baden," *Every Saturday: An Illustrated Weekly Journal*, 9 September 1871.

Second epigraph: William Dean Howells, *Life in Letters of William Dean Howells*, vol. 2, ed. Mildred Howells (New York: Doubleday, Doran, 1929).

1. Myrta Lockett Avary, *Dixie after the War* (New York: Doubleday, Page, 1906), 150, 157, 168; Ted Ownby, *Subduing Satan: Religion, Recreation, and Manhood in the Rural South, 1865–1920* (Chapel Hill: University of North Carolina Press, 1990), 67; Lossing, quoted in John Hervey, *Racing in America, 1665–1865* (New York: The Jockey Club, 1944), vol. 2, 346. On the frustrations experienced by many Confederate women, see Drew Gilpin Faust, "Altars of Sacrifice: Confederate Women and the Narratives of War," *Journal of American History* 76 (1990): 1200–28.

2. Edward A. Wyatt IV, "Newmarket of the Virginia Turf," *William and Mary Quarterly* 17 (1937): 491; Edwin B. Houghton, *The Campaigns of the Seventeenth Maine* (Portland, ME: Short & Loring, 1866), 204; H. H. Cunningham, "Confederate General Hospitals: Establishment and Organization," *Journal of Southern History* 20 (1954): 383; Anthony Kaye, *Joining Places: Slave Neighborhoods in the Old South* (Chapel Hill: University of North Carolina Press, 2007), 185; Justin Behrend, *Reconstructing Democracy: Grassroots Black Politics in the Deep South after the Civil War* (Athens: University of Georgia Press, 2015), 22–23; Winthrop D. Jordan, *Tumult and Silence at Second Creek: An Inquiry into a Civil War Slave Conspiracy*, rev. ed. (Baton Rouge: Louisiana State University Press, 1995), 244.

3. *Census of the State of New York for 1865* (Albany, NY: Charles Van Benthuysen and Sons, 1867), lv; Jon Sterngass, *First Resorts: Pursuing Pleasure at Saratoga Springs, Newport and Coney Island* (Baltimore, MD: Johns Hopkins University Press, 2001), 7, 12; Will B. Mackintosh, *Selling the Sights: The Invention of the Tourist in American Culture* (New York: New York University Press, 2019), 37, 193; Adam Hodgson, *Remarks during a Journey through North America in the Years 1819,*

1820, and 1821 (New York: Samuel Whiting, 1823), 122; Thomas W. Doswell to Frances Doswell, 31 July 1875, Doswell Family Papers, Section 4, T. W. Doswell—Correspondence (1823–1890), Mss. 1 D7424, Virginia Historical Society, Richmond; Brian Patrick Tyrrell, "Bred for the Race: Thoroughbred Horses and the Politics of Pedigree" (PhD diss., University of California–Santa Barbara, 2019), 124; Gary Cross, "Saratoga Springs: From Genteel Spa to Disneyfied Family Resort," *Journal of Tourism History* 4 (2012): 76; Gideon M. Davison, *The Fashionable Tour: A Guide to Travellers Visiting the Middle and Northern States, and the Provinces of Canada*, 4th ed. (Saratoga Springs, NY: G. M. Davison, 1830), 164; Thomas A. Chambers, *Drinking the Waters: Creating an American Leisure Class at Nineteenth-Century Mineral Springs* (Washington, DC: Smithsonian Institution Press, 2002), 190; Rebecca Cawood McIntyre, *Souvenirs of the Old South: Northern Tourism and Southern Mythology* (Gainesville: University Press of Florida, 2011), 14; Charlene M. Boyer Lewis, *Ladies and Gentlemen on Display: Planter Society at the Virginia Springs, 1790–1860* (Charlottesville: University Press of Virginia, 2001), 101; Jon M. Sterngass, "African American Workers and Southern Visitors at Antebellum Saratoga Springs," *American Nineteenth-Century History* 2 (2001): 44; John Hayward, *A Gazetteer of the United States of America* (Hartford, CT: Case, Tiffany, 1853), 669; "The Saratoga Races," *Boston Daily Advertiser*, 14 August 1865; *New York World*, 8 August 1865, quoted in John Hope Franklin, ed., *A Southern Odyssey: Travelers in the Antebellum North* (Baton Rouge: Louisiana State University Press, 1976), 269.

4. Franklin, *A Southern Odyssey*, 269; Katherine C. Mooney, *Race Horse Men: How Slavery and Freedom Were Made at the Racetrack* (Cambridge, MA: Harvard University Press, 2014), 147; "The Metairie-Race Course," *Frank Leslie's Illustrated Newspaper*, 4 May 1872; *American Turf Register: A Correct Synopsis of Turf Events in the United States, Embracing, Running, Trotting and Pacing, for 1870* (New York: Bruce, 1871), 62; Craig A. Bauer, *A Leader among Peers: The Life and Times of Duncan Farrar Kenner* (Lafayette, LA: Center for Louisiana Studies, 1993), 198. The responsibilities of race-day officials are set out in "Rules of the Saratoga Association," in *Rules and Regulations for the Government of Racing, Trotting, and Betting, as Adopted by the Principal Turf Associations throughout the United States and Canada* (New York: M. B. Brown, 1866), 28–29.

5. Eugene D. Genovese, *The Sweetness of Life: Southern Planters at Home* (Cambridge, UK: Cambridge University Press, 2017), 204; George Fitzhugh, "Southern Thought—Its New and Important Manifestations," *De Bow's Review* 23, no. 4 (October 1857): 340; Nina Silber, *The Romance of Reunion: Northerners and the South, 1865–1900* (Chapel Hill: University of North Carolina Press, 1993); Silber, "Intemperate Men, Spiteful Women, and Jefferson Davis: Northern Views of the Defeated South," *American Quarterly* 41 (1989): 614, 624; Eric Homberger, *Mrs. Astor's New York: Money and Social Power in a Gilded Age* (New Haven, CT: Yale University Press, 2002), 166.

6. Daniel Kilbride, "Travel, Ritual, and National Identity: Planters on the European Tour, 1820–1860," *Journal of Southern History* 69 (2003): 553; Jane H. Pease, "A Note on Patterns of Conspicuous Consumption among Seaboard Planters, 1820–1860," *Journal of Southern History* 35 (1969): 391–92.

7. Elliott J. Gorn, *The Manly Art: Bare-Knuckle Fighting in America* (Ithaca, NY: Cornell University Press, 1986), 108–10, 126; "Death of John Morrissey," *New York Tribune*, 2 May 1878; T. J. Stiles, *The First Tycoon: The Epic Life of Cornelius Vanderbilt* (New York: Vintage, 2009), 398; Myra B.

Young Armstead, *Lord, Please Don't Take Me in August: African Americans in Newport and Saratoga Springs, 1870–1930* (Urbana: University of Illinois Press, 1999), 12.

8. James C. Nicholson, *The Notorious John Morrissey: How a Bare-Knuckle Brawler Became a Congressman and Founded Saratoga Race Course* (Lexington: University Press of Kentucky, 2016), 75.

9. Carole Case, *The Right Breed: America's Aristocrats in Thoroughbred Racing* (New Brunswick, NJ: Rutgers University Press, 2000), 7; Eli Perkins, *Saratoga in 1901* (New York: Sheldon, 1872), 23.

10. Lewis, *Ladies and Gentlemen on Display*, 14, 201–6; Jeffrey C. Benton, *Respectable and Disreputable: Leisure Time in Antebellum Montgomery* (Montgomery, AL: NewSouth Books, 2013), 59; Susan Nance, "Game Stallions and Other 'Horseface Minstrelsies' of the American Turf," *Theatre Journal* 65 (2013): 360; William J. Baker, *Sports in the Western World*, rev. ed. (Urbana: University of Illinois Press, 1988), 109; Jessica Dallow, *Race, Gender and Identity in American Equine Art: 1832 to the Present* (New York: Routledge, 2022), 60; Oliver Wendell Holmes, *The Autocrat of the Breakfast-Table* (Boston: Houghton, Mifflin, 1892), 34; italics in original; Nicholas J. Hoey to Dugregiy Dupuy, 20 April 1855, Dugregiy Dupuy Family Papers, 1852–1910, Louisiana and Lower Mississippi Valley Collection, Mss. 3816, Hill Memorial Library, Louisiana State University, Baton Rouge; Paul Johnson, "Northern Horse: American Eclipse as a Representative New Yorker," *Journal of the Early Republic* 33 (2013): 714; "Druid," "Racing Prospects in Louisiana," *Spirit of the Times*, 27 June 1857; italics in original.

11. Nicholson, *The Notorious John Morrissey*, 12; Bernard Livingston, *Their Turf: America's Horsey Set and Its Princely Dynasties* (New York: Arbor House, 1973), 22; Nancy L. Struna, "The North-South Races: American Thoroughbred Racing in Transition, 1823–1850," *Journal of Sport History* 8 (1981): 32; William Gleason, "Grounds for Fun: The Place of Play in 19th-Century American Culture," *Nineteenth-Century Contexts* 35 (2013): 465; Hamilton Busbey, "The Running Turf in America: First Paper," *Harper's New Monthly Magazine* 41 (June 1870), 93, 94; Steven A. Riess, "The Cyclical History of Horse Racing: The USA's Oldest and (Sometimes) Most Popular Spectator Sport," *International Journal of the History of Sport* 31 (2014): 32, 34; Thomas L. Nichols, *Forty Years of American Life* (London: John Maxwell, 1864), vol. 1, 393. The "Knickerbockers" were the descendants of the Dutch settlers of colonial New York and constituted the majority of the city's elite until the middle decades of the nineteenth century, when they were supplanted by newly rich industrialists and financiers (Benson John Lossing, *History of New York City* [New York: Perine Engraving and Publishing, 1884], vol. 1, 66).

12. Holly Kruse, *Off-Track and Online: The Networked Spaces of Horse Racing* (Cambridge, MA: MIT Press, 2016), 55; "The Turf: Saratoga Race Meeting," *New York Herald*, 6 August 1863; Hugh Bradley, *Such Was Saratoga* (New York: Doubleday, Doran, 1940), 143; Henry Horenstein and Brendan Boyd, *Racing Days* (New York: Viking, 1987), 26.

13. Andrew K. Frank, *The Routledge Historical Atlas of the American South* (New York: Routledge, 1999), 74.

14. Bradley, *Such Was Saratoga*, 143; "Life at Saratoga," *Milwaukee Daily Sentinel*, 14 August 1863; T. J. Carty, *A Dictionary of Literary Pseudonyms in the English Language*, 2nd ed. (New York: Routledge, 2015), 29; Lewis, *Ladies and Gentlemen on Display*, 26. Although respectable women

did not want their full names to appear in newspaper reports, as this type of public notice was generally considered improper, plenty of female racegoers were content to be referred to, and identified by those in the know, by their initials, such as "Mrs H———h of New York," in her lilac silk dress trimmed with Honiton lace, or "Miss A. F———h, of Washington," whose gown of black silk was augmented with velvet point and illusion netting (Edward Hotaling, *They're Off!: Horse Racing at Saratoga* [Syracuse, NY: Syracuse University Press, 1995], 53). The simply dressed women of whom "Burleigh" expressed his approval were at the war's end soon replaced by "showy, dashing, and *insouciant*" female spectators ("The Saratoga Races"; italics in original).

15. Herbert Manchester, *Four Centuries of Sport in America, 1490–1890* (1931; New York: Benjamin Blom, 1968), 207; Henry William Herbert, *Frank Forester's Horse and Horsemanship of the United States and British Provinces of North America* (New York: George E. Woodward, 1871), vol. 1, 375; Dennis Brailsford, "Sporting Days in Eighteenth-Century England," *Journal of Sport History* 9 (1982): 44; "Horse Races," *Little Rock Daily Gazette*, 24 August 1865; Edward Hotaling, *The Great Black Jockeys: The Lives and Times of the Men Who Dominated America's First National Sport* (Rocklin, CA: Forum, 1999), 101; John Rickards Betts, "The Technological Revolution and the Rise of Sport, 1850–1900," *Mississippi Valley Historical Review* 40 (1953): 241; *The Atlantic Telegraph: Its History, from the Commencement of the Undertaking in 1854, to the Final Success in 1866* (London: Bacon, 1866), 88; Joel H. Wiener, *The Americanization of the British Press, 1832–1914: Speed in the Age of Transatlantic Journalism* (Houndmills, UK: Palgrave Macmillan, 2011), 169. When William Howard Russell, a journalist for the *Times* of London, visited Duncan Kenner at Ashland in June 1861, he noted that one of Kenner's friends "knew all about the winners of Epsom Oaks, and Ascot, and took delight in showing his knowledge of the 'Racing Calendar'" (Russell, *My Diary, North and South* [London: Bradbury and Evans, 1863], vol. 1, 414).

16. Linda Carroll and David Rosner, *Duel for the Crown: Affirmed, Alydar, and Racing's Greatest Rivalry* (New York: Gallery, 2014), 293; Deb Bennett, "Secrets of Secretariat's Speed," *Equus* 434 (November 2013): 44, 46; Mel Heimer, *Fabulous Bawd: The Story of Saratoga* (New York: Henry Holt, 1952), 99; James Chrystie White, *History of the British Turf, from the earliest period to the present day* (London: Henry Colburn, 1840), vol. 2, 22; Richard Nash, "'Honest English Breed': The Thoroughbred as Cultural Metaphor," in *The Culture of the Horse: Status, Discipline, and Identity in the Early Modern World*, ed. Karen Raber and Treva J. Tucker (New York: Palgrave, 2004), 248; Richard Nash, "Turf Wars: Violence, Politics, and the Newmarket Riots of 1751," in *Sporting Cultures, 1650–1850*, ed. Daniel O'Quinn and Alexis Tadie (Toronto: University of Toronto Press, 2018), 99; Pierce Egan, *Sporting Anecdotes, Original and Selected* (London: Sherwood, Jones, 1825), 356, 431; William Hamilton Maxwell, *The Field Book: or, Sports and Pastimes of the United Kingdom* (London: Effingham Wilson, 1833), 501; Frederick Marryat, *A Diary in America, With Remarks on Its Institutions* (London: Longman, Orme, Brown, Green, & Longmans, 1839), vol. 4, 7; William H. P. Robertson, *The History of Thoroughbred Racing in America* (Englewood Cliffs, NJ: Prentice-Hall, 1964), 32; "American Racing, by a Veteran of the Turf," *Outing: An Illustrated Monthly of Sport, Travel and Recreation* 16 (1890): 412; Mooney, *Race Horse Men*, 18; Anne Lambton and John Offen, *Thoroughbred Style: Racing Dynasties—The Horses, The Owners, The Studs* (London: Stanley

Paul, 1987), 196; Walter D. Osborne, *The Thoroughbred World* (New York: World, 1971), 55. As the British soldier, rider, and veterinarian Captain M. Horace Hayes opined, English Thoroughbreds' advantages lay in their speed and their early maturity, and their defects were their weak legs and their general "weediness" (thin, weak builds); they were "light-weight sprinters that are incapable of standing much work," rather than "sound 'stayers' which can carry a fair weight, and will 'train on'" (Hayes, *Points of the Horse*, 2nd. ed. [London: W. Thacker, 1897], 253).

17. Hotaling, *They're Off!*, 43; Jane Smiley, "The Sporting Life," *New Yorker*, 7 June 1999, 33.

18. Untitled article, *Milwaukee Daily Sentinel*, 25 July 1865; Sterngass, *First Resorts*, 148. The term "plug ugly" was coined in the 1850s, and referred initially to any urban brawler and subsequently to the members of gangs of white working-class men in New York City and Baltimore, who took the name as a testament to their ferocity (Irving Lewis Allen, *The City in Slang: New York Life and Popular Speech* [New York: Oxford University Press, 1993], 211).

19. Field Horne, *The Saratoga Reader: Writing about an American Village, 1749–1900* (Saratoga Springs, NY: Kiskatom, 2004), 196; John Edward Hilary Skinner, *After the Storm; Or, Jonathan and His Neighbours in 1865–6* (London: Richard Bentley, 1866), 62; William N. Thompson, "Horse Racing," in Thompson, *Gambling in America: An Encyclopedia of History, Issues, and Society* (Santa Barbara, CA: ABC-Clio, 2001), 169; Bradley, *Such Was Saratoga*, 162; *Saratoga Illustrated: The Visitor's Guide to Saratoga Springs* (New York: Taintor Brothers, 1876), 105; "Horse-Racing at Saratoga," *Harper's Weekly*, 26 August 1865.

20. Ian Bradley, *Water Music: Making Music in the Spas of Europe and North America* (Oxford: Oxford University Press, 2010), 180; Sterngass, *First Resorts*, 127, 135.

21. "The Saratoga Races," *Daily National Intelligencer* (Washington, DC), 14 August 1865; "The Saratoga Races," *Daily National Intelligencer*, 11 August 1865.

22. Untitled article, *New Haven (CT) Daily Palladium*, 19 August 1865; "Saratoga: The Hotels, the Women, and the Fashion," *Boston Daily Advertiser*, 11 August 1866. On Union women's activities in the Sanitary Commission, see Judith Ann Giesberg, *Civil War Sisterhood: The U.S. Sanitary Commission and Women's Politics in Transition* (Boston: Northeastern University Press, 2000). Waterfalls, cascades, and frizzles were popular hairstyles for women in the mid-nineteenth century.

23. William Dean Howells, *A Hazard of New Fortunes* (New York: Harper, 1911), 362; John K. Reeves, "The Way of a Realist: A Study of Howells' Use of the Saratoga Scene," *PMLA* 65 (1950): 1035.

24. "The Baden-Baden of America," *Milwaukee Daily Sentinel*, 29 July 1870. On Saratogian imitations of Continental leisure practices, see Avery Novitch, "There Must Be Something in the Water: Fashion, Wellness, and Class at Saratoga Springs, 1875–1925" (master's thesis, SUNY Fashion Institute of Technology, 2020), 46.

25. Henry James, "Saratoga," in *Portraits of Places*, by James (London: Macmillan, 1883), 327–33, *passim;* Hotaling, *They're Off!*, 86.

26. James, "Saratoga," 333–34, 328; Hotaling, *They're Off!*, 87. Cheltenham, in Gloucestershire, had gained great popularity among the English gentry in the 1780s, when George III and his family visited in order to take the waters, and it remained "a town of great resort and importance" throughout the following century (John Goding, *Norman's History of Cheltenham* [London: Longman, Green, Longman, Roberts, & Green, 1863], 289; Jane M. Adams, *Healing with Water: English*

Spas and the Water Cure, 1840–1960 [Manchester, UK: Manchester University Press, 2015], 66). Mackintosh, *Selling the Sights*, 87.

27. "Editorial Chit-Chat: Newport and Saratoga," *Peterson's Magazine* 50, no. 1 (July 1866): 70; Homberger, *Mrs. Astor's New* York, 166; Henry James, "The Sense of Newport," *Harper's Magazine* 113 (August 1906): 348; James, "Newport," in *Portraits of Places*, 341, 342; Eliza Putnam Heaton, "Saratoga Reforms," *Galveston Daily News*, 26 August 1895. The English politician Sir Charles Wentworth Dilke made a similar complaint during his visit to the United States just after the Civil War, observing that "among New-Yorkers there is not even the affectation of a search for rest," whereas in England successful businessmen craved escape from the world of work to "the comparative quiet of the country house" (Dilke, *Greater Britain: A Record of Travel in English-Speaking Countries during 1866 and 1867*, 6th ed. [London: Macmillan., 1872], 33). In Frances Hodgson Burnett's 1907 novel *The Shuttle*, the daughter of a self-made New York millionaire is described as having grown up in "a community in which even rich men worked, and in which young and able-bodied men would have felt rather indignant if aunts or uncles had thought it necessary to pension them off" (Burnett, *The Shuttle*, chap. 4, unpaginated, www.gutenberg.org/files/506/506-h/506-h.htm). See also Martin J. Wiener, *English Culture and the Decline of the Industrial Spirit, 1850–1890* (Cambridge, UK: Cambridge University Press, 1981).

28. Skinner, *After the Storm*, 61, 62; untitled article, *San Francisco Daily Evening Bulletin*, 23 August 1869.

29. George William Curtis, *The Potiphar Papers* (New York: Harper & Brothers, 1858), 206, 207, 205; Winifred Morgan, *An American Icon: Brother Jonathan and American Identity* (Newark: University of Delaware Press, 1988), 17, 22, 23.

30. The phrase is from Sven Beckert, *The Monied Metropolis: New York City and the Consolidation of the American Bourgeoisie, 1850–1896* (Cambridge, MA: Harvard University Press, 2003). On Americans' anxieties about the rise of finance capitalism, see Peter Knight, *Reading the Market: Genres of Financial Capitalism in Gilded Age America* (Baltimore, MD: Johns Hopkins University Press, 2016).

31. Gary L. Bunker and John J. Appel, "'Shoddy' Antisemitism and the Civil War," in *Jews and the Civil War: A Reader*, ed. Jonathan D. Sarna and Adam Mendelsohn (New York: New York University Press, 2010), 316, 323, 325.

32. Bunker and Appel, "'Shoddy' Antisemitism," 325, 326; Skinner, *After the Storm*, 62, 63; Field Horne, "Saratoga Springs: Evolution of a Resort," in New York State Archives Partnership Trust, *The Best of "New York Archives": Selections from the Magazine, 2001–2011* (Albany: State University of New York Press, 2017), 116; Sterngass, *First Resorts*, 127; Kate Field, "A Pre-Raphaelite at Saratoga," *Lippincott's Magazine of Literature, Science and Education* 2 (September 1868): 260, 261; Jennie E. Hicks, *Sparkles from Saratoga* (New York: American News Company, 1873), 49; John Clay Jr., *New World Notes: An Account of Journeyings and Sojournings in America and Canada* (Kelso, UK: J. & J. H. Rutherfurd, 1875), 188, 189; C. A. Faxon, *Faxon's Illustrated Handbook of Travel to Saratoga, Lakes George and Champlain, the Adirondacks, Niagara Falls, Montreal, Quebec, the Saguenay River, the White Mountains, Lakes Memphremagog and Winnepiseogee*, rev. ed. (Boston: C. A. Faxon, 1874), 54; Taintor, *Saratoga Illustrated*, 22; George Augustus Sala, *My Diary in America in the Midst of War* (London: Tinsley Brothers, 1865), vol. 2, 230, 270–71. According to the aforementioned Sir Charles

Wentworth Dilke, even "the new-men, the 'petroleum aristocracy' . . . unite with the oldest families [of New York] in thundering against 'Shoddy'" (Dilke, *Greater Britain*, 33).

33. Hotaling, *They're Off!*, 44; Steven A. Riess, *The Sport of Kings and the Kings of Crime: Horse Racing, Politics, and Organized Crime in New York, 1865–1913* (Syracuse, NY: Syracuse University Press, 2011), 18; "Sporting Intelligence: The Turf," *New York Herald*, 7 August 1863; "'Pools,' and Their Inventor," *Maryland Sentinel*, 3 August 1866; Gary A. O'Dell, "Under Siege: Kentucky and the Transformation of American Thoroughbred Racing, 1865–1936," *Register of the Kentucky Historical Society* 118 (2020): 404; Bradley, *Such Was Saratoga*, 163; Sterngass, *First Resorts*, 97.

34. Hotaling, *They're Off!*, 119, 138, 156; Riess, *The Sport of Kings*, 40, 41; Edwin G. Burrows and Mike Wallace, *Gotham: A History of New York City to 1898* (New York: Oxford University Press, 1999), 1164.

35. Lyman Horace Weeks, *The American Turf: An Historical Account of Racing in the United States, with Sketches of Turf Celebrities* (New York: Historical Company, 1898), 47; Robertson, *The History of Thoroughbred Racing in America*, 103; Kimberly Gatto, *Saratoga Race Course: The August Place to Be* (Charleston, SC: History Press, 2011); Riess, *The Sport of Kings*, 105; Brien Bouyea, *Bare Knuckles and Saratoga Racing: The Remarkable Life of John Morrissey* (Charleston, SC: History Press, 2016).

36. Arne K. Lang, *Sports Betting and Bookmaking: An American History* (Lanham, MD: Rowman & Littlefield, 2016), 62, 63; "Outlaws of the Turf," *New Orleans Daily Picayune*, 2 January 1892; Riess, *The Sport of Kings*, 108, 110; "Saratoga Springs," *New York Age*, 22 August 1891.

37. "Surprises at Guttenberg," *Daily Inter-Ocean* (Chicago), 17 January 1892; "Race Track Men Sentenced," *Milwaukee Journal*, 17 February 1895; "The 'Big Four' Go Free," *North American* (Philadelphia), 17 May 1895; Gatto, *Saratoga Race Course;* Riess, *The Sport of Kings*, 173.

38. Anthony Comstock and J. M. Buckley, *Traps for the Young* (1883; New York: Cosimo, 2009), 125; Nellie Bly, "Our Wickedest Summer Resort," *New York World*, 19 August 1894. Walbaum was not universally disparaged; newspaperwoman Elizabeth Tompkins described him as "the most progressive man who has ever had anything to do" with the Saratoga course and praised him for "develop[ing] [the Guttenberg] from a poor little half-mile track into a well equipped mile track, and all the time coined money out of it" (Tompkins, "Saratoga As It Is," *Daily Inter-Ocean*, 30 July 1893).

39. Cornelius E. Durkee, comp., *Reminiscences of Saratoga* (Saratoga Springs, NY: *The Saratogian*, 1928), 43; "Saratoga in the 'Soup,'" *Daily Inter-Ocean*, 16 July 1895; Walter Hines Page, ed., *The World's Work* (New York: Doubleday Page, 1903), vol. 6, 3916; Heaton, "Saratoga Reforms"; "Gossip of the Eastern Resorts," *Milwaukee Journal*, 11 June 1896; Hotaling, *They're Off!*, 159. Throughout the nineteenth century and well into the twentieth, the Boston area was notorious throughout the United States for its prudery with regard not only to drinking and gambling but to any element of popular culture that could be considered risqué, giving rise to the popular phrase "Banned in Boston" (Kevin Mattson, *Creating a Democratic Public: The Struggle for Urban Participatory Democracy during the Progressive Era* [University Park: Pennsylvania State University Press, 1998], 88).

40. "General Sporting Gossip," *Commercial-Appeal* (Memphis), 6 September 1898; Hotaling, *They're Off*, 158; "Mr. Whitney Inspects Saratoga Track," *New York Times*, 27 October 1901; Livingston, *Their Turf*, 238; Reeves, "The Way of a Realist," 1047.

6. NEW YORK CITY: CREATING A NATIONAL TURF ELITE

First epigraph: James D. McCabe Jr., *Lights and Shadows of New York Life; or, the Sights and Sensations of the Great City* (1872; New York: Farrar, Straus and Giroux, 1870), 675.

Second epigraph: W. S. Vosburgh, "The Passing of Jerome Park," *Outing Magazine*, 1901, 520.

1. During the first half of the nineteenth century Almack's, located on King Street in London's West End, was the city's most elite private social venue. Admission to its weekly balls was by invitation only, and the selection process was managed by its "Lady Patronesses," six of London's leading women of fashion (see Jennifer Davey, "'Wearing the Breeches'? Almack's, the Female Patroness, and Public Femininity, c. 1764–1848," *Women's History Review* 26 [2017]: 822–39).

2. Eric Homberger, *Mrs. Astor's New York: Money and Social Power in a Gilded Age* (New Haven, CT: Yale University Press, 2002), 86, 239.

3. Ward McAllister, *Society As I Have Found It* (New York: Cassell, 1890), chap. 16, *passim;* Elizabeth L. Bradley, *Knickerbocker: The Myth behind New York* (New Brunswick, NJ: Rutgers University Press, 2009), 77–78, 87; Charles Astor Bristed, *The Upper Ten Thousand*, quoted in Bradley, *Knickerbocker*, 81; Dana Cooper, *Informal Ambassadors: American Women, Transatlantic Marriages, and Anglo-American Relations, 1865–1945* (Kent, OH: Kent State University Press, 2014), 22; Maureen E. Montgomery, *"Gilded Prostitution": Status, Money and Transatlantic Marriages, 1870–1914* (New York: Routledge, 1989), 36. The Knickerbockers formed a cohesive elite in Manhattan from the American Revolution through the early nineteenth century, after which time they began to intermarry with members of mercantile dynasties transplanted from New England (Homberger, *Mrs. Astor's New York*, 9, 135; Roy Rosenzweig and Elizabeth Blackmar, *The Park and the People: A History of Central Park* [Ithaca, NY: Cornell University Press, 1992], 215). Sven Beckert, *The Monied Metropolis: New York and the Consolidation of the American Bourgeoisie, 1850–1896* [New York: Cambridge University Press, 2001], 156). The term originated with Washington Irving's 1809 novel *A History of New-York from the Beginning of the World to the End of the Dutch Dynasty, by Diedrich Knickerbocker* and is still in use today as the name of the city's professional basketball team. But although the writer Edith Wharton became renowned as a chronicler of "Old New York," she echoed the assertion of her mother, Lucretia Rhinelander Jones, that the Knickerbockers were simply "Dutch and British middle-class families, and that only four or five could show a pedigree leading back to the aristocracy of their ancestral country" (Wharton, *A Backward Glance* [New York: D. Appleton-Century, 1934], 10–11).

4. Beckert, *The Monied Metropolis*, 156. See, for example, "How the 400 Dance," *Los Angeles Herald*, 18 January 1891. On the rise of the society pages in American newspapers, see Julia Guarneri, *Newsprint Metropolis: City Papers and the Making of Modern Americans* (Chicago: University of Chicago Press, 2017), 139, 290.

5. "Ephemeral New York," 3 February 2014, https://ephemeralnewyork.files.wordpress.com/2014/02/sundayjournalfrontpage.jpg; David R. Spencer, *The Yellow Journalism: The Press and America's Emergence as a World Power* (Evanston, IL: Northwestern University Press, 2007), xi. Although, as Julia Guarneri has noted, papers aimed at a working-class audience drew their revenues primarily from classified ads rather than from the major advertisers who patronized the *Times* and other dailies favored by the urban bourgeoisie, and thus "could afford to make fun of

high society and consumer culture when they wished," the *Journal* depicted the ball in a favorable, even romanticized light (Guarneri, *Newsprint Metropolis*, 99).

6. "Shero, "New York Society," *North American*, 29 November 1880; "A Society Boss in New York," *San Francisco Daily Evening Bulletin*, 27 January 1882.

7. Dan M. Bowmar III, *Giants of the Turf* (Lexington, KY: The Blood-Horse, 1960), 51; *New York Times*, quoted in Beckert, *The Monied Metropolis*, 259; "An American Jockey Club," *Boston Daily Advertiser*, 24 September 1866; "Racing at Jerome Park," *New York Times*, 31 May 1885; Steven A. Riess, *The Sport of Kings and the Kings of Crime: Horse Racing, Politics, and Organized Crime in New York, 1865–1913* (Syracuse, NY: Syracuse University Press, 2011), 31; Homberger, *Mrs. Astor's New York*, 181, 182; Lloyd Morris, *Incredible New York: High Life and Low Life from 1850 to 1950* (Syracuse, NY: Syracuse University Press, 1951), 47. The Bathgate estate's sole previous claim to importance in the history of American racing was that in 1829 the celebrated Medoc, the get of American Eclipse, was born there (Brian Patrick Tyrrell, "Bred for the Race: Thoroughbred Horses and the Politics of Pedigree" [PhD diss., University of California–Santa Barbara, 2019], 126).

8. Morris, *Incredible New York*, 48; James D. McCabe Jr., *Lights and Shadows of New York Life; or, The Sights and Sensations of the Great City* (1872; New York: Farrar, Straus and Giroux, 1970), 676; Bill Twomey, *The Bronx in Bits and Pieces* (Bloomington, IN: Rooftop, 2007), 57; Bennett Liebman, "There Used to Be a New York Racetrack There: But Where Was It?," http://dx.doi.org/10.2139/ssrn.1510317; Matthew Hale Smith, *Twenty Years among the Bulls and Bears of Wall Street* (Hartford, CT: J. B. Burr, 1870), 255; Montgomery, *"Gilded Prostitution,"* 150; Junius Henri Browne, *The Great Metropolis: A Mirror of New York* (Hartford, CT: American, 1869), 569; Edward L. Bowen, *Belmont Park: A Century of Champions* (Lexington, KY: Eclipse, 2005), 11; Pamela Grundy and Benjamin Rader, *American Sports: From the Age of Folk Games to the Age of Televised Sports*, 7th ed. (New York: Routledge, 2016), 62; Riess, *The Sport of Kings*, 25.

9. Bradley, *Knickerbocker*, 90; "Mrs John King Van Rensselaer Explodes a Bomb at Annual Meeting," *New York Times*, 3 January 1917; May King Van Rensselaer, *The Social Ladder* (New York: Henry Holt, 1924), 53; Rhoda Nathan, "Ward McAllister: Beau Nash of *The Age of Innocence*," *College Literature* 14 (1987): 280.

10. Thomas L. Nichols, *Forty Years of American Life* (London: John Maxwell, 1864), vol. 1, 393. On vanished racetracks in and around New York City, see Jonathan Silverman, "Two Turns around the Digital: Horse Racing, Maps, and Process," *Journal of Sport History* 44 (2017): 188.

11. Bowen, *Belmont Park*, 10, 11; Henry Horenstein and Brendan Boyd, *Racing Days* (New York: Viking, 1987), 26; William Newnham Blane, *An Excursion through the United States and Canada during the years 1822–23, by an English Gentleman* (1824; New York: Negro Universities Press, 1969), 315, 316; Charles A. Murray, *Travels in North America during the Years 1834, 1835, & 1836* (London: Richard Bentley, 1839), vol. 2, 341; italics in original. On the "Great Match Races," see John Eisenberg, *The Great Match Race: When North Met South in America's First Sports Spectacle* (Boston: Houghton Mifflin, 2006). The St. Leger Stakes, run annually at Doncaster, South Yorkshire, from 1776, is the oldest of the English turf's five "Classic" races, and the Derby, held at Epsom, Surrey since 1780, is the richest and most famous.

12. See Kenneth Cohen, *They Will Have Their Game: Sporting Culture and the Making of the Early American Republic* (Ithaca, NY: Cornell University Press, 2017).

13. Clay McShane and Joel A. Tarr, *The Horse in the City: Living Machines in the Nineteenth Century* (Baltimore, MD: Johns Hopkins University Press, 2007), 92; Ed Hotaling, *They're Off!: Horse Racing at Saratoga* (Syracuse, NY: Syracuse University Press, 1995), 14, 24; William Gleason, "Grounds for Fun: The Place of Play in Nineteenth-Century American Culture," *Nineteenth-Century Contexts* 35 (2013): 465; Arne K. Lang, *Sports Betting and Bookmaking: An American History* (Lanham, MD: Rowman & Littlefield, 2016), 35.

14. "New York Urbanized Area: Population & Density from 1800," http://demographia.com/db-nyuza1800.htm); Silverman, "Two Turns around the Digital," 188.

15. Morris, *Incredible New York*, 93, 94; McCabe, *Lights and Shadows*, 675; Beckert, *The Monied Metropolis*, 259; McShane and Tarr, *The Horse in the City*, 85; McShane and Tarr, "The Decline of the Urban Horse in American Cities," *Journal of Transport History* 24 (2003): 177; Rosenzweig and Blackmar, *The Park and the People*, 15.

16. Rosenzweig and Blackmar, *The Park and the People*, 223.

17. Homberger, *Mrs. Astor's New York*, 240; Clifton Hood, "An Unusable Past: Urban Elites, New York City's Evacuation Day, and the Transformation of Memory Culture," *Journal of Social History* 37 (2004): 897, 901; Kathryn Wilkins, "Travel Narratives of the Victorian Elite: The Case of the London Season," in *Narratives of Travel and Tourism*, ed. Jacqueline Tivers and Tijana Rakic (Farnham, UK: Ashgate, 2012), 15; Whitman quoted in Rosenzweig and Blackmar, *The Park and the People*, 224. On Anglophilia in the nineteenth-century United States, see Elisa Tamarkin, *Anglophilia: Deference, Devotion, and Antebellum America* (Chicago: University of Chicago Press, 2007).

18. Steven A. Riess, "Harness Racing," in *Sports in America from Colonial Times to the Twenty-First Century*, ed. Riess (Abingdon, UK: Taylor & Francis, 2011), 444; Morris, *Incredible New York*, 95, 961; Carole Case, *The Right Blood: America's Aristocrats in Thoroughbred Racing* (New Brunswick, NJ: Rutgers University Press, 2001), 11.

19. Rosenzweig and Blackmar, *The Park and the People*, 215.

20. Donald Mrozek, "Sporting Life as Consumption, Fashion, and Display: The Pastimes of the Rich at the Turn of the Century," in *Major Problems in American Sport History: Documents and Essays*, ed. Steven A. Riess (Boston: Houghton Mifflin, 1997), 81, 82; John Steele Gordon, "The Country Club," *American Heritage* 41 (October/November 1990): 1, www.americanheritage.com/country-club; Riess, *City Games: The Evolution of American Urban Society and the Rise of Sports* (Urbana: University of Illinois Press, 1989). On elite women's participation in sports, see Roberta J. Park, "Sport, Gender and Society in a Transatlantic Victorian Perspective," *International Journal of the History of Sport* 24 (2007): 1574.

21. Riess, *The Sport of Kings*, 30, 31, 34; Hood, "An Unusable Past," 900; John Pinfold, "Horse Racing and the Upper Classes in the Nineteenth Century," *Sport in History* 28 (2008): 414–15; "Sporting Intelligence: The Derby," *The Times* (London), 20 May 1858; McCabe, *Lights and Shadows*, 676; Riess, *City Games*, 25; Carole Case, *Down the Backstretch: Racing and the American Dream* (Philadelphia: Temple University Press, 1991), 23. On the role of spectatorship at the antebellum

American racetrack, see Natalie Zacek, "Spectacle and Spectatorship at the Nineteenth-Century American Racetrack," *European Journal of American Studies* 14 (2019): 1–15.

22. Homberger, *Mrs. Astor's New York*, 193; Browne, *The Great Metropolis*, 569, 570; Riess, *The Sport of Kings*, 31; Allan Nevins and Milton Halsey Thomas, eds., *The Diary of George Templeton Strong; The Turbulent Fifties, 1850–1859* (New York: Macmillan, 1952), 275; John Allen Krout, *Annals of American Sport* (New Haven, CT: Yale University Press, 1929), 36.

23. John Dizikes, *Yankee Doodle Dandy: The Life and Times of Tod Sloan* (New Haven, CT: Yale University Press, 2000), 99–100, 18.

24. "The Races at Jerome Park," *Harper's Weekly*, 13 October 1866, 654.

25. "Wanted—A Derby Racing Park," *Harper's Weekly*, 16 November 1867, 733.

26. John O'Connor, *Wanderings of a Vagabond: An Autobiography* (New York: privately published, 1873), 118.

27. Melvin Adelman, *A Sporting Time: New York City and the Rise of Modern Athletics, 1820–70* (Urbana: University of Illinois Press, 1986), 86; italics in original; George Fredrickson, *The Black Image in the White Mind: The Debate on Afro-American Character and Destiny, 1817–1914* (New York: Harper & Row, 1971), 61; *Charleston Courier*, 24 February 1830, quoted in Maurie D. McInnis, *The Politics of Taste in Antebellum Charleston* (Chapel Hill: University of North Carolina Press, 2005), 26. The term "codfish aristocracy" was frequently deployed in the middle decades of the nineteenth century to satirize the United States' urban upper classes, particularly that of New York (John Evelev, "The City Sketch: Writing Middle-Class Identity on the Streets of Antebellum New York," in *Class and the Making of American Literature: Created Unequal*, ed. Andrew Lawson [New York: Routledge, 2014], 82).

28. Shamus Khan, "The New Elitists," *New York Times*, 7 July 2012.

29. "Black New Yorkers," https://blacknewyorkers-nypl.org/new-york-citys-black-population-by-gender-1850-1880/.

30. The history of African American jockeys, and their eventual replacement after the Civil War by white men, is recounted in Ed Hotaling, *The Great Black Jockeys: The Lives and Times of the Men Who Dominated America's First National Sport* (New York: Three Rivers, 1999); and Katherine C. Mooney, *Race Horse Men: How Slavery and Freedom Were Made at the Racetrack* (Cambridge, MA: Harvard University Press, 2014).

31. In the late nineteenth century, London's Black population was "desperately poor, composed largely of West Indian sailors, living in Canning Town in the East End"; "this tiny population [was] smaller, less advantaged, less politically experienced, [and] more despised than the Irish or Indian communities in London" (Jonathan Schneer, *London 1900: The Imperial Metropolis* [New Haven, CT: Yale University Press, 2001], 203).

32. Quoted in Reiss, *The Sport of Kings*, 25.

33. "Jerome-Park Reservoir," *Journal of the Society of Arts* 44, no. 2286 (11 September 1896): 810; "Closing Day at Jerome Park," *New York Times*, 25 August 1894; W. S. Vosburgh, "The Passing of Jerome Park," *Outing Magazine*, 1901, 520. Glenelg, Hanover, and Kingfisher were leading American Thoroughbreds of the 1870s and early 1880s, and the Withers and Belmont Stakes were the most prestigious of Jerome Park's annual races (Richard Sowers, *The Kentucky Derby, Preakness and Belmont Stakes: A Comprehensive History* [Jefferson, NC: McFarland, 2014], 11, 12; Amanda Barnes

and Juliet Wright, *The Butcher Boys: Part Two—The Breaking of the Brooklyn Stable* [Morrisville, NC: Lulu, 2019], 180; Dizikes, *Yankee Doodle Dandy*, 72).

34. On Americans' encounters with the stock market in the later nineteenth century, see Peter Knight, *Reading the Market: Genres of Financial Capitalism in Gilded Age America* (Baltimore, MD: Johns Hopkins University Press, 2016).

35. Dizikes, *Yankee Doodle Dandy*, 78.

36. John E. Morris, "August Belmont Jr.: The Forgotten Financier of the Gilded Age," *Financial History* 136 (2021): 18; R. B. Dooley, "A Footnote to Edith Wharton," *American Literature* 26 (1954): 81–83; Jay Sexton, "Transatlantic Financiers and the Civil War," *American Nineteenth Century History* 2 (2001): 31, 38; Bowmar, *Giants of the Turf*, 49, 53; Homberger, *Mrs. Astor's New York*, 174, 176; quoted in David Black, *The King of Fifth Avenue: The Fortunes of August Belmont* (New York: Dial, 1981), ix.

37. James Grant Wilson, "William Collins Whitney," *New York Genealogical and Biographical Sketch* 35 (1904): 11, 12; Edward L. Bowen, *Belmont Park: A Century of Champions* (Lexington, KY: Eclipse, 2005), 34; Mooney, *Race Horse Men*, 218; Ann Clymer Bigelow, "An Affair of Class: Western Virginia Eccentric versus New York Tobacco Magnate," *West Virginia History* 10 (2016): 93.

38. Dizikes, *Yankee Doodle Dandy*, 79; John H. Davis, *The American Turf with Personal Reminiscences* (New York: John Polhemus Printing, 1907), 108, 109; Henry Clews, *Fifty Years in Wall Street* (1908; Hoboken, NJ: Wiley, 2006), 318, 185; "James R. Keene," *New York Times*, 5 January 1913.

39. "Jesse Lewisohn Dies at 46," *New York Times*, 1 December 1918; "Mrs. Marcus Daly, 88, Mining Man's Widow," *New York Times*, 15 July 1941; Dizikes, *Yankee Doodle Dandy*, 79, 80, 30.

40. Riess, *The Sport of Kings*, 35, 40, 44, 88.

41. John I. Day, "Horse Racing and the Pari-Mutuel," *Annals of the American Academy of Political and Social Science* 269 (1950): 57.

42. Bennett Liebman, "There Used to Be a New York Racetrack There: But Where Was It?," p. 2, http://dx.doi.org/10.2139/ssrn.1510317); "A Most Successful Opening Day at the Finest Race Track in the World," *New York Times*, 21 August 1889; Vosburgh, "The Passing of Jerome Park," 520; Dizikes, *Yankee Doodle Dandy*, 72. Although the Morris Park course was both popular and glamourous, like Jerome Park it stood literally in the way of New York City's expansion, in this case that of the subway system and the concomitant development of this part of the Bronx as a residential community. As the Westchester Racing Association's lease on the site neared its end, its members chose to relocate to Elmont, in Nassau County, a site convenient for travel from Manhattan but seen as unlikely to be redeveloped for residential purposes (Riess, *The Sport of Kings*, 245).

43. Day, "Horse Racing and the Pari-Mutuel," 57; W. S. Vosburgh, *Racing in America, 1866–1921* (New York: privately published, 1922), 43; Riess, *The Sport of Kings*, 135, 147; "Three Jockeys Suspended," *Daily Inter-Ocean* (Chicago), 4 July 1891; "The Turf," *San Francisco Daily Evening Bulletin*, 4 August 1891; "Winter Turfmen Protest," *Milwaukee Daily Sentinel*, 25 December 1891; "Tricks on the Turf," *St. Paul Daily News*, 24 January 1893.

44. Carole Case, *Down the Backstretch*, 18, 19; David T. Swidler, *All about Thorobred* [sic] *Horse Racing: Aristocrat of Sports* (Miami: Hialeah Guild, 1967), 113; Riess, *The Sport of Kings*, 138; Day, "Horse Racing and the Pari-Mutuel," 57; Riess, *The Sport of Kings*, 161–63.

45. Bradley, *Knickerbocker*, 107; Beckert, *The Monied Metropolis*, 247; Steven A. Riess, "From Pitch to Putt: Sport and Class in Anglo-American Sport," *Journal of Sport History* 21 (1994): 142; Riess, *Sports in America*, 988.

46. Beckert, *The Monied Metropolis*, 18, 258; Julia Brock and Daniel Vivian, introduction to *Leisure, Plantations, and the Making of a New South: The Sporting Plantations of the South Carolina Lowcountry and Red Hills Region, 1900–1940*, ed. Brock and Vivian (Lanham, MD: Lexington, 2015), 6.

47. Case, *The Right Blood*, 2, 8, 11, 18, 30–31. The writer Nathaniel Parker Willis coined the phrase "the Upper Ten" in 1845 to describe the ten thousand New Yorkers whom he deemed the social leaders of the city (Homberger, *Mrs. Astor's New York*, 1).

48. Quoted in Cooper, *Informal Ambassadors*, 25.

49. "American Race Horses Going to Europe," *Pittsfield (MA) Sun*, 21 August 1856.

50. Dizikes, *Yankee Doodle Dandy*, 104.

51. Allen Guttmann, "English Sports Spectators: The Restoration to the Nineteenth Century," *Journal of Sport History* 12 (1985): 112.

52. Stephen Tuffnell, "'Uncle Sam Is to Be Sacrificed': Anglophobia in Late Nineteenth-Century Politics and Culture," *American Nineteenth Century History* 12 (2011): 80; Hood, "An Unusable Past," 897; Beckert, *The Monied Metropolis*, 258.

53. Rebecca Cassidy, *Horse People: Thoroughbred Culture in Lexington and Newmarket* (Baltimore, MD: Johns Hopkins University Press, 2007), 67; Bowmar, *Giants of the Turf*, 116.

54. Riess, "From Pitch to Putt," 142.

55. Christopher McGrath, *Mr. Darley's Arabian: High Life, Low Life, Sporting Life: A History of Racing in 25 Horses* (New York: Pegasus, 2017), 248.

56. Riess, *The Sport of Kings*, xiv.

57. Bowmar, *Giants of the Turf*, 15; Deb Bennett, "Secrets of Secretariat's Speed," *Equus* 434 (November 2013): 46; Herbert Manchester, *Four Centuries of Sport in America, 1490–1890* (1931; New York: Benjamin Blom, 1961), 207, 208; Walter D. Osborne, *The Thoroughbred World* (New York: World, 1971), 75.

58. John Rickard Betts, "The Technological Revolution and the Rise of Sport, 1850–1900," *Mississippi Valley Historical Review* 40 (1953): 241, 258, 259; Joel H. Wiener, *The Americanization of the British Press, 1832–1914: Speed in the Age of Transatlantic Journalism* (Houndmills, UK: Palgrave, 2011), 169. Eadweard Muybridge's experiments with photographing animals in motion were supported by the California turfman Leland Stanford.

59. John Gleaves, "Enhancing the Odds: Horse Racing, Gambling and the First Anti-Doping Movement in Sport, 1889–1911," *Sport in History* 32 (2012): 30, 31.

60. Case, *Down the Backstretch*, 19; Day, "Horse Racing and the Pari-Mutuel," 57–58.

61. Riess, *The Sport of Kings*, xix. On Knickerbockers' sense of their identity, see Clifton Hood, "Journeying to 'Old New York': Elite New Yorkers and Their Invention of an Idealized City History in the Late Nineteenth and Early Twentieth Centuries," *Journal of Urban History* (2002): 699–716.

62. Allen Guttmann, *From Ritual to Record: The Nature of Modern Sports*, updated ed. (New York: Columbia University Press, 2004); 54; Gleaves, "Enhancing the Odds," 28–29.

7. CHURCHILL DOWNS: THE NEW SOUTH'S OLD SOUTH

First epigraph: Ann J. Pearce to her brother Judge William S. Bodley, 5 June 1843, Bodley Family Papers, 1773–1939, Filson Historical Society, Louisville, Kentucky.

Second epigraph: "Daisy L" to "Friend Will," 21 May 1882, Mss. C D Daisy L., Filson Historical Society, Louisville, Kentucky.

1. John L. O'Connor, *The Kentucky Derby, 1875–1921* (White Plains, NY: privately published, 1921), 5–6.

2. James C. Nicholson, *The Kentucky Derby: How the Run for the Roses Became America's Premier Sporting Event* (Lexington: University of Kentucky Press, 2012), 24.

3. Preakness online shop, https://shop.1st.com.

4. NYRA Belmont Stakes online shop, https://shop.nyra.com/belmont-stakes/?utm_source=-belmontstakes&utm_medium=nav&utm_campaign=website&sort=featured&page=1; Belmont Stakes Instagram, www.instagram.com/p/Celi65uA2hW/.

5. "What to Wear," www.kentuckyderby.com/visit/what-to-wear; "Kentucky Derby 148 At Home Menu," www.kentuckyderby.com/party/recipes/kentucky-derby-148-at-home-menu.

6. "Kentucky Derby 2022 Clothes and Style," www.vineyardvines.com/kentucky-derby/?eq=kentucky%20derby; "Kentucky Derby at Home," www.kentuckyderby.com/party/williams-sonoma.

7. "An Ultimate Southern Tradition: The Kentucky Derby,"www.poshcouturerentals.com/blog/an-ultimate-southern-tradition-the-kentucky-derby; "The Kentucky Derby: A Race Like No Other," www.americasbestracing.net/the-sport/2022-the-kentucky-derby-race-no-other; "Celebrate the Kentucky Derby in Style," www.southernladymagazine.com/celebrate-the-kentucky-derby-in-style/4/; Henry Deedes, *Sketches of the South and West, or Ten Months' Residence in the United States* (Edinburgh: William Blackwood and Sons, 1869), 30.

8. Kenneth C. Crain, *They're Off: The Romance of the Kentucky Derby* (Chicago: Kenford, 1930), 23; Jeff Meyer, "Henry Clay's Legacy to Horse Breeding and Racing," *Register of the Kentucky Historical Society* 100 (2002): 474; Ulrich Bonnell Phillips, *Life and Labor in the Old South* (Boston: Little, Brown, 1929), 81; Rebecca Cassidy, *Horse People: Thoroughbred Culture in Lexington and Newmarket* (Baltimore, MD: Johns Hopkins University Press, 2007), 17; George G. Kendall, *The Story of the Kentucky Derby* (New Albany, IN: Daniel H. Thompson, 1926), 9; Kentucky Jockey Club, *The Kentucky Jockey Club: Lexington, Churchill Downs, Latonia* (Lexington: Kentucky Jockey Club, 1920), unpaginated.

9. J. Winston Coleman Jr., "Old Kentucky Watering Places," *Filson Club Historical Quarterly* 16 (1942): 3, 13; "Georgetown Races," *American Turf Register* (hereafter *ATR*) 2, no. 10 (June 1831): 516; "Hopkinsville Races," *ATR* 5, no. 8 (April 1834): 441; "Madison Races," *ATR* 7, no. 2 (October 1835): 93; "Versailles Races," *Spirit of the Times* (hereafter *Spirit*), 3 October 1846, 378; "Hickman Races," *Spirit*, 26 December 1846, 523.

10. Crain, *They're Off*, 24; John Nauright and Charles Parrish, eds., *Sports around the World: History, Culture, and Practice* (Santa Barbara, CA: ABC-CLIO, 2012), vol. 1, 256; "Horseracing's

Heritage," Speed Art Museum, Louisville, Kentucky, www.speedmuseum.org/collections/oakland-house-and-race-course/; John D. Dutton to John Thomson Mason, 25 September 1832, Miscellaneous Manuscripts Collection, Filson Historical Society (hereafter FHS), Louisville, Kentucky. See also *Constitution for the Louisville Association for Improvement of the Breed of Horses, and Rules and Regulations for the Government of the Course* (Louisville: W. W. Worsley, 1832).

11. Ann J. Pearce to Judge William S. Bodley, 5 June 1843, Bodley Family Papers, 1773–1839, Mss. A B668e; Joshua F. Bullitt to John C. Bullitt, 6 June 1839, Bullitt Family Papers, Oxmoor Collection, 1683–2003, Mss. A B937c, both FHS; Kentucky Jockey Club, *The Kentucky Jockey Club;* John Gilmer Speed, *The Horse in America* (New York: McClure, Phillips, 1905), 51; Lynn S. Renau, *Jockeys, Belles, and Bluegrass Kings* (Louisville, KY: Herr House, 1995), 24.

12. Gary A. O'Dell, "At the Starting Post: Racing Venues and the Origins of Thoroughbred Racing in Kentucky, 1783–1865," *Register of the Kentucky Historical Society* 116 (2018): 30; "History of the Kentucky Turf: Racing at Lexington, from 1787 to 1860," *Spirit,* 17 December 1859, 534; Nauright and Parrish, *Sports around the World,* vol. 1, 256; Meyer, "Henry Clay's Legacy," 477; John Wirt, "Lexington Races," *ATR* 2, no. 4 (December 1830): 198; "Louisville Races," *Spirit,* 15 June 1839, 175; Maryjean Wall, *How Kentucky Became Southern: A Tale of Outlaws, Horse Thieves, Gamblers, and Breeders* (Lexington: University Press of Kentucky, 2010), 54–55; "Kentucky Association," *Spirit of the Times,* 4 June 1842, 162; Renau, *Jockeys,* 23; Bradley Smith, *The Horse and the Blue Grass Country* (Garden City, NY: Doubleday, 1955), 26, 27. The *Kentucky Gazette* published a notice in August 1789 regarding a three-day race meeting to be held in Lexington, but this event appears to have been a one-off (Catriona Margaret Paul, "The Horsemen Got the Start: Horse Ownership and Advantage in Kentucky, 1770–1830" [PhD diss., University of Dundee, 2012], 259).

13. Jimmie Pinnell to Judge William S. Bodley, 16 September 1851, Bodley Family Papers, FHS; Charles Caldwell, *A Discourse on the Vice of Gambling* (Lexington, KY: J. Clarke, 1835), 34; "Race Courses and Jockey Clubs," *ATR* (July 1842): 404–5; "Sporting Epistle from Kentucky," *Spirit,* 7 February 1857, 618; "Kentucky—the Race Horse Region," *Spirit,* 14 August 1858, 319; Sir Charles Augustus Murray, *Travels in North America during the years 1834, 1835 & 1836* (London: Richard Bentley, 1841), vol. 1, 220; Gary A. O'Dell, "Under Siege: Kentucky and the Transformation of American Thoroughbred Racing, 1865–1936," *Register of the Kentucky Historical Society* 118 (2020): 391; Smith, *The Horse and the Blue Grass Country,* 30. Billingsgate was a London fish market long renowned for the profanity of its vendors.

14. T. B. Thorpe, "The Great Four Mile Day," in *The Hive of the 'Bee-Hunter': A Repository of Sketches, Including Peculiar American Character, Scenery, and Rural Sports,* by Thorpe (New York: D. Appleton, 1854), 286.

15. Stephen Aron, *How the West Was Lost: The Transformation of Kentucky from Daniel Boone to Henry Clay* (Baltimore, MD: Johns Hopkins University Press, 1996), 124. On the socioeconomic liminality of most antebellum Kentuckian turfmen, see Alison Bell et al., "'All My Little Might of Money': Signaling, Structure, and Mobility among the Middling in Nineteenth-Century Virginia and Kentucky," *Historical Archaeology* 53 (2019): 372–92.

16. Laura Ellyn Smith, "Anti-Jackson Democratization: The First National Political Party Conventions," *American Nineteenth Century History* 21 (2020): 158.

17. Norris W. Yates, *William T. Porter and the Spirit of the Times: A Study of the Big Bear School of Humor* (Baton Rouge: Louisiana State University Press, 1957), 116. Louisville was, however, the first locale west of the Allegheny Mountains to stage a ring tournament (see "Grand Tournament at Louisville Ky.," *Spirit of the Times*, 4 November 1854).

18. Bruce L. Bennett, "Sports in the South up to 1865," *Quest* 27 (1977): 17; Cassidy, *Horse People*, 16; John Allen Krout, *Annals of American Sport* (New Haven, CT: Yale University Press,1929), 34; John Jeremiah Sullivan, *Blood Horses: Notes of a Sportswriter's Son* (New York: Farrar, Straus and Giroux, 2004), 61; Gary A. O'Dell, "Under Siege," 392. Fearing that guerrillas from either side of the conflict might seize their stock, several leading Kentucky breeders sent their horses to the Woodburn stud farm outside Lexington, hoping that the British nationality of its owner, R. A. Alexander, the man who bought Lexington from Richard Ten Broeck, would protect the estate from being raided (William Preston Mangum II, "Disaster at Woodburn Farm: R.A. Alexander and the Confederate Guerrilla Raids of 1864–1865," *Filson Club History Quarterly* 70 [1996]: 152, 153). See also Danael Christian Suttle, "Horse Racing during the Civil War: The Perseverance of the Sport during a Time of National Crisis" (bachelor's thesis, University of Arkansas-Fayetteville, 2019).

19. The seminal text about this phenomenon is Nina Silber, *The Romance of Reunion: Northerners and the South, 1865–1900* (Chapel Hill: University of North Carolina, 1993).

20. "The Southern Transformation," *The Nation* 8 (8 November 1866): 371.

21. Rebecca Cawood McIntyre, *Souvenirs of the Old South: Northern Tourism and Southern Mythology* (Gainesville: University Press of Florida, 2011), 156, 157.

22. John William DeForest's 1867 novel *Miss Ravenel's Conversion from Secession to Loyalty* was the first entry in this genre (see Silber, *The Romance of Reunion*, 40).

23. Robert C. Reinders, *End of an Era: New Orleans, 1850–1860* (Gretna, LA: Pelican, 1964), 9; Nicholson, *The Kentucky Derby*, 10.

24. Robert Bruce Symon Jr., "'Child of the North': Louisville's Transition to a Southern City, 1879–1885" (master's thesis, University of Louisville, 2005), 17, 23; B. C. Hall and C. T. Wood, *The South* (New York: Scribner, 1995), 241; Gary A. O'Dell, "Under Siege," 407–8.

25. Peter Lee, *Spectacular Bid: The Last Superhorse of the Twentieth Century* (Lexington: University Press of Kentucky, 2019), 76; James J. Holmberg, "The Clark Family and the Kentucky Derby," *Filson News Magazine* 4, no. 1 (2003), www.filsonhistorical.org/archive/news_v4n1_clarkderby.html; Lee A. Farrow, "When Russian Royalty Met Southern Hospitality: Grand Duke Alexis in Kentucky, 1872," *Ohio Valley History* 22 (2022): 6; *Constitution of the Louisville Association for the Improvement of the Breed of Horses*, 6; Kendall, *The Story of the Kentucky Derby*, 10; Renau, *Jockeys, Belles, and Bluegrass Kings*, 34, 35. In France, Clark met with Vicomte Darn, the vice president of the French Jockey Club, but this aspect of his European sojourn seems to have had less effect on his plans for his home city (Nauright and Parrish, eds., *Sports around the World*, vol. 1, 257).

26. Renau, *Jockeys, Belles, and Bluegrass Kings*, 24; Bryan S. Bush, *Louisville Gambling Barons* (Charleston, SC: History Press, 2023), 17; Mildred A. Bullitt to Tom Bullitt, 22 May 1860, Bullitt Family Papers, FHS. Although Woodlawn was in existence for only a decade, its trophy, the Woodlawn Vase, which spent the war years buried on the ground of R. A. Alexander's Woodburn Farm lest it be stolen by marauders, long outlived the track for which it was created by Tiffany and Company.

It then passed through the hands of various turfmen until it came to Baltimorean Thomas C. Clyde, who gave it to the Maryland Jockey Club, of which he was a director. Since that time it has been presented to the winner of each running of the Preakness Stakes at Pimlico; it is kept at Baltimore's Maryland Historical Society for the rest of the year (Mangum, "Disaster at Woodburn Farm," 184; Avalyn Hunter, *American Classic Pedigrees [1914–2002]* [Lexington, KY: Eclipse Press, 2003], 29, 30).

27. William Weaver, "Samuel Clemens Lectures in Kentucky," *Mark Twain Journal* 17 (1974): 21; Lee, *Spectacular Bid*, 76; Pamela K. Brodowsky and John Philbin, *Two Minutes to Glory: The Official History of the Kentucky Derby* (New York: Collins, 2007), 4, 5; Marjorie Rieser, "Horse Racing in Central Kentucky and Jefferson County (with special reference to Churchill Downs) (master's thesis, University of Louisville, 1944), 41–42. The original Galt House had opened in 1835 and burned down in 1865; the second, which opened in 1869, was modeled on Rome's Palazzo Farnese, and its huge frescoed rotunda boasted a medallion that depicted the Kentucky state seal (Farrow, "When Russian Royalty Met Southern Hospitality," 10).

28. Margaretta Brown to her son Orlando Brown, 7 July 1819, quoted in Aron, *How the West Was Lost*, 126; Farrow, "When Russian Royalty Met Southern Hospitality," 3, 5, 12.

29. Brodowsky and Philbin, *Two Minutes to Glory*, 5; Crain, *They're Off*, 25.

30. Deb Bennett, "Secrets of Secretariat's Speed," *Equus* 434 (November 2013): 46; Cassidy, *Horse People*, 17.

31. *Louisville Courier-Journal*, 17 May 1875, quoted in *They're Off: A Century of Kentucky Derby Coverage by "The Courier-Journal" and "The Louisville Times"* (Louisville, KY: Pinaire Lithographing, 1975).

32. John Henry, *Galloping Ghosts: The Story of the Kentucky Derby, 1885–1933* (Louisville, KY: Herald Post Incorporated, 1934), 11; O'Connor, *The Kentucky Derby*, 17. Chuck-a-luck was a dice game associated with casinos, and spindle, often known as "squeeze spindle," was a portable version of the roulette wheel.

33. John H. Davis, *The American Turf* (New York: John Polhemus Printing, 1907), 29, 30; Henry, *Galloping Ghosts*, 13; "The Great Race of Wednesday," *Louisville Courier-Journal*, 11 May 1876 (typescript at FHS).

34. Henry, *Galloping Ghosts*, 15; "Mrs. Sallie Downs," *Boston Daily Advertiser*, 9 July 1896; unknown to Lizzie Haldeman, 21 May 1879, Haldeman Family Papers, 1843–1985, Mss. A HI59 85, FHS; Daisy L. to William Lower, 21 May 1882, FHS.

35. *Louisville Courier-Journal*, 24 May 1883, in *They're Off*; Henry, *Galloping Ghosts*, 23, 26 42.

36. Henry, *Galloping Ghosts*, 15; Wall, *How Kentucky Became Southern*, 179; "A Reception by General Mite and Lucia Zarate," *Philadelphia Times*, 21 April 1885; "Celebrities at the Kentucky Derby," TMZ, www.tmz.com/photos/image_jpg_20190504_0bf1356f33d857209461e00aa5f30828/.

37. Renau, *Jockeys, Belles, and Bluegrass Kings*, 40, 41, 54; O'Dell, "At the Starting Post," 76; Nicholson, *The Kentucky Derby*, 13, 21; "Official Programme of the Louisville Jockey Club, 27 September 1876," Nicola Marschall Scrapbook, 1846–1917, FHS; Steven A. Riess, *The Sport of Kings and the Kings of Crime: Horse Racing, Politics, and Organized Crime in New York, 1865–1913* (Syracuse, NY: Syracuse University Press, 2011), 60, 61, 65; James Robert Saunders and Monica Renae Saunders, *Black Winning Jockeys in the Kentucky Derby* (Jefferson, NC: McFarland, 2003), 34, 35.

38. John Samuel Ezell, *The South since 1865*, 2nd ed. (Norman: University of Oklahoma Press, 1975) 336; Ted Ownby, *Subduing Satan: Religion, Recreation, and Manhood in the Rural South, 1865–1920* (Chapel Hill: University of North Carolina Press, 1990), 68, 76; Nicholson, *The Kentucky Derby*, 21; *Louisville Courier-Journal*, 18 May 1891, in *They're Off*; Renau, *Jockeys, Belles, and Bluegrass Kings*, 41.

39. *Louisville Courier-Journal*, 14 May 1886, in *They're Off.*

40. Andrew P. Patrick, "The Kentucky Association for the Improvement of Breeds of Stock: Natural Advantages and Market Motivations," http://works.bepress.com/andrew_patrick/2.

41. Bennett Liebman, "The Naming of the Triple Crown," http://dx.doi.org/10.2139/ssrn.264 9997.

42. Important works on the Lost Cause myth include Gaines M. Foster, *Ghosts of the Confederacy: Defeat, the Lost Cause, and the Emergence of the New South, 1865–1913* (New York: Oxford University Press, 1988); Jason Phillips, *Diehard Rebels: The Confederate Cult of Invincibility* (Athens: University of Georgia Press, 2007); and Charles Reagan Wilson, *Baptized in Blood: The Religion of the Lost Cause, 1865–1920* (Athens: University of Georgia Press, 2011). The phrase comes from the journalist Edward A. Pollard's 1866 book *The Lost Cause: A New Southern History of the War of the Confederates.* On women's activism, see Karen L. Cox, *Dixie's Daughters: The United Daughters of the Confederacy and the Preservation of Confederate Culture* (Gainesville: University Press of Florida, 2003); and Caroline E. Janney, *Burying the Dead but Not the Past: Ladies' Memorial Associations and the Lost Cause* (Chapel Hill: University of North Carolina Press, 2008).

43. The case is analyzed in detail in Patricia Cline Cohen, *The Murder of Helen Jewett: The Life and Death of a Prostitute in Nineteenth-Century New York* (New York: Knopf, 1998).

44. The phrase is from Karen Halttunen's seminal study of the mid-nineteenth-century American urban bourgeoisie, *Confidence Men and Painted Women: A Study of Middle-Class Culture in America, 1830–1870* (New Haven, CT: Yale University Press, 1982).

45. Wall, *How Kentucky Became Southern*, 203, 204.

46. Ownby, *Subduing Satan*, 75.

47. "Saratoga: The Hotels, the Women, and the Fashion," *Boston Daily Advertiser*, 11 August 1866; Edward Sullivan, Esq., *Rambles and Scrambles in North and South America* (London: Richard Bentley, 1852), 37; "A Settled Gentleman," "Letter from the White Sulphur Springs," *National Intelligencer*, 24 August 1867.

48. Nicholson, *The Kentucky Derby*, 17–18.

49. Nicholson, *The Kentucky Derby*, 21, 23–24.

50. Nicholson, *The Kentucky Derby*, 22; 42–45; William S. Ward, "The Literature of Three Delectable Kentucky Vices, Part I: Racing," *Kentucky Review* 9 (1989): 13; Marshall, *Creating a Confederate Kentucky*, 134.

51. Nicholson, *The Kentucky Derby*, 28, 32; Wall, *How Kentucky Became Southern*, 211; Ward, "Kentucky Vices," 13; Marshall, *Creating a Confederate Kentucky*, 133.

52. Wall, *How Kentucky Became Southern*, 203. On plantation literature, see Jeremy Wells, *Romances of the White Man's Burden: Race, Empire, and the Plantation in American Literature, 1880–1936* (Nashville, TN: Vanderbilt University Press); and Peter Templeton and Andrew Dix, "'Old,' 'New,' and 'Problem' Souths in Thomas Nelson Page's *In Ole Virginia*," *Mississippi Quarterly* 74 (2022): 313–33

53. Wall, *How Kentucky Became Southern,* 206, 207–8; Marshall, *Creating a Confederate Kentucky,* 133, 144, 145; F. Scott Fitzgerald, "Bernice Bobs Her Hair," in *Flappers and Philosophers,* by Fitzgerald (1920; New York: Open Road Integrated Media, 2016), 87.

54. Morgan Elizabeth Byrd, "Unbridled Elegance: Examining African American Representation through the Kentucky Derby" (master's thesis, University of Arizona, 2022), 26; Wall, *How Kentucky Became Southern,* 212; Jeanne Harrah-Conforth, "The Landscape of Possibility: An Ethnography of the Kentucky Derby" (PhD diss., Indiana University, 1992), 71; Nicholson, *The Kentucky Derby,* 104.

55. Matthew Saul Perreault, "Jockeying for Position: Horse Racing in New Orleans, 1865–1920" (master's thesis, Louisiana State University, 2016), 16, 18; David K. Wiggins, *Glory Bound: Black Athletes in a White America* (Syracuse, NY: Syracuse University Press, 1997), 32; Lyman Horace Weeks, ed., *The American Turf: An Historical Account of Racing in the United States, with Biographical Sketches of Turf Celebrities* (New York: Historical Company, 1898), 370. See also Katherine C. Mooney, *Race Horse Men: How Slavery and Freedom Were Made at the Racetrack* (Cambridge, MA: Harvard University Press, 2014).

56. Charles Stewart, "My Life as a Slave," *Harper's Monthly Magazine,* October 1884, 730–37.

57. Michael Leeds and Hugh Rockoff, "Jim Crow in the Saddle: The Expulsion of African American Jockeys from American Racing," National Bureau of Economic Research Working Paper 28167, December 2020, 3, 4, www.nber.org/system/files/working_papers/w28167/w28167.pdf; Steven A. Riess, "The American Jockey, 1865–1910," *Transatlantica* 2 (2011): 4; Rebecca Richart, "The "Backside' of the Track: Race, Recognition, and Labor Shifts in Thoroughbred Horse Racing," *Ohio Valley History* 19 (2019): 58. Katherine C. Mooney's *Isaac Murphy: The Rise and Fall of a Black Jockey* (New Haven, CT: Yale University Press, 2023) further illuminates the virtual disappearance of African American jockeys from American racetracks throughout the twentieth century. Kevin Krigger, who was born in the US Virgin Islands and who rode in the 2013 Derby, was the first African American to do so since Winkfield more than a century earlier (Gabe Bullard, "A Black Jockey at the Kentucky Derby, Once Again," National Public Radio, 3 May 2013, www.npr.org/sections/codeswitch/2013/05/03/180555617/a-black-jockey-at-the-kentucky-derby-once-again).

58. "My Old Kentucky Home," www.kentuckyderby.com/history/traditions/my-old-kentucky-home; Alex Lubet and Steven Lubet, "The Complicated Legacy of 'My Old Kentucky Home,'" *Smithsonian* blog, 3 September 2020, www.smithsonianmag.com/arts-culture/complicated-legacy-my-old-kentucky-home-180975719/. See also Emily Bingham, *My Old Kentucky Home: The Astonishing Life and Reckoning of an Iconic American Song* (New York: Knopf, 2022).

59. Anthony Harkins, "Colonels, Hillbillies, and Fightin': Twentieth-Century Kentucky in the National Imagination," *Register of the Kentucky Historical Society* 113 (2015): 432–33; Mooney, *Race Horse Men,* 6; Elizabeth A. Perkins, "The Forgotten Victorians: Louisville's Domestic Servants, 1880–1920," *Register of the Kentucky Historical Society* 85 (1987): 119–20, 128–29.

60. Nicholson, *The Kentucky Derby,* 67; F. Kevin Simon, ed., *The WPA Guide to Kentucky* (1939; Lexington: University Press of Kentucky, 1996), 97.

61. *The Kentucky Derby, 1875–1932,* 30, 32. 52.

62. Nicholson, *The Kentucky Derby*, 47, 48; Mooney, *Race Horse Men*, 146. Prices for reserved seats at the 2023 Derby started at seven hundred dollars, but general admission was just seventy-seven dollars, as Churchill Downs' management considers the attendance of less affluent spectators not just acceptable but desirable; these guests are seen as contributing more to the event's carnival atmosphere than the rich people and celebrities who pay ten to twenty times as much for their tickets. Louisville native Hunter S. Thompson's famous essay about his visit to the 1970 Derby gave a notorious description of the infield: "'That whole thing,' I said, 'will be jammed with people; fifty thousand or so, and most of them staggering drunk. It's a fantastic scene—thousands of people fainting, crying, copulating, trampling each other and fighting with broken whiskey bottles. We'll have to spend some time out there, but it's hard to move around, too many bodies'" (Matthew Glowicki, "How Much Are Tickets to the Kentucky Derby? Here's Your Complete 2023 Guide," *Louisville Courier-Journal*, 23 January 2023; Hunter S. Thompson, "The Kentucky Derby Is Decadent and Depraved," *Scanlan's Magazine* [June 1970], https://grantland.com/features/looking-back-hunter-s-thompson-classic-story-kentucky-derby/). Antebellum southern turfmen would have been mortified had their home tracks' atmosphere been described as "decadent and depraved," but Churchill Downs' managers seem unfazed by Thompson's claims.

CONCLUSION

1. Edward Hotaling, *They're Off!: Horse Racing at Saratoga* (Syracuse, NY: Syracuse University Press, 1995), 225.

2. The photographic archive of the area's most widely read local newspaper, the *Albany Times-Union*, includes pictures of many famous visitors to the track, including restaurateur Bobby Flay (2017), musician Josh Groban (2016), comedian Joan Rivers (2007), actor Paul Newman (2006), and sexologist Dr. Ruth Westheimer (2000) ("Photos: Celebrity Sightings in Saratoga, *Times-Union*, www.timesunion.com/entertainment/article/Photos-Celebrities-in-Saratoga-6180119.php#photo-7746281).

3. Lawrence Van Gelder, "Marylou Whitney: Life at the Gallop," *New York Times*, 10 January 1997; Leonard Shapiro and Vicky Moon, "At the Track, the Betting's on the Queen of Saratoga," *Washington Post*, 9 August 2006.

4. "Food & Drink at Saratoga Race Course," www.saratoga.com/race-track/coolers-food-drink-tips/; Dennis Yusko, "Drinkin' at the Track," *The Saratoga Blog, Times-Union*, 19 May 2011, https://blog.timesunion.com/saratogaseen/horse-racing-beer/8778/; "Saratoga Race Course Dress Code," www.saratoga.com/race-track/dress-code/; Gary Cross, "Saratoga Springs: From Genteel Spa to Disney-fied Resort," *Journal of Tourism History* 4 (2012): 82. Saratoga was an important stop on the "Fashionable Tour" of the Northeast, from Manhattan to Quebec, that became popular in the 1820s (Will B. Mackintosh, *Selling the Sights: The Invention of the Tourist in American Culture* [New York: New York University Press, 2019], 10). See also Jon Sterngass, *First Resorts: Pursuing Pleasure at Saratoga Springs, Newport, and Coney Island* (Baltimore, MD: Johns Hopkins University Press, 2001).

5. Eric Banks, "Saratoga's Sesquicentennial Shindig," *Town & Country,* 14 August 2013, www.townandcountrymag.com/leisure/sporting/a1126/saratoga-racing-150th-anniversary/; Carter Wilkie, "At Saratoga, A Step Back in Time," *New York Times,* 20 July 2012; "Cultural Resources," New York Racing Association, www.nyra.com/uploads/wysiwyg/assets/uploads/15_Cultural.pdf.

6. Wendy Liberatore, "Saratoga Meet Breaks Betting Record Again to Close 2020–21 Horse Racing Season," *Times-Union,* 6 September 2021, www.timesunion.com/news/article/Saratoga-meet-breaks-handle-record-again-16438528.php; "Saratoga Meet Concludes with Record Handle, 'Robust' Audience," *Paulick Report,* 5 September 2022.

BIBLIOGRAPHY

MANUSCRIPT SOURCES

California

Henry E. Huntington Library, San Marino
Brock Collection

Kentucky

Filson Historical Society, Louisville
Bodley Family Papers
Bullitt Family Papers, Oxmoor Collection
"The Great Race of Wednesday," typescript from the *Louisville Courier Journal*, 11 May 1876
Haldeman Family Papers
Nicola Marschall Scrapbook
Miscellaneous Manuscripts Collection
Mss. C D Daisy L.
Louis Allahwyn Walker Additional Papers

Louisiana

Louisiana and Lower Mississippi Valley Collection, Hill Library, Louisiana State University, Baton Rouge
Rosella Kenner Brent Recollections
Dugregiy Dupuy and Family Papers
Morris-Sibley Papers

South Carolina

South Carolina Historical Society, Charleston
Gaillard Family Papers
Ms 43/375
Ms 43/568
Read Family Papers
Rules of the Santee Jockey Club, 1791, typescript
James Shoolbred Letterbooks and Journals
South Carolina Jockey Club Rules, 1828
Thomas P. Ravenel Collection
Charleston Library Society, Charleston
South Carolina Jockey Club Records

Virginia

Albert and Shirley Small Special Collections Library, University of Virginia, Charlottesville
Tappahannock Jockey Club Minute Book, 1796–1801, Marion du Pont Scott Papers
Valentine Richmond History Center, Richmond
Wirt Armistead Cate, "History of Richmond," typescript (ca. 1943)
Virginia Historical Society, Richmond
Doswell Family Papers
McIntosh Family Papers
Michael Gretter Papers
Norfolk Jockey Club Book
Richmond Jockey Club Records
Tayloe Family Papers
Virginia Landscape Surveys

NEWSPAPERS AND PERIODICALS

Albany (NY) Times-Union
Alexandria (VA) Gazette & Advertiser
All the Year Round
American Turf Register and Sporting Magazine
The Argonaut
Atlantic Monthly

Baily's Magazine of Sports and Pastimes
Bell's Life in London and Sporting Chronicle
Boston Daily Advertiser
Boston Evening Transcript
Cambridge (MA) Chronicle
Charleston (SC) Mercury
Charleston (SC) News and Courier
Christian Reflector
Commercial-Appeal (Memphis)
Cosmopolitan: A Monthly Outing Magazine
Daily Evening Bulletin (San Francisco)
Daily Inter-Ocean
Daily National Intelligencer
Daily Picayune
Daily True Delta
Easton (MD) Gazette
Every Saturday: An Illustrated Weekly Journal
The Exposition
Frank Leslie's Illustrated Newspaper
Galveston (TX) Daily News
Harper's Magazine
Harper's New Monthly Magazine
Harper's Weekly
Illustrated American
Independent Gazetteer
Journal of the Society of Arts
Los Angeles Herald
Lippincott's Magazine of Literature
Little Rock (AR) Daily Gazette
Louisville Courier-Journal
Maryland Sentinel
Milwaukee Daily Sentinel
Misissippi [sic] Herald & Natchez Gazette
Mississippi Free Trader
Mississippi Free Trader and Natchez Gazette
Mississippi State Gazette
Munsey's Magazine
The Nation

National Intelligencer
New England Magazine
New Haven Daily Palladium
New Orleans Times-Picayune
New York Age
New York Evening Post
New York Herald
New York Times
New York Tribune
New York World
Niles' Weekly Register
The North American
Outing: An Illustrated Monthly Magazine of Recreation
Peterson's Magazine
Philadelphia Times
Pittsfield (MA) Sun
Porter's Spirit of the Times
Racing Times
Richmond (VA) Examiner
Richmond (VA) Whig
San Francisco Morning Call
Spirit of the Times
St. Paul (MN) Daily News
Times (London)
Traveller and Spirit of the Times
United States Magazine and Democratic Review
Virginia Gazette
Virginia Religious Magazine
Wallace's Monthly
Washington Post
Wilkes' Spirit of the Times

PRINTED SOURCES

Books

Adams, Henry. *History of the United States during Thomas Jefferson's Administration.* New York: Charles Scribner's Sons, 1891.

Adams, Jane M. *Healing with Water: English Spas and the Water Cure, 1840–1960.* Manchester, UK: Manchester University Press, 2015.

Adelman, Melvin. *A Sporting Time: New York City and the Rise of Modern Athletics, 1820–70.* Urbana: University of Illinois Press, 1986.

Alcott, William Alexander. *The Young Man's Guide.* 2nd. ed. Boston: Lilly, Wait, Colman, and Holden, 1834.

Alexander, David. *The History and Romance of the Horse, Told with Pictures.* New York: Cooper Square, 1965.

Alexander, James Waddell. *The Life of Archibald Alexander, D.D.* New York: Charles Scribner, 1854.

Allen, Irving Lewis. *The City in Slang: New York Life and Popular Speech.* New York: Oxford University Press, 1993.

American Turf Register: A Correct Synopsis of Turf Events in the United States, Embracing, Running, Trotting and Pacing, for 1870. New York: Bruce, 1871.

Anburey, Thomas. *Travels through the Interior Parts of America.* London: William Lane, 1789.

Anderson, Dorothy Middleton, and Margaret Middleton Rivers Eastman. *St. Philip's Church of Charleston: An Early History of the Oldest Parish in South Carolina.* Charleston, SC: History Press, 2014.

Anderson, James Douglas. *Making the American Thoroughbred.* Norwood, MA: Plimpton, 1916.

Anzilotti, Cara. *In the Affairs of the World: Women, Patriarchy, and Power in Colonial South Carolina.* Westport, CT: Greenwood, 2002.

Armstead, Myra B. Young. *Lord, Please Don't Take Me in August: African Americans in Newport and Saratoga Springs, 1870–1930.* Urbana: University of Illinois Press, 1999.

Armstrong, Zella, comp. *Notable Southern Families.* Chattanooga, TN: Lookout, 1922.

Aron, Stephen. *How the West Was Lost: The Transformation of Kentucky from Daniel Boone to Henry Clay.* Baltimore, MD: Johns Hopkins University Press, 1996.

Arthur, Stanley Clisby, and George Campbell Huchet de Kernion. *Old Families of Louisiana.* 1931. Baltimore, MD: Genealogical Publishing, 2009.

Asbury, Francis. *The Journal of the Rev. Francis Asbury.* New York: N. Bangs and T. Mason, 1821.

The Atlantic Telegraph: Its History, from the Commencement of the Undertaking in 1854, to the Final Success in 1866. London: Bacon, 1866.

Avary, Myrta Lockett. *Dixie after the War.* New York: Doubleday, Page, 1906.

Baker, William J. *Sports in the Western World.* Rev. ed. Urbana: University of Illinois Press, 1988.

Baptist, Edward E. *The Half Has Never Been Told: Slavery and the Making of American Capitalism.* New York: Basic, 2014.

Barker, Thomas, and Marjie Britz. *Jokers Wild: Legalized Gambling in the Twenty-First Century*. Westport, CT: Praeger, 2000.

Barnes, Amanda, and Juliet Wright. *The Butcher Boys: Part Two—The Breaking of the Brooklyn Stable*. Morrisville, NC: Lulu, 2019.

Barrere, Albert, and Charles G. Leland, eds. *A Dictionary of Slang, Jargon & Cant*. Edinburgh: Ballantyne, 1890.

Bauer, Craig Anthony. *A Leader among Peers: The Life and Times of Duncan Farrar Kenner*. Lafayette, LA: Center for Louisiana Studies, 1993.

Beckert, Sven. *Empire of Cotton: A Global History*. New York: Knopf, 2014.

———. *The Monied Metropolis: New York City and the Consolidation of the American Bourgeoisie, 1850–1896*. New York: Cambridge University Press, 2001.

Behrend, Justin. *Reconstructing Democracy: Grassroots Black Politics in the Deep South after the Civil War*. Athens: University of Georgia Press, 2015.

Benfey, Christopher. *Degas in New Orleans: Encounters in the Creole World of Kate Chopin and George Washington Cable*. Berkeley: University of California Press, 1997.

Benton, Jeffrey C. *Respectable and Disreputable: Leisure Time in Antebellum Montgomery*. Montgomery, AL: NewSouth, 2013.

Bernard, John. *Retrospections of America, 1797–1811*. Edited by Mrs. Bayle Bernard. New York: Harper & Brothers, 1887.

Betts, Edwin Morris. *Thomas Jefferson's Farm Book*. Princeton, NJ: Princeton University Press, 1953.

Billings, Warren M., ed. *The Old Dominion in the Seventeenth Century: A Documentary History of Virginia, 1606–1700*. Rev. ed. Chapel Hill: University of North Carolina Press, 2007.

Bingham, Emily. *My Old Kentucky Home: The Astonishing Life and Reckoning of an Iconic American Song*. New York: Knopf, 2022.

Birkbeck, Morris. *Notes on a Journey in America*. London: James Ridgeway, 1818.

Black, David. *The King of Fifth Avenue: The Fortunes of August Belmont*. New York: Dial, 1981.

Black, Patti Carr. *Art in Mississippi, 1720–1980*. Jackson: University Press of Mississippi, 1998.

Black, Robert. *Horse-Racing in France: A History*. London: Sampson Low, Marston, Searle, & Rivington, 1886.

Blanchard, Elizabeth, and Manly Wade Wellman. *The Life and Times of Sir Archie: The Story of America's Greatest Thoroughbred, 1805–1833*. Chapel Hill: University of North Carolina Press, 1958.

Blane, William Newnham. *An Excursion through the United States and Canada during the Years 1822–23, by an English Gentleman*. 1824. New York: Negro Universities Press, 1969.

Blight, David W. *Race and Reunion: The Civil War in American Memory*. Cambridge, MA: Harvard University Press, 2001.

Bostick, Douglas W. *The Union Is Dissolved!: Charleston and Fort Sumter in the Civil War*. Charleston, SC: History Press, 2009.

Bourdieu, Pierre. *Outline of a Theory of Practice*. Translated by Richard Nice. Cambridge, UK: Cambridge University Press, 1977.

Bourgeois, Lillian C. *Cabanocey: The History, Customs and Folklore of St. James Parish*. 1957. Gretna, LA: Pelican, 1998.

Bouyea, Brien. *Bare Knuckles and Saratoga Racing: The Remarkable Life of John Morrissey*. Charleston, SC: History Press, 2016.

Bowen, Edward L. *Belmont Park: A Century of Champions*. Lexington, KY: Eclipse, 2005.

Bowmar, Dan M., III. *Giants of the Turf*. Lexington, KY: The Blood-Horse, 1960.

Bradley, Elizabeth L. *Knickerbocker: The Myth behind New York*. New Brunswick, NJ: Rutgers University Press, 2009.

Bradley, Hugh. *Such Was Saratoga*. New York: Doubleday, Doran, 1940.

Bradley, Ian. *Water Music: Making Music in the Spas of Europe and North America*. Oxford: Oxford University Press, 2010.

Brazy, Martha Jane. *An American Planter: Stephen Duncan of Antebellum Natchez and New York*. Baton Rouge: Louisiana State University Press, 2006.

Bridenbaugh, Carl. *Myths and Realities: Societies of the Colonial South*. Baton Rouge: Louisiana State University Press, 1952.

Brissot de Warville, Jacques-Pierre. *New Travels in the United States of America, Performed in 1788*. Dublin: W. Corbet, 1792.

Bristol, Douglas Walter, Jr. *Knights of the Razor: Black Barbers in Slavery and Freedom*. Baltimore, MD: Johns Hopkins University Press, 2009.

Brock, Julia, and Daniel Vivian. Introduction to *Leisure, Plantations, and the Making of a New South: The Sporting Plantations of the South Carolina Lowcountry and Red Hills Region, 1900–1940*, edited by Brock and Vivian. Lanham, MD: Lexington, 2015.

Brodowsky, Pamela K., and John Philbin. *Two Minutes to Glory: The Official History of the Kentucky Derby*. New York: Collins, 2007.

Browne, Junius Henri. *The Great Metropolis: A Mirror of New York*. Hartford, CT: American, 1869.

Bruce, William Cabell. *John Randolph of Roanoke, 1773–1833*. New York: G. P. Putnam's Sons, 1922.

Buchanan, Thomas C. *Black Life on the Mississippi: Slaves, Free Blacks, and the Western Steamboat World*. Chapel Hill: University of North Carolina Press, 2004.

Buckingham, James Silk, *The Slave States of America*. London: Fischer, 1842.

Budd, Graham. *Racing Art and Memorabilia.* London: Philip Wilson, 1997.

Burke, Peter. *Popular Culture in Early Modern Europe.* New York: Harper & Row, 1978.

Burnard, Trevor. *Planters, Merchants, and Slaves: Plantation Societies in British America, 1650–1820.* Chicago: University of Chicago Press, 2013.

Burrows, Edwin G., and Mike Wallace. *Gotham: A History of New York City to 1898.* New York: Oxford University Press, 1999.

Bush, Bryan S. *Louisville Gambling Barons.* Charleston, SC: History Press, 2023.

Bush, Francis Marion. *Colonial Downs and More.* Bloomington, IN: iUniverse, 2011.

Butler, Christina Rae. *Charleston Horse Power: Equine Culture in the Palmetto City.* Columbia: University of South Carolina Press, 2023.

Butler, Nicholas Michael. *Votaries of Apollo: The St. Cecilia Society and the Patronage of Concert Music in Charleston, South Carolina, 1766–1820.* Columbia: University of South Carolina Press, 2007.

Caldwell, Charles. *A Discourse on the Vice of Gambling.* Lexington, KY: J. Clarke, 1835.

Cantwell, Robert. *Bluegrass Breakdown: The Making of the Old Southern Sound.* Urbana: University of Illinois Press, 1984.

Carmichael, Peter S. *Lee's Young Artillerist: William R. J. Pegram.* Charlottesville: University Press of Virginia, 1995.

Carroll, Linda, and David Rosner. *Duel for the Crown: Affirmed, Alydar, and Racing's Greatest Rivalry.* New York: Gallery, 2014.

Carson, Jane. *Colonial Virginians at Play.* Williamsburg, VA: Colonial Williamsburg, 1965.

Carty, T. J. *A Dictionary of Literary Pseudonyms in the English Language.* 2nd ed. New York: Routledge, 2015.

Case, Carole. *Down the Backstretch: Racing and the American Dream.* Philadelphia: Temple University Press, 1991.

———. *The Right Breed: America's Aristocrats in Thoroughbred Racing.* New Brunswick, NJ: Rutgers University Press, 2000.

Cassidy, Rebecca. *Horse People: Thoroughbred Culture in Lexington and Newmarket.* Baltimore, MD: Johns Hopkins University Press, 2007.

Census of the State of New York for 1865. Albany: Charles Van Benthuysen and Sons, 1867.

Chambers, Thomas A. *Drinking the Waters: Creating an American Leisure Class at Nineteenth-Century Mineral Springs.* Washington, DC: Smithsonian Institution Press, 2002.

Childs, Arney R., ed. *Rice Planter and Sportsman: The Recollections of J. Motte Alston, 1821–1909.* Columbia: University of South Carolina Press, 1953.

Claiborne, J. F. H. *Life and Times of Gen. Sam Dale, the Mississippi Partisan.* New York: Harper & Brothers, 1860.

Clark, Emily. *The Strange History of the American Quadroon: Free Women of Color in the Revolutionary Atlantic World.* Chapel Hill: University of North Carolina Press, 2013.

Clark, Thomas D., and John D. W. Guice. *The Old Southwest, 1795–1830: Frontiers in Conflict.* 1989. Norman: University of Oklahoma Press, 1995.

Clay, John, Jr. *New World Notes: An Account of Journeyings and Sojournings in America and Canada.* Kelso, UK: J. & J. H. Rutherfurd, 1875.

Clews, Henry. *Fifty Years in Wall Street.* 1908. Hoboken, NJ: Wiley, 2006.

Click, Patricia J. *The Spirit of the Times: Amusements in Nineteenth-Century Baltimore, Norfolk, and Richmond.* Charlottesville: University Press of Virginia, 1989.

Clinton, Catherine. *Fanny Kemble's Civil Wars.* New York: Oxford University Press, 2001.

Cobb, Jasmine Nichole. *Picture Freedom: Remaking Black Visuality in the Early Nineteenth Century.* New York: New York University Press, 2015.

Coffin, Charles Carleton. *The Boys of '61; or, Four Years of Fighting.* Boston: Estes and Lauriat, 1884.

Cohen, Hennig, ed. *The South Carolina Gazette, 1732–1775.* Columbia: University of South Carolina Press, 1953.

Cohen, Kenneth. *They Will Have Their Game: Sporting Culture and the Making of the Early American Republic.* Ithaca, NY: Cornell University Press, 2017.

Cohen, Patricia Cline. *The Murder of Helen Jewett: The Life and Death of a Prostitute in Nineteenth-Century New York.* New York: Knopf, 1998.

Coleman, W. H. *Historical Sketch Book and Guide to New Orleans and Environs.* New York: William H. Coleman, 1885.

Comstock, Anthony, and J. M. Buckley. *Traps for the Young.* 1883. New York: Cosimo, 2009.

Conn, Dr. George H. *The Arabian Horse in America.* Woodstock, VT: Countryman, 1957.

Connolly, Cyril. *Enemies of Promise.* 1948. Rev. ed. Chicago: University of Chicago Press, 2008.

Constitution for the Louisville Association for Improvement of the Breed of Horses, and Rules and Regulations for the Government of the Course. Louisville: W. W. Worsley, 1832.

Conway, Moncure Daniel. *Barons of the Potomack and the Rappahannock.* New York: Grolier Club, 1892.

Cooke, John Esten. *Henry St. John, Gentleman, of "Flower of Hundreds," in the County of Prince George, Virginia: A Tale of 1774–'75.* New York: Harper & Brothers, 1860.

———. *The Virginia Comedians: or, Old Days in the Old Dominion.* New York: D. Appleton, 1854.

Cooper, Dana. *Informal Ambassadors: American Women, Transatlantic Marriages, and Anglo-American Relations, 1865–1945.* Kent, OH: Kent State University Press, 2014.

Cote, Richard N. *Mary's World: Love, War, and Family Ties in Nineteenth-Century Charleston.* Mount Pleasant, SC: Corinthian, 2001.

Cowan, Walter G., et al. *New Orleans Yesterday and Today.* Baton Rouge: Louisiana State University Press, 1983.

Cox, Karen L. *Dixie's Daughters: The United Daughters of the Confederacy and the Preservation of Confederate Culture.* Gainesville: University Press of Florida, 2003.

Crain, Kenneth C. *They're Off: The Romance of the Kentucky Derby.* Chicago: Kenford, 1930.

Cram, Mildred. *Old Seaport Towns of the South.* New York: Dodd, Mead, 1917.

Creecy, James R. *Scenes of the South.* Washington, DC: Thomas McGill, 1860.

Crevecoeur, J. Hector St. John de. *Letters from an American Farmer.* 1782. Edited by Susan Manning. Oxford: Oxford University Press, 1997.

Crooks, Esther J., and Ruth W. Crooks. *The Ring Tournament in the United States.* Richmond, VA: Garrett and Massie, 1936.

Cruz, Jesus. *The Rise of Middle-Class Culture in Nineteenth-Century Spain.* Baton Rouge: Louisiana State University Press, 2011.

Culver, Francis Barnum. *Blooded Horses of Colonial Days.* Baltimore: privately published, 1922.

Curtis, George William. *The Potiphar Papers.* New York: Harper & Brothers, 1858.

Cutler, William Parker, and Julia Perkins Cutler. *Life, Journals, and Correspondence of Rev. Manasseh Cutler, LL.D.* Cincinnati, OH: Robert Clarke, 1888.

Dabney, Virginius. *Richmond: The Story of a City.* Charlottesville: University Press of Virginia, 1976.

Dallow, Jessica. *Race, Gender and Identity in American Equine Art: 1832 to the Present.* New York: Routledge, 2022.

Dalzell, Robert F., Jr. *Enterprising Elite: The Boston Associates and the World They Made.* Cambridge, MA: Harvard University Press, 1987.

Davis, Edwin Adams, and William Ransom Hogan. *The Barber of Natchez.* Baton Rouge: Louisiana State University Press, 1954

Davis, John H. *The American Turf with Personal Reminiscences.* New York: John Polhemus Printing, 1907.

Davis, Reuben. *Recollections of Mississippi and Mississippians.* Boston: Houghton, Mifflin, 1891.

Davison, Gideon M. *The Fashionable Tour: A Guide to Travellers Visiting the Middle and Northern States, and the Provinces of Canada,* 4th ed. Saratoga Springs, NY: G. M. Davison, 1830.

Day, Louise Haskell. *Alexander Cheves Haskell: The Portrait of a Man.* Norwood, MA: privately published, 1934.

Deedes, Henry. *Sketches of the South and West, or Ten Months' Residence in the United States.* Edinburgh: William Blackwood and Sons, 1869.

Denton, Daniel. *A Brief Description of New-York, Formerly Called New-Netherlands.* Edited by Gabriel Furman. New York: William Gowans, 1845.

DeRosier, Arthur H., Jr. *William Dunbar: Scientific Pioneer of the Old Southwest.* Lexington: University Press of Kentucky, 2007.

Devol, George H. *Forty Years a Gambler on the Mississippi*, 2nd ed. New York: George H. Devol, 1926.

Dibdin, Charles. *The Songs of Charles Dibdin.* London: G. H. Davidson, 1848.

Dilke, Sir Charles Wentworth. *Greater Britain: A Record of Travel in English-Speaking Countries during 1866 and 1867.* 6th ed. London: Macmillan, 1872.

Dizikes, John. *Sportsmen and Gamesmen.* Columbia: University of Missouri Press, 2002.

———. *Yankee Doodle Dandy: The Life and Times of Tod Sloan.* Lincoln: University of Nebraska Press, 2000.

Donald, Diana. *Picturing Animals in Britain, 1750–1850.* New Haven, CT: Yale University Press, 2007.

Drayton, John. *A View of South-Carolina, as Respects Her Natural and Civil Concerns.* Charleston, SC: W. P. Young, 1802.

Dunn, Susan. *Dominion of Memories: Jefferson, Madison, and the Decline of Virginia.* New York: Basic, 2007.

Durkee, Cornelius E., comp. *Reminiscences of Saratoga.* Saratoga Springs, NY: The Saratogian, 1928.

Early, Eleanor. *New Orleans Holiday.* New York: Rhinehart, 1947.

Eberle, Kevin R. *A History of Charleston's Hampton Park.* Charleston, SC: History Press, 2012.

Edgar, Patrick Nisbett. *The American Race-Turf Register, Sportsman's Herald, and General Stud Book.* New York: Henry Mason, 1838.

Edgar, Walter. *South Carolina: A History.* Columbia: University of South Carolina Press, 1998.

Egan, Pierce. *Sporting Anecdotes, Original and Selected.* London: Sherwood, Jones, 1825.

Eisenberg, John. *The Great Match Race: When North Met South in America's First Sports Spectacle.* Boston: Houghton Mifflin, 2006.

Evans, Emory J. *A "Topping People": The Rise and Decline of Virginia's Old Political Elite, 1680–1790.* Charlottesville: University Press of Virginia, 2009.

Extracts from the Votes and Proceedings of the American Continental Congress. London: J. Almon, 1774.

Ezell, John Samuel. *The South since 1865.* 2nd ed. Norman: University of Oklahoma Press, 1975.

Fant, Jennie Holton, ed. *The Travelers' Charleston: Accounts of Charleston and Lowcountry South Carolina, 1666–1861.* Columbia: University of South Carolina Press, 2016.

Faust, Drew Gilpin. *James Henry Hammond and the Old South: A Design for Mastery.* Baton Rouge: Louisiana State University Press, 1985.

Faxon, C. A. *Faxon's Illustrated Handbook of Travel to Saratoga, Lakes George and Champlain, the Adirondacks, Niagara Falls, Montreal, Quebec, the Saguenay River, the White Mountains, Lakes Memphremagog and Winnepiseogee.* Rev. ed. Boston: C. A. Faxon, 1874.

Featherstonhaugh, G. W. *An Excursion to the Slave States.* New York: Harper & Brothers, 1844.

Federal Writers' Project. *Mississippi: A Guide to the Magnolia State.* New York: Viking, 1938.

Finn, Margot, and Kate Smith. Introduction to *The East India Company at Home, 1757–1857*, edited by Finn and Smith. London: UCL, 2018.

Fischer, David Hackett, and James C. Kelly. *Bound Away: Virginia and the Westward Movement.* Charlottesville: University Press of Virginia, 2000.

Fitzgerald, F. Scott. *Flappers and Philosophers.* 1920. New York: Open Road Integrated Media, 2016.

Flint, Timothy. *Recollections of the Last Ten Years.* Boston: Cummings, Hilliard, 1826

Foote, William Henry, D.D. *Sketches of Virginia, Historical and Biographical.* Philadelphia: William S. Martien, 1849.

Ford, Lacy K., Jr. *Origins of Southern Radicalism: The South Carolina Upcountry, 1800–1860.* New York: Oxford University Press, 1988.

Forret, Jeff. *Race Relations at the Margins: Slaves and Poor Whites in the Antebellum Southern Countryside.* Baton Rouge: Louisiana State University Press, 1996.

Foster, Gaines M. *Ghosts of the Confederacy: Defeat, the Lost Cause, and the Emergence of the New South, 1865–1913.* New York: Oxford University Press, 1988.

Foster, Lillian. *Wayside Glimpses North and South.* New York: Rudd and Carleton, 1860.

Fourteenth Annual Report of the Board of Public Works, to the General Assembly of Virginia. Richmond: Samuel Shepherd, 1830.

Fox-Genovese, Elizabeth, and Eugene D. Genovese. *The Mind of the Master Class: History and Faith in the Southern Slaveholders' Worldview.* New York: Cambridge University Press, 2005.

Frank, Andrew K. *The Routledge Historical Atlas of the American South.* New York: Routledge, 1999.

Franklin, John Hope, ed. *A Southern Odyssey: Travelers in the Antebellum North.* Baton Rouge: Louisiana State University Press, 1976.

Fraser, Charles. *Reminiscences of Charleston.* 1854. Charleston, SC: Garnier, 1969.

Frederickson, George M. *The Black Image in the White Mind: The Debate on Afro-American Character and Destiny, 1817–1914.* New York: Harper & Row, 1971.

Freehling, William W. *Prelude to Civil War: The Nullification Crisis in South Carolina, 1816–1836.* 1965. New York: Oxford University Press, 1992.

Gandolfo, Henri A. *Metairie Cemetery: An Historical Memoir.* New Orleans: Stewart Enterprises, 1981.

Garland, Hugh A. *The Life of John Randolph of Roanoke*. New York: D. Appleton, 1856.

Gatto, Kimberly. *Belmont Park: The Championship Track*. Charleston, SC: History Press, 2013.

———. *Saratoga Race Course: The August Place to Be*. Charleston, SC: History Press, 2011.

Genovese, Eugene D. *The Sweetness of Life: Southern Planters at Home*. Cambridge, UK: Cambridge University Press, 2017.

Giesberg, Judith Ann. *Civil War Sisterhood: The U.S. Sanitary Commission and Women's Politics in Transition*. Boston: Northeastern University Press, 2000.

Gilman, Caroline. *Recollections of a Southern Matron*. New York: Harper & Brothers, 1838.

Glazier, Captain William. *Peculiarities of Great American Cities*. Philadelphia: Hubbard Brothers, 1884.

Goding, John. *Norman's History of Cheltenham*. London: Longman, Green, Longman, Roberts, & Green, 1863.

Gorn, Elliott J. *The Manly Art: Bare-Knuckle Fighting in America*. 1986. Updated ed. Ithaca, NY: Cornell University Press, 2012.

Gorn, Elliott J., and Warren Goldstein. *A Brief History of American Sports*. Urbana: University of Illinois Press, 1993.

Gould, Virginia Meacham. Preface to *Chained to the Rock of Adversity: To Be Free, Black, and Female in the Old South*, edited by Gould. Athens: University of Georgia Press, 1998.

Greene, Ann Norton. *Horses at Work: Harnessing Power in Industrial America*. Cambridge, MA: Harvard University Press, 2008.

Groves, Joseph A. *The Alstons and Allstons of North and South Carolina*. Atlanta: Franklin Printing, 1901.

Grundy, Pamela, and Benjamin Rader. *American Sports: From the Age of Folk Games to the Age of Televised Sports*. 7th ed. New York: Routledge, 2016.

Guarneri, Julia. *Newsprint Metropolis: City Papers and the Making of Modern Americans*. Chicago: University of Chicago Press, 2017.

Guilbeau, James. *The Saint Charles Streetcar, or, the History of the New Orleans and Carrollton Railroad*. New Orleans: Louisiana Landmarks Society, 1975.

Guttmann, Allen. *From Ritual to Record: The Nature of Modern Sports*. Updated ed. New York: Columbia University Press, 2004.

Hall, A. Oakey. *The Manhattaner in New Orleans; or, Phases of Crescent City Life*. New York: J. S. Redfield, 1851.

Hall, B. C., and C. T. Wood. *The South*. New York: Scribner, 1995.

Hall, Basil. *Travels in North America in the Years 1827 and 1828*. Edinburgh: Cadell, 1829.

Halttunen, Karen. *Confidence Men and Painted Women: A Study of Middle-Class Culture in America, 1830–1870*. New Haven, CT: Yale University Press, 1982.

Hammond, Gerald. *The Language of Horse Racing*. London: Routledge, 2016.

Hampton, Ann Fripp, ed. *A Divided Heart: Letters of Sally Baxter Hampton, 1853–1862.* Columbia, SC: Phantom, 1994.

Harlow, Luke E. *Religion, Race, and the Making of Confederate Kentucky, 1830–1880.* New York: Cambridge University Press, 2014.

Harris, Sharon M. Introduction to *Selected Writings of Judith Sargent Murray*, ed. Harris. New York: Oxford University Press, 1995.

Harrison, Eliza Cope, ed. *Best Companions: Letters of Eliza Middleton Fisher and Her Mother, Mary Hering Middleton, from Charleston, Philadelphia, and Newport, 1839–1846.* Columbia: University of South Carolina Press, 2001.

Harrison, Fairfax. *The Belair Stud, 1747–1761.* Richmond, VA: Old Dominion, 1929.

———. *Early American Turf Stock, 1730–1830.* Richmond, VA: Old Dominion, 1934.

———. *The John's Island Stud.* Richmond, VA: Old Dominion, 1931.

———. *The Roanoke Stud, 1795–1833.* Richmond, VA: Old Dominion, 1930.

Hart, Emma. *Building Charleston: Town and Society in the Eighteenth Century.* Charlottesville: University Press of Virginia, 2010.

Hawkins, J. *Reports of Cases Argued and Determined in the Supreme Court of Louisiana.* Vol. 21. New Orleans: Office of the *Daily Republican*, 1869.

Hayes, Captain M. Horace. *Points of the Horse.* 2nd. ed. London: W. Thacker, 1897.

Haynes, Robert V. *The Mississippi Territory and the Southwest Frontier, 1795–1817.* Lexington: University Press of Kentucky, 2010.

Hayward, John. *A Gazetteer of the United States of America.* Hartford, CT: Case, Tiffany, 1853.

Heimer, Mel. *Fabulous Bawd: The Story of Saratoga.* New York: Henry Holt, 1952.

Hennessey, Louis C. *Diamond Jubilee: The Fair Grounds, New Orleans.* New Orleans: New Orleans Fair Ground Corporation, 1947.

Henry, John. *Galloping Ghosts: The Story of the Kentucky Derby, 1885–1933.* Louisville, KY: Herald Post Incorporated, 1934.

Herbert, Henry William. *Frank Forester's Horses and Horsemanship of the United States and British Provinces of North America.* New York: Stringer & Townsend, 1857.

Herbert, Robert L. *Impressionism: Art, Leisure, and Parisian Society.* New Haven, CT: Yale University Press, 1988.

Hervey, John. *Racing & Breeding in America and the Colonies.* London: London & Counties Press Association, 1931.

———. *Racing in America, 1665–1865.* New York: The Jockey Club, 1944.

Hicks, Jennie E. *Sparkles from Saratoga.* New York: American News Company, 1873.

Hodgson, Adam. *Letters from North America, Written during a Tour in the United States and Canada.* London: Hurst, Robinson, 1824.

———. *Remarks during a Journey through North America in the Years 1819, 1820, and 1821.* New York: Samuel Whiting, 1823.

Hogan, William Ransom, and Edwin Adams Davis, eds. *William Johnson's Natchez: The Ante-Bellum Diary of a Free Negro.* Baton Rouge: Louisiana State University Press, 1979.

Holliman, Jennie. *American Sports [1785–1835].* Durham, NC: Seeman, 1931.

Hollingsworth, Kent. *The Kentucky Thoroughbred.* Lexington: University Press of Kentucky, 2009.

Holmes, Oliver Wendell. *The Autocrat of the Breakfast-Table.* Boston: Houghton, Mifflin, 1892.

Homberger, Eric C. *Mrs. Astor's New York: Money and Social Power in a Gilded Age.* New Haven, CT: Yale University Press, 2002.

Horenstein, Henry, and Brendan Boyd. *Racing Days.* New York: Viking, 1987.

Horne, Field. *The Saratoga Reader: Writing about an American Village, 1749–1900.* Saratoga Springs, NY: Kiskatom, 2004.

Hotaling, Edward. *The Great Black Jockeys: The Lives and Times of the Men Who Dominated America's First National Sport.* New York: Three Rivers, 1999.

———. *They're Off!: Horse Racing at Saratoga.* Syracuse, NY: Syracuse University Press, 1995.

Houghton, Edwin B. *The Campaigns of the Seventeenth Maine.* Portland, ME: Short & Loring, 1866.

Houstoun, Mrs. [Matilda C. F.]. *Hesperos; or, Travels in the West.* London: John W. Parker, 1850.

Howells, Mildred, ed. *Life in Letters of William Dean Howells.* New York: Doubleday, Doran, 1928.

Howells, William Dean. *A Hazard of New Fortunes.* New York: Harper, 1911.

Huber, Leonard V., et al. *The Cemeteries.* Vol. 3 of *New Orleans Architecture.* Gretna, LA: Pelican, 2004.

Hume, Sophia. *An Exhortation to the Inhabitants of the Province of South-Carolina, to bring their deeds to the light of Christ, in their own consciences.* London: Luke Hinde, 1752.

Hundley, Esq., D. R. *Social Relations in Our Southern States.* New York: Henry B. Price, 1860.

Hunter, Avalyn. *American Classic Pedigrees (1914–2002).* Lexington, KY: Eclipse, 2003.

Ingraham, Joseph Holt. *The South-West by a Yankee.* New York: Harper & Brothers, 1835.

Irving, John Beaufain. *The South Carolina Jockey Club.* Charleston, SC: Russell & Jones, 1857.

Isaac, Rhys H. *The Transformation of Virginia, 1740–1790.* Chapel Hill: University of North Carolina Press, 1982.

Jackson, Joy J. *New Orleans in the Gilded Age: Politics and Urban Progress, 1880–1896.* Baton Rouge: Louisiana State University Press, 1969.

Jacobs, Thornwell, ed. *Diary of William Plumer Jacobs.* Oglethorpe University, GA: Oglethorpe University Press, 1937.

James, D. Clayton. *Antebellum Natchez.* Baton Rouge: Louisiana State University Press, 1968.

James, Henry. *Portraits of Places.* London: Macmillan, 1883.

Janney, Caroline E. *Burying the Dead but Not the Past: Ladies' Memorial Associations and the Lost Cause.* Chapel Hill: University of North Carolina Press, 2008.

Jett, Dora Chinn. *In Tidewater Virginia.* Richmond, VA: Whittet & Shepperson, 1924.

Jewell, Edwin L. *Crescent City Illustrated: The Commercial, Social, Political and General History of New Orleans.* New Orleans: privately published, 1873.

Jockey Club, The. *22nd Annual Roundtable Conference on Matters Relating to Racing.* New York: The Jockey Club, 1974.

Johnson, Odai. *London in a Box: Englishness and Theatre in Revolutionary America.* Iowa City: University of Iowa Press, 2017.

Johnson, Rashauna. *Slavery's Metropolis: Unfree Labor in New Orleans during the Age of Revolutions.* New York: Cambridge University Press, 2016.

Johnson, Walter. *River of Dark Dreams: Slavery and Empire in the Cotton Kingdom.* Cambridge, MA: Harvard University Press, 2013.

Jones, Arthur F., and Bruce Weber. *The Kentucky Painter: From the Frontier Era to the Great War.* Lexington: University of Kentucky Art Museum, 1981.

Jones, Hugh. *The Present State of Virginia.* New York: Joseph Sabin, 1865.

Jordan, Winthrop D. *Tumult and Silence at Second Creek: An Inquiry into a Civil War Slave Conspiracy.* Baton Rouge: Louisiana State University Press, 1999.

Kamoie, Laura Croghan. *Irons in the Fire: The Business History of the Tayloe Family and Virginia's Gentry, 1700–1860.* Charlottesville: University Press of Virginia, 2007.

Kane, Harnett T. *Natchez on the Mississippi.* New York: William Morrow, 1947.

———. *Plantation Parade: The Grand Manner in Louisiana.* New York: William Morrow, 1945.

———. *Queen New Orleans.* New York: William Morrow, 1949.

Kaye, Anthony. *Joining Places: Slave Neighborhoods in the Old South.* Chapel Hill: University of North Carolina Press, 2007.

Kemble, Frances Anne. *Journal of a Residence on a Georgia Plantation in 1838–1839.* Edited by John Anthony Scott. Athens: University of Georgia Press, 1984.

Kendall, George G. *The Story of the Kentucky Derby.* New Albany, IN: Daniel H. Thompson, 1926.

Kennedy, Cynthia M. *Braided Lives, Entwined Relations: The Women of Charleston's Urban Slave Society.* Bloomington: Indiana University Press, 2005.

Kennedy, Mary Selden. *Seldens of Virginia and Allied Families.* New York: Frank Allaben Genealogical Company, 1911.

Kentucky Jockey Club, The. *The Kentucky Jockey Club: Lexington, Churchill Downs, Latonia.* Lexington: Kentucky Jockey Club, 1920.

Kierner, Cynthia A. *Beyond the Household: Women's Place in the Early South, 1700–1835*. Ithaca, NY: Cornell University Press, 1998.

Kimball, Gregg. *American City, Southern Place: A Cultural History of Antebellum Richmond*. Athens: University of Georgia Press, 2000.

King, Grace Elizabeth. *Creole Families of New Orleans*. New York: Macmillan, 1921.

King, Grace [Elizabeth]. *New Orleans: The Place and the People*. New York: Macmillan, 1896.

Kipling, Rudyard. *Selected Poetry*. London: Penguin, 1992.

Knight, Peter. *Reading the Market: Genres of Financial Capitalism in Gilded Age America*. Baltimore, MD: Johns Hopkins University Press, 2016.

Krawczynski, Keith. *William Henry Drayton: South Carolina Revolutionary Patriot*. Baton Rouge: Louisiana State University Press, 2001.

Krout, John Allen. *Annals of American Sport*. New Haven, CT: Yale University Press, 1929.

Kruse, Holly. *Off-Track and Online: The Networked Spaces of Horse Racing*. Cambridge, MA: MIT Press, 2016.

Lambert, John. *Lambert's Travels through Lower Canada and the United States*. London: Richard Phillips, 1810.

Lambton, Anne, and John Offen. *Thoroughbred Style: Racing Dynasties—The Horses, The Owners, The Studs*. London: Stanley Paul, 1987.

Landry, Donna J. *Noble Brutes: How Eastern Horses Transformed English Culture*. Baltimore, MD: Johns Hopkins University Press, 2009.

Landry, Stuart D. *History of the Boston Club*. New Orleans: Pelican, 1938.

Lang, Arne K. *Sports Betting and Bookmaking: An American History*. Lanham, MD: Rowman & Littlefield, 2016.

Latrobe, Benjamin Henry. *The Journal of Latrobe: The Notes and Sketches of an Architect, Naturalist and Traveler in the United States from 1796 to 1820*. New York: D. Appleton, 1905.

Lawrence, John. *The History and Delineation of the Horse, in All His Varieties*. 1809. New York: Olms, 1979.

Lears, T. J. Jackson. *Something for Nothing: Luck in America*. New York: Viking, 2003.

LeClercq, Anne Sinkler Whaley, ed. *Between North and South: The Letters of Emily Wharton Sinkler, 1842–1865*. Columbia: University of South Carolina Press, 2001.

———, ed. *Elizabeth Sinkler Coxe's Tales from the Grand Tour, 1890–1910*. Columbia: University of South Carolina Press, 2006.

Lee, Peter. *Spectacular Bid: The Last Superhorse of the Twentieth Century*. Lexington: University Press of Kentucky, 2019.

Lepler, Jessica M. *The Many Panics of 1837: People, Politics, and the Creation of a Transatlantic Financial Crisis*. New York: Cambridge University Press, 2013.

Levasseur, A[uguste]. *Lafayette in America in 1824 and 1825; or, Journal of a Voyage to the United States*. Translated by John D. Godman. Philadelphia: Carey & Lea, 1829.

Levi-Strauss, Claude. *Le totemisme aujourd'hui*. Paris: Presses Universitaires de France, 1962.

Levine, Lawrence H. *Highbrow/Lowbrow: The Emergence of Cultural Hierarchy in America*. Cambridge, MA: Harvard University Press, 1990.

Lewis, Charlene M. Boyer. *Ladies and Gentlemen on Display: Planter Society at the Virginia Springs, 1790–1860*. Charlottesville: University Press of Virginia, 2001.

Lewis, Robert W. *The Stadium Century: Sport, Spectatorship and Mass Society in Modern France*. Manchester, UK: Manchester University Press, 2017.

Lipscomb, Terry W. *South Carolina in 1791: George Washington's Southern Tour*. Columbia: South Carolina Department of Archives and History, 1993.

Livesay, Daniel. *Children of Uncertain Fortune: Mixed-Race Jamaicans in Britain and the Atlantic Family, 1733–1833*. Chapel Hill: University of North Carolina Press, 2018.

Livingston, Bernard. *Their Turf: America's Horsey Set and its Princely Dynasties*. New York: Arbor House, 1973.

Long, Alecia P. *The Great Southern Babylon: Sex, Race, and Respectability in New Orleans, 1865–1920*. Baton Rouge: Louisiana State University Press, 2004.

Longacre, Edward G. *Gentleman and Soldier: A Biography of Wade Hampton III*. Nashville, TN: Rutledge Hill, 2003.

Lossing, Benson John. *History of New York City*. New York: Perine Engraving and Publishing, 1884.

Luskey, Brian. *On the Make: Clerks and the Quest for Capital in Nineteenth-Century America*. New York: New York University Press, 2010.

Macey, Alan. *The Romance of the Derby Stakes*. London: Hutchinson, 1930.

Mackay-Smith, Alexander. *The Race-Horses of America, 1832–1872: Portraits and Other Paintings by Edward Troye*. Saratoga Springs, NY: National Museum of Racing, 1981.

———. *The Thoroughbred in the Lower Shenandoah Valley, 1785–1842*. Winchester, VA: Pifer Printing, 1948.

Mackie, J. Milton. *From Cape Cod to Dixie and the Tropics*. New York: G. P. Putnam, 1864.

Mackintosh, Will B. *Selling the Sights: The Invention of the Tourist in American Culture*. New York: New York University Press, 2019.

Macon, T. J. *Life Gleanings*. Richmond: W. H. Adams, 1913.

Malavesec, Alice Elizabeth. *The F Street Mess: How Southern Senators Rewrote the Kansas-Nebraska Act*. Chapel Hill: University of North Carolina Press, 2017.

Manarin, Louis H., and Clifford Dowdey. *The History of Henrico County*. Charlottesville: University Press of Virginia, 1984.

Manchester, Herbert. *Four Centuries of Sport in America*. 1931. New York: Benjamin Blom, 1968.

Mandell, Daniel R. *The Lost Tradition of Economic Equality in America*. Baltimore, MD: Johns Hopkins University Press, 2020.

Marler, Scott P. *The Merchants' Capital: New Orleans and the Political Economy of the Nineteenth-Century South.* New York: Cambridge University Press, 2013.

Marryat, Frederick. *A Diary in America, With Remarks on its Institutions.* London: Longman, Orme, Brown, Green, & Longmans, 1839.

Marshall, Anne E. *Creating a Confederate Kentucky: The Lost Cause and Civil War Memory in a Border State.* Chapel Hill: University of North Carolina Press, 2010.

Mathew, William M., ed. *Agriculture, Geology, and Society in Antebellum South Carolina: The Private Diary of Edmund Ruffin, 1843.* Athens: University of Georgia Press, 1992.

Mattson, Kevin. *Creating a Democratic Public: The Struggle for Urban Participatory Democracy during the Progressive Era.* University Park: Pennsylvania State University Press, 1998.

Maxwell, William Hamilton. *The Field Book: or, Sports and Pastimes of the United Kingdom.* London: Effingham Wilson, 1833.

May, Robert E. *John A. Quitman: Old South Crusader.* Baton Rouge: Louisiana State University Press, 1985.

Mazur, Zbigniew. *The Power of Play: Leisure, Recreation and Cultural Hegemony in Colonial Virginia.* Lublin, Poland: Wydawnictwo Uniwersytetu Marii Curie Sklodowskiej, 2010.

McAllister, Ward. *Society As I Have Found It.* New York: Cassell, 1890.

McBee, May Wilson, comp. *The Natchez Court Records, 1767–1805: Abstracts of Early Records.* 1953. Baltimore, MD: Genealogical Publishing Group, 1994.

McCabe, James, Jr. *Lights and Shadows of New York Life; or, The Sights and Sensations of the Great City.* 1872. New York: Farrar, Straus and Giroux, 1970.

McDonnell, Lawrence. *Performing Disunion: The Coming of the Civil War in Charleston, South Carolina.* Cambridge, UK: Cambridge University Press, 2018.

McGrath, Christopher. *Mr. Darley's Arabian: High Life, Low Life, Sporting Life: A History of Racing in 25 Horses.* New York: Pegasus, 2017.

McInnis, Maurie D. *The Politics of Taste in Antebellum Charleston.* Chapel Hill: University of North Carolina Press, 2005.

McIntyre, Rebecca Cawood. *Souvenirs of the Old South: Northern Tourism and Southern Mythology.* Gainesville: University Press of Florida, 2011.

McKinney, Louise. *New Orleans: A Cultural History.* New York: Oxford University Press, 2006.

McLemore, Richard Aubrey. *A History of Mississippi.* Jackson: University Press of Mississippi, 1973.

McShane, Clay, and Joel A. Tarr. *The Horse in the City: Living Machines in the Nineteenth Century.* Baltimore, MD: Johns Hopkins University Press, 2007.

Merritt, Keri Leigh. *Masterless Men: Poor Whites and Slavery in the Antebellum South.* New York: Cambridge University Press, 2017.

Mesick, Jane Louise. *The English Traveller in America, 1785–1835.* New York: Columbia University Press, 1922.

Miles, Tiya. *All That She Carried: The Journey of Ashley's Sack, a Black Family Keepsake*. New York: Random House, 2021.

Mills, Quincy T. *Cutting along the Color Line: Black Barbers and Barber Shops in America*. Philadelphia: University of Pennsylvania Press, 2013.

Montgomery, Maureen E. *"Gilded Prostitution": Status, Money and Transatlantic Marriages, 1870–1914*. New York: Routledge, 1989.

Mooney. Katherine C. *Isaac Murphy: The Rise and Fall of a Black Jockey*. New Haven, CT: Yale University Press, 2023.

———. *Race Horse Men: How Slavery and Freedom Were Made at the Racetrack*. Cambridge, MA: Harvard University Press, 2014.

Moore, John Hebron. *The Emergence of the Cotton Kingdom in the Old Southwest: Mississippi, 1770–1860*. Baton Rouge: Louisiana State University Press, 1988.

Mordecai, Samuel. *Richmond in By-Gone Days: Reminiscences of an Old Citizen*. Richmond, VA: George M. West, 1856.

———. *Virginia, Especially Richmond, in By-Gone Days; with a Glance at the Present: Being Reminiscences of an Old Citizen*, 2nd ed. Richmond, VA: West and Johnston, 1860.

Morgan, Philip D. *Slave Counterpoint: Black Culture in the Eighteenth-Century Chesapeake and Lowcountry*. Chapel Hill: University of North Carolina Press, 1998.

Morgan, Winifred. *An American Icon: Brother Jonathan and American Identity*. Newark: University of Delaware Press, 1988.

Morris, Lloyd. *Incredible New York: High Life and Low Life from 1850 to 1950*. Syracuse, NY: Syracuse University Press, 1951.

Morrison, A. J., ed. *Travels in Virginia in Revolutionary Times*. Lynchburg, VA: J. P. Bell, 1922.

Moser, Harold D., and J. Clint Clift, eds. *The Papers of Andrew Jackson*, Vol. 6. Knoxville: University of Tennessee Press, 2002.

Murray, Hon. Amelia M. *Letters from the United States, Cuba and Canada*. New York: G. P. Putnam, 1856.

Murray, Sir Charles Augustus. *Travels in North America during the Years 1834, 1835, & 1836*. London: Richard Bentley, 1839.

Myers, Amrita Chakrabarti. *Forging Freedom: Black Women and the Pursuit of Liberty in Antebellum Charleston*. Chapel Hill: University of North Carolina Press, 2011.

Nadelhaft, Jerome J. *The Disorders of War: The Revolution in South Carolina*. Orono: University of Maine Press, 1981.

Nauright, John, and Charles Parrish, eds. *Sports around the World: History, Culture, and Practice*. Santa Barbara, CA: ABC-CLIO, 2012.

Nelson, Lynn A. *Pharsalia: An Environmental Biography of a Southern Plantation, 1780–1880*. Athens: University of Georgia Press, 2010.

Nevins, Allan, and Milton Halsey Thomas, eds. *The Diary of George Templeton Strong; The Turbulent Fifties, 1850–1859*. New York: Macmillan, 1952.

Nichols, Thomas L. *Forty Years of American Life*. London: John Maxwell, 1864.

Nicholson, James C. *The Kentucky Derby: How the Run for the Roses Became America's Premier Sporting Event*. Lexington: University Press of Kentucky, 2012.

———. *The Notorious John Morrissey: How a Bare-Knuckle Brawler Became a Congressman and Founded Saratoga Race Course*. Lexington: University Press of Kentucky, 2016.

Norman, Benjamin Moore. *Norman's New Orleans and Environs*. New Orleans: B. M. Norman, 1845.

O'Connor, John. *Wanderings of a Vagabond: An Autobiography*. New York: privately published, 1873.

O'Connor, John L. *The Kentucky Derby, 1875–1921*. White Plains, NY: privately published, 1921.

Olivarius, Kathryn. *Necropolis: Disease, Power, and Capitalism in the Cotton Kingdom*. Cambridge, MA: Harvard University Press, 2022.

Olmsted, Frederick Law. *A Journey in the Back Country in the Winter of 1853–4*. New York: Mason Brothers, 1860

———. *A Journey in the Seaboard Slave States; with Remarks on Their Economy*. London: Sampson, Low, Son, 1856.

Olsen, Christopher J. *Political Culture and Secession in Mississippi*. New York: Oxford University Press, 2000.

Ordinances of the City Council of Charleston. Charleston, SC: A. Timothy, 1789.

Osborne, Walter D. *The Thoroughbred World*. New York: World, 1971.

Osterweis, Rollin G. *Romanticism and Nationalism in the Old South*. New Haven, CT: Yale University Press, 1949.

Ownby, Ted. *Subduing Satan: Religion, Recreation, and Manhood in the Rural South, 1865–1920*. Chapel Hill: University of North Carolina Press, 1990.

Page, Walter Hines, ed. *The World's Work*. New York: Doubleday Page, 1903.

Parent, Anthony S., Jr. *Foul Means: The Formation of a Slave Society in Virginia, 1660–1740*. Chapel Hill: University of North Carolina Press, 2003.

Parrish, T. Michael. *Richard Taylor: Soldier Prince of Dixie*. Chapel Hill: University of North Carolina Press, 1992.

Parton, James. *Life of Andrew Jackson*. New York: Mason Brothers, 1859.

Pease, William H., and Jane H. Pease. *The Web of Progress: Private Values and Public Styles in Boston and Charleston, 1828–1843*. New York: Oxford University Press, 1985.

Peeples, Scott. *The Man of the Crowd: Edgar Allan Poe and the City*. Princeton, NJ: Princeton University Press, 2020.

Perkins, Eli. *Saratoga in 1901*. New York: Sheldon, 1872.

Pharo, Elizabeth B., ed. *Reminiscences of William Hasell Wilson (1811–1902)*. Philadelphia: Patterson and White, 1937.

Phillips, Jason. *Diehard Rebels: The Confederate Cult of Invincibility*. Athens: University of Georgia Press, 2007.

Phillips, Ulrich Bonnell. *Life and Labor in the Old South*. Boston: Little, Brown, 1929.

Power, Tyrone. *Impressions of America: During the Years 1833, 1834, and 1835*. Philadelphia: Carey, Lea & Blanchard, 1836.

Powers, Bernard E. Jr. *Black Charlestonians: A Social History, 1822–1885*. Fayetteville: University of Arkansas Press, 1994.

Ramsay, David. *The History of South-Carolina, from Its First Settlement in 1670, to the Year 1808*. Charleston, SC: David Longworth, 1809.

Ranck, George W. *History of Lexington, Kentucky: Its Early Annals and Recent Progress*. Cincinnati: Robert Clarke, 1872.

Ranney, Garner, ed. *A Man of Pleasure, and a Man of Business: The European Travel Diaries of Duncan Farrar Kenner, 1833–4*. Lafayette, LA: Center for Louisiana Studies, 1991.

Rasmussen, William M. S., and Robert S. Tilton. *Old Virginia: The Pursuit of a Pastoral Ideal*. Charlottesville, VA: Howell, 2003.

Ravenel, Mrs. St. Julien. *Charleston: The Place and the People*. New York: Macmillan, 1906.

Reber, Thomas. *Proud Old Natchez: History and Romance*. Natchez: privately published, 1909.

Reid, Whitelaw. *After the War: A Tour of the Southern States, 1865–1866*. Edited by C. Vann Woodward. 1866. New York: Harper & Row, 1965.

Reinders, Robert C. *End of an Era: New Orleans, 1850–1860*. New Orleans: Pelican, 1964.

Renau, Lynn S. *Jockeys, Belles, and Bluegrass Kings*. Louisville, KY: Herr House, 1995.

Riess, Steven A. *City Games: The Evolution of American Urban Society and the Rise of Sports*. Urbana: University of Illinois Press, 1989.

———. *The Sport of Kings and the Kings of Crime: Horse Racing, Politics, and Organized Crime in New York, 1865–1913*. Syracuse, NY: Syracuse University Press, 2011.

———, ed. *Sports in America from Colonial Times to the Twenty-First Century: An Encyclopedia*. Abingdon, UK: Taylor & Francis, 2011.

Rightor, Henry. *Standard History of New Orleans*. New Orleans: Lewis, 1900.

Ripley, Eliza. *Social Life in Old New Orleans: Being Recollections of My Girlhood*. New York: D. Appleton, 1912.

Roach, Joseph. *Cities of the Dead: Circum-Atlantic Performance*. New York: Columbia University Press, 1996.

Robertson, William H. *The History of Thoroughbred Racing in America*. Englewood Cliffs, NJ: Prentice-Hall, 1964.

Robinson, Lura. *It's an Old New Orleans Custom.* New York: Vanguard, 1948.

Roche, Daniel. *France in the Enlightenment.* Translated by Arthur Goldhammer. Cambridge, MA: Harvard University Press, 1998.

Rodrigue, John C. *Freedom's Crescent: The Civil War and the Destruction of Slavery in the Lower Mississippi Valley.* Cambridge, UK: Cambridge University Press, 2023.

Rogers, George C., Jr. *The History of Georgetown, South Carolina.* 1970. Spartanburg, SC: Reprint Company, 1990.

Rosen, Robert N. *A Short History of Charleston.* San Francisco: Lexikos, 1982.

Rosenzweig, Roy, and Elizabeth Blackmar. *The Park and the People.* Ithaca, NY: Cornell University Press, 1992.

Rothman, Joshua. *The Ledger and the Chain: How Domestic Slave Traders Shaped America.* New York: Basic, 2021.

———. *Notorious in the Neighborhood; Sex and Families across the Color Line in Virginia, 1787–1861.* Chapel Hill: University of North Carolina Press, 2003.

Rozbicki, Michal J. *The Complete Colonial Gentleman: Cultural Legitimacy in Plantation America.* Charlottesville: University Press of Virginia, 1998.

Rules and Regulations for the Government of Racing, Trotting, and Betting, as Adopted by the Principal Turf Associations throughout the United States and Canada. New York: M. B. Brown, 1866.

Rules and Regulations of the Fairfield Jockey Club. Richmond, VA: C. H. Wynne's Steam-Power Presses, 1853.

Russell, William Howard. *My Diary North and South.* London: Bradbury and Evans, 1863.

Rutledge, Anna Wells. *Artists in the Life of Charleston: Through Colony and State from Restoration to Reconstruction.* Philadelphia: American Philosophical Society, 1949.

Sala, George Augustus. *My Diary in America in the Midst of War.* London: Tinsley Brothers, 1865.

Sansing, David, et al. *Natchez: An Illustrated History.* Natchez, MS: Plantation, 1992.

Saratoga Illustrated: The Visitor's Guide to Saratoga Springs. New York: Taintor Brothers, 1876.

Saunders, James Robert, and Monica Renae Saunders. *Black Winning Jockeys in the Kentucky Derby.* Jefferson, NC: McFarland, 2003.

Schneer, Jonathan. *London 1900: The Imperial Metropolis.* New Haven, CT: Yale University Press, 2001.

Schoonover, Thomas J. *The Life and Times of Gen. John A. Sutter.* 1895. Sacramento, CA: Bullock-Carpenter Printing, 1907.

Schopf, Johann David. *Travels in the Confederation, 1783–1784.* Edited and translated by Alfred J. Morrison. Philadelphia: William J. Campbell, 1911.

Searight, Sarah. *New Orleans.* New York: Stein and Day, 1973.

Severens, Kenneth. *Charleston: Antebellum Architecture and Civic Destiny.* Knoxville: University of Tennessee Press, 1988.

Shields, David S. *Southern Provisions: The Creation and Revival of a Cuisine.* Chicago: University of Chicago Press, 2015.

Shippee, Lester B., ed. *Bishop Whipple's Southern Diary, 1843–1844.* New York: Da Capo, 1968.

Silber, Nina. *The Romance of Reunion: Northerners and the South, 1865–1900.* Chapel Hill: University of North Carolina Press, 1993.

Simon, F. Kevin, ed., *The WPA Guide to Kentucky.* 1939. Lexington: University Press of Kentucky, 1996.

Skeel, Emily Ellsworth Fowler Ford. *Notes on the Life of Noah Webster.* New York: privately published, 1912.

Skinner, Edward Hilary. *After the Storm; Or, Jonathan and His Neighbours in 1865–6.* London: Richard Bentley, 1866.

Smart, Christopher, trans. *The Works of Horace.* New York: Harper & Brothers, 1863.

Smith, Bradley. *The Horse and the Blue Grass Country.* Garden City, NY: Doubleday, 1955.

Smith, James H. *History of Madison and Chenango Counties.* Syracuse: D. Mason, 1880.

Smith, Matthew Hale. *Twenty Years among the Bulls and Bears of Wall Street.* Hartford, CT: J. B. Burr, 1870.

Smith, Thomas Ruys, ed. *Blacklegs, Card Sharps, and Confidence Men: Nineteenth-Century Mississippi River Gambling Stories.* Baton Rouge: Louisiana State University Press, 2010.

———. *Southern Queen: New Orleans in the Nineteenth Century.* London: Continuum, 2011.

Smucker, Philip G. *Riding with George: Sportsmanship and Chivalry in the Making of America's First President.* Chicago: Chicago Review Press, 2017.

Smyth, J. F. D. *A Tour in the United States of America.* London: G. Robinson, 1784.

Somers, Dale A. *The Rise of Sports in New Orleans, 1850–1900.* Baton Rouge: Louisiana State University Press, 1972.

Sowers, Richard. *The Kentucky Derby, Preakness and Belmont Stakes: A Comprehensive History.* Jefferson, NC: McFarland, 2014.

Sparks, Randy J. *Religion in Mississippi.* Jackson: University Press of Mississippi, 2001.

Sparks, W. H. *The Memories of Fifty Years.* Philadelphia: Claxton, Remsen, & Haffelfinger, 1870.

Speed, John Gilmer. *The Horse in America.* New York: McClure, Phillips, 1905.

Spencer, David L. *The Yellow Journalism: The Press and America's Emergence as a World Power.* Evanston, IL: Northwestern University Press, 2007.

Stanard, Mary Newton. *Richmond, Its People and Its Story.* Philadelphia: J. B. Lippincott, 1938.

Stanley, Louisa Cheves, ed. *Autobiographical Notes, Letters and Reflections, by Thomas Smyth, D.D.* Charleston, SC: Walker, Evans & Cogswell, 1914.

Sterngass, Jon. *First Resorts: Pursuing Pleasure at Saratoga Springs, Newport and Coney Island.* Baltimore, MD: Johns Hopkins University Press, 2001.

Stiles, T. J. *The First Tycoon: The Epic Life of Cornelius Vanderbilt.* New York: Vintage, 2009.

Stott, Richard. *Jolly Fellows: Male Milieus in Nineteenth-Century America.* Baltimore, MD: Johns Hopkins University Press, 2009.

Struna, Nancy L. *People of Prowess: Sport, Leisure, and Labor in Early Anglo-America.* Urbana: University of Illinois Press, 1996.

Stuart, James. *Three Years in North America.* 3rd ed. Edinburgh: R. Cadell, 1833.

Sullivan, Edward, Esq. *Rambles and Scrambles in North and South America.* London: Richard Bentley, 1852.

Sullivan, John Jeremiah. *Blood Horses: Notes of a Sportswriter's Son.* New York: Farrar, Straus and Giroux, 2004.

Swidler, David T., *All About Thorobred [sic] Horse Racing: Aristocrat of Sports.* Miami: Hialeah Guild, 1967.

Sydnor, Charles S. *A Gentleman of the Old Natchez Region: Benjamin L.C. Wailes.* Durham, NC: Duke University Press, 1938.

———. *Gentlemen Freeholders: Political Practices in Washington's Virginia.* Chapel Hill: University of North Carolina Press, 1952.

Szczesiul, Anthony. *The Southern Hospitality Myth: Politics, Race, and American Memory.* Athens: University of Georgia Press, 2017.

Tamarkin, Elisa. *Anglophilia: Deference, Devotion, and Antebellum America.* Chicago: University of Chicago Press, 2007.

Taylor, William R. *Cavalier and Yankee: The Old South and National Character.* New York: Oxford University Press, 1957.

They're Off: A Century of Kentucky Derby Coverage by "The Courier-Journal" and "The Louisville Times." Louisville: Pinaire Lithographing, 1975.

Thomas, J., and T. Baldwin, eds. *A Complete Pronouncing Gazetteer, or Geographical Dictionary of the World.* Philadelphia: J. B. Lippincott, 1859.

Thompson, Jack. *Charleston at War: The Photographic Record, 1860–1865.* Gettysburg, PA: Thomas, 2000.

Thompson, M. Agnes. *Metairie and Other Aunt Tilda of New Orleans Sketches.* New Orleans: privately published, 1892.

Thomson, William Norman. *Gambling in America: An Encyclopedia of History, Issues, and Society.* Santa Barbara, CA: ABC-CLIO, 2001.

Tillson, Albert H., Jr. *Accommodating Revolution: Virginia's Northern Neck in an Era of Transformations, 1760–1810.* Charlottesville: University Press of Virginia, 2010.

Timbs, John. *Curiosities of London.* London: David Bogue, 1855.

Tinling, Marion, ed. *The Correspondence of the Three William Byrds of Westover.* Charlottesville: University Press of Virginia, 1977.

Trevathan, Charles E. *The American Thoroughbred.* New York: Macmillan, 1905.

Trumpbour, Robert C. *The New Cathedrals: Politics and Media in the History of Stadium Construction*. Syracuse, NY: Syracuse University Press, 2007.

Truth Is Stranger Than Fiction, or, New Orleans As It Is. Utica, NY: DeWitt C. Grove, 1849.

Tunnard, W. H. *A Southern Record: The History of the Third Regiment Louisiana Infantry*. Baton Rouge: privately published, 1866.

Twain, Mark. *Life on the Mississippi*. Boston: James R. Osgood, 1883.

Twomey, Bill. *The Bronx in Bits and Pieces*. Bloomington, IN: Rooftop, 2007.

Tyler-McGraw, Marie. *At the Falls: Richmond, Virginia, and Its People*. Chapel Hill: University of North Carolina Press, 1994.

United States Department of the Interior. *Final Environmental Statement for the Natchez Trace Parkway*. Washington, DC: United States Department of the Interior, 1978.

Van Rensselaer, May King. *The Social Ladder*. New York: Henry Holt, 1924.

Vosburgh, W. S. *Racing in America, 1866–1921*. New York: privately published, 1922.

Wall, Maryjean. *How Kentucky Became Southern*. Lexington: University Press of Kentucky, 2010.

Wallace, John H. *The Horse of America, in his Derivation, History, and Development*. New York: privately published, 1897.

Wallace, Sarah Agnes, and Frances Elma Gillespie, eds. *The Journal of Benjamin Moran, 1857–1865*. Chicago: University of Chicago Press, 1948.

Wallenstein, Peter. *Cradle of America: A History of Virginia*. 2nd ed. Lawrence: University Press of Kansas, 2014.

Walsh, Norman Sinkler. *Plantations, Pineland Villages, Pinopolis and Its People*. Virginia Beach: Donning, 2006.

Watson, Ritchie Devon, Jr. *The Cavalier in Virginia Fiction*. Baton Rouge: Louisiana State University Press, 1985.

Wayne, Michael. *The Reshaping of Plantation Society: The Natchez District, 1860–80*. Urbana: University of Illinois Press, 1990.

Webb, Allie B. Windham, ed. *Mistress of Evergreen Plantation: Rachel O'Connor's Legacy of Letters, 1823–1845*. Albany: State University of New York Press, 1983.

Weddell, Alexander Wilbourne. *Portraiture in the Virginia Historical Society*. Richmond: Virginia Historical Society, 1945.

Weeks, Lyman Horace. *An Historical Account of Racing in the United States*. New York: Historical Company, 1898.

Weil, Francois. *Family Trees: A History of Genealogy in America*. Cambridge, MA: Harvard University Press, 2013.

Weld. Isaac, Jr. *Weld's Travels through the States of North America, and the Provinces of Upper and Lower Canada during the Years 1795, 1796, and 1797*. 4th ed. London: John Stockdale, 1807.

Wells, Jeremy. *Romances of the White Man's Burden: Race, Empire, and the Plantation in American Literature, 1880–1936*. Nashville, TN: Vanderbilt University Press, 2011.

Wendorf, Richard. *America's Membership Libraries*. New Castle, DE: Oak Knoll, 2007.

Wharton, Edith. *A Backward Glance*. New York: D. Appleton-Century, 1934.

White, James Chrystie. *History of the British Turf, from the Earliest Period to the Present Day*. London: Henry Colburn, 1840.

Wiener, Joel H. *The Americanization of the British Press, 1832–1914: Speed in the Age of Transatlantic Journalism*. Houndmills, UK: Palgrave Macmillan, 2011.

Wiener, Martin J. *English Culture and the Decline of the Industrial Spirit, 1850–1890*. Cambridge, UK: Cambridge University Press, 1981.

Wiggins, David K. *Glory Bound: Black Athletes in a White America*. Syracuse, NY: Syracuse University Press, 1997.

Williams, John Rogers, ed. *Philip Vickers Fithian: Journal and Letters, 1767–1774*. Princeton, NJ: University Library, 1900.

Wilson, Charles Reagan. *Baptized in Blood: The Religion of the Lost Cause, 1865–1920*. Athens: University of Georgia Press, 2011.

Wood, Harry M. *Richmond: An Illustrated History*. Northridge, CA: Windsor, 1985.

Wright, Louis B., and Marion Tinling, eds. *Quebec to Carolina in 1785–1786: Being the Travel Diary of Robert Hunter, Jr., a Young Merchant of London*. San Marino, CA: Huntington Library, 1943.

Yates, Norris W. *William T. Porter and the "Spirit of the Times": A Study of the Big Bear School of Humor*. Baton Rouge: Louisiana State University Press, 1957.

Young, Jacob. *Autobiography of a Pioneer: On the Nativity, Experience, Travels, and Ministerial Labors of Rev. Jacob Young; with incidents, observations, and recollections*. Cincinnati, OH: Cranston & Curtis, 1857.

Zagarri, Rosemarie. *The Politics of Size: Representation in the United States, 1776–1850*. Ithaca, NY: Cornell University Press, 1987.

Zahniser, Marvin R. *Charles Cotesworth Pinckney: Founding Father*. Chapel Hill: University of North Carolina Press, 1967.

Journal Articles and Book Chapters

Ames, Joseph S. "Cantey Family." *South Carolina Historical and Genealogical Magazine* 11 (1910): 203–58.

Aslakson, Kenneth M. "The 'Quadroon-*Placage*' Myth of Antebellum New Orleans: Anglo-American (Mis)Interpretations of a French-Caribbean Phenomenon." *Journal of Social History* 45 (2012): 709–34.

Bachand, Marise. "Gendered Mobility and the Geography of Respectability in Charleston and New Orleans, 1790–1861." *Journal of Southern History* 81 (2015): 41–78.

Baptist, Edward E. "'Cuffy,' 'Fancy Maids,' and 'One-Eyed Men': Rape, Commodification, and the Domestic Slave Trade in the United States." *American Historical Review* 106 (2001): 1619–50.

Behrend, Justin. "Rebellious Talk and Conspiratorial Plots: The Making of a Slave Insurrection in Civil War Natchez." *Journal of Southern History* 77 (2011): 17–52.

Beliles, Mark A. "The Christian Communities, Religious Revivals, and Political Culture of the Central Virginia Piedmont, 1737–1813." In *Religion and Political Culture in Jefferson's Virginia,* edited by Garrett Ward Sheldon and Daniel L. Dreisbach. Lanham, MD: Rowman & Littlefield, 2000.

Bell, Alison, et al. "'All My Little Might of Money': Signaling, Structure, and Mobility among the Middling in Nineteenth-Century Virginia and Kentucky." *Historical Archaeology* 53 (2019): 372–92.

Bellows, Barbara L. "Of Time and the City: Charleston in 1860." *South Carolina Historical Magazine* 112 (2011): 157–72.

Bennett, Bruce L. "Sports in the South up to 1865." *Quest* 27 (1977): 4–18.

Bennett, Deb. "Secrets of Secretariat's Speed." *Equus* 434 (November 2013): 35–57.

Bergmann, Iris. "He Loves to Race—or Does He? Ethics and Welfare in Racing." In *Equine Cultures in Transition: Ethical Questions,* edited by Jonna Bornemark et al. New York: Routledge, 2019.

Betts, John Rickards. "Sporting Journalism in Nineteenth-Century America." *American Quarterly* 5 (1953): 39–56.

———. "The Technological Revolution and the Rise of Sport, 1850–1900." *Mississippi Valley Historical Review* 40 (1953): 231–56.

Bigelow, Ann Clymer. "An Affair of Class: Western Virginia Eccentric versus New York Tobacco Magnate." *West Virginia History* 10 (2016): 93–109.

Boulware, Hunt. "'Unworthy of Modern Refinement': The Evolution of Sport and Recreation in the Early South Carolina and Georgia Lowcountry." *Journal of Sport History* 35 (2008): 429–48.

Boyle, Raymond. "'We Are Celtic Supporters. . . .': Questions of Football and Identity in Modern Scotland." In *Game without Frontiers: Football, Identity and Modernity,* edited by Richard Giulianotti and John Williams. London: Routledge, 2017.

Brailsford, Dennis. "Sporting Days in Eighteenth-Century England." *Journal of Sport History* 9 (1982): 41–54.

Breen, T. H. "Horses and Gentlemen: The Cultural Significance of Gambling among the Gentry of Virginia." *William and Mary Quarterly,* ser. 3, vol. 34, no. 2 (April 1997): 239–57.

Bronner, Edwin B., ed. "Notes and Documents: A Philadelphia Quaker Visits Natchez." *Journal of Southern History* 27 (1961): 513–20.

Broussard, Joyce L. "Stepping Lively in Place: The Free Black Women of Antebellum Natchez." In *Mississippi Women: Their Histories, Their Lives,* edited by Elizabeth Ann Payne et al. Athens: University of Georgia Press, 2010.

Brown, David. "A Vagabond's Tale: Poor Whites, Herrenvolk Democracy, and the Value of Whiteness in the Late Antebellum South." *Journal of Southern History* 79 (2013): 799–840.

Buckner, Timothy R. "A Crucible of Masculinity: William Johnson's Barbershop and the Making of Free Black Men in the Antebellum South." In *Fathers, Preachers, Rebels, Men: Black Masculinity in U.S. History and Literature, 1820–1945,* edited by Buckner and Peter Caster. Columbus: Ohio State University Press, 2011.

———. "Vicksburg's War on Vice: Drinking, Gambling, and Race in the Antebellum South." *Journal of Mississippi History* 67 (2005): 311–30.

Bunker, Gary L., and John J. Appel. "'Shoddy' Antisemitism and the Civil War." In *Jews and the Civil War: A Reader,* edited by Jonathan D. Sarna and Adam Mendelsohn. New York: New York University Press, 2010.

Burke, Peter. "Viewpoint: The Invention of Leisure in Early Modern Europe." *Past & Present* 146 (1995): 136–50.

Campanella, Richard. "An Ethnic Geography of New Orleans." *Journal of American History* 94 (2007): 704–15.

Campbell, Richard. "Family Practices and Domestic Problems in a Transatlantic World: Reconstructing the Curious Case of Maria Alston." *South Carolina Historical Magazine* 113 (2012): 315–37.

Carnes, Mark C. "Middle-Class Men and the Solace of Fraternal Ritual." In *Meanings for Manhood: Constructions of Masculinity in Victorian America,* edited by Carnes and Clyde Griffen. Chicago: University of Chicago Press, 1990.

Cheves, Langdon. "Izard of South Carolina," *South Carolina Historical and Genealogical Magazine* 2 (1901): 205–40.

"The Cocke Family of Virginia." *Virginia Historical Magazine* 4 (1896): 212–17.

Cockrell, Dale. "William Johnson: Barber, Musician, Parable." *American Music* 32 (2014): 1–23.

Cohen, Kenneth. "Well Calculated for the Farmer: Thoroughbreds in the Early National Chesapeake, 1790–1850." *Virginia Magazine of History and Biography* 115 (2007): 370–411.

Coit, Margaret L. "Moses Waddel: A Light in the Wilderness." *Georgia Review* 5 (1951): 34–47.

Coleman, J. Winston, Jr. "Old Kentucky Watering Places." *Filson Club Historical Quarterly* 16 (1942): 1–26.

Cross, Gary. "Saratoga Springs: From Genteel Spa to Disneyfied Family Resort." *Journal of Tourism History* 4 (2012): 75–84.

Cunningham, H. H. "Confederate General Hospitals: Establishment and Organization." *Journal of Southern History* 20 (1954): 376–94.

Dal Lago, Enrico. "The City as Social Display: Landed Elites and Urban Images in Charleston and Palermo." *Journal of Historical Sociology* 14 (2001): 374–96.

Davey, Jennifer. "'Wearing the Breeches'? Almack's, the Female Patroness, and Public Femininity, c. 1764–1848." *Women's History Review* 26 (2017): 822–39.

Day, John I. "Horse Racing and the Pari-Mutuel." *Annals of the American Academy of Political and Social Science* 269 (1950): 55–61.

Dinces, Sean. "The Attrition of the Common Fan: Class, Spectatorship, and Major League Stadiums in Postwar America." *Social Science History* 40 (2016): 339–65.

Dooley, R. B. "A Footnote to Edith Wharton." *American Literature* 26 (1954): 78–85.

Doscher, Sallie A. "Art Exhibitions in Nineteenth-Century Charleston." In *Art in the Lives of South Carolinians: Nineteenth-Century Chapters*, edited by David Moltke-Hansen. Charleston, SC: Carolina Art Association, 1979.

Dresser, Rebecca M. "Kate and John Minor: Confederate Unionists of Natchez." *Journal of Mississippi History* 64 (2002): 188–216.

Duplantier, Crozet J. "A Sportsman's Town." In *The Past as Prelude: New Orleans, 1718–1968*, edited by Hodding Carter. New Orleans: Pelican, 1968.

Ellwanger, Ella Hutchinson. "Famous Steamboats and their Captains on Western and Southern Waters," part 2. *Register of the Kentucky State Historical Society* 18 (1920): 18–32.

Evans, Richard Xavier. "Letters from Robert Mills." *South Carolina Historical and Genealogical Magazine* 39 (1938): 110–24.

Evelev, John. "The City Sketch: Writing Middle-Class Identity on the Streets of Antebellum New York." In *Class and the Making of American Literature: Created Unequal*, edited by Andrew Lawson. New York: Routledge, 2014.

Farrow, Lee A. "When Russian Royalty Met Southern Hospitality: Grand Duke Alexis in Kentucky, 1872." *Ohio Valley History* 22 (2022): 3–21.

Faust, Drew Gilpin. "Altars of Sacrifice: Confederate Women and the Narratives of War." *Journal of American History* 76 (1990): 1200–28.

Ferrari, Mary C. "Charity, Folly, and Politics: Charles Town's Social Clubs on the Eve of the Revolution." *South Carolina Historical Magazine* 112 (2001): 50–83.

Fitzhugh, George. "Southern Thought—Its New and Important Manifestations." *De Bow's Review* 23, no. 4 (October 1857): 347.

Formwalt, Lee W. "An English Immigrant Views American Society: Benjamin Henry Latrobe's Virginia Years, 1796–1798." *Virginia Magazine of History and Biography* 85 (1977): 387–410.

Frink, Sandra. "'Strangers are Flocking Here': Identity and Anonymity in New Orleans, 1810–1860." *American Nineteenth Century History* 11 (2010): 155–81.

Geertz, Clifford. "Deep Play: Notes on the Balinese Cockfight." *Daedalus* 101 (1972): 1–37.

Gill, Harold B., Jr. "A Sport Only for Gentlemen." *Colonial Williamsburg* 20 (1997): 49–53.

Gleason, William. "Grounds for Fun: The Place of Play in 19th-Century American Culture." *Nineteenth-Century Contexts* 35 (2013): 463–78.

Gleaves, John. "Enhancing the Odds: Horse Racing, Gambling and the First Anti-Doping Movement in Sport, 1889–1911." *Sport in History* 32 (2012): 26–52.

Goudsouzian, Aram. "House of Cards: Leisure, Freedom, Authority, Revolution, and the Diary of Landon Carter." *Journal of Sport History* 49 (2022): 1–19.

Graydon, Nell S. "Some Letters from John Christopher Schulz, 1829–1833." *South Carolina Historical Magazine* 56 (1955): 1–7.

Gruesz, Kristen Silva. "Delta *Desterrados:* Antebellum New Orleans and New World Print Culture." In *Look Away! The U.S. South in New World Studies*, edited by Jon Smith and Deborah Cohn. Durham, NC: Duke University Press, 2004.

Guttmann, Allen. "English Sports Spectators: The Restoration to the Nineteenth Century." *Journal of Sport History* 12 (1985): 103–25.

Harkins, Anthony. "Colonels, Hillbillies, and Fightin': Twentieth-Century Kentucky in the National Imagination." *Register of the Kentucky Historical Society* 113 (2015): 421–52.

Harrell, Laura D.S. "Horse Racing in the Old Natchez District, 1783–1830." *Journal of Mississippi History* 13 (1951): 123–37.

Harrison, Fairfax. "The Equine FFVs: A Study of the Evidence for the English Horses Imported into Virginia before the Revolution." *Virginia Magazine of History and Biography* 35 (1927): 329–70.

Harrower, John. "Diary of John Harrower, 1773–1776." *American Historical Review* 6 (1900): 65–107.

Hilliard, Kathleen M. "'In the Days of Her Power and Glory': Visions of Venice in Antebellum Charleston." In *The U.S. South and Europe: Transatlantic Relations in the Nineteenth and Twentieth Centuries*, edited by Cornelis A. van Minnen and Manfred Berg. Lexington: University Press of Kentucky, 2013.

Hood, Clifton. "Journeying to 'Old New York': Elite New Yorkers and Their Invention of an Idealized City History in the Late Nineteenth and Early Twentieth Centuries." *Journal of Urban History* (2002): 699–716.

Horne, Field. "Saratoga Springs: Evolution of a Resort." In New York State Archives Partnership Trust, *The Best of "New York Archives": Selections from the Magazine, 2001–2011*. Albany: State University of New York Press, 2017.

Howe, Mark A. DeWolfe, ed., "Journal of Josiah Quincy, Junior, 1773." *Proceedings of the Massachusetts Historical Society* 50 (1916): 433–71.

Howland, Joan S. "Let's Not 'Spit the Bit' in Defense of 'The Law of the Horse': The Historical and Legal Development of American Thoroughbred Racing." *Marquette Sports Law Review* 14 (2004): 473–507.

Huggins, Mike. "The Proto-Globalisation of Horseracing, 1730–1900: Anglo-American Interconnections." In *Sport as History: Essays in Honour of Wray Vamplew*, edited by Tony Collins. Abingdon, UK: Routledge, 2011.

Ingle, Larry H. "Joseph Wharton Goes South." *South Carolina Historical Magazine* 96 (1995): 304–28.

Jeter, Katherine Brash. "A Racing Heritage." *Louisiana History* 30 (1989): 5–22.

Johnson, Paul. "Northern Horse: American Eclipse as a Representative New Yorker." *Journal of the Early Republic* 33 (2013): 701–26.

Johnson, Pegram, III. "The *American Turf Register and Sporting Magazine:* A 'Quaint and Curious Volume of Forgotten Lore.'" *Maryland Historical Magazine* 89 (1994): 5–21.

Keller, Mark A. "Reputable Writers, Phony Names: Identifying Pseudonyms in the *Spirit of the Times.*" *Papers of the Bibliographical Society of America* 75 (1981): 198–209.

Kierner, Cynthia A. "'The Dark and Dense Cloud Perpetually Lowering Over Us': Gender and the Decline of the Gentry in Postrevolutionary Virginia." *Journal of the Early Republic* 20 (2000): 185–218.

Kilbride, Daniel. "Class, Region, and Memory in a South Carolina-Philadelphia Marriage." *Journal of Family History* 28 (2003): 540–60.

———. "Cultivation, Conservatism, and the Early National Gentry: The Manigault Family and Their Circle." *Journal of the Early Republic* 19 (1999): 221–56.

———. "Travel, Ritual, and National Identity: Planters on the European Tour, 1820–1860." *Journal of Southern History* 69 (2003): 549–84.

Klingberg, Frank Wysor. "The Case of the Minors: A Unionist Family within the Confederacy." *Journal of Southern History* 13 (1947): 27–45.

Ledbetter, Bonnie S. "Sports and Games of the American Revolution." *Journal of Sport History* 6 (1979): 29–40.

Link, Stefan, and Noam Maggor. "The United States as a Developing Nation: Revisiting the Peculiarities of American History." *Past & Present* 246 (2020): 269–306.

Lockhart, Matthew. "'Under the Wings of Columbia': John Lewis Gervais as Architect of South Carolina's 1786 Capital Relocation Legislation." *South Carolina Historical Magazine* 104 (2003): 176–97.

Mangum, William Preston, II. "Disaster at Woodburn Farm: R. A. Alexander and the Confederate Guerrilla Raids of 1864–1865." *Filson Club History Quarterly* 70 (1996): 143–85.

McGuane, Tanya, et al. "'You Wanna Ride, Then You Waste': The Psychological Impact of Wasting in National Hunt Jockeys." *Human Kinetics Journal* 33 (2018): 129–36.

McShane, Clay, and Joel A. Tarr. "The Centrality of the Horse in the Nineteenth-Century American City." In *The Making of Urban America*, edited by Raymond A. Mohl. 2nd ed. Lanham, MD: SR, 1997.

———. "The Decline of the Urban Horse in American Cities." *Journal of Transport History* 24 (2003): 177–98.

Meyer, Jeff. "Henry Clay's Legacy to Horse Breeding and Racing." *Register of the Kentucky Historical Society* 100 (2002): 473–96.

Mills, W. H. "The Thoroughbred in South Carolina." *Proceedings of the South Carolina Historical Association* (1937): 15–19.

Mohl, Raymond A. "'The Grand Fabric of Republicanism': A Scotsman Describes South Carolina, 1810–1811." *South Carolina Historical Magazine* 71 (1970): 170–88.

Mooney, Katherine C. "'I Got the Horse Right Here': New Directions in Sporting History." *Register of the Kentucky Historical Society* 115 (2017): 645–60.

Morris, John E. "August Belmont Jr.: The Forgotten Financier of the Gilded Age." *Financial History* 136 (2021): 18–22.

Mrozek, Donald. "Sporting Life as Consumption, Fashion, and Display: The Pastimes of the Rich at the Turn of the Century." In *Major Problems in American Sport History: Documents and Essays*, edited by Steven A. Riess. Boston: Houghton Mifflin, 1997.

Myerson, Joel, and Michael C. Weisenburg. "'I Liked the Town No Better at Our Second Interview': A New Emerson Letter from Charleston in 1827." *New England Quarterly* 89 (2016): 493–504.

Nance, Susan. "Game Stallions and Other 'Horseface Minstrelsies' of the American Turf." *Theatre Journal* 65 (2013): 355–72.

Nash, Richard. "'Honest English Breed': The Thoroughbred as Cultural Metaphor." In *The Culture of the Horse: Status, Discipline, and Identity in the Early Modern World*, edited by Karen Raber and Treva J. Tucker. New York: Palgrave, 2004.

———. "Turf Wars: Violence, Politics, and the Newmarket Riots of 1751." In *Sporting Cultures, 1650–1850*, edited by Daniel O'Quinn and Alexis Tadie. Toronto: University of Toronto Press, 2018.

Nathan, Rhoda. "Ward McAllister: Beau Nash of *The Age of Innocence*." *College Literature* 14 (1987): 277–84.

"A New York Turf Editor Discovers a Richmond Race Track." *Richmond Literature and History Quarterly* 2 (1979): 39–40.

Noll, Mark A. "The Election Sermon: Situating Religion and the Constitutional in the Eighteenth Century." *DePaul Law Review* 59 (2010): 1223–48.

Nuwer, Deanne Stephens, and Greg O'Brien, "Mississippi's Oldest Pastime." In *Resorting to Casinos: The Mississippi Gambling Industry*, edited by Denise von Herrmann. Jackson: University Press of Mississippi, 2006.

Nye, Joseph. "Soft Power." *Foreign Policy* 80 (1990): 153–71.

O' Brien, Michael. "Italy and the Southern Romantics." In *Rethinking the South: Essays in Intellectual History*, by O'Brien. Baltimore, MD: Johns Hopkins University Press, 1988.

O'Dell, Gary A. "At the Starting Post: Racing Venues and the Origins of Thoroughbred Racing in Kentucky, 1783–1865." *Register of the Kentucky Historical Society* 116 (2018): 29–78.

———. "Under Siege: Kentucky and the Transformation of American Thoroughbred Racing, 1865–1936." *Register of the Kentucky Historical Society* 118 (2020): 389–446.

O'Malley, Gregory E. "Slavery's Converging Ground: Charleston's Slave Trade as the Black Heart of the Lowcountry," *William and Mary Quarterly*, 3rd ser., vol. 74, no. 2 (April 2017): 271–302.

Otis, Lara. "Washington's Lost Racetracks: Horseracing from the 1760s to the 1930s." *Washington History* 24 (2012): 136–54.

Park, Roberta J. "Sport, Gender and Society in a Transatlantic Victorian Perspective." *International Journal of the History of Sport* 24 (2007): 1570–1603.

Pearson, Edward. "'Planters Full of Money': The Self-Fashioning of the Eighteenth-Century South Carolina Elite." In *Money, Trade, and Power: The Evolution of Colonial South Carolina's Plantation Society*, edited by Jack P. Greene et al. Columbia: University of South Carolina Press, 2001.

Pease, Jane H. "A Note on Patterns of Conspicuous Consumption among Seaboard Planters, 1820–1860." *Journal of Southern History* 35 (1969): 381–93.

Peck, W. F. G. "Four Years under Fire at Charleston." *Harper's New Monthly Magazine* 31 (August 1865): 358–66.

Perkins, Elizabeth A. "The Forgotten Victorians: Louisville's Domestic Servants, 1880–1920." *Register of the Kentucky Historical Society* 85 (1987): 111–37.

Peters, Martha Ann. "The St. Charles Hotel: New Orleans Social Center, 1837–1860." *Louisiana History* 1 (1960): 191–211.

"Petersburg Jocky [*sic*] Club Book, 1785." *William and Mary Quarterly*, 2nd ser., vol. 18 (1938): 210–16.

Pinfold, John. "Horse Racing and the Upper Classes in the Nineteenth Century." *Sport in History* 28 (2008): 414–30.

Rasmussen, Hans C. "The Culture of Bullfighting in Antebellum New Orleans." *Louisiana History* 55 (2014): 133–76.

———. "The Spoils of the Turf," *Civil War Book Review* 24 (2022): 1–5.

Reeves, John C. "The Way of a Realist: A Study of Howells' Use of the Saratoga Scene." *PMLA* 65 (1950): 1035–52.

Richart, Rebecca. "The "Backside' of the Track: Race, Recognition, and Labor Shifts in Thoroughbred Horse Racing." *Ohio Valley History* 19 (2019): 57–71.

Riess, Steven A. "The Cyclical History of Horse Racing: The USA's Oldest and (Sometimes) Most Popular Spectator Sport." *International Journal of the History of Sport* 31 (2014): 29–54.

———. "From Pitch to Putt: Sport and Class in Anglo-American Sport." *Journal of Sport History* 21 (1994): 138–84.

———. "The New Sports History." *Reviews in American History* 18 (1990): 311–25.

Riley, Franklin L. "Extinct Towns and Villages of Mississippi." In *Publications of the Mississippi Historical Society*, ed. Riley. Oxford: Mississippi Historical Society, 1902.

Roberts, Blain, and Ethan J. Kytle. "Looking the Thing in the Face: Slavery, Race, and the Commemorative Landscape in Charleston, South Carolina, 1865–2010." *Journal of Southern History* 78 (2012): 639–84.

Roche, Daniel. "Equestrian Culture in France from the Sixteenth to the Nineteenth Century." *Past and Present* 199 (2008): 113–45.

Roeber, A. G. "Authority, Law, and Custom: The Rituals of Court Day in Tidewater Virginia, 1720 to 1750." *William and Mary Quarterly*, 3rd ser., vol. 37, no. 1 (1980): 29–52.

Rothman, Joshua. "The Contours of Cotton Capitalism: Speculation, Slavery, and Economic Panic in Mississippi, 1832–184." In *Slavery's Capitalism: A New History of American Economic Development*, edited by Sven Beckert and Seth Rockman. Philadelphia: University of Pennsylvania Press, 2016.

———. "The Hazards of the Flush Times: Gambling, Mob Violence, and the Anxieties of America's Market Revolution." *Journal of American History* 95 (2008): 651–77.

Rothstein, Morton. "The Changing Social Networks and Investment Behavior of a Slaveholding Elite in the Ante-Bellum South: Some Natchez 'Nabobs,' 1800–1860." In *Entrepreneurs in Cultural Context*, edited by Sidney M. Greenfield et al. Albuquerque: University of New Mexico Press, 1978.

———. "'The Remotest Corner': Natchez on the American Frontier." In *Natchez before 1830*, edited by Noel Polk. Jackson: University Press of Mississippi, 1989.

Schweninger, Loren. "A Negro Sojourner in Antebellum New Orleans." *Louisiana History* 20 (1979): 305–14.

Seay, Kelley N. "Jousting and the Evolution of Southernness in Maryland." *Maryland Historical Magazine* 99 (2004): 50–80.

Sexton, Jay. "Transatlantic Financiers and the Civil War." *American Nineteenth Century History* 2 (2001): 29–46.

Shelley, Fred, ed. "The Journal of Ebenezer Hazard in Virginia, 1777." *Virginia Magazine of History and Biography* 62 (1954): 400–423.

Shulman, Cecilia. "The Bingamans of Natchez." *Journal of Mississippi History* 63 (2001): 285–315.

Silverman, Jonathan. "Two Turns around the Digital: Horse Racing, Maps, and Process." *Journal of Sport History* 44 (2017): 178–92.

Sitterson, J. Carlyle. "The William J. Minor Plantations: A Study in Ante-Bellum Absentee Ownership." *Journal of Southern History* 9 (1943): 59–74.

Smiley, Jane. "The Sporting Life." *New Yorker*, 7 June 1999, 33–34.

Smith, D. E. Huger. "Nisbett of Dean and Dean Hall." *South Carolina Historical and Genealogical Magazine* 24 (1923): 17–29.

Smith, Hayden R. "Reserving Water: Environmental and Technological Relationships with South Carolina Inland Rice Plantations." In *Rice: Global Networks and New Histories*, edited by Francesca Bray et al. Cambridge, UK: Cambridge University Press, 2015.

Smith, Laura Ellyn. "Anti-Jackson Democratization: The First National Political Party Conventions." *American Nineteenth Century History* 21 (2020): 149–69.

Somers, Dale A. "War and Play: The Civil War in New Orleans." *Mississippi Quarterly* 26 (1972): 3–28.

Sparks, Randy J. "Gentleman's Sport: Horseracing in Antebellum Charleston." *South Carolina Historical Magazine* 93 (1992): 15–30.

———. "Mary Fisher, Sophia Hume, and the Quakers of Colonial Charleston." In *South Carolina Women: Their Lives and Times*, edited by Marjorie J. Spruill et al. Athens: University of Georgia Press, 2009.

"The St. George's Club." *South Carolina Historical and Genealogical Magazine* 8 (1907): 88–94.

Stanard, W. G. "Racing in Colonial Virginia." *Virginia Magazine of History and Biography* 2 (1895): 293–305.

Stauffer, John. "Interspatialism in the Nineteenth-Century South: The Natchez of Henry Norman." *Slavery and Abolition* 29 (2008): 247–63.

Sterngass, Jon M. "African American Workers and Southern Visitors at Antebellum Saratoga Springs." *American Nineteenth-Century History* 2 (2001): 35–59.

Stroup, Rodger. "Up-Country Patrons: Wade Hampton II and His Family." In *Art in the Lives of South Carolinians: Nineteenth-Century Chapters*, edited by David Moltke-Hansen. Charleston, SC: Carolina Art Association, 1979.

Struna, Nancy L. "The Formalizing of Sport and the Formation of an Elite: The Chesapeake Gentry, 1650s–1720s." *Journal of Sport History* 13 (1986): 212–34.

———. "The North-South Races: American Thoroughbred Racing in Transition, 1823–1850." *Journal of Sport History* 8 (1981): 28–57.

———. "Sport and Society in Early America." *International Journal of the History of Sport* 5 (1988): 292–311.

Sturtz, Linda L. "The Ladies and the Lottery: Elite Women's Gambling in Eighteenth-Century Virginia." *Virginia Magazine of History and Biography* 104 (1996): 165–84.

Sutton, Robert P. "Nostalgia, Pessimism, and Malaise: The Doomed Aristocrat in Late-Jeffersonian Virginia." *Virginia Magazine of History and Biography* 76 (1968): 41–55.

Taylor, Rosser Howard. "The Gentry of Ante-Bellum South Carolina." *North Carolina Historical Review* 17 (1940): 114–31.

Taylor, William Banks. "Southern Yankees: Wealth, High Society, and Political Economy in the Late Antebellum Natchez Region." *Journal of Mississippi History* 59 (1997): 79–122.

Templeton, Peter, and Andrew Dix. "'Old,' 'New,' and 'Problem' Souths in Thomas Nelson Page's *In Ole Virginia*." *Mississippi Quarterly* 74 (2022): 313–33.

Thorpe, T. B. "The Great Four Mile Day." In *The Hive of the 'Bee-Hunter': A Repository of Sketches, Including Peculiar American Character, Scenery, and Rural Sports*, by Thorpe. New York: D. Appleton, 1854.

"Tracing the Tracks of Time." *Charleston Stagebill* 1, no. 9 (February 1993): 56.

Tuffnell, Stephen. "'Uncle Sam Is to Be Sacrificed': Anglophobia in Late Nineteenth-Century Politics and Culture." *American Nineteenth Century History* 12 (2011): 77–99.

Vanderford, Chad. "Peter Little and the Pennsylvania Connection in Antebellum Natchez." *Journal of Mississippi History* 71 (2009): 317–41.

Ward, William S. "The Literature of Three Delectable Kentucky Vices, Part I: Racing." *Kentucky Review* 9 (1989): 10–23.

Warden, Margaret Lindsley. "The Fine Horse Industry in Tennessee." *Tennessee Historical Quarterly* 6 (1947): 134–47.

Wates, Wylma. "Precursor to the Victorian Age: The Concept of Marriage and Family as Revealed in the Correspondence of the Izard Family of South Carolina." In *In Joy and in Sorrow: Women, Family, and Marriage in the Victorian South, 1830–1900*, edited by Carol Bleser. New York: Oxford University Press, 1991.

Weaver, William. "Samuel Clemens Lectures in Kentucky." *Mark Twain Journal* 17 (1974): 20–21.

Weddell, Alexander Wilbourne. "Samuel Mordecai: Chronicler of Richmond, 1786–1865." *Virginia Magazine of History and Biography* 53 (1945): 265–87.

Welch, Kimberly. "Arteries of Capital: William Johnson and the Practice of Black Money-lending in the Antebellum U.S. South." *Slavery and Abolition* 41 (2020): 304–26.

———. "Black Litigiousness and White Accountability: Free Blacks and the Rhetoric of Reputation in the Antebellum Natchez District." *Journal of the Civil War Era* 5 (2015): 372–98.

Whitelegg, Drew. "From Smiles to Miles: Delta Air Lines Flight Attendants and Southern Hospitality." *Southern Cultures* 11 (2005): 7–27.

Wilkins, Kathryn. "Travel Narratives of the Victorian Elite: The Case of the London Season." In *Narratives of Travel and Tourism,* edited by Jacqueline Tivers and Tijana Rakic. Farnham, UK: Ashgate, 2012.

Wilson, James Grant. "William Collins Whitney." *New York Genealogical and Biographical Sketch* 35 (1904): 11–12.

Wyatt, Edward A. "Newmarket of the Virginia Turf." *William and Mary Quarterly* 17 (1937): 481–95.

———. "Petersburg Plans a Turf Museum." *Commonwealth* 6, no. 1 (January 1939): 13.

Young, Cory James. "From North to Natchez during the Age of Gradual Abolition." *Pennsylvania Magazine of History and Biography* 143 (2019): 117–39.

Zacek, Natalie A. "Spectacle and Spectatorship at the Nineteenth-Century American Racetrack." *European Journal of American Studies* 14 (2020): 1–15.

UNPUBLISHED THESES, DISSERTATIONS, AND ESSAYS

Akard, Carrie Meitzner. "Southern Genre Painting and Illustration from 1830 to 1890." Master's thesis, University of North Texas, 1997.

Bachand, Marise. "A Season in Town: Plantation Women and the Urban South, 1790–1877." PhD diss., University of Western Ontario, 2011.

Banker, Tollie Jean. "A Peculiar Diversion: The Social Ramifications of Quarter-Racing in the Eighteenth-Century Tidewater Virginia." Master's thesis, University of Tennessee–Knoxville, 2006.

Bauer, Craig Anthony. "A Leader among Peers: The Life and Times of Duncan Farrar Kenner." PhD diss., University of Southern Mississippi, 1989.

Berry, Matthew S. "Evangelical Religion and Benevolent Reform in the Antebellum Urban Southwest: Natchez and Vicksburg, Mississippi, 1800–1860." Master's thesis, Eastern Illinois University, 2008.

Bevan, Alana K. "'We Are the Same People': The Leverich Family of New York and Their Antebellum American Inter-Regional Network of Elites." PhD diss., Johns Hopkins University, 2010.

Bodek, Richard. "Racing in Charleston." Unpublished manuscript in author's possession.

Burman, Nathan. "Two Histories, One Future: Louisiana Sugar Planters and the Anglo-Creole Schism, 1815–1865." PhD diss., Louisiana State University, 2013.

Busch, Jason T. "'Such a Paradise Can Be Made on Earth': Furniture Patronage and Consumption in Antebellum Natchez, Mississippi, 1828–1863." Master's thesis, University of Delaware, 1998.

Hannan, Madelyn. "Horseracing in New Orleans: The Eclipse Course as a Case Study, 1837–1849." Master's thesis, University of New Orleans, 2002.

Harrah-Conforth, Jeanne. "The Landscape of Possibility: An Ethnography of the Kentucky Derby." PhD diss., Indiana University, 1992.

Novitch, Avery. "There Must Be Something in the Water: Fashion, Wellness, and Class at Saratoga Springs, 1875–1925." Master's thesis, SUNY Fashion Institute of Technology, 2020.

Paul, Catriona Margaret. "The Horsemen Got the Start: Horse Ownership and Advantage in Kentucky, 1770–1830." PhD diss., University of Dundee, 2012.

Perreault, Matthew Saul. "Jockeying for Position: Horse Racing in New Orleans, 1865–1920." Master's thesis, Louisiana State University, 2016.

Raichelson, Richard M. "Black Religious Folksong: A Study in Generic and Social Change." PhD diss., University of Pennsylvania, 1975.

Roberts, Hugh. "Territorial Politics: Formative Identities and Networks in the Mississippi Territory, 1798–1817." PhD diss., University of Kent, 2020.

Sergeant, Daniel. "Place Bonding, Fan Identification, and Nostalgia and Fenway's Future: Observations about Red Sox Nation." PhD diss., University of Florida, 2012.

Suttle, Danael Christian. "Horse Racing during the Civil War: The Perseverance of the Sport during a Time of National Crisis." Bachelor's thesis, University of Arkansas–Fayetteville, 2019.

Symon, Robert Bruce, Jr. "'Child of the North': Louisville's Transition to a Southern City, 1879–1885." Master's thesis, University of Louisville, 2005.

Tyrrell, Brian Patrick. "Bred for the Race: Thoroughbred Horses and the Politics of Pedigree." PhD diss., University of California–Santa Barbara, 2019.

Wingfield, Charles L. "The Sugar Plantations of William J. Minor, 1830–1860." Master's thesis, Louisiana State University, 1950.

Wojcik, Piotr. "Tracks/Traces: The New Deal Transformation of Lexington, Kentucky's Landscapes of Horseracing and Housing." Master's thesis, University of Kentucky, 2022.

ONLINE RESOURCES

Banks, Eric. "Saratoga's Sesquicentennial Shindig." *Town & Country*, 14 August 2013. www.townandcountrymag.com/leisure/sporting/a1126/saratoga-racing-150th-anniversary/.

Battuello, Patrick. "Shuttered U.S. Racetracks (since 2000)." *Horseracing Wrongs*. https://horseracingwrongs.com/shuttered-u-s-racetracks-since-2000/.

Belmont Stakes, Longines Prize for Elegance. www.instagram.com/p/Celi65uA2hW/.

"Black New Yorkers." https://blacknewyorkers-nypl.org/new-york-citys-black-population-by-gender-1850-1880/.

Braga, Heather. "35 Things You Can Wear to Watch the Kentucky Derby." *BuzzFeed*, 22 April 2019. www.buzzfeed.com/hbraga/things-to-wear-to-a-kentucky-derby-party.

Bray, Sarah. "Inside the Kentucky Derby's Exclusive, Secret Clubhouse." *Town & Country*, 12 May 2016. www.townandcountrymag.com/leisure/sporting/news/a6127/kentucky-derby-the-mansion/.

Bullard, Gabe. "A Black Jockey at the Kentucky Derby, Once Again." National Public Radio, 3 May 2013. www.npr.org/sections/codeswitch/2013/05/03/180555617/a-black-jockey-at-the-kentucky-derby-once-again.

Burnett, Frances Hodgson. *The Shuttle*. www.gutenberg.org/files/506/506-h/506-h.htm.

"Celebrate the Kentucky Derby in Style." *Southern Lady*, 28 April 2018. www.southern-ladymagazine.com/celebrate-the-kentucky-derby-in-style/4/.

"Celebrities at the Kentucky Derby." TMZ. www.tmz.com/photos/image_jpg_20190504_0bf1356f33d857209461e00aa5f30828/.

Churchill Downs Annual Report 2019. https://ir.churchilldownsincorporated.com/static-files/0526f0e6-66ee-4363-8cf3-c758657a48db.

"Cultural Resources." New York Racing Association. www.nyra.com/uploads/wysiwyg/assets/uploads/15_Cultural.pdf.

Dallow, Jessica. "Antebellum Sports Illustrated: Representing African Americans in Edward Troye's Equine Paintings." *Nineteenth-Century Art Worldwide* 12, no. 2 (Autumn 2013). www.19thc-artworldwide.org/autumn13/dallow-on-edward-troye-s-equine-paintings.

Dizikes, John. "Richard Ten Broeck." *American National Biography Online*. https://doi.org/10.1093/anb/9780198606697.article.1900217.

Evans, Jace, and Sam Schmieder. "At Pimlico, Racing Fans Remember When Tracks, Not Casinos, Drew Crowds." *Capital News Service*. https://cnsmaryland.org/gambling/community/pimlico.html.

Gordon, John Steele. "The Country Club." *American Heritage* 41 (October/November 1990). www.americanheritage.com/country-club.

Holmberg, James J. "The Clark Family and the Kentucky Derby." *Filson News Magazine* 4, no. 1 (2003). www.filsonhistorical.org/archive/news_v4n1_clarkderby.html.

"Horse-Racing: Pimlico Track Should Be Demolished and Rebuilt, Study Says." *Reuters*, 15 December 2018. www.reuters.com/article/us-horseracing-pimlico-idUSKBN1OE0RM.

"Horseracing's Heritage." Speed Art Museum, Louisville, Kentucky. www.speedmuseum.org/collections/oakland-house-and-race-course/.

"How the Kentucky Derby Makes a Business Impact Each Year." *Business First Family*, 19 February 2019. https://businessfirstfamily.com/business-impact-kentucky-derby/.

"Kentucky Derby Museum Celebrates Best Year Ever." 8 October 2019. www.derbymuseum.org/Media-And-Press/Article/323/Kentucky-Derby-Museum-celebrates-Best-Year-Ever.

"Kentucky Derby 2022 Clothes and Style." www.vineyardvines.com/kentucky-derby/?eq =kentucky%20derby.

Kentucky Derby website. www.kentuckyderby.com.

King, Martha J. King. "Clementina Rind (d. 1774)." *Encyclopedia Virginia*. https://encyclopediavirginia.org/entries/rind-clementina-d-1774/.

Leeds, Michael, and Hugh Rockoff. "Jim Crow in the Saddle: The Expulsion of African American Jockeys from American Racing." National Bureau of Economic Research Working Paper 28167. December 2020. www.nber.org/system/files/working_papers/w28167/w28167.pdf.

Liebman, Bennett. "The Naming of the Triple Crown." http://dx.doi.org/10.2139/ssrn.2649997.

———. "There Used to Be a New York Racetrack There: But Where Was It?" http://dx.doi.org/10.2139/ssrn.1510317.

Lubet, Alex, and Steven Lubet. "The Complicated Legacy of 'My Old Kentucky Home.'" *Smithsonian* blog, 3 September 2020. www.smithsonianmag.com/arts-culture/complicated-legacy-my-old-kentucky-home-180975719/.

Maryland Jockey Club Reports Record Preakness Weekend." *Bloodhorse*, 19 May 2019. www.bloodhorse.com/horse-racing/articles/233774/maryland-jockey-club-reports-record-preakness-weekend.

Maryland Stadium Authority website. www.mdstad.com/.

McGrath, Maggie. "Kentucky Derby Special: How 143-Year-Old Churchill Downs Keeps Betting—and Winning—on a Dying Sport." *Forbes.com*, 3 May 2018. www.forbes.com/sites/maggiemcgrath/2018/05/03/churchill-downs-doubles-down-on-the-success-of-the-kentucky-derby/#4b94cc3f1c80.

McKee, Mark. "A Day at the Races: How to Dress for the Kentucky Derby." *The Manual*, 4 May 2023. www.themanual.com/fashion/best-kentucky-derby-mens-outfits/.

Meares, Hadley. "The Glitz and Glamour of Hollywood Park." *Curbed Los Angeles*, 20 September 2018. https://la.curbed.com/2018/9/20/17691686/hollywood-park-inglewood-race-track-history.

Measuring Worth. www.measuringworth.com.

National Archives of the United Kingdom, Currency Converter, 1270–2017. www.nationalarchives.gov.uk/currency-converter.

Nelson, Adam. "Hot to Trot: Why Dressage Is Yielding Such Interest from Fans and Sponsors." *Sport Business*, 28 September 2017. www.sportbusiness.com/2017/09/hot-to-trot-why-dressage-is-yielding-such-interest-from-fans-and-sponsors/.

New York Racing Association, Belmont Stakes online shop. https://shop.nyra.com/belmont-stakes/?utm_source=belmontstakes&utm_medium=nav&utm_campaign=website&sort=featured&page=1.

"New York Urbanized Area: Population & Density from 1800." http://demographia.com/db-nyuza1800.htm.

Patrick, Andrew P. "The Kentucky Association for the Improvement of Breeds of Stock: Natural Advantages and Market Motivations." http://works.bepress.com/andrew_patrick/2.

Preakness Stakes online shop. https://shop.1st.com.

Rhode, Paul, and Koleman Strumpf. "Historical Political Futures Markets: An International Perspective." National Bureau of Economic Research Working Paper 14377. October 2008. www.nber.org/papers/w14377.

Riess, Steven A. "The American Jockey, 1865–1910." *Transatlantica* 2 (2011). https://journals.openedition.org/transatlantica/5480#quotation.

"Saratoga Meet Concludes with Record Handle, 'Robust' Audience." *Paulick Report*, 5 September 2022. https://paulickreport.com/news/the-biz/saratoga-meet-concludes-with-record-handle-robust-attendance/.

Saratoga, New York, website. www.saratoga.com.

Shields, David. "Madeira When Charleston Was Madeira Mad." Paper presented at the Madeira Dinner, Gadsden House, Charleston, South Carolina, 25 September 2015. www.facebook.com/SlowFoodSouthern/posts/954654747926114.

"Slots Money Could Fund Racetrack Improvements." Maryland Department of Agriculture, 15 February 2013. https://news.maryland.gov/mda/news-clippings/2013/02/15/slots-money-could-fund-racetrack-improvements/.

Southern Hospitality Natural Foot Care website. www.sohofeet.com/.

"Sunday Journal Front Page." Ephemeral New York, 3 February 2014. https://ephemeralnewyork.files.wordpress.com/2014/02/sundayjournalfrontpage.jpg.

Thompson, Hunter S. "The Kentucky Derby Is Decadent and Depraved." *Scanlan's Magazine*, June 1970. https://grantland.com/features/looking-back-hunter-s-thompson-classic-story-kentucky-derby/.

"The 20th Century Awards: *Sports Illustrated* Honors World's Greatest Athletes." *Sports Illustrated*, 3 December 1999. https://vault.si.com/vault/1999/11/29/honoring-the-best-the-sports-illustrated-20th-century-sports-awards.

Vespe, Frank. "Pimlico to Run 12 Days of Racing in 2017." *Bloodhorse*, 21 December 2016. www.bloodhorse.com/horse-racing/articles/218545/pimlico-to-run-12-days-of-racing-in-2017.

INDEX